Studies on Modern China

UNITED STATES
ATTITUDES
AND
POLICIES
TOWARD
CHINA
THE IMPACT OF
AMERICAN MISSIONARIES

PATRICIA NEILS
editor

JOHN C. BREWER
MARGARET B. DENNING
ARLINE T. GOLKIN
LAWRENCE D. KESSLER
MARJORIE KING
TONY LADD
KATHLEEN L. LODWICK
JESSIE GREGORY LUTZ
JOHN RAWLINSON
KENNETH W. REA
MURRAY A. RUBINSTEIN
CHARLES W. WEBER
EDMUND S. WEHRLE
JEAN-PAUL WIEST

An East Gate Book

M. E. Sharpe, Inc.
ARMONK, NEW YORK
LONDON, ENGLAND

Library of Congress Cataloging-in-Publication Data

United States attitudes and policy toward China : the impact of American
    missionaries / edited by Patricia Neils.
        p.   cm.
    Papers from an international conference held Oct. 23–24, 1987 at the
    University of San Diego and sponsored by the Asia Pacific Rim Insti-
    tute of the United States International University.
    Includes bibliographical references
    ISBN 0-87332-632-6
    1. United States—Relations—China—Congresses.   2. China—Rela-
    tions—United States—Congresses.   3. Missionaries—China—Politi-
    cal activity—Congresses.   4. Americans—China—Politics and
    government—Congresses.   I. Neils, Patricia, 1945– .   II. United
    States International University. Asia Pacific Rim Institute.
    E183.8.C5U59   1990
    303.48′251073—dc20   89-78510
                                                                CIP

Printed in the United States of America

MV   10   9   8   7   6   5   4   3   2   1

CONTENTS

UNITED STATES
ATTITUDES
AND
POLICIES
TOWARD
CHINA

1

INTRODUCTION

Patricia Neils

The first international conference to examine the impact of American missionaries on U.S. attitudes, images, and policies toward China was held October 23 and 24, 1987, at the University of San Diego. It was sponsored by the Asia Pacific Rim Institute of United States International University. Along with twenty featured speakers, commentators included Daniel Bays, director of the Center for East Asian Studies at the University of Kansas; David Buck, East Asian history professor from the University of Wisconsin at Milwaukee; *Missiology* editor Ralph R. Covell; History Professor William Head from Mercer University; Richard Madsen, director of the China Studies program at the University of California at San Diego; James McCutcheon, director of the American Studies program at the University of Hawaii; Raymond G. O'Connor, retired history professor from the University of Miami; and Peter Chen-main Wang, associate professor of history at Tamkang University in Taipei.

The scholarly interest in missionaries demonstrated at this conference reflects a new climate of opinion in the study of Chinese history and in Sino-American relations. While anti-Communist attitudes colored scholarly writings in the late 1940s and on through the 1950s, the New Left historiography of the late 1960s and early 1970s evoked exaggerated sympathy for the Chinese Communist regime under Mao, and hypercritical assessments of America's overall role in China. Not only was America's political and journalistic support for the ''inefficient, corrupt and moribund'' regime Chiang Kai-shek condemned, but the religious and human-itarian work of missionaries was also derided. Today, however, the passionate ideological controversies of the 1940s and 1950s have cooled, and the New Left climate of opinion that pervaded the 1960s and 1970s has dissipated. Hence, in the 1980s a more balanced view of America's role in China is emerging.[1]

In response to current trends, there have been two complementary conferences this past decade that focused on nonmissionary groups of Americans who played significant roles in China-American interactions. One conference on American journalists in China met in Scottsdale, Arizona, in November 1982, and one on

American foreign service officers met at the University of Montana's Maureen and Mike Mansfield Center for Asian Studies in Missoula in April 1984. A book related to the Scottsdale conference has been written by the director, Steve MacKinnon, and his associate, Oris Friesen.[2] Also a compilation of the papers presented in Missoula has been edited with an introduction by Paul Lauren, director of the Mansfield Center.[3]

Reflecting upon America's changing images and attitudes toward China at the Arizona conference, Harvard Professor John Fairbank remarked, "We all tried but we failed in one of the great failures of history. We could not educate or communicate. We were all superficial—academics, government officials, journalists. We were a small thin stratum." This same sentiment was expressed by the conferees in Montana. Approaching the decade of the 1990s, scholars have come to recognize that the junior foreign service officers, like the liberal journalists, were unfairly castigated by McCarthyism in the 1950s, but too highly exalted by the New Left writers of the 1960s. As new questions are asked and new conclusions are drawn, the time has come to reexamine the role of missionaries in China along with the other types of Americans who lived and worked there. It seems that the missionaries have been too euphorically praised as messengers of the gospel on the one hand, and too categorically denounced as cultural iconoclasts on the other.

The historical origins of scholarship regarding the role and impact of missionaries in China can be traced back at least as far as Kenneth Scott Latourette (1884–1967). He emerged as not only one of America's foremost scholars of Chinese history, but also as the nation's leading authority on the expansion of Christianity. As a young adult, Latourette attended Yale University and became involved in its Student Volunteer Movement which had as its motto, "The evangelization of the world in this generation." Yale University itself had a continuous historical commitment to foreign and home missions since 1818. By 1909 it was leading all other colleges in its missionary activities and monetary donations.

Like his mentor, Frederick Wells Williams, Latourette was trained as a scientific historian of the Leopold Von Ranke tradition. He believed, however, that this training did not always adequately explain the flow of events in human history. Thus a supernatural explanation was required when the natural causes were insufficient. He probably offered the clearest description of this view of history in his 1949 presidential address to the American Historical Association, which he entitled, "The Christian Understanding of History." He described the missionary enterprise as a partial fulfillment of the "Great Commission" to bring "all phases of the human scene into subjection to Christ."[4] He saw a divine plan at work and was convinced that ultimately God's will would be accomplished. "All reality," he wrote, "is one and under the control of God."[5]

Latourette was not looking for rapid success, however. He reminded his listeners that the nominal conversion of the Roman Empire, even with a much smaller population than China, required over three hundred years. And the "superficial" conversion of northern Europe was achieved by missionaries who were accepted as members of a superior civilization and who were often backed by the authority of the state. Still, its conversion was accomplished only in about a thousand years. China, with its sophisticated culture and religious-philosophical belief systems, would predictably take much longer. Nevertheless, it would be greatly hastened if Christian contact were to bring about a general disintegration of Chinese culture and thereby eliminate all solid opposition from existing institutions. In Latourette's view, this would be a likely and desirable eventuality.

Hence, Kenneth Latourette saw the missionary enterprise as the most important part of the inexorable Western expansion that dominated nineteenth-century global movements. In his view, it compensated to a great extent for the faults and failings of the nonmissionary merchants and diplomats. In his introduction to *A History of Christian Missions in China* (1926), Latourette predicted that the missionary enterprise would inevitably have an enduring and an increasing share in shaping the culture and destiny of China. "Should Christianity stamp its impress upon the new China even half as firmly as it has upon Europe and America," he prophesized, "the future historian may see in missions in China one of the most important movements of the past three centuries."[6] Latourette's views were in accord with what nineteenth-century missionary writers such as Timothy Richard, Young J. Allen, and W. A. P. Martin had also been saying.

To be sure, while the missionaries never converted more than a very small percentage of the Chinese people, the China Christian colleges introduced Western (modern) education. A preponderance of the leadership of the Republic from 1911 to 1949 was Christian, and of the total Chinese population, there remains even today a dedicated core of Christian enthusiasts. Though still miniscule, they have outlasted Maoist efforts to suppress them and are growing in numbers and vitality.

Nevertheless, scholars of more recent times give little credence to the divine providence theory in China-American relations. John K. Fairbank who, even in his retirement from Harvard, remains one of America's foremost Sinologists, serves as a noteworthy contrast to Latourette. He writes, "My upbringing was almost entirely irreligious. Today my acquired religion is Harvard and what it stands for in the secular world. That is, I put my faith in our ongoing institutions devoted to fostering the free working of the mind. Irrational faith appalls me."[7]

While Latourette's cosmic view of Christian expansion saw the penetration of missionaries into China as a providential blessing to a beleaguered civilization, Fairbank has contended that the opposite point of view has just as much validity. He has argued that the missionaries were revolutionaries, a threat to the Confucian world order. For example, Christianity was diametrically opposed to the concept of ancestor worship, which included not only the spirits of family and clan lineage, but also patron deities of guilds and communities as well as cultic rituals performed by officials and gentry. Christianity, therefore, was not only an ideological threat but an institutional one as well. Fairbank once proclaimed that, "The threat was potentially much more devastating than mere Communism, a Western heresy, could ever be in America of the 1950s."[8]

Besides teaching religion, the missionaries also did what they could to eliminate what they regarded as evil, such as opium smoking, gambling, prostitution, foot-binding, concubinage, the exposure of infants, famine, and poor labor conditions. They provided numerous medical facilities and unprecedented educational opportunities. Although Latourette had no doubt that these were worthwhile accomplishments, Fairbank has been far from profuse in his praise. He has argued that while such good works were probably praiseworthy in themselves, these efforts became a major factor in the destructive upheavals with which China was wrought throughout the first half of the twentieth century.

Historical Survey of Missionaries in China

As early as the sixteenth and seventeenth centuries the European missionaries had already set the stage for the American experience in the nineteenth century. For the missionaries, the Chinese were not only corrupted by superstitions and false ideas but were also ignorant of the Revelation. On this subject, Jacques Gernet has written, "All that was necessary was to undeceive them. And if Christianity found little success in China, if it was the object of violent attacks, it could only be for reasons that reflected poorly on the Chinese."[9]

From the Chinese point of view, Christianity was a religion that changed customs, called into question accepted ideas, and above all threatened to undermine existing institutions. Gernet says, "The missionaries, just like the Chinese literary elite, were the unconscious bearers of a whole civilization."[10] Matteo Ricci's struggle in formulating a concept of heaven and the Sovereign on high that would be compatible with the Chinese classics is legendary. According to Gernet, "The reason why [missionaries] so often came up against difficulties of translation is that different languages express, through different logics, different visions of the world and man."[11]

Nevertheless, in the early years of the seventeenth century, the missionaries had as yet attracted few critics, and many members of the literate elite were won over by the "Western man of letters." They were delighted by the analogies they thought they detected between his teachings and those of the Chinese tradition. The scholar gentry admired Matteo Ricci for his observation of the Chinese rules of politeness; his knowledge of the classics and the written language; his astonishing memory; his approval of Confucius; his mathematical learning and map of the world; as well as for the curiosities that he brought with him such as paintings, books, clocks, and astronomical instruments.[12]

Although Catholics had been in China since the sixteenth century, it wasn't until 1807 that Robert Morrison, under the London Missionary Society, became the first

Protestant missionary to take up residence there. While working for the East India Company at Portuguese Macao, Morrison undertook the task of translating the Bible into Chinese. In 1824, he published his Bible and a six-volume English-Chinese dictionary. Meanwhile, he established the Anglo-Chinese College at Malacca in 1818. By 1842, there were about twenty Protestant missionaries representing eight missionary societies in China and about one hundred converts of Chinese nationality.

Although American commercial contacts with China began as early as 1784 when America's first ship, the *Empress of China* arrived there, American missionaries did not establish themselves in China until the 1830s. By then, however, America's sense of manifest destiny was firmly established. As early as 1782, St. Jean Crevecoeur captured the exhilarating spirit in his famous volume *Letters from an American Farmer*. In it he spoke of America as "the most perfect society now existing in the world" and Americans, he said, "are the western pilgrims, who are carrying along with them that great mass of arts, sciences, vigor, and industry, which began long since in the east. They will finish the great circle."[13] From an American Studies perspective, Crevecoeur's view fit in with the

> Romantic thought that civilization had followed what was termed the "westward course of empire." Having begun in the East, in China and India, it was said, civilization had moved steadily westward in its successive stages of development—from the Far East, through Persia and Egypt, to Greece, Rome, the Italian city states, France and Spain, Britain, and finally America. The dynamic elements in this movement had been the growth of progress and enlightenment. From the Catholicism and monarchism of the Mediterranean world, for example, civilization had developed toward the liberal Protestant and parliamentary regime of Britain, and eventually matured in the republicanism of the United States.[14]

American missionaries began their enterprise in China during what Harold Isaacs has termed the nineteenth-century "Age of Hostility" in China-American relations. American high school textbooks as well as newspapers, films, comic books, and even literary magazines such as *Scribner's, Century*, and *The Atlantic Monthly* at that time conveyed unattractive images of the Chinese. Also, popular journals such as *Outlook* and *Independent* with reputations for unbiased reporting, religious magazines, popular weeklies, and professional journals, including the *Political Science Quarterly*, all shared in the anti-Chinese sentiment.[15]

According to Sherwood Eddy, most nineteenth-century missionaries "preached only about eternal punishment, with constant images of 'millions of heathen' going every hour into 'Christian graves.' "[16] Though discouraged at times with their slow progress and the anti-Christian sentiment they often faced, the missionaries did not despair. They believed they were participating in a divine plan and that the ultimate Christianization of China was inevitable.

Typifying these trends was the missionary author Karl Gützlaff. As Jessie Lutz points out in her essay below, Gützlaff was a great publicist who wrote frequently to a number of American mission, tract, and Bible society journals; in addition, he published such works as *Journal of Three Voyages Along the Coast of China, A Sketch of Chinese History* and *China Opened* during the 1830s. Extracts from these works were widely reprinted in American mission journals. With his insistence that China was accessible to missionaries despite government prohibition, he stirred up great interest in China and in China missions. Professor Lutz contends that, although Gützlaff was an independent evangelist from Prussia, he shared a common language and frame of reference with American pietistic Protestantism. Like the evangelists of the Great Awakening, he emphasized the sinfulness of mankind and the necessity of individual rebirth leading to moral reformation and reconciliation with God.

In addition to identifying with Gützlaff's brand of Protestantism, Americans, according to Lutz, derived a vicarious pleasure from reading about his adventures and exploits in China. Gützlaff, it seemed, was a frontiersman and an entrepreneur who exemplified the ideas and ideals of Jacksonian America.

The enthusiasm that he generated, however, was quickly followed by disillusionment as Gützlaff's exaggerations were revealed. While he deserves credit for fostering friendship toward and interest in China, he is also at least partially responsible for purveying inaccurate and distorted images and attitudes that have plagued China-American intercultural relations.

As Charles Weber explains, the impact of the Baptist missionary enterprise in China paralleled the influence of Karl Gützlaff. More than most other denominations, the Baptists tried to counter rationalism and Deism with the conviction that each individual must make a personal commitment to faith in Christ and then lead others into a life of personal piety and devotion to God. Weber's essay stresses what he sees as the uniqueness of the Baptist vocation, and he traces the historical development of Baptist missions in China from the 1830s until the beginning of the twentieth century. He focuses particularly on their efforts in education with the conviction that Baptist mission schools in China played an important role in communicating one culture to another. Weber demonstrates that the Baptists differed from some of the other missionary groups in a number of ways, including their efforts to keep themselves free of political involvement, their emphasis on evangelizational work over social work, their insistence that religion be taught in Chinese rather than English, and their quest to establish an indigenous and self-supporting church of devout Christian believers.

For the most part, difficulties and privations encountered by all the missionary groups in China were assuaged by the elite status afforded them. The missionary compound itself was walled off from the rest of Chinese society and was staffed with servants to perform all the menial tasks of everyday life. By the second half of the nineteenth century, furthermore, missionaries were confident that their home governments would protect them whenever conflicts with the Chinese arose. Extraterritorial rights guaranteed by treaties applied not only to merchants and diplomats, but to all other foreign residents, including missionaries. As Professor James Thomson explains, "The legal provisions of extraterritoriality gave the agents of alien culture a cocoon of inviolability. They also gave foreigners a class status most of them had never known at home. After 1860, the Westerner in China was the automatic recipient of most of the perquisites of officialdom."[17]

Until the end of the nineteenth century, missionaries continued to believe that they were dearly needed by the Chinese and had a major contribution to make to a civilization that many thought was stagnant, superstitious, and repressive. By contrast, the United States seemed to be, at that same time, marching forward with dynamic progress and prosperity. The standard of living was rising rapidly and there were many opportunities for ambitious entrepreneurs as the United States was becoming the richest and most powerful nation in the world.

In spite of the difficulties encountered and their lack of success in winning converts during their first few decades, missionary efforts were revitalized in the 1890s partly as a response to the fear of spiritual stagnation. Just as theorists contended that overseas markets would alleviate the danger of economic stagnation, overseas crusaders were sought to maintain religious fervor in the United States.

The expanding economy and accelerated industrial output, meanwhile, coincided with what Frederick Jackson Turner memorialized as the closing of the American frontier. With opportunities seemingly limited at home, the quest began for foreign markets. Adam Smith's theories of laissez-faire and Herbert Spencer's social Darwinism were generally accepted and seemed to justify America's political and cultural expansion abroad.

One particularly noteworthy missionary organization that contributed to intercultural understanding and epitomized the crusading spirit of the 1890s was the Student Volunteer Movement (SVM) of the YMCA. It was formed in the 1880s at Northfield, Massachusetts, the home of the popular evangelical preacher, Dwight Moody. Before long, students from two hundred colleges pledged their commitment to rapid, worldwide conversion. In 1891, six thousand students agreed to become foreign missionaries. In the next decade, the movement expanded and played a significant role in spreading American cultural influence around the world. The SVM made East Asia, particularly China, the focus of its attention. "Although other missionary groups existed, the SVM was probably the most important missionary arm of American Protestantism."[18] And the Protestant Missionary enterprise as a whole served as the primary image maker for Americans who were forming their first impressions of China in the nineteenth and early twentieth centuries.

The missionary movement was not only zealous and optimistic, it was also enthusiastically admired and respected by the American people. Educated, dedicated, and devout men and women who were willing to leave the comforts of their homeland in order to become missionaries in China were not, for the most part, subjected in their own day to the cynicism that dominated American perceptions of missionaries in later generations.

Scholars have consistently pointed out that, largely because they were generally admired by audiences back home, missionaries, in their letters to their families and to their mission boards, created the images of China that were held by hundreds of thousands of Americans before World War II. Professor John W. Masland noted that the New York office of the Associated Boards for Christian Colleges in China often distributed as many as thirty-five hundred mimeographed copies of letters from its representatives in China to prominent and influential people in the United States. He commented:

> It is apparent that these letters arouse considerable interest among those who receive them. In the aggregate they provide a great deal of information about China to a large body of people in this country. The sincerity and urgency of their appeals and the natural sympathy of those receiving them must not be forgotten. Their cumulative effect is undoubtedly of considerable influence. In this connection it should be observed that the public which they reach is of considerable breadth, including many persons who have achieved positions of leadership in their social, business or professional communities and whose opinions are of commanding influence.[19]

In one of the selections for this volume, Lawrence Kessler examines the Southern Presbyterian mission station at Kiangyin (Jiangyin, Jiangsu) and its special relationship with its home church, the First Presbyterian Church of Wilmington, North Carolina. By studying private and circular letters of missionaries in Kiangyin, missionary journals such as *The Missionary, Missionary Survey, Bi-Monthly Bulletin*, the private papers of several missionaries, records of the First Presbyterian Church, and through personal interviews, Kessler found that the missionaries at this station assiduously cultivated a relationship with backers in the United States through a steady stream of personal and institutional correspondence, talks, and ''lantern-slide'' presentations when home on furlough, and by naming buildings in honor of home supporters. Kiangyin missionaries thereby informed their home constituency about events in China and the progress and needs of mission work. Kessler's essay demonstrates that the missionaries were better situated than most other Americans to observe the activities and attitudes of Chinese people at the basic level of village and town and, in turn, grass-roots Americans often gained their first and lasting impressions of this faraway civilization through missionary reports.

Similarly, Kathleen Lodwick, in her essay on the Hainan missionaries (which is based on her book-length study on the history of the Hainan station), gives a detailed account of mission reports that informed American audiences about conditions in China. Lodwick argues that readers of these church publications probably obtained a more intimate view of China than did most other Americans, although the view was not especially favorable. Lodwick also demonstrates that while these reports were often, if not usually, oriented toward justifying financial assistance for the missions and were not always accurate, they were nonetheless informative and influential in creating images and attitudes toward the Chinese people.

As the Gilded Age in America gave way to the Progressive Era, writings such as those of Herbert Croly inspired the humanitarian movement, which was characterized by the reform efforts of individuals like Jacob Riis, Jane Addams, and Katherine Philips Edson. Progressive presidents Theodore Roosevelt and Woodrow Wilson were also caught up in the spirit of the era and promoted such altruistic efforts both at home and abroad. Both Roosevelt and Wilson gave China missionaries their full support. In their view, missionaries played an important role in America's duty to lead the world in the ways of peace and righteousness.[20]

Meanwhile in China, in spite of (or, perhaps as Professor Latourette suggested, because of) Japan's victory in the Sino-Japanese War (1894–95)—which accompanied the breakdown of Chinese institutions, the aborted republic, and the rise of warlordism—missionaries enjoyed unprecedented success during the early years of the twentieth century. Deeply shaken, the Middle Kingdom became ever more vulnerable, if not receptive, to American Protestantism and "sentimental imperialism." Thousands of Chinese students poured into mission schools and dozens of new mission societies entered the China field. Major foundations as well as private American funds through churches and schools made generous contributions to the endowment of schools and hospitals in China.

In the spirit of Emersonian optimism, however, a few missionaries like Henry Winters Luce began to question the stereotypical images of the past and fostered a greater awareness and appreciation of the Chinese religious philosophy and culture. In this sense, some became "missionaries in reverse." That is, rather than adhering to the political-theological doctrine that was convinced that God had given America His particular blessing and had entrusted the nation to spread Christianity and democracy to heathen backward nations, Luce felt that it was at least equally important for him to educate Americans to the philosophies, traditions, and achievements of the Chinese. "He must become a missionary from China to his own native land."[21]

As John Rawlinson's essay masterfully demonstrates in this volume, his missionary father, Frank Rawlinson, experienced a similar transformation. In the writing of his father's biography (forthcoming), John Rawlinson has had access to a wealth of materials in the archives of the Southern Baptist Convention and the American Board of Commissioners for Foreign Missions, to voluminous personal correspondence saved by his late mother, and to the entire run of his father's editorials in *The Chinese Recorder*, which he presided over from 1914 to 1937. These sources reveal a dramatic transition from Rawlinson's smug talks in 1907–1908 on how splendidly the heathen were following the light of the Gospel, to his almost entirely political reportage in the 1930s suffused with a sense of

Western and Christian failure. In the later years his primary concern was to adjust Christianity to fit Chinese proclivities, rather than the other way around, and to search for a way that Americans and Chinese alike could together find a viable world religion, transcending all cultures.

The life, work, and writings of Frank Rawlinson are particularly significant for this volume because of the probable impact he had on Americans back home. Rawlinson had six furloughs over his thirty-five years in the field, and although some were timed to accommodate his health needs, and others were largely occupied by study, he did a great deal of deputation talking designed to influence home-base opinion. In addition, he wrote numerous reports to his boards, articles to U.S. publications such as *World Unity* or the *Christian Century*, and letters to his supporting churches, which were usually read from the pulpit.

In a similar vein, Marjorie King summarizes Ida Pruitt's work as the founder and head of the Department of Social Services at the Peking Union Medical College, 1921–29; as the executive secretary of the American Committee of the Chinese Industrial Cooperatives, 1939–52; and as the author of perhaps the most widely read American book about traditional Chinese women. According to King, Pruitt was both a representative and a critic of foreign missionaries in China in terms of their impact on American attitudes and policies toward China. Although Pruitt saw her own professional, literary, and political work on behalf of the Chinese people and nation as a departure from missionary efforts, King argues that these efforts were really a continuation and elaboration in secular terms of earlier missionary impulses to save China in a spiritual sense.

The heyday of American missionaries in terms of China-American relations was from the late nineteenth through the early twentieth century. By the mid-twenties, American churches were supporting a missionary enterprise in China that included some 13 Christian colleges with 3,500 students, over 200 middle schools with 26,000 students, 250,000 pupils in primary schools, about 100 hospital, YMCA, and YWCA centers, as well as a great variety of other activities in social welfare and agricultural production.[22]

Meanwhile, as seen in the life and work of Ida Pruitt, postwar liberal theology was promoting Christian humanism in missionary programs, in contradistinction to the primary emphasis on evangelism that characterized the earlier missionaries. Concurrently, in the 1920s, there was a general decline in church participation. The introduction of the automobile, the radio, and the moving picture theater in the Roaring Twenties, no doubt, contributed to church apathy in American society. But also significant were the teachings of the natural and social sciences, which challenged the intellectual validity of church teachings. Religious liberals were influenced by new intellectual trends in psychology and philosophy, which seemed to find only one justification for remaining within the institutional frame-work of the church. This justification lay in their faith that the new social order must be based on Christian ethics and ideals such as charity, mercy, the worth of the individual, and the fostering of international goodwill.

Some intellectuals, influenced by new trends in anthropology, were not only critical of church doctrines in general, but overtly hostile toward missionary work.

> Anthropologists had now successfully diffused among the reading public the culture concept. In the light of this each society was considered a unit by itself and its religious expression a product of its peculiar historical experience. This not only ran counter to the notion that Christianity had a universal applicability, but it made any attempt to engraft Christianity onto an Oriental society of great antiquity seem foolish. Every native custom had some validity, and for the Western missionary to destroy these customs was to help bring about the collapse of the moral order of that society.[23]

In this climate of opinion, missionaries of the 1920s were often subjected to criticism, cynicism, satire, and lampooning in America such as they never before had to endure.

According to Paul Varg, church apathy and theological liberalism "had a delayed impact on the missionary enterprise in China. [I]n the years immediately after the war the movement continued along the lines of rapid development characteristic of the years before 1917. Indeed," he says, "from 1919 to 1925, the number of volunteers and the amount of contributions far surpassed the marks set in the peak years 1910 to 1916."[24]

Beginning in 1926, however, the missionary enterprise responded to the secularization of religion in the United States, and China's wartime suffering. The "social gospel" group among China missionaries attempted to adapt the gospel to conditions in China by emphasizing the humanitarianism rather than evangelization. Traditional missionaries, however, tried to say that the root of China's problems was spiritual. Neither group enjoyed much success.[25]

Serving as an interesting comparison with, and contrast to, Lodwick's Hainan study is the essay by Jean-Paul Wiest. Though focusing on a somewhat later time period and on Catholics rather than on Presbyterians, Wiest relies on similar source material. He notes that the Maryknoll missionaries have been historically bold and imaginative in their use of mass media. Wiest demonstrates that their most successful means of spreading mission information has been the magazine, *Maryknoll*, which was started by James A. Walsh in 1907 under the title *The Field Afar*. One of its clearly defined goals, Wiest explains, was to educate American Catholics about foreign missions. His study of the thousands of stories and articles published in this magazine between 1918 and 1953 reveals that the Maryknoll missionaries painted a highly favorable, but not always accurate, picture of China. Themes that the Maryknolls tried to impress upon the minds of Americans emphasized that China was a great civilization, a country attracted to Christianity by its works of charity, and a country threatened by communism. The Maryknolls also applauded the faith and patriotism of Chinese Catholics.

Looking at the missionaries' interpretation of events in China from a broader perspective is the essay by Murray Rubinstein. In focusing on problems of images and their impact, Rubinstein presents three case studies of evangelically or charismatically oriented mission bodies, and examines how members of these representative mission communities saw events in twentieth-century China and how they reported these events to their superiors. His essay shows how the leaders of these mission boards made use of the missionary reports in spreading the word to their own church constituencies. And it assesses the extent to which these reports affected the way these Americans in their churches scattered throughout the length and breadth of the United States saw China and its traumatic and sometimes tragic revolution.

Rubinstein's essay also leads into Part II of this volume, which illustrates how American political expansion often went hand in hand with religious, cultural, and economic expansion. As these essays testify, American missionaries in China became involved not only in religious and humanitarian work, but also played prominent roles in diplomacy. For example, the Yale graduate, Rev. Peter Parker, not only founded modern medical missions in China, he was also integrally involved in diplomacy as the American charge d'affaires and commissioner. In 1841, he was invited to address a joint session of Congress on the subject of American relations with China and to submit a written report. The Sino-American Treaty of 1844, which governed relations between the two countries for many years, was based primarily on this report and included the "toleration of Christianity" clause. It was negotiated primarily by the newly appointed commissioner to China, Caleb Cushing, but Parker and fellow missionaries, Samuel Wells Williams and Elijah C. Bridgman, assisted him.[26]

Subsequent treaties of the late nineteenth century benefited the merchants still further by providing tariff restrictions and foreign concessions in some of the cities. But the treaties also provided additional security and proselytizing opportunities for missionaries. Extraterritoriality provisions, for example, benefited merchants and missionaries alike.

For the missionaries, such treaty provisions were not only desirable, they were necessary if they were to have any hope of success. "So strong and so continuous was the antagonism toward the missionary," says Professor Varg, "that he could never have attempted to Christianize the country had not the Western nations with their superior force upheld his right to be there."[27] Hence, in nineteenth-century policy matters missionaries and diplomats were in agreement, at least for the most part.

In their involvement with the formulation of foreign policy, China missionaries had personal contacts, under varying situations and circumstances, with State Department officials in Washington, as well as with American diplomatic and consular representatives in China. Government officials regularly received in large quantity copies of resolutions and declarations on American East Asian policy passed by the Foreign Missions Conference or its committees, the many denominational foreign missions boards, and thousands of church congregations and ministerial associations.[28]

After the Boxer Rebellion the missionaries, encouraged by Chinese attempts at reform, were more positive in their outlook and became defenders of China. While American missionaries were generally sympathetic to Chinese aspirations, however, they were not very effective in winning support from the American government. American East Asian policy had become, by then, the product of a whole set of considerations beyond the concerns of missionaries. Economic interests, for example, as well as relations with Japan and Europe, were of considerable significance.

In 1915, all of Wilson's zeal and lofty rhetoric about the integrity of China were overcome by pressures from Japan. And all the missionaries' sympathy and calls for righteousness had no appreciable influence in safeguarding China's interests.

Arline T. Golkin's essay on the politics of famine relief verifies that the years 1928–30 were characterized by American withdrawal from involvement in providing relief for Chinese famine victims in spite of intensive efforts on the part of missionaries. American missionary communities in China and in the United States could not convince State Department and Red Cross officials that famine relief was either possible or justifiable. The debates that characterized missionary appeals and official responses demonstrated that private endeavors could not succeed without official sanction and support and that, in the case of famine intervention during the late 1920s, the impact of American missionaries on U.S. policies toward China was negligible.

While little China assistance was forthcoming from the American government, some revisionist missionaries[29] placed great hope in many Chinese Christian leaders. These leaders were generally ardent advocates of treaty revision and, by this time, revisionist missionaries who were sympathetic toward Chinese nationalism no longer thought it necessary or wise to rely on treaty provisions for themselves. The missionaries came to believe that only by surrendering treaty rights could they hope to rescue their fragile enterprise from the onrushing holocaust of Chinese nationalism. It is virtually impossible to prove influence, but the preponderance of evidence indicates that American missionaries deserve a great deal of credit for the fact that it was the United States that eventually led the way in granting China tariff autonomy. Missionaries met with considerable opposition from business interests and old China hands in the diplomatic service,[30] but by July 1928 their view prevailed, and Secretary of State Frank Kellogg was ready to proceed with negotiations.

With the Japanese invasion of Manchuria in 1931 and its bombing of Chinese cities throughout the 1930s, American missionaries served as eyewitnesses to the suffering inflicted upon China. Not only did they send detailed accounts to the American press but they also dispatched ''to the President, the State Department and to members of Congress countless airmail letters and cables lodging protests against Japan or demanding some particular action by the American government."[31] Letters and articles vividly described Japanese atrocities and also alerted the American people and the American government to Japan's ultimate aims of conquering and commercially exploiting all of China. They warned furthermore that Japan had "aggressive designs against the Philippines, and the British, French and Dutch colonies further South."[32] At the same time, missionaries emphasized the strength of China and the refusal of Chiang Kai-shek's government to yield. They incessantly demanded that the American government extend material assistance to China in its war against Japan. Most missionaries, however, were opposed to any military involvement on the part of the United States to halt Japan.

Secretary of State Henry L. Stimson resisted both economic and military measures against Japan, in spite of missionary advocacy for the former. Instead, Stimson announced a nonrecognition doctrine, stating that the United States would not recognize territorial changes resulting from use of force and violation of treaty agreements. Although Stimson was not in total agreement with missionary thinking, it appears that he was influenced by it. Although nonrecognition had no effect in deterring Japan, Stimson himself confirmed that in formulating it he was moved by a knowledge of

> incalculable harm which would be done immediately to American prestige in China and ultimately to the material interests of America and her people in that region, if after having for many years assisted by public and private effort in the education and development of China towards the ideals of modern Christian civilization, and having taken the lead in the movement which secured the covenant of all the great powers, including ourselves, "to respect her sovereignty, her independence and her territorial and administrative integrity," we should now cynically abandon her to her fate when this same covenant was violated.[33]

While most missionaries favored some kind of economic sanctions against Japan, they opposed a complete embargo for fear that it would lead to war.[34] A few notable missionaries, however, believed that point of view was moral irresponsibility and insisted that only an embargo could halt Japan's aggression.

Particularly influential in this connection was the American medical missionary and later congressman, Dr. Walter Henry Judd. Although he is best known for his so-called "China Lobby" efforts in the late 1940s and early 1950s, his interest in China began much earlier.[35] Upon receiving his medical degree in 1923, Judd remained active in church and mission organizations such as the Student Volunteer Movement. In early 1926, under the sponsorship of the Congregational Foreign Missionary Board, he began his career as a medical missionary in China. After suffering malaria and some unpleasant encounters with Communist guerrillas in the late 1920s and early 1930s, Judd contributed to local mission programs not only through his practice of medicine but also by teaching music and English. During the period of coalition between the Nationalists and Communists, Judd provided medical assistance to many Communist leaders, including Lin Piao.

As the Japanese aggression in China intensified, Dr. Judd resigned his position in China, and returned to the United States to speak out against the Japanese. During a two-year span, from 1939 to 1941, he delivered some fourteen hundred lectures on behalf of the American Committee for Non-Participation in Japanese Aggression, a group seeking to prevent scrap iron from being shipped to Japan for use in China.

Although Judd felt that he was a voice crying in the wilderness, he did not give up. Besides giving speeches, he appealed to the media, writing numerous articles for newspapers and magazines. In February 1941, *Reader's Digest* published his piece entitled simply, "Let's Stop Arming Japan." Judd's article cited a Gallup Poll finding that 82 percent of the American people favored shutting off war supplies to Japan.

Missionaries like Judd may have finally won over the general public, but they had not yet won over the American businessmen. In assessing their views in September 1940, *Fortune* magazine found that 40.1 percent of representative American businessmen still favored appeasement of Japan and recognition of her claim to a sphere of influence, while 35 percent would let nature take its course, and only 19.1 percent favored an embargo or other meaningful threats of force.[36] Thus, in molding an organized vocal opinion demanding that the government act against its established trade relations, the missionary movement ran counter to business interests, but was belatedly successful.

After Pearl Harbor when China officially became America's honored ally, all those who so strongly sympathized with China's plight were hopeful that some substantial assistance would be forthcoming. But Margaret Denning demonstrates in her essay that such hopes were in vain. She points out that United States diplomatic and military personnel in China during World War II relied on a varied cast of sources in obtaining information about both free and Japanese-occupied China. As the Japanese proceeded to expand and consolidate their control over areas throughout China, many observers—such as business people, educators, journalists, and government officials—withdrew in the face of hardships and uncertainties precipitated by the wartime conditions and the Japanese presence. Although some missionaries departed as well, Professor Denning says, others remained to continue their work. It is from these remaining eyewitnesses that U.S. news services, military observers, and diplomatic personnel drew many facts and impressions concerning Japanese treatment of civilians, the Chinese response to the war, and the internal strife that resulted from Kuomintang and Chinese Communist differences.

In examining the extent to which U.S. governmental agencies referred to American missionaries in China for information during the war years, Denning relied on U.S. government documents and statements of both officials and missionaries in China at that time. In assessing the impact of that contribution on overall U.S. policy toward China and on the attitude of U.S. officials toward the Chinese, she concluded that American missionaries played no small role in arousing both the sympathy and the impatience reflected by U.S. officials. But, sadly, she could find little substantial evidence that in spite of all the emotion they aroused, the missionaries had much of an impact on the actual formulation of policy.

Meanwhile, the Pearl Harbor attack convinced some of Judd's friends that his knowledge of Asia qualified him to be an effective wartime congressman. After due consideration and several refusals, he launched his campaign, won the election, and on January 6, 1943, began his career as a congressman from Minnesota. He remained in office for twenty years. From his first days in Washington, Walter H. Judd was widely regarded as the "China expert" among policy makers and was one of Congress's most sought-after speakers not only for partisan Republican rallies, but for civic, religious, and professional groups. "During his congressional days Judd received an average of eight invitations a day to speak at some function." He accepted over a hundred invitations a year and his personality and platform style seldom failed to arouse considerable comment and debate from both his critics and his admirers.[37]

Judd made one of his most memorable speeches before the House of Representatives shortly after the end of World War II (November 20, 1945) to plead for American aid to China and to urge the U.S. government to keep the American marines in Asia until the civil war was settled.

During the war years, missionaries had but little impact on either policy makers or the general American public. In the Gallup Poll of July 1946, which asked a cross section of Americans what they thought the United States should do about the situation in China, 50 percent of those polled gave responses such as "Nothing," "Stay out," and "Leave them alone." Only 13 percent of those queried were in favor of giving aid to Chiang in his struggle against the Communists.[38]

According to the essay by Tony Ladd, Walter Judd felt that his crusade against trade with Japan in the 1930s, as well as his subsequent twenty-year congressional career, was an extension of his missionary service in China. He preached in Congress an American crusade as zealously as he had preached his religion in China. Nevertheless, Ladd concludes, Judd's mission to Capitol Hill and his attempt to impact American policies relative to China, when measured by legislative accomplishment, were small at best.

Because of his unwillingness to compromise, Judd drew a great deal of criticism in later years. He was blamed for creating a political climate of polarized ideologies that characterized the Cold War era. For good or ill, his highly charged speaking in Congress certainly promoted the containment of communism policy that dominated the 1950s, and Ladd suggests that Judd's influence may have extended beyond the 1950s as well by indirectly affecting the positions of Lyndon Johnson in the 1960s and Ronald Reagan in the 1980s. The American policies relative to

Vietnam, Grenada, and Nicaragua, Ladd argues, reflect basic containment ideas outlined by Judd.

Besides Judd, another noteworthy missionary who played a prominent role in policy making during the war years was John Leighton Stuart. As the essays by John Brewer and Edmund S. Wehrle explain, it was in July 1946, while president of Peking's Yenching University, that this veteran American missionary was personally selected by General George C. Marshall to become the American ambassador to China. His principle duty was to assist General Marshall, President Truman's special representative, in negotiating a settlement between the National Government and the Communist party.

A missionary-educator who spent most of his life in China, Stuart, according to John Brewer, brought to his office a deep understanding of the Chinese, which was lacking in Washington.[39] Stuart's role in the Marshall mission negotiations, and on through his term as the United States ambassador to China (1946–49) varied from an active participant to that of an observer. According to Ed Wehrle, Stuart was steadfast in his proclivity to see things from the Nationalist point of view, and had considerable influence on Marshall's negative attitudes toward the Chinese Communists.

Professor Wehrle is probably correct, but it is impossible to measure scientifically the impact of American missionaries on U.S. attitudes and policies toward China. A volume such as this probably raises more questions than it answers. Nevertheless, recent scholarship demonstrates that, beyond a doubt, China mission history has played an integral part in the history of the complex relationship between China and the United States. The role has not always been positive, consistent, or decisive, but overall it has most definitely been significant and calls for further study.

Notes

1. At the annual meeting of the Association for Asian Studies, which met in Boston, April 10–12, 1987, Professor Andrew Nathan of Columbia University's East Asian Institute prepared a paper for the panel on "New Views of Chinese Foreign Relations." In it he summarized some of the recent scholarship that challenges, for example, the cliché that Mao Tse-tung had "won the hearts and minds of the people." Scholars today are taking a more critical look at Mao's political, social, and economic policies vis-à-vis those of Chiang Kai-shek.

2. Paul Gordon Lauren, *The China Hands' Legacy: Ethics and Diplomacy* (Boulder, CO: Westview Press, 1987).

3. Stephen R. MacKinnon and Oris Friesen, *China Reporting: An Oral History of American Journalism in the 1930s and 1940s* (Berkeley, CA: University of California Press, 1987).

4. Kenneth Scott Latourette, "The Christian Understanding of History," *American Historical Review* Vol. 104, No. 2 (January 1949): 259–76. See also Latourette's *The Emergence of a World Christian Community* (New Haven: Yale University Press, 1949), p. 35; Latourette's *History of Christian Missions in China* (New York: Macmillan, 1926);

Latourette's *A History of the Expansion of Christianity*, especially Vol. 6: *The Great Century in Northern Africa and Asia, A.D. 1800–A.D. 1914* (New York: Harper & Brothers, 1945); and Latourette's *Missions and the American Mind* (Indianapolis: National Foundation Press, 1949).

5. Kenneth S. Latourette, *The Emergence of a World Christian Community* (New Haven: Yale University Press, 1949), p. 35.

6. Kenneth S. Latourette, *History of Christian Missions in China* (New York: Macmillan, 1926), pp. 5, 44–45.

7. John K. Fairbank, *Chinabound: A Fifty-Year Memoir* (New York: Harper & Row, 1982), p. 5.

8. John K. Fairbank, *Chinese-American Interaction: A Historical Summary* (New Brunswick, NJ: Rutgers University Press, 1975), p. 22.

9. Jacques Gernet, *China and the Christian Impact* (Cambridge, MA: Cambridge University Press, 1985), p. 1.

10. Ibid.

11. Ibid., p. 2.

12. Ibid., p. 24.

13. James Thomson, Jr., Peter W. Stanley, and John Curtis Perry, *Sentimental Imperialists: The American Experience in East Asia* (New York: Harper & Row, 1985), p. 16. This same notion of America being the fulfillment of history and the dawn of the future permeates the poetry of Walt Whitman and is reflected in Henry Nash Smith's classic study, *The Virgin Land: The American West as Symbol and Myth* (Cambridge: Harvard University Press, 1950).

14. Thompson, Stanley, and Perry, p. 16.

15. Harold Isaacs, in *Images of Asia: American Views of China and India* (New York: G. P. Putnam, 1970), traces the historical development of America's ever-changing images of China.

16. Sherwood Eddy, *Pathfinders of the World Missionary Crusade* (New York: Abingdon-Cokesbury, 1945), p. 54.

17. Thomson, p. 4.

18. Emily S. Rosenberg, *Spreading the American Dream: American Economic and Cultural Expansion, 1890–1945* (New York: Hill and Wang, 1982), p. 28.

19. John W. Masland, "Missionary Influence Upon American Far Eastern Policy," *The Pacific Historical Review*, Vol. 10 (September 1941) 2: 81–82. For previous discussions on the influence of missionaries on China policy see Joseph L. Grabill, "The 'Invisible' Missionary: A Study in American Foreign Relations," *Journal of Church and State*, Vol. 14 (Winter 1972): 93–105; and the seminal study by James Reed, *The Missionary Mind and American East Asia Policy, 1911–1915* (Cambridge: Council on East Asian Studies, Harvard University, 1983).

20. See Theodore Roosevelt, "The Awakening of China," *The Outlook*, November 28, 1908, p. 666. Wilson's enthusiasm for the Christianization of China can be found in *Missionary Review of the World* (February 1916): 97.

21. B. A. Garside, *One Increasing Purpose: The Life of Henry Winters Luce* (New York: Fleming H. Revell, 1948), pp. 116–17.

22. Jessie Gregory Lutz, *China and the Christian Colleges, 1850–1950* (Ithaca, NY: Cornell University Press, 1971).

23. Paul A. Varg, *Missionaries, Chinese and Diplomats: The American Protestant Missionary Movement In China, 1890–1952* (Princeton: Princeton University Press, 1958), p. 162.

24. Ibid., p. 147. See also Kenneth Scott Latourette, "What Is Happening to Missions?" *The Yale Review* (September 1928): 76–77; Charles H. Fahs, "Recruiting and Selecting New

Missionaries," *Laymen's Foreign Missions Inquiry Fact-Finders' Reports*, ed. Orville A. Petty, Vol. 7 (New York: Harper & Brothers, 1932); Jesse R. Wilson, "Missionaries Sent Out By North American Boards," *The Foreign Missions Conference of North America: Report of 34th Annual Meeting*, ed. Fennell P. Turner, 214 (New York: Foreign Missions Conference of North America, 1927).

25. The missionary controversy over whether to Christianize or evangelize is dealt with extensively in William R. Hutchinson, *Errand to the World: American Protestant Thought and Foreign Missions* (Chicago: The University of Chicago Press, 1987). See especially introduction, pp. 12–13, and chapter 1.

26. Frederick Wells Williams, *The Life and Letters of Samuel Wells Williams, L.L.D.* (New York: G. P. Putnam's Sons, 1889), p. 127. For details on some of the negotiations involving Peter Parker, see Peter Parker to Robert M. McLane, November 10, 1854, U.S. Congress, Senate, 2nd Session, 35th Congress, Ex. Doc. Vol. 7, No. 22, 303.

27. Varg, *Missionaries*, p. 31.

28. Masland, p. 283.

29. By the late 1920s, Paul Varg categorizes China missionaries into three groups: fundamentalists, conservatives, and liberals (or revisionists). The fundamentalists and conservatives by that time were comparatively few in number, "devoted almost all their energies to the traditional program of evangelization" and "were essentially nonpolitical." Varg, *Missionaries*, p. 214.

30. For American views that opposed treaty revision in the late 1920s, see Dorothy Borg, *American Policy and the Chinese Revolution, 1925–1928* (New York: American Institute of Pacific Relations and Macmillan, 1947); "American Association of China," *The North China Herald*, June 27, 1925; "The N.C.C. Again," *The North China Herald*, July 25, 1925; "The Powers' Attitude Toward China," *The North China Herald*, August 1925. Quoted in Varg, *Missionaries*, pp. 198–99.

31. Masland, pp. 283–84.

32. Letters distributed by Associated Boards for Christian Colleges in China, New York, September 1, 1939, January 18, 1940. Referred to by Masland, p. 286. See also *Christian Century* articles, January 3, 1940, p. 29, and April 24, 1940, p. 557. And letters on file in Missionary Research File, Union Theological Seminary in New York, referred to by Varg, *Missionaries*, p. 253.

33. Henry L. Stimson and McGeorge Bundy, *On Active Service in Peace and War* (New York: Harper & Brothers, 1947), p. 90. Quoted in Varg, *Missionaries*, p. 254.

34. See, for example, Kenneth Scott Latourette, "A Church-Made War with Japan," *The Christian Century*, January 31, 1940; A. L. Warnshuis, "The Way to Peace in East Asia," *The Christian Century*, January 3, 1940; and Hugh Vernon White to editor, *The Christian Century*, March 13, 1940, p. 356.

35. In addition to the information offered here by Tony Ladd, sources on Walter Judd include Stanley Bachrack, *The Committee of One Million: The China Lobby in American Politics, 1953–71* (New York: Columbia University Press, 1976); Floyd Russel Goodno's "Walter H. Judd: Spokesman for China in the United States House of Representatives" (unpublished dissertation, Oklahoma State University, 1970); Walter Judd's voluminous personal papers, which are still unorganized but available for scholars at the Hoover Institution, Stanford University; and an oral interview with Dr. Judd by Paul Hopper is also available at the Dwight D. Eisenhower Library in Abilene, Kansas.

36. *Fortune*, Vol. 22 (September 1940): 73.

37. Goodno, pp. 67–68. As early as 1939, having been called as a witness before the Senate Foreign Relations Committee, Judd impressed his listeners to such a degree that according to Senator Lewis B. Schwellenbach D–WA, "It was the unanimous opinion of those present at that meeting that the testimony of Dr. Judd had been so outstanding, and

had so clearly and exhaustively outlined the situation in the Far East, that there was no need to call any other witnesses." *Congressional Record*, 76th Congress, 1st Sess., 1939, 84, Part 10, 10753. Quoted by Nancy Bernkopf Tucker in *Patterns in the Dust: Chinese-American Relations and the Recognition Controversy, 1949–1950* (New York: Columbia University Press, 1983), p. 89. Tucker also notes that Judd was highly respected by the *New York Times*. Tucker, p. 256. In April 1944, Mike Mansfield, a liberal Democratic congressman from Montana who had served in East Asia as a marine during the early 1920s and served as a special emissary to China for President Franklin D. Roosevelt in the 1940s, said of Judd, "I have a high regard for the gentleman and consider him one of the outstanding authorities on the Far East in the entire country." Mike Mansfield, *Congressional Record*, 78th Cong., 2nd Sess., 1944, Part 3, 3552.

38. A. T. Steele, *The American People and China* (New York: McGraw-Hill, 1966), p. 31.

39. For more information on John Leighton Stuart, see his own account: *Fifty Years in China: The Memoirs of John Leighton Stuart, Missionary and Ambassador* (New York: Random House, 1954); eds. Kenneth W. Rea and John C. Brewer, *The Forgotten Ambassador: The Reports of John Leighton Stuart, 1946–1949* (Boulder, CO: Westview, 1981); and the John Leighton Stuart Papers in the United Board for Christian Higher Education Collection, Yale Divinity School Archives.

Part I

Missionary Contributions to Intercultural Understanding

2

CONFLICTING CULTURAL TRADITIONS IN CHINA
Baptist Educational Work in the Nineteenth Century

Charles W. Weber

Introduction

A major aspect of missions is the extent to which they are involved in acculturation. China in the nineteenth century provides an interesting case study for acculturation since, during this period, a resurgent industrializing Western culture and an activist, mission-minded church were making a more concerted impact on the Ching dynasty. The dynamic interaction of Western culture and Christianity with Chinese civilization is a model of cross-cultural analysis.

Focusing on mission-provided education contributes significantly to an understanding of Western versus Chinese cultures because education is a socialization process. Therefore, mission schools become a means of communicating one culture to another, and in this process the comparisons between the West and China become apparent as divergent customs and values come into contact with one another. In the efforts of missionaries to foster their religious beliefs nurtured in their own cultural and historic traditions, the difficulties of transplanting these beliefs into another cultural milieu became manifest. Missionary educational efforts can be used to highlight this cultural clash.

The missionary was the agent for both this clash and cultural interaction. As John K. Fairbank has observed, "In China's nineteenth-century relations with the West, Protestant missionaries are still the least studied but most significant actors in the scene."[1] It might be claimed in this connection that one of the least studied groups of these early Protestant missionaries are the Baptist missions. This paper attempts to examine one aspect of Baptist missionary activity in Chinese society, that of mission schools.

The Growth of American and English Baptist Mission Work in China During the Nineteenth Century

Modern missions were largely an outgrowth of the Pietist and Evangelical movements in Protestantism in the eighteenth and nineteenth centuries. These movements revitalized the Protestant churches of the Western world, including America, as they countered the impact of rationalism and Deism with the conviction that each individual must make a personal commitment to live a new life through faith in Christ and then lead others into this life of personal piety and devotion to God. It was out of this religious atmosphere, stressing the necessity of individual salvation through Christ and the conversion experience for all people, that the modern missionary movement had its inception.

The growth of Baptist missions was also the result of the impact of the Pietist and Evangelical movements. In 1792 the English Baptists organized the first modern missionary society and sent their first missionaries to India and Burma. The English Baptists were supported in their Asian enterprise by the American Baptists who gave between $7,000 and $8,000 to the English Baptists in a twenty-year period before founding the American Baptists' own mission society, the General Missionary Convention, in 1814.[2] By 1833 the American Baptists had thirty-three missionaries and wives working in Burma and about four hundred converts.[3]

In 1833 one of the American Baptist missionaries, John Taylor Jones, was impressed with the need for someone to work with the Chinese in Bangkok and he requested that the mission send someone. The next year, Rev. and Mrs. William Dean started work among the community in Bangkok and found the ethnic Chinese there more responsive than the Siamese. Thus, the first work of Baptists among the Chinese people was not in China but rather among the overseas Chinese. One important reason for this situation was that from the mid-eighteenth century to 1828 there was an almost continual nationwide persecution of Christians in China and from 1828 to 1858 the persecution continued but more intermittently.[4]

However, in 1807, before the Baptists commenced their work, a most resourceful man, Robert Morrison, went to Portuguese Macao under the London Missionary Society and became the first Protestant missionary to reside in China. In Macao Morrison translated for the East India Company and also worked on a personal project of translating the Bible into middle Chinese with the aid of Chinese helpers and Chinese Catholics. In 1824 he published his Bible and a six-volume English-Chinese dictionary. Publication of Morrison's Bible occurred two years after the publication of the Marshman-Lassar translation (Marshman being an English Baptist) in Mandarin at Serampore, India. Despite the crude nature of these translations, the early Baptist missionaries relied on them heavily (especially Morrison's version) and the translations provided the missionaries with success in circumventing the Chinese imperial decree against Chinese teaching their language to foreigners.

In addition to his translation, Morrison established the Anglo-Chinese College at Malacca in 1818 with the purpose, in his own words, of teaching both "English and Chinese literature in order to spread the gospel of Jesus Christ." Many Chinese attended this school and then went into trade or employment with foreigners.[5] In

1850 the London Missionary Society moved Morrison's school to Hong Kong.

From 1807 to 1842 there were only about twenty Protestant missionaries evangelizing the Chinese; they represented eight missionary societies. A few of these missionaries were in Canton or Macao, but most were outside China in Singapore, Malacca, or Bangkok. In fact, by 1842 it was estimated that there were only about a hundred actual converts of Chinese nationality.[6]

In this period the only Baptist group active among the Chinese was the American Baptists. In 1836 they sent Rev. and Mrs. J. Shuck from Bangkok to Macao to open up the South China Mission. The next year, Issacher Roberts and the Rev. and Mrs. William Dean joined the Shucks in Macao.

After 1842, missions in general benefited from the treaties that followed the Opium War of 1839 to 1842, forcing Chinese concessions. First, Hong Kong was ceded to the British and the ports of Canton, Amoy, Foochow, Ningpo, and Shanghai were opened to foreign residences and trade, although the presence of foreigners was restricted to these ports. Also, the privilege of extraterritoriality was granted to all foreigners as well as the right of foreigners to study the Chinese language. In addition, each of the treaties contained a most-favored-nation clause. Actually very little was said in the treaties about religion except that in the French and American treaties the Chinese granted permission for houses, hospitals, schools, and places of worship to be built in the open ports. Of course, under the most-favored-nation clause this provision could also be claimed by the other European powers.[7] The significance of these treaties concluding the Opium War was that it allowed Europeans, including missions, to become established within imperial China.

Missions took advantage both of these treaty provisions as well as of the imperial edicts of toleration issued in 1842 and 1844 allowing the Chinese to practice Christianity. Missionary societies, such as the American Board of Commissioners for Foreign Missions, the American Presbyterians, the American Methodists, English Wesleyans, and English Presbyterians, initiated and expanded their efforts in China at this time. However, not all missions were as eager, particularly the London Missionary Society (LMS), the Church Missionary Society (CMS), and the British Mission Society (BMS), all of whom hesitated to take advantage of privileges exacted after a disgraceful war fought over a commodity, opium, which they morally repudiated.[8]

The American Baptists continued to expand their South China Mission begun in 1836. In 1842 the Shucks moved to Hong Kong and began the important work of revising the Scriptures and of opening three elementary schools for both boys and girls. In 1845 the Shucks established a new station in Canton where they stayed until 1854 when they returned to America to work with the Chinese on the West Coast. Also in 1845, the British General Baptists, after numerous appeals from Rev. Shuck, sent two missionaries to Ningpo. However, the Ningpo station was turned over to the English Methodists in the 1870s.

The year 1845 marked an important development among the American Baptists when the denomination split over the issue of slavery to form two groups, the American Baptist Missionary Union (ABMU) and the Southern Baptist Convention (SBC). The mission work already begun in South China was continued by the Southern Baptists who made Canton and Shanghai their first foreign mission field.

During this early period, indeed throughout the nineteenth century, there was generally good cooperation among all Protestant missions. Part of this has to do with their common religious heritage coming out of Evangelicalism and Pietism and their common interest in evangelization. The cooperation was especially apparent in the area of translating Scripture and of writing Christian literature that they felt was their primary means of evangelization.[9] Tremendous effort was put into making translations of the Chinese dialects with romanized letters. These literary accomplishments were met with contempt by the Chinese scholars, but they resulted in a tremendous production of books, tracts, hymns, texts, dictionaries, grammars, histories, and so on in both Mandarin and the dialects. To the Protestants the spreading of the gospel was seen as a common endeavor emphasizing Scripture translation and the production of a religious literature available to a literate Chinese populace.

The renewal of warfare between the Ching state and Europeans at the end of the 1850s led to the further expansion of missions through the provisions in treaties of 1858 and the Convention of 1860. The new concessions most important for missions were: (1) the opening of more ports to foreigners, (2) the freedom for foreigners to travel outside the treaty ports and for missions to acquire property within the Chinese Empire, (3) requiring the Chinese to pay indemnities to Britain and France for damages to foreigners and their property, and (4) imperial toleration of Christianity and a promise of protection to Chinese and foreign Christians in China, insured if necessary by the direct intervention of the foreign powers themselves. Payment of indemnities and state protection of Christians in China were used mostly by the French and the Roman Catholics, while Britain, the United States, and the Protestant missions were more reluctant to become involved, although on occasion they also made use of these treaty provisions.[10]

The result of this Second Treaty Settlement was that Protestant missions, including the LMS, CMS, and BMS, decided to take advantage of the opportunity these treaties provided. Thus, from 1860 to 1900 missions began to penetrate extensively throughout China accompanied by the expansion of the West under the ''new imperialism'' and by the intensification of religious fervor with the growth of Fundamentalism in the West during this same period. The English and American Baptists were not exempted from these influences.

In order to understand the extent of Baptist work, the following section traces the expansion of Baptist missions in China. Special emphasis is given to the concern of the missions with the establishment of schools. References to this map,

Protestant Missions in China in 1900

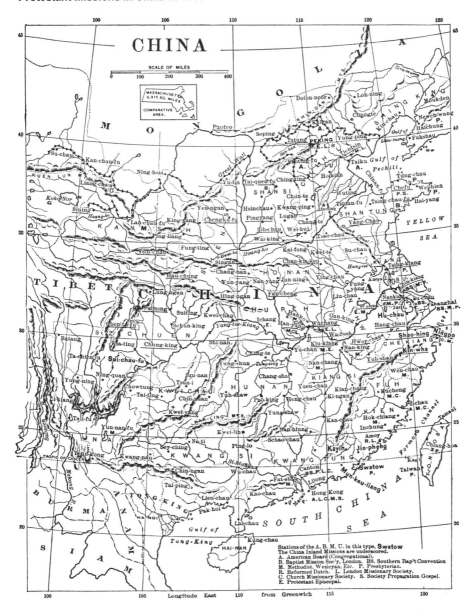

Source: British Missionary Magazine, Vol. 80:8 (August 1900), p. 485.

reprinted from the *Baptist Missionary Magazine* (1900), may be helpful in locating the places mentioned in the following material.

Baptist Missionary Society (English)

In 1859 the BMS opened its work in North China by going into Shanghai. In 1860–61 they expanded their work up the Yangtze River as far as Nanking where they came into contact with areas under the influence of the Taipings. After an initial period of optimism concerning the nature of the Taiping movement, the BMS, as well as other Protestant missions, became disenchanted and saw the Taipings as morally and spiritually decadent. In 1861 the BMS tried to establish a mission in Peking but this never became established. The city of Chefoo in Shantung Province was another station opened in 1861, but it also failed. The reason for these failures was that death and disease struck many of the missionaries who also were hindered by the bands of robbers so prevalent at the time. In 1875 the Chefoo station was handed over to the Scotch Presbyterian mission. Actually, by 1869 the BMS counted only 35 members.[11]

However, after 1869 the fortunes of the BMS in Shantung Province changed under the dynamic leadership of Timothy Richard. Richard was an energetic person who felt that in order to be successful in China, Christianity must first appeal to the scholars, officials, and leaders of Chinese society and then filter down the social ladder. In 1875 Richard put his ideas into action when he left his work at Chefoo to the American Baptists and established a new work 250 miles away in Ching-Chau-Fu. Here he started by ministering to the sick and starving in the area; this activity made him so popular that he was asked twice to lead the Chinese in a revolt against the authorities.[12] His first missionary efforts consisted of organizing local churches, personally working with the local leaders and establishing schools for orphans in elementary education with additional training in carpentry, iron work, and silk spinning. In the 1880s, more BMS missionaries joined Richard in China and the work increased through opening up a training school (1884) and two boarding schools for girls (1894). In 1893 these training schools became the Gotch-Robinson Institute with a full four- to five-year course for teachers, evangelists, and preachers in villages and a special two-year course for lay leaders. By the end of the nineteenth century, this work in Shantung Province had prospered, including the addition of a new station at Tsou-ping (1889) and a total church membership in the province of 4,117.[13]

From 1877 to 1879, Richard went on a famine relief mission to Shansi Province where it is estimated as many as 13 million Chinese died. Richard was credited with saving 70,000 people from death, and after the famine relief he turned to evangelization and book distribution with the particular objective of reaching the scholars and mandarins. In fact, for three years Richard gave popular monthly illustrated lectures on the sciences, history, geography, and religion to appeal to the Chinese fascination with Western learning. He also opened day schools in the Shansi provincial capital of Tai-Yuan-Fu. But by 1900 there were only 256 church members in Shansi and 150 students in the schools. In addition, all the BMS missionaries in Shansi were killed during the Boxer Rebellion.[14]

The BMS opened a new mission in Shensi Province in 1890 when 50 former Chinese Christian residents of Shantung Province migrated to Shensi (under government auspices to open up more arable land) and asked Richard to start a BMS mission in their new area. The zeal of these people was reflected in their active evangelization and the establishment of boys' and girls' day schools as well as a boys' and a girls' boarding school (1892). By the early twentieth century there were 720 church members in Shensi, 25 day schools, 2 boarding schools, and 2 Bible training schools (totaling 400 students in all schools).[15] Again the Boxer Rebellion intervened by forcing all BMS missions to seek refuge in Shanghai.

American Baptist Missionary Union

As mentioned earlier, in 1845 the South China mission field of the American Baptists was the first transferred to the auspices of the SBC after their denominational split. However, the ABMU continued to maintain a work in this area under the enthusiastic leadership of Rev. and Mrs. William Ashmore who arrived in Hong Kong in 1858 and in 1863 moved the headquarters of the ABMU's South China work to Swatow. From here the mission work quickly expanded. In 1873 Swatow Women's Bible Training School was established to train women to go to homes and evangelize their neighbors. This program was highly regarded by the missionaries and by the mid-1890s, 212 women had received instruction.[16] By 1879 four boys' schools had been started. But by 1900 the educational program had expanded to include a boys' and girls' boarding school attended by 36 and 34 students, respectively, with a primary or grammar school curriculum, as well as 31 other schools with 371 male and 38 female students in lower primary grades.[17] In addition, Ashmore soon founded a theological seminary to train national church leadership and by 1898 he had trained 9 ordained and 42 unordained preachers. This emphasis on education was successful for the mission because in 1900 there were 5 main stations, 90 outstations, 12 churches, and 2,073 baptized church members in the South China field of the ABMU.[18] In 1893 the center of the mission was moved from Swatow to Ungkung (thirty miles northeast of Swatow) and from here the work was extended into Fukien Province.

The East China field was located in Cheking Province with the center at Ningpo. The field was opened for the ABMU in 1843 by Dr. D. J. Macgowan and was quickly expanded emphasizing evangelism and literature translation as well as educational and medical facilities. In 1866 Hangchow and Kinhwa were opened (in 1888 a day school for boys was established in Hangchow). In 1870 a church was organized in Shaohsing and in 1888 a mission station was established in

Huckow after years of missionary preaching in the area and strong opposition from the literati. By 1900 the East China field included 3 boarding schools (in 1872 a girls' school, in 1873 a theological training class, in 1880 a boys' school), 5 other primary schools, 13 organized churches, 22 outstations, 683 church members, 9 ordained and 19 unordained Chinese preachers, and 6 Bible women.[19]

The West China field was the third started by the ABMU in China and it provides a worthwhile illustration of the motivation and perseverance of these early missionaries. In 1889 the Baptists opened their first station in Suifu of Szechuan Province, which they viewed as a vast and beautiful land with many people who knew nothing of the Gospel. The original plan had been to open a station in Suchow, but a fire in that city in 1889 proved to be disastrous and the missionaries decided to go to Suifu instead. One missionary's comment on the Suchow fire was, "A hundred souls a day passing into eternity in one city, and not one of them ever heard of Jesus!"[20] It was this attitude that accompanied the missionaries in their pioneering effort. In 1894 two new stations were opened in Kaiting and Yachow. In 1895 a boys' and a girls' school were started in Suifu; however, an antiforeign rebellion in the same year made the missionaries flee for their lives. No missionary was killed and, in addition, their attitude in light of this crisis, which seems typical of the response of other missionaries when they faced hardship and hostility, was one of determination and of faith in God's Providence. For example, Rev. George Hill in West China wrote, "May these disappointments and trials to our West China work, be the means of better preparation on our part, and inspire more prayer for this Christless land."[21] Rev. C. A. Salquist expressed a similar view when he wrote:

> It seems like a heavy blow and makes us all disappointed, still we do not despair. We all fully believe that this can be allowed for nothing else than the glory of the Lord. Far from giving up the thought of going back to [Szechwan], we are only gathering strength and experience for further work there, if God is willing to send us all back.[22]

Another wrote, "But the outcome is in God's hands."[23] By the end of 1895 an American embassy to Szechwan had obtained a guarantee of protection for foreigners and the mission work continued, although it did not really grow extensively until after the Boxer Rebellion. Up until 1900, it included three churches and sixty-eight members.[24] Yet the establishment of the West China field was indicative of the conviction under which the missionaries were working.

In 1893 the ABMU opened a Central China field in Hupei Province at Hanyang (extending to the nearby cities of Hankow and Wuchang) "if for nothing else, in order to render much needed support to the resolute band of Christian workers who have planted the banner of the cross near the western boundary of the vast empire."[25] Actually, a Chinese couple from the ABMU's East China field helped in opening this new station which was in their homeland. But the work here showed little growth before 1900, although it did have day schools, 3 churches, and 120 baptized members.[26]

This was the extent of the ABMU China mission until 1900. The staff included sixty-five missionaries including wives and unmarried missionaries. The work had prospered despite some rather immense obstacles.

Southern Baptist Convention

The SBC mission in China was not as extensive as the ABMU's work, but one important reason was that the American Civil War severely limited the resources available for missions. Nevertheless, the SBC contributed significant advances in evangelizing China.

As mentioned previously, the SBC assumed the responsibility for the ABMU's work that had been started in South China by 1845. Their early efforts were centered on Hong Kong and Canton but they were beset with many problems, particularly the poor health of the missionaries. In 1856 Rev. Robert Graves arrived and took charge of the South China field by sustaining an active evangelization program, translating literature, and setting up schools. Under his leadership the mission expanded to 13 stations around Canton, 7 schools including a theological school, and 530 church members by 1871.[27] By 1900 the three main stations were at Yingtak, the open port of Wuchow, and Canton City as the headquarters, and by 1907 there were 20 chapels and 418 church members.[28]

In 1847 the SBC founded a church at Shanghai with six foreigners and four Chinese to start their Central field. Three years later a new station was opened in Okadjau (twenty miles southeast of Shanghai) and this was the first permanently owned Protestant station in the interior. By 1853 the mission work directed from Shanghai had five day schools with an average attendance of a hundred. In 1879 a new outstation was started in Quinsan (fifty miles northwest of Shanghai). Then in 1883 two new mission stations were opened in Chinkiang and Soachow and in 1891 a mission station was established in Yangshaw. Thus, by 1906 the Central China field of the SBC had 4 main stations with the main center at Shanghai, 9 churches, and a membership of 409.[29]

The North China mission of the SBC was started in 1861 when missionaries came to Chefoo and Tengchowfu, which had a boarding school by 1863. However, the American Civil War intervened and the field did not grow rapidly until the 1880s. In 1891 the Pingtu region was opened and by 1900 it had three main stations with the headquarters in Tengchowfu.[30]

Thus, growth of these three Baptist missions, as outlined above, shows the extent and areas of involvement of Baptist mission work in China during the nineteenth century. However, a mere listing of new stations and schools says nothing of the hardship from disease, even death and persecution, to which most missionaries were subjected as they attempted to carry their Gospel message to China. They firmly believed that their activities were within the Providence of God to demonstrate God's great love for men as manifest in Scripture and to thwart the power of the Devil and thus redeem both lost souls and a lost world. This religious conviction, along with the realization of the immense potential of China, which is a recurrent theme in the mission literature, resulted in a dedication and a sense of immediacy among the missionaries that made Christianizing China a compelling priority in the nineteenth-century Protestant mission effort. The sincere intentions of missionaries to China should not be lost among the factual data because these intentions are the motivating force. Rev. E. P. Burtt provided a fitting summary of the missionary attitude when he said, ''So the church filled and actuated by the blessed Spirit of God has but one life and one mission. It is a life of love; it is a mission of service.''[31] This attitude stimulated missionaries in their work and attracted the interest of their home constituencies in Christianizing the Chinese Empire, an immense mission field containing the world's largest population.

The Development of Baptist Educational Work in the Nineteenth Century

Western missionaries to China entered a society where education was already highly esteemed, although only a small percentage of the Chinese were literate. Chinese education provided a means to social mobility through a series of civil service examinations. These exams were based on the Chinese classical literature of Confucius and Mencius as well as the commentaries on these ancient sages. The government administered these exams, which emphasized memorization of the classics and the ability to write a good essay. Passing these exams assured a person of a post in the imperial bureaucracy (many became clerks or teachers). However, despite the importance of education to the Chinese, the traditional education was not provided by the government but had to be sought out by a student from a private teacher who would give instruction in the classics for the exams (later, after exams had been passed, the imperial government supplied further instruction).

Western missionaries to China immediately recognized the important role of this educational system to Chinese life, yet they were prone to criticize it as ''unworthy'' or ''effete'' because the Chinese emphasis on the classics appeared sterile and backward.[32] Western learning, which was viewed by the European as the most advanced, was taught exclusively by the mission schools in China in the period before the twentieth century.

The Baptist missionaries of the nineteenth century advocated an educational policy in contrast to that of both the Chinese and many other missionary societies. The educational policy espoused by the Baptists was intended to supplement their view of the nature of missions.

The Baptist sects of Protestantism have traditionally held to the religious dogmas of the Reformation and the various pietist movements. The churches were noncreedal and deemphasized hierarchical church governance. Their main stress has been on the authority of Scripture as the sole guide to faith and practice, the priesthood of all believers, the need for an individual commitment to God, a belief in adult baptism by immersion, and an insistence on the separation of church and state, including in China where they tried to keep themselves free of political involvement.[33]

It was with this perspective in mind that the Baptist mission enterprise in China emphasized the following five areas:[34]

1. Evangelistic preaching. This was always considered preeminent. The instructions of the Executive Committee of the ABMU in 1850 underscored this when they told their new missionaries both to spread the Gospel of Jesus Christ and not Western science, art, and culture, and never to let translation or educational work take too much time from evangelization.[35] In carrying out evangelization, the missionaries used as a model the example of St. Paul in Athens. Thus, they drew upon the local Chinese situation and quoted from the classics in their attacks on Chinese customs and superstition while stressing their Christian themes of one's duty to God, the need for redemption and purity of heart, God's love and brotherly love, God as father and creator, and a coming day of judgment.[36] The missionaries were very active in their ministry and often ventured into the countryside around the cities to preach even before mission stations had been established.

2. Personal evangelism. The missionaries were also involved in a concerted effort to instruct inquirers and converts individually and in groups on the meaning of living the Christian life. One of the most effective ways of accomplishing this Christian nurture was to establish congregations and churches. The common procedure for carrying out this more intensive evangelization was to establish a mission station according to the following pattern. First, the missionary tried to obtain a house, which often was difficult because the Chinese did not want to rent or sell to foreigners. After obtaining a house, the missionary would invite Chinese into their home in an attempt to convert them. Then the missionaries would get a building to be used as a street chapel where as many as two or three services would be held each day consisting of prayer, Scripture reading, and preaching.[37] The last stage in setting up a mission station was for the Chinese to create their own congregation and to build a church. The mission objective was to develop an indigenous and self-supporting church of sound, devout Christian believers.

3. Literature distribution. The tremendous emphasis on Christian literature in the Chinese language has already been mentioned. Literature distribution was seen as an integral part of evangelism. The missionaries spent much time translating portions of the Bible, tracts, catechisms, and textbooks into the various Chinese dialects, oftentimes in romanized script. The production of Chinese literature was most impressive. As early as 1867 a press at Shanghai was able to report in a volume entitled "Memorials of Protestant Missionaries" that there were 746 publications

in Chinese of which 189 were in dialects. As one might expect, most of these were listed in such categories as sacred biography, catechism, hymns, prayers, educational and linguistic, history, government, geography, mathematics, astronomy, medicine, botany, physics, almanacs, and serials. In addition, this 1867 work listed a number of Chinese works that had been translated into English and German, most notably the *Chinese Classics* by James Legge, who was a Scottish LMS missionary and head of the Anglo-Chinese College in Hong Kong for thirty years beginning in 1839, along with his own introduction and commentary.[38] The pace of literature translation quickened through to the end of the nineteenth century with the degree of literalness of the translation being the major controversy among missionaries.[39]

4. Training children and converts in Christian doctrine and ethics. In the second half of the nineteenth century, there was a gradual shift from tract distribution to schools as the favored method of making an impact on Chinese culture and training Christian leaders. The impetus for this came from an imperial requirement ''that Confucius should be honoured in all schools with rites which Chinese Christians regarded as tantamount to worship.'' This policy created a conflict ''with the conscience of Christian parents'' and encouraged both Chinese Christians and missionaries to establish Christian elementary schools to avoid government interference and to nurture youngsters with Christian influences.[40]

The clear intention here was to further implement the building of an indigenous and self-supporting church by training lay leaders and by preparing native evangelists, teachers, and pastors under the auspices of the mission. The issue that continually appeared during this period was how much effort should be diverted from the job of winning converts in order to initiate and maintain schools, which were meant to supplement evangelism.

5. The establishment of hospitals, orphanages, and dispensaries. This was usually low on the priority list unless trained personnel were available, such as doctors and nurses. Nevertheless, work in these areas was considered an important asset to evangelism and of meeting Chinese social needs.

The purpose of Baptist missions as it related to education was perhaps best summed up by William Ashmore when he stated that education is to be the natural outgrowth of evangelism with the education designed to serve the evangelization process and not the secular interests of society. He said, ''Our schools follow our churches.''[41] With such a view, the educational approach of the Baptists was very practical, stressing mastery of the vernacular languages, Bible studies and memorization of Scripture, preaching and evangelism, and learn-by-doing techniques.[42] Thus, the objective of Baptist mission work in China and the role of education in that plan were carefully correlated.

Pattern of the Baptist Educational System

Taking into consideration the Baptists' distinctive doctrinal beliefs and view of missions, a unique pattern for their educational system might be expected. This became increasingly true as the nineteenth century progressed and as many other Protestant groups changed their focus. In the second half of the nineteenth century there was in Protestant circles at large a general questioning of the belief in Christianity as the only true religion and a tendency toward cultural and religious relativism that justified missions as a kind of humanitarian activity, which included a heavy emphasis on education and social action done in the name of Christian love and a deemphasis on a more activist proselytizing. However, the Baptists were identified with an alternative movement known as Fundamentalism and staunchly defended the traditional sanctions for missions and the supplementary role education should play in missions.[43]

The main motivating force for Baptist mission education was the feeling that "an illiterate church would soon drift back to idolatry" and "besides the children of Christians have an inherent claim to be educated," giving special attention to "character-building."[44] Thus, Baptist mission education was perceived as a means of strengthening the indigenous church, to which the Chinese Christians responded positively.[45]

The educational program of the Baptists was formulated on four levels. The curriculum was always essentially the same. The Bible was the main text. The students' responsibility was to master reading and writing in the vernacular and learn basic doctrines from a catechism and the teacher.[46] The Baptists were practical in their curricular approach and thus desired to avoid an educational program oriented to the liberal arts. Their objective was to provide leadership training for their parishioners. In order to accomplish these purposes, their educational system was organized on the following four levels.

First, there were the day schools. These were located in the villages and were placed under the auspices of the local church and the Christian teacher. Many churches wanted these schools as ways of training their parishioners' children and as a good means of evangelism. However, the mission insisted these schools be supported by the Chinese and thus not be a drain on the mission's budget. As Ashmore stated, "The school is theirs not ours."[47]

The content of the day school education centered on the three Rs, some history and geography, and Bible study. An interesting example was a survey taken of the curricula of 29 elementary schools in South China (ABMU) between 1835 and 1881, which showed the following courses most frequent: all schools taught religion (Christianity) and Chinese, 19 taught handiwork, 7 arithmetic, 4 history, 2 general subjects, and 1 practice teaching.[48]

The teaching technique employed was the Chinese custom of reading aloud and memorizing coupled with an attempt to gradually replace this with Western ideas of pedagogy, such as visual and audio aids, questions and answers, and review procedures. These were seen as more conducive to the assimilation of the material. However, erratic attendance made any substantial, sustained instruction difficult. The only real mission reward to this approach was if children would become

Christian and then reach their parents with the Gospel.

A second level of education was that provided by the boarding schools for both boys and girls. These "boarding schools were looked on as training centers for the children of the church," whereas the day schools were meant as evangelizing institutions.[49] As training centers for the children of Christians, the boarding schools were primarily intended to provide teachers, evangelists, and ministerial candidates for the Chinese churches.

The curriculum centered on the Bible and Christian doctrine, but also included elementary training in areas such as geography, physiology, Chinese classics, domestic arts, and hygiene.[50] The boys were trained to become teachers for mission schools and preachers. Their salaries in these vocations were low as a kind of repayment to the mission for their earlier education. The girls' schools, for which there was a precedent in traditional Chinese society with private Chinese girls' schools that appealed to girls from wealthy families,[51] were used by the Baptist missionaries to train women as teachers and housewives (especially for graduates of the boys' boarding schools). Also, the curriculum for the girls was meant to demonstrate to the Chinese the abilities of women and to demonstrate why their treatment should improve.[52]

The boarding schools were centrally located for easy access and they were set up to be models for the various day schools in the surrounding area. However, difficulties in staffing and financing often made the boarding school programs erratic, yet usually successful in their overall purpose of augmenting the Chinese Christian community. The size of the schools was between 29 to 35 students with an average age of about 17 or higher.[53]

The Baptists did not have any secondary schools until after 1900 because their emphasis on evangelism left little time, strength, or inclination for this kind of higher education. Yet, after 1870, the pressure from Chinese Baptist converts for training for government service and professional leadership in their country, like that provided by the Roman Catholics and Episcopalians, was increasing and the Baptists realized they were in danger of losing converts over this issue,[54] but the policy of Baptist mission boards and the lack of money and adequate staff delayed higher education facilities until the twentieth century.

The third level of education was that of the theological "schools" or training. These were usually composed of a small group of men with essentially a primary education who were under the tutorship of a missionary training them for ordination. Many of the theological students were busy as pastors and evangelists meeting with the missionary every few months for more instruction. Their studies emphasized the Pentateuch, the New Testament, and apologetics to meet Chinese criticisms of Christianity. This training was deemed sufficient since "the intellectual caliber of the church members did not seem to demand a highly trained ministry."[55] One of the outstanding examples of this kind of training was that accomplished by William Ashmore, who in 1878 had 15 theological students between the ages of

21 and 55 years old under his tutorship and who, up to 1898, produced 9 ordained and 42 unordained preachers.[56] Ordination was not easily granted. The missionaries wanted to be certain of the sincerity of the student's conversion as well as his doctrinal purity and devotion to evangelism before granting ordination.

Lastly, a fourth method of education, which proved very successful, was the training of "Bible women." Some of the Bible women were from the boarding schools, but most were trained by the women missionaries who instructed groups of Chinese Christian women in their homes. The lessons were in stories and Scripture after which the women were sent out two-by-two to visit the homes of other women in the community. Then the Bible women returned for more instruction. The use of Bible women was important to the missionaries because it was felt that the training of women and daughters was essential if the Gospel was to be successful in China.[57] Also, Bible women needed to visit homes because Chinese women would seldom attend public meetings such as the street chapels or churches. Actually, the example of Bible women and girls' boarding schools aided in the liberation of the Chinese woman by increasing sentiment for female suffrage and encouraging the entry of women into various occupations.[58]

The use of Western pedagogy has already been mentioned as a way of improving the traditional Chinese method of memorization and recitation. However, there is one major area where the Baptists, both American and English, refused to Westernize. They did not use English as the medium of teaching. Their reasons were basically threefold. First, a knowledge of English by the Chinese "opened the doors to temptation," in other words, they were more prone to go to work for the traders than to stay in mission work. Second, the missionaries wanted Christianity to be presented as naturally in Chinese as in English, thus emphasizing the idea that Christianity is a world religion that can be expressed in various cultures.[59] As we have seen, this resulted in a vast literature in the colloquial languages which, although disliked by the Chinese literati, did facilitate the work of Bible women and preachers. Teaching was in the vernacular with the Bible as the main text. Lastly, although English was needed most in the teaching of science, the Baptists did not emphasize science in their schools, namely because they thought it was too Westernizing, so they insisted on the vernacular. For these reasons, the Baptists in the nineteenth century did not employ English either as a subject in their schools or as a medium of instruction. English was considered a hindrance to the overall purposes of their work.

To most Chinese, the problem of all mission education in the nineteenth century was that it was under the auspices of the distrusted foreigner and it did not help in passing the civil service exams until 1898 when the emperor revised the civil service exam to include Western subjects. Besides, the Baptists never had a comprehensive plan of educational development since they saw education as a buttress for spreading the Gospel.[60] Despite these problems, the Baptists did make noticeable advances in the area of mission education. To do this, Baptists empha sized the expression of Christianity in the Chinese language and within the local Chinese community with an active national leadership in the churches by both lay and ordained leaders.

Cultural Difficulties Existing
Between the Missionaries and Chinese

The penetration of China by the Christian missionary with evangelism and education resulted in a bitter cultural clash. Both the Chinese and the Westerners perceived the situation from different perspectives and the barrier thus created was difficult to overcome.

For the most part, the missionaries were puzzled by Chinese culture primarily because "their thoughts and modes of expression are so totally different from ours."[61] In addition, the Chinese were perceived as very materialistic with a religion based on a pantheistic animism especially designed to bestow material well-being and to get rid of evil. What the missionaries desired to do was to take the moral and spiritual inclinations of the Chinese along with their disciplined minds and transfer them to Christianity and the Bible.[62] They hoped the result would be a transformation of what was perceived as Chinese materialism and selfishness into a demonstration of Christian love and service. So the missionaries confronted a culture very alien to their own with the anticipation of changing its emphases.[63] Of course, this problem was compounded by the fact that the missionaries had great difficulty learning the Chinese language and dialects, yet as mentioned previously, they, especially Baptists, would not use English.

Furthermore, the Chinese were convinced of the superiority of their own views and culture and, to be sure, the Chinese were often unclear of the real nature of Western culture. Still, they contended that Westerners were only "clever barbarians" with a material and technological superiority but no superiority in ideas or culture.[64] After all, Confucius and Mencius had taught many ideas similar to those of the Westerners, and really anything worthy in Christianity had already been expressed better in the beautiful literature of the classics. Besides, the Buddhists traditionally believed in incarnations and the Taoists in miracles and fulfilled prophecy.[65] Thus, the Chinese were convinced that Christian doctrine offered no improvement over what they already had. The Christian insistence on individual redemption was seen as unnecessary and the numerous denominations only served to confuse the Chinese.

Not only were the Chinese convinced of the superiority of their own beliefs, but they were insulted when the missionaries undermined their customs. The missionaries did not hide their feelings that, in general, the Chinese were depraved, immoral, and dishonest. In Ashmore's words, "The first source of China's corruption then, is the natural depravity of the human heart; the second is an emasculated ethics."[66] This kind of attitude hurt the self-esteem of the Chinese. The animosity of many Chinese was further aroused when the missionaries taught such things as the emperor needing salvation as much as the poor, men and women meeting together, banning the practice of foot-binding, and eliminating ancestor worship and idolatry among good Christians. However, when Chinese gave up these traditional customs, especially ancestor worship, they were suspect by neighbors and subject to ridicule and persecution. Superstition remained very strong in China and often natural calamities such as famines, fires, death, and disease were blamed on evil spirits in the guise of Chinese Christians or missionaries.[67] Most Chinese jealously guarded their traditions and were insulted to have them criticized by foreigners; even though many scholars themselves had contempt for the gods, they still respected societal norms.

On the other hand, the Chinese were willing to be syncretic and often drew correlations between the two belief systems. But the missionaries took the position that "in origin, principles, operations, influence, and ultimate design, the two (religions) are utterly incongruous,"[68] so it was not that the Chinese refused to worship the Christian God or the divinity of Christ, but that they were not willing to make it exclusive. In fact, in a seventeenth-century catalog of Chinese gods, Jesus was listed as a god of the West and one of the emperor's gods, which the Chinese of the nineteenth century felt should be honor enough for the Westerners.[69] The Chinese even were willing to accept the Bible as God's authoritative word, but not exclusively.[70]

Yet even this tendency towards sycretism proved difficult. For example, the Protestants disputed for the second half of the nineteenth century over the Chinese term to use for their God, *Siang-te* or *Shing*. Another example is the confusion by the Chinese over Christian symbolism. To illustrate, the Chinese considered the left rather than the right the seat of honor, so for the resurrected Christ to be seated on the right hand of God was not understood as honorable. They revered the serpent or dragon, whereas in the West the serpent is a source of temptation. Western missionaries referred to one's sins being made "white as snow" through conversion and thus, ensuring eternal salvation. However, to Chinese this seemed incongruous because white was the color of death and mourning. Thus, some of the literature of the early missions contained symbolism, terminology, and customs that did not carry the same meaning, or were meaningless or contradictory, to the Chinese.[71] The communication barrier was great.

Another hindrance to the acceptance of Christianity by the Chinese was that missionaries were Westerners, part of the resented foreigners. In fact, in the interior of China the presence of missionaries was often the only real manifestation of the foreigner.[72] In addition, the missionaries had the privilege of property ownership and extraterritoriality, which engendered among Chinese a reminder and dislike of the treaties. Of course, the Chinese could always challenge the teachings of the missionaries by pointing to the Western traders of opium and coolie labor, as well as to drunken sailors, pirates, and dishonest merchants and then take the attitude of "physician heal thyself." In other words, many Chinese could never really understand why the missionaries would only come for religious or altruistic reasons and not as agents of a foreign power. The Boxer Rebellion's attacks on missionaries were in part a result of this attitude.

Another problem in mission work was the "rice Christian" syndrome. Some Chinese helpers worked with the missionaries and Chinese churches just to make a living in a poor country or to receive benefits available from the mission, such as food or education. There were also incidents where individuals got into trouble with the law and sought the help, protection, or intervention of the missionaries or where the mission was asked to take sides in the frequent clan or village disputes.[73] Baptists, unlike some other missions, generally refused to get involved in these legal or partisan disputes.[74] Nevertheless, the problem of determining ulterior motives for Chinese becoming Christians was a continual one for missions.

Alienation of the Chinese convert was also a problem. The missionaries often waited a long time before they baptized a Chinese inquirer because they wanted to be sure that the convert had gotten rid of the old customs hindering living the Christian way of life. This meant that many Chinese under Christian instruction might be separated for long periods of time both from their countrymen and from full participation in the church, and so many became discouraged.[75] Yet the Baptists insisted on assurance of conversion before allowing one to join the church.

Conclusion

Certainly credit must be given to the Baptist mission work for its attempt to understand China and its customs and for its role in spreading information to Westerners concerning the Chinese and their traditions. This they did through frequent articles in their denominational papers like the *Baptist Missionary Magazine* and *Baptist Missionary Review* (both used extensively for this paper) and through reports disseminated to local congregations in America through letters and personal appearances while on furlough. Despite their biases, the Baptists produced some worthy scholarship and their purpose was always good intentioned. They came with their desire to share something extremely important to them, namely eternal life, to a people living outside the revelation of Christ Jesus. Their efforts were sacrificial in an attempt to reach all Chinese with the Gospel. Their aim was to improve the Chinese, first through evangelism and then through character building. Their efforts in literature translation and printing, in building mission stations, hospitals, and schools, and in active evangelizing represented the time, effort, and resources of many people both in China and in the home churches in the United States and England.

This mission endeavor was a major project and through it all another factor seemed apparent. The Baptists in the nineteenth century held a firm stance in their beliefs as to the relationship between evangelism and education and between the two cultural traditions. There seemed to be little or no room for compromise. Their beliefs, methods, and personal dedication were all well established and, despite innumerable obstacles, the size of the Baptist community in China grew. In 1905 the British Missionary Society had 332 stations and 4,403 communicants, while the American Baptist Missionary Union had 240 stations and 15,509 communicants, and the Southern Baptist Convention had 105 stations and 5,049 communicants.[76]

These results are indicative of the intense enterprise the Baptist missions undertook in the nineteenth century with their own distinct approach to missions and mission education, and in spite of imposing hindrances. The potentialities of China as a mission field stimulated their missionary enthusiasm and provided a mission field that captured the attention and imagination of their supporters in the pews of America and Britain.

Notes

1. Suzanne Wilson Barnett and John K. Fairbank, *Christianity in China: Early Protestant Missionary Writings* in the introduction by Fairbank (Cambridge: Harvard University Press, 1985), p. 2.

2. Robert G. Torbet, *Venture of Faith: The Story of the American Baptist Foreign Mission Society and the Woman's American Baptist Foreign Mission Society, 1814–1954* (Philadelphia: The Judson Press, 1955), p. 13.

3. Ibid., p. 51.

4. H. R. Williamson, *British Baptists in China, 1845–1952* (London: The Cary Kingsgate Press, 1957), p. 7.

5. Kenneth Scott Latourette, *A History of Christian Missions in China* (New York: Macmillan, 1932), p. 215.

6. Williamson, *British Baptists*, p. 11.

7. Latourette, *History of Missions,* p. 229.

8. Williamson, *British Baptists*, p. 17.

9. Latourette, *History of Missions,* pp. 263–64.

10. Ibid., p. 280.

11. Williamson, *British Baptists*, p. 31.

12. Ibid., p. 39.

13. Ibid., pp. 45–48.

14. D. MacGillivray, ed., *A Century of Protestant Missions in China, 1807–1907* (Shanghai: American Presbyterian Mission Press, 1907), p. 80.

15. Ibid., p. 84.

16. Torbet, *Venture of Faith,* p. 297.

17. Kenneth Gray Hobart, "A Comparative History of the East China and South China Missions of the American Baptist Foreign Mission Society, 1833–1935: A Study of the Intensive versus the Extensive Policy in Mission Work" (unpublished Ph.D. dissertation, Yale University), p. 157.

18. Ibid., p. 150.

19. Torbet, *Venture of Faith,* p. 308.

20. *The British Missionary Magazine,* Vol. 69:10 (October 1889), 387. Hereafter referred to as *BMM.*

21. *BMM,* Vol. 75:9 (September 1895), 488.

22. Ibid., 513.

23. Ibid., 509.

24. Torbet, *Venture of Faith*, p. 290.

25. *BMM*, Vol. 73:7 (July 1893), 300.

26. *BMM*, Vol. 81:7 (July 1901), 447.

27. Latourette, *History of Missions*, p. 371.

28. MacGillivray, *A Century of Missions,* pp. 314, 316.

29. Ibid., pp. 317–18, 322.

30. Edmund F. Merriam, *A History of American Baptist Missions* (Philadelphia: American Baptist Publication Society, 1900), p. 159.

31. *BMM*, Vol. 70:1 (January 1890), 14.

32. *BMM*, Vol. 53:3 (March 1873), 74.

33. *Annual Report of the American Baptist Foreign Mission Society* for 1845, p. 155.

34. See Ashmore's comments in *BMM*, Vol. 81:1 (January 1901), 10.

35. *Annual Report of the A.B.F.M.S.* for 1850, pp. 224–25.

36. L. N. Wheeler, *The Foreigner in China* (Chicago: S. C. Griggs, 1881), p. 170.

37. Paul A. Varg, *Missionaries, Chinese and Diplomats: The American Protestant Missionary Movement in China, 1890–1952* (Princeton: Princeton University Press, 1958), p. 20.

38. Wheeler, *The Foreigner in China*, p. 164.

39. See Mary Raleigh Anderson, *Protestant Mission Schools for Girls in South China (1827 to the Japanese Invasion)* (Mobile, AL: Heiter-Starke Printing Company, 1943), pp. 294–96 for an example of a popular Christian tract entitled *Three Character Classic* modeled after a Chinese text of the same title.

40. Williamson, *History of Missions*, p. 223.

41. *BMM*, Vol. 59:8 (August 1879), 294–95.

42. This approach was supported by the General Missionary Conference in Shanghai in 1877. Samuel H. Leger, *Education of Christian Ministers in China: An Historical and Critical Study* (Shanghai: n.n., 1925), pp. 13–15.

43. Torbet, *Venture of Faith*, pp. 120–21.

44. Henry C. Vedder, *A Short History of Baptist Missions* (Philadelphia: The Judson Press, 1927), p. 176.

45. Torbet, *Venture of Faith*, p. 169.

46. *Annual Report of the A.B.F.M.S.* for 1879, p. 58. Schools at Swatow are good examples.

47. *BMM*, Vol. 59:8 (August 1879), 295.

48. Anderson, *Mission Schools for Girls*, p. 279.

49. Ibid., p. 152.

50. Hobart, "A Comparative History of the East China and South China Missions of the A.B.F.M.S., 1833–1935," p. 237.

51. Anderson, *Mission Schools for Girls*, pp. 52–53.

52. Ibid., pp. 306–307.

53. *Annual Report of the A.B.F.M.S.* for 1883, p. 267.

54. Torbet, *Venture of Faith*, p. 148.

55. Hobart, "A Comparative History," p. 161.

56. Ibid., p. 160.

57. Ibid., p. 87.

58. Vedder, *A Short History of Baptist Missions*, p. 138.

59. Anderson, *Mission Schools for Girls*, p. 282.

60. Hobart, "A Comparative History," p. 158. I have no statistics as to the number of students receiving instruction throughout the nineteenth century.

62. William Ashmore, *BMM*, Vol. 62:9 (September 1882), 331.

63. Vedder, *A Short History of Baptist Missions*, p. 137.

64. An interesting account in Wheeler, *The Foreigner in China*, pp. 176–83, quotes a Chinese tract critical of Westerners and Christianity entitled, "Expulsion of the Non-Human Species."

65. Timothy Richard notes the similarities between Christianity and Buddhism in his introduction to *The New Testament of Higher Buddhism* (Edinburgh: T. and T. Clark, 1910).

66. *The Baptist Missionary Review*, Vol. 5:1 (January 1899), 1.

67. See Lida Scott Ashmore, *The South China Mission of the American Baptist Foreign Mission Society: A Historical Sketch of Its First Cycle of Sixty Years* (Shanghai: Methodist Publishing House, n.d.), pp. 51–52, and *BMM*, Vol. 27:2 (February 1847), 48 for examples.

68. *BMM*, Vol. 25:5 (May 1845), 111.

69. *BMM*, Vol. 38:5 (May 1858), 153.

70. Hobart, "A Comparative History," p. 261.

71. Varg, *Missionaries, Chinese and Diplomats*, p. 23.

72. Paul A. Cohen, *China and Christianity: The Missionary Movement and the Growth of Chinese Anti-foreignism, 1860–1870* (Cambridge: Harvard University Press, 1963), pp. 51–52 relates this to antiforeignism.

73. Examples may be found in *BMM*, Vol. 41:4 (April 1861), 101 and *BMM*, Vol. 42:12 (December 1862), 454–55.

74. Ashmore says involvement in these disputes leads to the loss of converts. *Baptist Missionary Review*, Vol. 3:3 (March 1897), 117.

75. *BMM*, Vol. 34:11 (November 1854), 445.

76. Figures are from W. Nelson Britton, "Statistics of Protestant Missions in China for the Year Ending 1905," in MacGillivray, *A Century of Missions,* frontispiece. I have no figures for the total number of Baptist converts up to 1900; however, there are figures for the total growth of Protestant missions. The number of Protestants grows from 6 in 1842, to 53 in 1853, to 2,000 in 1865, to 13,065 in 1876, to 28,000 in 1886, to 37,287 in 1889, to 55,093 in 1893, according to Kenneth Scott Latourette, *A History of the Expansion of Christianity*, Vol. VI: *The Great Century in Northern Africa and Asia, A.D. 1800–A.D. 1914* (New York: Harper & Brothers, 1944), p. 337.

3

THE GRAND ILLUSION
Karl Gützlaff and Popularization of
China Missions in the United States during the 1830s

Jessie Gregory Lutz

The Optimism-Depression Cycle of China Missions

"A great and effectual door is opening to China." "The fields are white unto harvest." During the middle 1830s these two sentences were picked up by American churches and religious organizations, to be repeated over and over again in mission magazines and annual reports, preached from church pulpits, and featured at annual meetings of the American Bible Society and American Tract Society. Though Robert Morrison had gone to China in 1807 as the first Protestant missionary and had conscientiously tried to arouse interest in China, it was not until the 1830s that China became a major focus of attention for American and British missions. Much of the credit for the rapid popularization of China missions among Americans belongs to Karl Gützlaff, an independent evangelist from Prussia.

Since China was officially closed to Christian evangelization until the imperial edicts of toleration in 1844 and 1846, Gützlaff's earliest work in 1828–31 was in Southeast Asia. Between June 1831, and September 1832, however, Gützlaff made two journeys from Southeast Asia up along the China coast. These treks, one on a Chinese junk and one on a British East India Company vessel, included brief forays into villages to distribute Scriptures, religious tracts, and simple medicines. Extracts from Gützlaff's journals, first published in *The Chinese Repository* of 1832, were reprinted in dozens of American and British mission magazines and were frequently cited at mission society meetings; they came out in book form in 1833.[1] As one report puts it, it was almost like the discovery of a new coast of some fertile and prosperous continent for the mercantile and religious community.[2]

A third tour, from October 1832 to April 1833, was on the "Sylph," an opium smuggler that helped to initiate regular runs up the coast of China by "smugs." Gützlaff's publicity regarding these exploits heightened hopes of evangelizing within China and created the impression that the Chinese populace thirsted for the

Gospel. *The Journal of Three Voyages* went through three English language editions and was widely excerpted; variant translations of the journals were published in Germany, Sweden, the Netherlands, and Switzerland.[3] The *Baptist Missionary Magazine*, quoting Gützlaff's journals, stated in 1835 that 400 millions of souls are drowned in superstition and sin and demand the attention of the whole world. "So large a portion of Christ's inheritance . . . is a fact to rouse all the slumbering energy of Christian zeal." The American Tract Society exulted in 1834: to China the eyes of the church are now turned with an interest and ardor of expectation that has had no parallel in previous years. "The late voyages of Mr. Gützlaff . . . will probably constitute an era in the commercial and religious history of [China]," according to the American Board of Commissioners for Foreign Missions (ABCFM).[4]

A father named his son for Gützlaff, and upon the death of little Charles Gützlaff Hildreth at the age of three, he sent the $5 savings account set up for the son to the American Tract Society for Gützlaff's distribution of religious tracts in China; Gützlaff replied with a small Chinese tract based on the quotation, "Come unto me all ye who are heavily laden and I will give you rest."[5] He expressed the hope that the death of the child would contribute to life eternal for millions. Others sent donations with the specific request that the monies be conveyed to Gützlaff for his work. In 1835 the Auxiliary Bible Society of Montgomery County, New York answered Gützlaff's plea for thousands of Bibles by starting a campaign to collect funds for a Bible a day for China, 365 Bibles a year. Thereby, "the number of individuals constantly enjoying the privilege of reading, or hearing the word of God, will not be less than 2,064. . . . If [other Bible societies] approve such a plan, they have the privilege to go and do likewise."[6]

Deciding in 1834 to send its first missionary to the "vast empire" of China, the Baptist Board of Missions stated that Robert Morrison's residence on the borders had encouraged them, and the recent journals and communications of the "devoted missionary Gützlaff" had made them doubly sure of the practicality of such a venture.[7] The Church Missionary Society (Episcopal), contemplating entrance to the China field, wrote to Robert Morrison and Karl Gützlaff in 1834 requesting advice and recommendations. Though Morrison had died by the time the inquiry reached Macao, Gützlaff sent cheering words about the work to be done for the largest nation of heathens on earth. Mr. and Mrs. E. B. Squire set sail in 1836 as the first American Episcopal missionaries to the Chinese.[8] At Dr. Peter Parker's consecration in 1834 as the first American medical missionary to China, Robert Morrison and Karl Gützlaff were commended to Parker as mentors and models.[9]

Morrison and Gützlaff were not, of course, the only advocates of China Protestant missions during the 1830s. Elijah Bridgman, David Abeel, Jacob Tomlin, and Walter Medhurst were indefatigable publicists. Even so, examples of the burgeoning American interest in China that specifically cite Gützlaff could be multiplied several times.

Firing the imagination and hopes of pious Americans during the 1830s was the flamboyant Gützlaff, exuding optimism and enthusiasm in hyperbolic calls for laborers. While Chinese edicts still forbade Christian proselytism in China, the conversion of Chinese to Christianity, and foreign residence except in Canton, the annual number of Protestant missionaries sent to East Asia increased severalfold and the amount of literature on China available to Western Christians multiplied even more dramatically. For the first time the American Bible Society voted in 1832 to extend its activities overseas, while in 1835 China and Southeast Asia began to rival the much more accessible India in the appropriations of the American Tract Society.[10] "Gutzlaff declares that the nation received him with open arms. . . . In no part of Asia . . . is there such a great demand for Bibles and tracts as in China. . . . Blot out from your missionary publications that China is shut," rejoiced the *Missionary Record*.[11] "The attention of the whole Christian world is turned extensively toward China," according to *The New York Observer*.[12] The 1834 annual meeting of the American Tract Society concluded, "*Who will pray for Gützlaff? Who will send him Tracts to distribute?* Who can doubt that a great and glorious work is commenced in China? . . . The way must be opened and the glorious work proceed. Already other hearts are burning to be enlisted in this service."[13]

Following the meteoric popularity of China missions during the mid-1830s came depression and disillusionment. American supporters began to realize that the China mainland was not open to Christian missionaries and, furthermore, that Chinese conversion did not automatically follow upon receipt of the Gospel. With the opening of five treaty ports in the Treaty of Nanking, 1842, and the imperial edicts of toleration in 1844 and 1846, however, another high point came. Missionaries and mission societies alike praised God who in His Providence had opened China; they hailed the treaty in extravagant language: "We say, then, that viewed politically and commercially, the recent treaty with China is the most important event which has occurred since the discovery of America, and as respects the moral interests of our race, we must go back to the Reformation for an event of equal interest and importance."[14] China missionaries united in a call for vastly greater efforts. Again the number of Protestant missionaries sent out annually increased from one in 1839 and one in 1840 to seventeen in 1847 and eighteen in 1848.

The year 1848 was the peak, however (see chart). Optimism once more gave way to sobering reassessments, for converts remained embarrassingly few, while disease and Chinese hostility took their toll on the missionary communities.[15] China was still not open and Chinese were not yet flocking to the cross. Word of the Taiping Christians briefly revived hopes that all China was on the eve of conversion. The Taipings were reprinting Gützlaff's translation of the New Testament! Millions of Chinese would be clamoring for Bibles! In October 1853, the British and Foreign Bible Society launched a campaign to supply the demand, and by June 1854 it had actually collected enough money to send more than two million

Missionaries Arriving in China

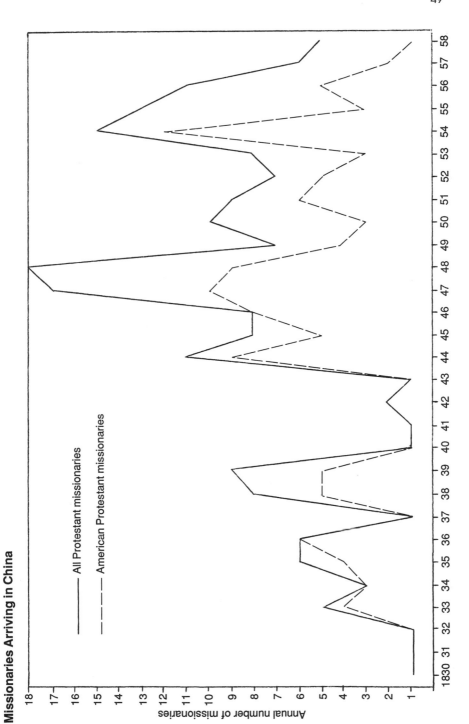

Annual number of missionaries

copies of the New Testament to China.[16] Again, hopes were belied as Westerners learned more about the Taipings and concluded that Taiping Christianity was heretical. Eventually, of course, the Taipings were defeated and in the minds of many Chinese the association of Christianity with subversion seemed confirmed. Conversion was not made easier, and opposition by upholders of Chinese tradition was strengthened.

The experiences of American Protestant missions between the 1830s and 1850s raise several questions. How does one explain the rapid popularization of China missions during the 1830s, and what was the special appeal of Karl Gützlaff to Americans during this decade? What was the legacy of the optimism-depression cycle for Sino-American relations and perceptions? What was Gützlaff's lasting influence on mission methodology and Chinese Christianity?

First, a few biographical details regarding Gützlaff.[17] Gützlaff was born in 1803 in Stettin, Prussia, son of a tailor. He volunteered for mission service under the influence of the Protestant revivalist movement but, lacking financial support, he embarked with characteristic zeal on a program of self-instruction. Through a typically ostentatious gesture—presentation of a poem to the visiting Prussian king—he found a patron. Frederick William III offered to send Gützlaff to the Jänicke Missionary School in Berlin. Following training in Berlin and Rotterdam, Gützlaff sailed for Southeast Asia in 1826 under the sponsorship of the Netherlands Missionary Society. He spent four years on the fringes of China assiduously studying Chinese, but finally could no longer resist the greatest of challenges, China with its one-third of humankind. In June of 1831, without the permission of the Netherlands Missionary Society, he embarked on the first of a series of journeys along the China coast which included frequent short incursions into the interior. In December 1834 Gützlaff inaccepted a position as Chinese secretary and interpreter with the British superintendent of trade, and thenceforth until his death in August 1851 combined civil duties with evangelistic activities. Macao was initially his home base, but after the Opium War he resided in Hong Kong.

Biographical details cannot convey the contradictions and the drama that were Gützlaff. Arthur Waley characterized him as "a cross between parson and pirate, charlatan and genius, philanthropist and crook."[18] Contemporary accounts during the 1830s, however, employed such terms as apostolic zeal, deep piety, quenchless ardor, self-denying labors, the apostle of China, luminous prophet, devoted servant of Christ, and the celebrated Gützlaff. I would argue that Gützlaff was less a charlatan than a tragic figure, victim of his own hyperbole in popularizing China missions and of self-delusion in commitment to the cause of Christianizing China. He was, simultaneously, a typical, if exaggerated, expression of the Protestant pietism that would continue to be important in China mission history and also in Chinese Christian history.

One reason Gützlaff became known as "the apostle to China" during the 1830s was his great success as a publicist. Though practically all the leading China missionaries appear to have been prolific correspondents, none perhaps equaled Gützlaff during the height of his evangelistic activity. Every sailing apparently carried a packet of letters from Gützlaff to a variety of recipients: secretaries of mission societies, editors of religious periodicals, contacts that he had made through merchants or his three successive English wives, individual donors, book publishers, seminary professors, branches of Bible and tract societies, women's auxiliary organizations, and the American Sunday School Union. The list seems almost endless. He even thanked anonymous donors as in the case of a letter printed in the *American Tract Magazine*:

> To the unknown Donor. Dear Sir,
> Though I am a perfect stranger to you, I cannot refrain from expressing my warmest thanks for the large donation of 110 dollars. With this sum I am going to print a new edition of the Life of our Savior in Chinese; and I shall forward to you a specimen as soon as it is out. I always like to dwell emphatically upon the work of Redemption and love towards the Savior, being persuaded that this is the end and beginning of our faith, and the only means of calling the heathen from darkness to light. May the Savior bless you for the zeal you have shown in promoting his glory in this dark country, and may souls be rescued from eternal perdition by perusal of this book.[19]

Surely the first contribution by the anonymous donor was not his last! Gützlaff had simultaneously employed this example of selfless charity to appeal to the tract magazine's whole audience of potential contributors.

Gützlaff was adept at using his materials in a variety of ways to gain maximum exposure. "An Appeal to American Churches" by Gützlaff appeared in numerous English and American magazines, was printed as a separate leaflet for circulation to churches and individuals, and became widely quoted at annual meetings of religious organizations and in fund raising campaigns.[20] His *Sketch of Chinese History* and *China Opened* relied heavily on previously published articles and reports, most of which, though not all, were his own.[21] As indicated above, the journals of his coastal tours circulated in numerous forms, publications, and languages. Not unlike such American leaders of religious revivals as Charles G. Finney and Peter Cartwright, Gützlaff appreciated the necessity of professional promotion and was skillful at it.

The Second Great Awakening was initially directed toward the unchurched at home: immigrant workers in the cities, the frontiersmen with their reputation for gambling, drinking, and lawlessness, rural villagers who had left the straight-and-narrow path, and such. Missions to the Indians also occupied attention and some argued that American Christians had enough to do at home. The popularization of China missions, however, expanded church horizons. The American effort to Christianize China represented one of the earliest international commitments of the young republic and, significantly, it was one with moral purpose.

Churches and Bible societies soon discovered that they benefited from the promotion of foreign missions. Overseas crusades, instead of detracting from home responsibilities, rejuvenated churches and helped keep the revivalist spirit alive. The image of millions of benighted heathens on the brink of hell because they had not received the Word inspired and united Christian congregations. It also opened pocketbooks so that fund drives for missions were more apt to increase church budgets than deplete them. The *New York Observer* of December 28, 1833 quoted the Prudential Committee of the ABCFM, "Such commitment abroad is not harmful but helpful to the home church. Since missions to the heathen were commenced by our churches, has not our land been blessed, to an extent hitherto unexampled, with revivals of religion? Haven't religious and benevolent institutions . . . grown almost in exact percent to the spirit of foreign missions?"[22]

The small American Lutheran Church, short of ministers for the expanding numbers of German immigrants, voted in 1837 to organize a German Foreign Missionary Society and to provide support for overseas missions.[23] The arguments employed in the report recommending such a step were revealing. They noted the intimate connection between efforts made for the conversion of the world and God's blessing upon the churches putting forth these efforts. The Lutheran Church had recently received letters from "the two most distinguished German missionaries, now in the foreign field, the celebrated Gutzlaff, and the indefatigable Rhenius," the latter having been inspired by Gützlaff to offer himself for service; we "acknowledge the hand of Providence; and regard this as a call of the Spirit for us to aid . . . in preaching the unsearchable riches of Christ to the benighted heathen." German ethnic pride clearly helped persuade the Lutheran synod to support overseas missions.

Gützlaff's Appeal in the Era of Manifest Destiny

What was the special appeal of a nonsectarian Prussian such as Gützlaff to American Baptists, Congregationalists, Presbyterians, and Episcopalians? Gützlaff, I think, spoke to the expansive, self-assertive, and optimistic mood of Jacksonian America. As the enterprising voyager, he seemed to embody the pioneer spirit of an America moving across the continent. As an exponent of Protestant pietism, he shared with Americans the belief that revival and moral reform were the cures for social evils. His emphasis on the friendliness of the Chinese people had a populist ring. His insistence on the right of free intercourse, both economic and religious, carried with it the conviction that material benefits would accrue to both China and the West as result of the adoption of Christian ethics and Western technology. Gützlaff, though not an American, became part of America's developing sense of identity, of a growing pride that was intertwined with a sense of mission.

Gützlaff's appeal to Americans may have been partially the result of shrewd calculation, but much it of seems to have been integral to his personality. Exuberant, even unbounded optimism, characterized Gützlaff. For him, the greater the challenge, the more glorious the opportunities. In "An Appeal in Behalf of China" in 1833, Gützlaff wrote of one of his coastal tours, "I had ample reason to praise our Savior for opening so wide a door to the introduction of the holy gospel . . . had I had a million of tracts, and fifty thousand copies of the Scriptures, they would all have been scattered amongst eager readers. My most sanguine expectations have been far surpassed. I marvel and adore in the dust. . . . *China is not shut;* He, the almighty conqueror of death and hell, will open the gates of heaven for these myriads—he has opened them." As a cautionary, he acknowledged that great difficulties might frequently arise, "but what are they before an omnipotent God? The decree of evangelizing China is passed in heaven; what therefore can all the contrary decrees of the pretended 'son of heaven' avail?"[24] The very thought that one-third of the population of the world awaited mission labors in China inspired Gützlaff to ever more expansive plans for conveying the Gospel to them; in his letters and articles, he reiterated the wonderful numbers time and again.

ABCFM's first representative in China was Elijah Bridgman, another major figure in the history of early Protestant missions to China.[25] As a publicist, he rivaled Gützlaff in volume of output. He exerted great influence through *The Chinese Repository*, which he edited, and through his Chinese-language history of America, *Mei-li-ko ho-sheng-kuo chih-lueh* (A short account of the united provinces of America) (Singapore, 1838). But Bridgman was more often than not depressed by the magnitude of the task and his reaction was to resort to shaming. The ABCFM Report of 1833 offered extracts from a Bridgman letter "written in a familiar strain," "Were it not for the exceeding great and precious promises, my heart would fail me—the work is so great, so vast, and the laborers so few and feeble. We are as nothing. I am not discouraged, my brother; I am not disheartened; but I am often, as now, *sad*. . . . The light of the Gospel cannot and must not be kept hid."[26] In a letter to the secretary of the American Bible Society, March 18, 1836, Bridgman expressed grief over how little was being done when so much remained to be done. "Unless our faith and strength are sustained, and increased, and our numbers greatly and speedily augmented, your high hopes and expectations will not soon be realized."[27] A later report by Bridgman and S. W. Williams, March 7, 1838, was even more defensive regarding the paucity of converts and the failure of the mission to live up to the expectations of the home society. Expressing frustration over their inability to make the home supporters understand the difficulties encountered, they remarked,

> If any in the churches ask us, Why these things are so? we beg they will first tell us, why so many Christians among themselves feel, and pray, and do so little for the heathen. . . . Why in such a land of liberty . . . are so many left to grow up in ignorance, profaning the Sabbath, revelling in dissipation. . . . Let our Christian friends at home answer these questions; then we will tell them some of the reasons why, that which was ordained unto life, is here rendered ineffectual.[28]

However accurate the observations of Bridgman and Williams, mission societies were more apt to quote Gützlaff's appeals and with good reason.

The slightest success inspired Gützlaff to elaborate more far-reaching plans. After he had witnessed the popular demand for books and the ineffectual opposition of Chinese officials during his first three coastal tours, he began to consider a journey all the way up the Yangtze River to Burma and Tibet; such a trip, he stated, was as practicable as a voyage from the Malaysian peninsular to Batavia.[29] To the secretary of the American Bible Society, he wrote, "The day of small things is past and it behooves us now to venture all upon the Lord. You can form no idea of the grand sphere upon which you are going to enter. . . ."[30] If only one Chinese in a hundred received a Bible, it would require a decade's income of the society. He intended to establish a hospital in the capital of Chekiang province. When he learned of Dr. Peter Parker's assignment to China, he talked of Parker's becoming the first Protestant missionary to reside within the empire. "No country in Asia, ruled by Native Princes, is so easy of access" as China, he claimed.[31]

Obstacles did not easily daunt Gützlaff. Appealing to populism and the frontier mentality, Gützlaff tried to allay concern over stiffening Chinese opposition by stating that gentlemen missionaries were not wanted in China. China was open to heroes and martyrs but was shut to those of weak faith and wavering mind, he wrote; we need pioneers who, not expecting much peace and comfort, will establish themselves in China, not just at Macao or Canton.[32] If enterprising merchants risked the unknown and the dangerous for the sake of profits, surely, said Gützlaff, there were also young American men willing to sacrifice all for the greatest of causes.

A constant theme of his journals was the basic good will of the general populace; they welcomed him with his medicines and tracts, some even accepting him as an adopted citizen of Fukien. Villagers offered him tea and shelter, even warned him that chair carriers were trying to take advantage of him.[33] He contrasted the eagerness of the masses for both trade and tracts with the hostility and opposition of the "despotic" emperor and high officials. On occasion, Gützlaff even insisted that Chinese merchants and lesser officials would welcome trade and free intercourse if they were not intimidated by their superiors.[34] He speculated, in true democratic fashion, that the central government could not enforce prohibitions against foreign contacts in the face of popular will. Westerners ought to take the initiative and be firm.

Gützlaff not only articulated the populist, pioneering ideal; he lived the life of a pioneer, deliberately courting danger, enduring hardships, and thoroughly enjoying adventure. His first tour up the coast, a single Westerner on a Chinese junk in defiance of Chinese law, was both risky and bold; at one point, he came in danger of losing his life as the sailors plotted to murder him for his supposed wealth.[35] On his third journey, the "Sylph" ran aground in the Gulf of Liaotung. Soon, a fierce cold wind had disabled the Indian sailors and iced the ship. Since they were unable to right the vessel, Gützlaff typically gathered a group of volunteers to seek help. Land was twenty-five miles distant, and by the time their boat had reached shore they were entirely covered with ice. One Indian froze to death even though Gützlaff gave him some of his own wraps; the others, in the words of Gützlaff, "were on the verge of eternity." Though they obtained no aid from the mandarins, "the ship got off by the interposition of God, who had ordered the south wind to blow. . . . His name be praised to all eternity."[36]

A trip to interior Fukien in 1834 to obtain tea plants and information about tea cultivation was truly a venture into the unknown for Gützlaff, three Europeans, and eight Indian soldiers accompanied by a single Chinese servant.[37] Gützlaff managed to hire a Chinese guide and the two of them led the way as the group traipsed up hilly footpaths until their feet were so swollen that they could no longer walk. Hiring chair carriers, they pressed on into the mountains despite warnings of bandits and despite the primitive facilities of village inns. Once, they had to negotiate the narrow footpaths by moonlight before they finally reached a village; here, Gützlaff managed to find lodging with a friendly peasant though they had to share the quarters with the farmer's pigs.

In 1837 several missionaries and traders tried to use the excuse of returning shipwrecked Japanese sailors to their homeland in order to test the possibility of opening Japan to evangelism and commerce.[38] Gützlaff characteristically insisted on being part of such a glamorous venture. And, since, with his voracious appetite for knowledge, he had been studying Japanese with some of the sailors, he was considered essential to the crew of the "Morrison"; he served as a primary intermediary in the futile negotiations with the Japanese.

Many other examples of Gützlaff's pioneering spirit could be given, all of them amply publicized in the journals of Gützlaff and his companions and quoted at length in numerous magazines. One more example may be presented in order to indicate that Gützlaff's unbounded energy and zest for adventure remained unabated even into middle age. After agreement on the terms of the Treaty of Nanking in August 1842, Chinese and Western officials exchanged ceremonial visits. A Chinese banquet, departure of the commissioners, and final tidying up of language and protocol by interpreters, Gützlaff, Robert Thom, and G. T. Lay, appeared to conclude the day. But Gützlaff suddenly proposed a visit to the famous porcelain tower of Nanking.[39] Even though it was already evening, none could resist the lark. Gützlaff and his wife's young cousin Harry Parkes hurried along toward the Buddhist shrine as Thom, Lay, and Chinese servants panted behind. After exploring the tower with the aid of lighted torches, they spent the night in a neighboring temple, the local magistrate providing them with supper and blankets for beds.

If the frequent excerpting of these exploits in magazines is any indication, Americans derived vicarious pleasure from reading about them. If the adjectives applied to Gützlaff—intrepid, remarkable, indefatigable, resolute, etc.—are any indication, Americans admired and identified with such an entrepreneur and gambler. Peter Parker doubtless expressed the view of many in his farewell address before embarking for China in June of 1834, "I would commend to you that [the example] of Morrison and Gutzlaff. To these I might refer you for illustrations of what *individual enterprise* united with *faith,* and *humble dependence* on God, may accomplish."[40] The ABCFM in 1834 cautioned against overoptimism concerning the openness of China; other missionaries could not necessarily do what Gützlaff had done, they said; even so, they pointed to the example of Gützlaff in calling for volunteers to enter the harvest field of China.[41] Gützlaff in China was a frontiersman and an entrepreneur; he exhibited many of the qualities and attitudes of venturesome spirits in America during the 1830s.

Gützlaff shared a common language and frame of reference with American pietistic Protestantism. Like the American revivalists of the first half of the nineteenth century, Gützlaff's themes were the sinfulness of humankind and the necessity of individual Christian rebirth leading to moral reformation and reconciliation with God. Evangelists of the Great Awakening depicted the sins of their listeners in the darkest possible colors; Gützlaff set forth the depravity of the Chinese in the amplest detail: infanticide, dishonesty, sensuality, cruelty.[42] All the more need for revivals, all the greater urgency of missions, all the more reason for benevolent guidance to the less fortunate. Gützlaff, ever sanguine, quickly went on to the saving grace of Jesus; there was no cause for despair—rather, Gützlaff gloried in the beneficence of Christ.

The Bible was for Gützlaff the inspired word of God; both its history and its teachings were to be accepted literally on faith. This assumption influenced the methodology of early Protestant missions. Though Gützlaff's reliance on the distribution of tracts and Scriptures was derived partly from the difficulty of long-term contacts with Chinese, he, like many pietists, had implicit faith in the power of the Word. He assumed that those who read and understood the Gospel could not but be impelled to accept the truth. Along with other early missionaries, he insisted that the Chinese were a reading people so tracts could carry the Word far into the interior. The myth that Buddhism had gained acceptance in China primarily through the written word became a part of mission literature during the 1830s; the implication, of course, was that Christianity could do the same.

To those who questioned the motives of the Chinese in clamoring for books, he responded in terms difficult to gainsay: the analogy of sowing seeds that might sprout who knows where and when, the contention that God worked in his own wondrous ways, and the argument that if one soul were saved from perdition, the efforts had not been in vain. For a time the British and American Bible and tract societies and numerous missionary organizations operated on these assumptions. Donations for the printing and distribution of tracts poured in; societies contributed toward the development of a set of movable metallic Chinese type in order to facilitate and expedite the production of tracts, more specifically, so that Gützlaff might have tens of thousands of tracts to distribute should he require them.[43]

Gützlaff was not so much interested in building church congregations as in spreading the Word of God, the sole means of salvation. He did not concern himself with denominational differences. Of converts, he required that they acknowledge the one true Christian God and Jesus as His son and the source of salvation. Gützlaff would, like many preachers of the Second Great Awakening, leave to his successors the task of organizing congregations and monitoring the theology of those who had experienced rebirth. He was a forerunner.

Gützlaff had no use for Roman Catholicism, or Popism, as he called it. Even though he expressed admiration for the dedication and determination of the early Jesuit missionaries to China, he was convinced that they had preached a false religion. He frequently lumped Buddhism and Roman Catholicism together as idolatrous superstitions. Believing that the Protestant Reformation had achieved a return to the true and original Christianity, he applied the term ''heterodoxy'' or even ''heresy'' to Catholicism. For him as for the pietists in general, the only orthodoxy was Protestantism. Few of the Chinese Catholics had been entirely ''reclaimed from paganism,'' he wrote, for this could be effected only by all-conquering grace; without the Holy Spirit touching the heart, total change was not possible.[44] Since, in the early nineteenth century, Americanism and Protestantism were accepted as almost synonymous, Gützlaff's intolerance was likely to offend few; rather, it harmonized with a developing concern over the increasing numbers of Catholic workers emigrating to America.

American Protestants in particular could understand and appreciate Gützlaff's faith that God is active in this world and that history represents the working out of God's will. In almost every letter, Gützlaff reiterated that his fate rested in God's hands. If he undertook perilous journeys at risk of his life, he did so in the belief that God would protect him; whether he lived or died depended on God's plan for him.[45] God had sent the southern wind that freed the ice-bound ''Sylph''; God had opened the door of China.[46] He shared with many missionaries and mission societies the conviction that God in his Providence had brought good out of evil, since the Opium War became the means for expanding evangelism to the five treaty ports.[47] The hostility of Chinese officials and the paucity of converts rarely dampened his enthusiasm, for he remained confident of the eventual triumph of Christianity. God's promise assured him that Christianity represented the wave of the future. Though he praised Confucius for fostering filial piety and respect for elders and for his useful lessons promoting social order, Gützlaff never doubted the universality of Christianity and Christian morality. The limitations and errors of Confucius were proof for Gützlaff that without divine revelation, man could attain only partial truth. Confucius, unfortunately, was concerned only with this world and believed that man could find happiness on the basis of a human ethic.[48]

In writing to the officials of American religious societies, Gützlaff deliberately cultivated the notion that God had a special mission for Americans.[49] He contrasted America's enthusiasm with Britain's ''specious contention'' that China remained inaccessible. On America, he said, God had abundantly poured out His Divine Spirit; to America, God had granted religious liberty. Americans he described to the secretary of the American Bible Society as a "great and free people eminently blessed by the Lord from on high." His obvious conclusion was that such a favored people incurred a unique obligation to extend the blessings of the Gospel to all the peoples of the world. America, of all nations, was destined to engage in the noble endeavor to communicate the treasures of knowledge to those in total darkness. Either consciously or instinctively he appreciated the sense of superiority that accompanies charity and he fed the growing sense of a distinctive American identity. Instead of pleading for workers or begging for funds, he often followed praises of America's reputation for benevolence and bounty with the confident assertion that God would provide. He expressed admiration for "your excellent Dr. Parker" and for "your countryman [Issachar] Roberts." The developing national pride of Americans should lead them to accept the greatest challenge of all: China, with one-third of humankind.

Nor does Gützlaff seem to have doubted for a moment that material rewards would accompany spiritual blessings. He believed as firmly in freedom of commercial relations as he did in the freedom to proselytize. On one occasion he circulated a pamphlet in which he quoted from Chinese classics to prove that China's early philosophers had been advocates of open interchange; he added, furthermore, that since God had created all men as brothers, free intercourse accorded with the natural laws of God.[50] Not only was China harming herself by cutting her people off from the benefits of Western Christendom; she was defying natural law. Gützlaff went one better than those who thought that Christian revivalism could serve as a civilizing force in the riotous American West. Christian missions could civilize the whole world and Americans were privileged to participate in the crusade to redeem the most numerous and most advanced people in Asia. America's secular destiny would merge with her benevolent mission as she shared in the opening of China to trade, to technology and science, and to Christianity. The three were for Gützlaff an inseparable triumvirate.

Contradictions

Gützlaff became, however, the victim of his own optimism and verbal embroidery. With respect to the possibility of evangelists penetrating the Chinese interior and the effectiveness of broadcasting Christian tracts, he deluded himself as well as Western religious societies. His ability to rationalize the use of every available means in the great cause of Christianizing China proved self-defeating. His naivete in believing that those who professed a sense of sin and rebirth were true Christians allowed Chinese field preachers to take advantage of him and recycle tracts for their own profit.

Gützlaff, of course, was far from unique in assuming that his mission made him subject to a higher law than Chinese regulations.[51] Both Catholic priests working underground in interior China and Protestant missionaries preaching on the fringes of China were defying imperial edicts against Christianity and proselytism. Most of the Protestant pioneers continued to distribute tracts despite the opposition of Chinese officials and even in the knowledge that these officials might be degraded for failure to prevent the incursions. Christ's commission to carry the Gospel to all the corners of the earth was their justification; in their view, this charge superseded all earthly authority.

Nor was Gützlaff unique in combining government office with evangelistic activities. Many of the early Protestant missionaries served their governments either temporarily or on a long-term basis, while Robert Morrison was an employee of the British East India Company for over two decades. Such a union of secular and religious occupations derived in part from the Chinese prohibition on evangelism and the need for missionaries to legitimize their residency in Canton and Macao. In most instances, however, the missionaries were pressed into service by Western diplomats because of the shortage of persons with a knowledge of Chinese. Unlike most foreign merchants and quite a few later missionaries, the early Protestant evangelists concentrated on acquiring facility in both spoken and written Chinese. Their acquaintance with Chinese language and customs made them indispensable to Western negotiators ignorant of both; it also allowed them to have considerable influence as advisers and intermediaries. Several missionaries, including Peter Parker, became diplomatic representatives of their government in China.

Even participation in the opium trade was not confined to Gützlaff and opium smugglers.[52] The opium business was so important and so pervasive that it permeated practically all facets of Sino-Western interaction. Banking, money exchange, and other fiscal arrangements depended upon opium. Mail, supplies, reports, and even salaries circulated through opium smugglers. Christian tracts were stored at the opium depot of Lintin. Not only did navigational information come from the captains of opium clippers, but missionaries frequently took passage on boats carrying opium. Among the most generous contributors to mission activities were companies heavily involved in the opium trade. Although a small number of merchants and most missionaries refused to have any direct dealings in opium, few could entirely avoid dependence on the trade in some fashion.

Gützlaff was never one for half measures, so all of the contradictions in the missionaries' activities were overstated in Gützlaff. In return for Gützlaff's acting as interpreter on opium clippers, the merchant shipowner William Jardine offered Gützlaff support for his Chinese language publications and the opportunity to make forays into coastal villages to preach the Gospel and distribute tracts and medicines.[53] Gützlaff hesitated, pondering the rectitude of accepting such an offer, but he couldn't resist the prospect of opening doors for proselytizing. Once having reconciled himself to employment in the "Sylph" journey, he served on opium smugglers in a half dozen subsequent tours. Typically, he performed his interpreter's duties with gusto, on occasion browbeating mandarins who tried to deter the "smugs" or who demanded bribes higher than the going rate.[54] Gützlaff simultaneously condemned opium smoking and even worked with addicts to try to help them break the habit by administering an emetic mixed with opium.

As the humanitarian movement in England kindled public attacks on opium, Gützlaff's known association with the trade became an embarrassment. Gützlaff apparently accepted a position as interpreter with the British superintendent of trade partly out of a desire to end his role in facilitating opium smuggling.[55] Despite this belated move, probably no other single missionary did more than Gützlaff to link opium and Christian evangelism in the minds of Chinese. When public opinion in the West turned increasingly against opium in the late nineteenth century, Gützlaff's notoriety would also inform later assessments of him.

Gützlaff's impatience with Protestant denominationalism and his tendency to view China missions as part of a global Protestant enterprise evidenced themselves early in his career. Protestants, including merchants, diplomats, and evangelists, Presbyterians, Congregationalists, and all denominations, should cooperate in the common goal of bringing the Gospel of salvation to lost souls. Chafing under restraint on his activities and also over what he considered timidity in trying to penetrate China, Gützlaff severed association with the Netherlands Missionary Society after only two years in Asia. He succeeded for a while in supporting his proselytizing activities by combining his deceased wife's inheritance, monies from interpreting work on the opium ships, and grants from various religious societies. Financial need was, however, a second reason for his decision in December 1834 to accept employment as Chinese secretary and interpreter with British commercial authorities.

To religious groups, he explained that his new position would offer greater opportunity to work for opening China to both missionaries and merchants.[56] Gützlaff was not being hypocritical. Out of his income and receipts, he contributed toward tracts distributed by Chinese and Western evangelists, his second wife's school for Chinese children, the support of several orphaned blind girls, and the publication of numerous Chinese Christian pamphlets and secular materials; he offered hospitality to numerous newly arrived missionaries.

Gützlaff believed that China's acceptance of Western technology, material goods, and Christianity was part of one process, indeed that the Christian heritage had made the difference in the advancement of modern science and technology in the West. China would benefit from opening wide her doors, and, in fact, should be required to do so. He acted accordingly. In 1833 Gützlaff founded a Chinese language magazine *Tung-Hsi-yang k'ao mei-yueh t'ung-chi-chuan* (The East West monthly magazine). Articles on European geography, government, history and customs, Western technology, and international commercial and diplomatic relations dominated the contents.[57] In editing such a secular magazine, Gützlaff's goal was two-fold: (1) to make available knowledge useful to the Chinese and (2) to demonstrate to the Chinese that Westerners were a civilized people and thereby to create among Chinese respect for Western Christendom. The magazine, which lasted until February 1839, was designed for Chinese readers and did actually fulfill the first function as it became a significant source for several Chinese literati seeking information about the West. Instead of creating a favorable attitude toward Christianity, however, it had the immediate effect of eliciting imperial edicts against foreign books.

During the "Lord Amherst" journey of 1832, Gützlaff and Hugh H. Lindsay circulated a pamphlet and plastered up posters advocating free trade. In defiance of imperial edicts, the literature appealed to the populace to oppose the policy of restricting intercourse to Canton.[58] Gützlaff and his companions challenged officials who tried to prevent their landing and exploring coastal towns. Despite opposition, they spent days at various ports gathering navigational and commercial data. The unexpectedness of their arrival, the superior maneuverability and speed of their craft, the weakness of Chinese defenses, and the reluctance of Chinese officials to engage in forceful confrontation, all enabled the foreigners to get by with their subversive activities.

But Gützlaff in his publicity implied that much more was possible.[59] China, he wrote to the West, was open. The general populace was friendly and the demand for Christian tracts was overwhelming. Not only were Chinese administrators unable to shut the doors, but most did not actually wish to do so. He reconstructed conversations with Chinese officials in which the latter seemed to agree with his arguments favoring free intercourse: the English permitted Chinese ships to trade at London and other British ports and so the Chinese should reciprocate; if the emperor were truly compassionate and benevolent toward all under heaven, he would permit both Chinese and Westerners to share the benefits of free exchange; Confucius had said that all men were brothers and so obviously would have desired unobstructed contacts.

When a Fukien official requested copies of Gützlaff's tracts to send to the emperor, Gützlaff happily made up a packet. Believing, of course, that the Gospel truth could not but carry its own conviction, Gützlaff gave a highly optimistic interpretation to the Fukien official's request. "Our Bibles and tracts have created a great sensation in the Chinese empire. Wei, the deputy-governor of Fukien . . . sent a copy of the Scripture lessons and our principal tracts to the emperor, and recommended him very earnestly to have the doctrines duly examined." "We adore the all-ruling Providence, which has permitted us to be the harbinger of good tidings."[60] By the fall of 1833, the tale had grown with the telling. The executive committee of the American Tract Society was hearing that the Chinese emperor had sent to Gützlaff for Christian tracts for his own examination; tracts had already found their way into the heart of China and possibly into the very palace of the august emperor. The committee unanimously voted to raise $20,000 for printing and distributing tracts.[61]

Difficulties, Opposition, and Disillusionment

Almost the exact opposite of the received perceptions of the Tract Society executives was occurring in China. Instead of doors opening, doors were shutting. With each subsequent report to Peking of incursions into China and of circulation of forbidden literature, imperial edicts became more adamant in charging officials to put a stop to all such activities. Military commanders and civil administrators were degraded for failure to oust the offending Westerners, while coastal fortifications began to be repaired and military units upgraded.[62]

In addition to an increase in Sino-Western contacts and the expansion of opium smuggling, other events were exacerbating relations. The Chinese evangelist Liang A-fa had distributed Christian tracts to Kwangtung examination candidates in 1833. In the summer of 1834 the new superintendent of British trade, Lord William Napier, made a vain attempt to negotiate directly with Chinese officials as an equal. Frustrated, he posted Chinese placards protesting his treatment and accusing the Chinese viceroy of ignorance and hostility. Napier's proclamation concluded, "The viceroy will find it as easy to stop the current of the Canton river, as to carry into effect the insane determinations of the hong. (Canton, August 25, 1834)"[63] The Chinese government's reaction was swift and harsh.[64] The Chinese translators working with Westerners were arrested; members of Liang A-fa's family and other converts were flogged and imprisoned; Liang, under the protection of missionaries, fled to Malacca; fonts for Christian tracts were seized and the Canton press had to close down. The Chinese became fearful of associating with evangelists and even the missionaries had to exercise discretion in their preaching and tract distribution in the Canton area.

Though the Chinese lacked the force to deter coastal journeys, officials were put on their mettle to prevent forays into the interior. A trip to the tea districts of Fukien in the spring of 1835 illustrates the hardening of opposition.[65] As Gützlaff and his companions made their way up the Min River, Chinese ships tracked them practically the whole distance. When they had gone some seventy miles into the province, they were surrounded by Chinese war boats and were fired on. They decided to turn back rather than contest the issue; finally, having lost their way, they were escorted out by the Chinese military. Gützlaff protested vehemently to Chinese administrators against such "atrocious" treatment but failed to secure a satisfactory reply. The repercussions were far reaching.

Copies of two tracts distributed by Gützlaff were sent to the emperor and occasioned new edicts. Declaring that no "Outside Foreigner" could have printed such works, the emperor in 1835 ordered the governor of Kwangtung to discover and seize the traitors who had prepared and circulated the works. The governor immediately demanded an investigation whereby the origins of the tracts would be "drawn out by grinding torture." Christian works were condemned as fabulous nonsense, as pernicious and depraved. Chinese language teachers and other assistants deserted the missionaries, and plans for reopening the Canton press had to be abandoned. An imperial edict in the spring of 1836 condemned Europeans for penetrating into the interior of China, for secretly printing books, for passing along the coast in disguise and distributing European pamphlets exhorting Chinese to believe and venerate the chief of their religion, named Jesus, and for preaching fables without foundation which only destroyed the human heart.[66]

Word of such difficulties eventually began to trickle back to the Western churches. The London Mission Society designated two representatives to test the waters themselves. Their experience confirmed what was becoming increasingly apparent: coastal journeys with brief excursions to nearby villages were possible, though the only vessels making such voyages were opium smugglers. Neither extended trips into the interior nor foreign residence outside Canton was feasible.[67] China was not open, or at least was open only in a very limited sense.

Gützlaff buoyantly put a good face on events. Over 50 million Chinese remained accessible in Southeast Asia and along the coasts of China. The imperial edicts, he wrote, were only for show, not meant to be enforced; they "harm us as little as Papal bulls."[68] Always the entrepreneur, he searched for other tactics. What was needed was a mission ship which could ply the coast continuously and plant the seeds of the Gospel. He joined other missionaries in pressing American businessmen and religious societies to support such a vessel and thereby obviate the need to employ opium smugglers.[69] He recommended increasing use of Chinese to itinerate in the interior; if they stayed away from government centers, they could freely distribute Christian tracts and preach the fundamental truths of sin and salvation.

Not all missionaries or Western congregations had the resiliency of Gützlaff. After the overblown expectations of 1834–35 came doubt and reassessment. There was, naturally, a lag in the realization of the actual state of affairs. Most China missionaries were reluctant to undercut enthusiasm and support so they gave more copy to the opportunities than to the obstacles. W. H. Medhurst stressed the foundation that had been laid in language study: preparation of dictionaries, grammars, and tracts; the education of thousands of Chinese youths and the baptism of a dozen converts.[70] Samuel Dyer of the London Mission Society gave a sober assessment of the ways in which China was and was not open. Though he ended on a positive note, he included a subtle criticism of Gützlaff, "We want something more than bare assertion [that China is open] to prove the point in question; we want ONE missionary to *settle* and . . . publish the gospel to the people." [71] David Abeel in a speech to an American congregation, May 15, 1835, was more forthright than many. After high praise for Gützlaff, who "accomplished more than any man of his age," Abeel characterized Gützlaff as "a mere bird of passage" alighting here and there. Abeel feared that a false impression had been created that missionaries might go to any part of China and remain there and he cautioned against a letdown; much could still be accomplished and volunteers should still try to breach the wall of China.[72]

Receiving such mixed signals, many religious groups managed to maintain a determined optimism well into 1836 and even into 1837. The ABCFM report for 1837 was temperate but it nevertheless found satisfaction in the knowledge that the means of assault were being multiplied and that the imperial prohibitions had created greater interest in working among the numerous Chinese in Southeast Asia. Quoting the missionaries who pointed to the millions of accessible Chinese, the American Tract Society concluded that the way was now open for incomparably more than the churches were now attempting. Despite growing evidence to the contrary, it asserted that interest in China remained unparalleled.[73] Gützlaff continued his persuasive appeals. A long letter to the American Bible Society detailing the opportunities awaiting a missionary ship concluded, "I think it is the peculiar province of you as a great and free people . . . to advocate His cause in these countries, which have so little engaged Christian benevolence, and to enter a vineyard, the largest on the face of the globe. Let me therefore entreat you to persevere under all circumstances and to render every facility for carrying the blessed Gospel to the most distant shore."[74] He assured the Church Missionary Society that his seven voyages had amply proved the accessibility of the coast and that free trade, with the abolition of the British East India Company monopoly, would actually extend the range.[75]

Nevertheless, negative data mounted. Estimates of the percentage of literate Chinese and of the influence of overseas Chinese and traders were downgraded. Reports that Chinese desired tracts for purposes unrelated to their content persisted and questions were raised about the tracts' intelligibility for individuals without a Christian frame of reference.[76] Deep divisions opened up between those favoring an idiomatic translation of the Bible and those who insisted that the revealed Word must be translated literally. A rancorous debate over the proper Chinese terms for God, Holy Spirit, and baptism began to emerge.[77] Not only did the number of converts remain depressingly few, but most of them were either employees of the mission or the fruit of Liang A-fa's efforts rather than of the Westerners'. Apostasy, or backsliding, as the missionaries termed it, occurred with a frequency that was unsettling.

In 1837 an exploratory journey to Southeast Asia on the *Himmaleh*, purchased and fitted out at a cost of $20,000, ended in utter shambles. Gützlaff, whose participation was considered vital because of his linguistic ability and his facility in gaining entree, could not secure a job release from the British Superintendent of Trade.[78] The one missionary who could speak Chinese died soon after the "Himmaleh" left Macao; his two replacements knew neither Chinese nor Malay and one of these survived only a short time in the tropical environment. The ship's captain proved timorous and unwilling to land at hostile or unfamiliar ports. It was hardly surprising, though it was disappointing, that plans for the "Himmaleh" to ply the China coast were abandoned and the British and Foreign Bible Society decided not to renew the contract of its agent on the trip.[79] The failure of the expensive "Morrison" venture to Japan in the same year further contributed to the sense of disillusionment. Even more dismaying was the fact that thousands of tracts and Scriptures had piled up at the Lintin opium depot, undistributed and a prey to white ants and the tropical climate.[80]

By 1839 donations to the American Tract Society were down and allocations for China had been cut. The American Bible Society was reporting that prospects for Bible distribution in China were dispiriting; furthermore, it had postponed further appropriations pending resolution of the controversy over which version of the Bible should be patronized.[81] Such gloom had settled upon the ABCFM missionaries to Canton that they no longer had the heart to try to offset the dreary picture. After listing the various obstacles, they lamented, "The delusion which appears to envelope almost everything pertinent to this country in the minds of those who have never been here, renders the prospect of doing justice to the subject very faint."[82] In an oblique reference to Gützlaff, they stated that the difficulty of ascertaining the truth was increased by authors who put forth their works with great pretensions and bewildered the inquirer with contrary opinions.

Amidst the disillusionment, Gützlaff published a new book entitled *China Opened*. To many, the subtitle, *A Display of the Topography, History, Customs, Manners, Arts, Manufactures, Commerce, Literature, Religion, Jurisprudence, etc. of the Chinese Empire*, was a more accurate description of its contents. The book was largely a compendium of Gützlaff's previous articles on China and concluded with a long section on China's foreign trade, strongly advocating a laissez-faire philosophy. Gützlaff may have intended a double entendre in the title, i.e., he was opening China to the West by providing an introduction to her culture. In 1838 the title was ill timed. Though later evaluations of the work have accorded it some merit, many of the reviews of the late 1830s were harsh.[83]

S. Wells Williams, who had often been the recipient of Gützlaff's hospitality and guidance, wrote in 1839, "Mr. Gutzlaff, some time ago published, as a discovery, that China was open; and this he repeated, until many persons in western lands believed it; but China still obstinately remaining shut as close [sic] as ever to all permanent general intercourse. . . . He describe[s] the country and its inhabitants that they shall be open to the minds of his readers." Williams admitted that the work would attract attention because of the eclat of the author, but he concluded that authentic information was mixed with crude theories, careless expressions, and partial misstatements; it was not a work such as a person of Gützlaff's advantages ought to produce.[84] Such vehemence reflected a feeling that Gützlaff had done a disservice to the cause of China missions. Gützlaff, with his flamboyance and hyperbole, was at least partially responsible for the sense of betrayal and the current dilemma of China missions.

Peter Parker, a former admirer of Gützlaff and a close associate in Macao and Canton, had expressed his misgivings even earlier: "The interest that upon false grounds was awakened is subsiding, and people are beginning to turn their attention to more inviting fields."[85] Parker tried to revive solicitude and support by emphasizing the populousness of China and the readiness of Catholic missionaries to move in. G. T. Lay, who had participated in the "Himmaleh" fiasco, expressed the hope that the Christian public would not allow itself to be tossed to and fro: China open, China not open. He also stated that the indiscriminate distribution of tracts had left little trace; running up the numbers of works handed out had more impact in the West than in China.[86]

Antagonism toward Gützlaff was mounting. The Reverend Robert W. Orr was even more blunt in his criticism of Gützlaff:

> At one time there was no part of the heathen world, which was thought to be so important, or awakened so deep an interest in the public mind, as China. It is well-known that the popular but extravagant and unguarded statements, of Mr. Gutzlaff, contributed more than any other cause, to excite this extraordinary interest in that country. A few years, however, passed by, and it was found that the high-wrought anticipations which had been raised, were not realized—it was discovered that after all that had been said and written on "China Opened," the Chinese Empire yet remained as effectually closed against all direct missionary effort, as it was twenty years ago. The discovery of these facts, and the disappointment given to the sanguine hopes of some, have, I think, produced a reaction in the public mind.

Orr, of course, went on to urge the importance of the China field and to emphasize the great numbers of accessible Chinese not currently being served by the church.[87]

Gützlaff's secretarial responsibilities, meanwhile, had become more demanding; first, there was the death of Robert Morrison in 1834 and heavier duties as interpreter, and then came the escalation of conflict between Chinese and British authorities over opium and trading conditions. It is difficult to know how to interpret Gützlaff's loyal fulfillment of the increasing demands, even to the point of declining participation in such a missionary venture as the "Himmaleh" tour. Was it the need for a regular salary or a sense of obligation to carry out the terms of his contract? Was it because of his belief that his civil position enhanced his possibilities of serving the mission cause through forcing China open, or was it because he derived pleasure from exercising authority vis-à-vis Chinese officials? Whatever the motivation, Gützlaff was forced to conduct his evangelistic activities within a more circumscribed locale. He still itinerated in the Macao-Canton area and maintained contact with numerous Western organizations and societies, but the phenomenal output of the mid-1830s was no longer possible. A letter to the American Bible Society in 1838 began with the crossed out sentence: "It is now the third year since I have not received a single line from you."[88] An enclosure accompanying a copy of his new version of the *Old Testament* was short and to the point, nothing like the long exhortatory letters of previous years. Gützlaff turned increasingly to emphasis on evangelism by Chinese preachers.

In the initial phases, the Opium War of 1839–42 further added to uncertainty regarding China missions. Contributions declined; the number of missionaries sent out touched bottom. Many Christians felt uncomfortable about a conflict so closely linked with opium. Dreams easily revived, however. The Treaty of Nanking, 1842, opening five Chinese ports to foreign residence, found mission societies eager to take advantage of the new opportunities. Some missionaries, in fact, had not awaited the conclusion of hostilities but had followed British troops to occupied cities and had benefited from Gützlaff's sponsorship.

Gützlaff himself had served as scout for British troops and interpreter for British military commanders; he had also acted as civil magistrate in several of the captured cities, always continuing, of course, his evangelistic efforts.[89] As indicated above, the emperor's edicts of 1844 and 1846 granting tolerance to Christianity and proselytism further heightened expectations.

Missionaries, convinced that hostility had originated with the central government rather than with the populace and that inaccessibility had been a major reason for the small number of converts, sent urgent pleas for colleagues. God worked in mysterious ways, they wrote, and through the distressing military conflict had opened China to the Gospel. "[W]e are all bending forward on the tiptoe of expectation. I can fancy that the angels are also stooping to look into that mighty empire."[90] Dozens, even hundreds of workers would be needed and they must come quickly, for the Catholics were already rushing through the open door. The call was answered, if not in the abundance desired by the missionaries. Interest in China, financial support, and the number of volunteers for the field all increased.

The numbers of converts did not, however, show commensurate growth, and the attrition rate for missionaries was appalling. Acrimony over the proper Chinese term for God so intensified that a new translation of the Bible had to be published with blank spaces left for insertion of the preferred term. Already by the late 1840s, disquieting reevaluations of methodology and cautions against unrealistic hopes had begun to pervade missionary reports and articles.

Gützlaff had turned his attention and energies toward forming a Chinese Union of salaried colporteurs who would go into interior China to circulate tracts and preach the Gospel. The Chinese themselves, not foreigners, would convert China to Christianity, he argued. Only thus, would a truly indigenous church come into existence. Perhaps the example of Liang A-fa came to mind, for the success of Liang in making converts contrasted with the frustrations of the Westerners. Gützlaff made ambitious plans for recruiting hundreds of Chinese who would reach every Chinese province; the membership of the Chinese Union multiplied. A trip to England and Europe in 1849–50 enabled Gützlaff to organize dozens of support societies for his Chinese Union. Gradually, however, it became clear that many colporteurs had taken advantage of Gützlaff's faith for their own economic benefit.[91] Many were confidence men from Hong Kong's underworld and had never left the area. Though they presented Gützlaff with journals of their itinerations and recorded baptisms, they were actually selling the tracts to local printers and booksellers to be repurchased by Gützlaff for recirculation again. Confronted with the revelations, Gützlaff at first contended that only a few of the rapidly burgeoning numbers of workers had deceived him. He returned to China determined to defend his Chinese colleagues, only to be presented with evidence that he had been victimized by a majority of the members of the Chinese Union. He died a broken man in August 1851. A backlash of indignation in Europe led to the rapid collapse of most support societies.

The story of the alternation of optimism and despondency does not, however, end with Gützlaff's death. Reports of the Taiping Christians in 1852–53 gave rise to illusions that the Chinese might indeed convert their own people to Christianity. Even before the defeat of the Taipings in 1864, however, Protestants had concluded that Taiping Christianity was a heresy.

Gützlaff's Legacy

Gützlaff was his own worst enemy as far as his historical reputation is concerned. In both his strengths and his deficiencies, he was almost bigger than life. Certainly he more than any single individual helped to originate the sense of a special relationship between China and America. He was integrally involved in the early phases of the love-hate relationship between America and China as he repeatedly raised expectations that could not be realized. His very success in stimulating American interest in China contributed in the long run to overreaction when images of conversions, trade, and even at times good will proved to be mirages. The myth of the open door, however, survived and survives even today.

Missions were for over a hundred years a major form of Sino-Western relations. For American Protestants in the late nineteenth and early twentieth centuries, China missions represented their heaviest overseas investment of personnel, funds, and hopes. American Protestant churches were, by the 1920s, supporting an establishment that involved some 5,000 workers including wives, 13 Christian colleges, over 200 middle schools, about 275 hospitals, YMCA and YWCA centers, plus a great variety of other activities. The grass-roots foundation of interest in China, laid down during the 1830s, never collapsed. Missionaries linked small-town America and village China as did no other participants in Sino-American relations.[92] Despite repeated disappointments, Protestant congregations continued to adopt ''their missionary'' in China and voluminous correspondence kept them in touch. Church and mission societies sponsored special mission Sundays and China appeals. Missionaries on home leaves were kept busy with lecture tours designed to maintain commitment to the China millions. Even American colleges and universities established abiding ties with China Christian colleges; these included exchange of personnel, scholarships for

Chinese students, and aid in the form of books, laboratory equipment, building funds, and short-term teachers for the China institutions. However significant the cultural interaction was, the religious achievements in terms of numbers of converts were modest at best. The history of Protestant missions in China, like the history of Sino-American diplomatic and economic relations, alternated between hopeful anticipation and a sense of frustration and estrangement.

For a hundred years missionaries acted as a significant source of popular information about China in the West; they were, also, particularly in the early period, important purveyors of information about the West to Chinese. With the exchanges came "scratches on our minds,"[93] to use Harold Isaacs' phrase: images and attitudes through which data filtered. Gützlaff did more than his share of building images. His bold initiatives certainly contributed to a hardening of official Chinese attitudes toward Christianity and Christian missions. While his dual secular and religious roles were not uncommon for the pioneer missionaries, they became for Chinese one more example of the symbiotic relationship between Christian missions and imperialism. Even though Gützlaff rode with the opium smugglers for only a few years, and despite the fact that there were numerous other examples of interdependence, Gützlaff came to symbolize the linkage.

Gützlaff's influence in China was not limited to these activities, however.[94] He also helped to provide data about the West and to alter perceptions in a great variety of ways. He composed dozens of pamphlets and distributed tens of thousands of tracts conveying his version of pietistic Protestantism to Chinese. He wrote articles, books, and pamphlets on secular aspects of Western civilization; materials from his *Tung-Hsi* magazine were subsequently incorporated into Chinese works on Western geography, history, and so on. His contributions to Chinese perceptions of Western civilization were as complex and contradictory as the whole Protestant missionary effort to convert China.

In the West Gützlaff's writings were reproduced in many forms and became a source for numerous accounts on China published by travelers and military campaigners.[95] The picture that emerged from Gützlaff's writings was replete with paradoxes. More than most missionaries, Gützlaff could adapt to the living style of the Chinese and was master of the popular idiom; he insisted on the basic friendliness of the people; he appreciated their industriousness and their family loyalty.

Yet, for Gützlaff, the Chinese could not but be depraved, for they were heathens. Christendom was both the norm and the good for Gützlaff as for most missionaries. The poverty, dirt, disease, corruption, and conservatism that Gützlaff and others portrayed so vividly were certainly prominent on the Chinese scene during the nineteenth century, but the picture was too rarely balanced by detailing the strengths and glories of Chinese civilization. The Chinese emphasis on ceremony, face saving, and compromise was interpreted as dishonesty, for the yardstick was a Western one. Little beauty could be found in Chinese rituals and temples, for they were idolatrous. Even the Chinese classics, not benefiting from God's revelation, could contain only partial truth. How widespread female infanticide was in China is impossible to know since it was a private, even secret act, but it received more than ample publicity in the writings of Gützlaff and his colleagues. Prostitution was legal in China, but whether it was more prevalent than in the West would be hard to say; at any rate the pietistic Protestants viewed the Chinese as a sensual people. Such examples could be multiplied. Nineteenth-century missionaries participated in the discrediting of the Jesuits' admiring representation of Chinese civilization during the seventeenth century and helped in replacing it with a much less favorable view. As they contributed to the sense of a special relationship between America and China, they also contributed to its ambivalences.[96]

Gützlaff's legacy for mission methodology has received little attention, most of it negative; only recently have more positive evaluations appeared.[97] The mainstream of Protestant missions, as for American Protestantism in general during the second half of the nineteenth century, came more and more under the dominance of denominational societies. Sectarian Christianity built on the work of the evangelists of the Second Great Awakening; it incorporated their converts and constructed extensive administrative structures at home and abroad. The age of entrepreneurial pioneers passed. Founding churches, cultivating congregations, and educating potential converts occupied missionaries' attention. China missions, however, continued to remain important to the health and wealth of the churches.[98]

An alternate line of mission methodology, theology, and life style survived, nevertheless. It was one that shared much with Liang A-fa and Gützlaff, and one that was initially directly influenced by Gützlaff. Issachar J. Roberts, who instructed the founder of the Taipings, and J. Hudson Taylor of China Inland Mission fame represented this strain, as did David Livingstone of African renown.[99] Roberts volunteered for China missions as the result of publicity by Morrison, Bridgman, Gützlaff, and others. Once in China, Roberts lived in Gützlaff's home during his first eight months there, studied Chinese with Gützlaff, and joined him on itinerations. After Roberts lost the support of the home society, Gützlaff helped to supplement his income. In a vain attempt to guide the Taipings toward a more orthodox Protestantism, Roberts, in pigtail and Chinese dress, spent over a year with the Taipings in their Nanking capital. The writings of Morrison and Gützlaff likewise inspired Hudson Taylor to choose a missionary career. One of Gützlaff's support societies for the Chinese Union apparently persuaded Taylor in December 1849 to select China as his field. Taylor's China Inland Mission, which eventually became the largest single mission agency in the country, was in many ways a successor to Gützlaff's efforts.

Gützlaff, Roberts, Taylor—all three preached a pietistic Christianity with the

Bible, prayer, and rebirth at the core of a minimal theology. All three believed in the direct intervention of God in history while accepting the role of Providence in working out their own lives. They were loners, rejecting control by home churches or denominations and sometimes founding their own instruments, as in the case of the Chinese Union and the China Inland Mission. Roberts did insist on Baptist teachings regarding immersion even after the Baptist Society ceased its support, but the goal of all three was to spread the Gospel, not to build replicas of Western churches. For Gützlaff and Taylor, denominationalism held no interest. Once the sinner had experienced revival, he or she should give evidence by moral reformation. If the former sinner wished to affiliate with a particular sect, Gützlaff and Taylor had no objection, but they, like many evangelists of the Second Great Awakening, left that sphere of work to others.

All three were intense individuals with a sense of drive and dedication beyond the norm even for evangelists. As self-contained personalities, the possibility of self-delusion was real. They worked closely with the poorest of the Chinese, even at times adopting Chinese dress and life style. Above all, they hoped for a Sinified Christianity. They were willing to depend heavily on Chinese evangelists and to allow them considerable latitude in their preaching. Because the doctrinal freight was minimal, the possibility of a Sinified Christianity was greater. Such attempts as the Chinese Union and the Taipings ended in disaster, but this approach survived the denominationalism of the late nineteenth and early twentieth centuries.

The pietistic Protestantism of Liang A-fa and these Western pioneers endured, to be popularized by some of China's best known pastors: Wang Ming-tao of the Christian Tabernacle in Peking; Chang I-ching, editor of *Chen-kwang tsa-chih* (True light review); and Chia Yu-ming of the Spiritual Training Institute in Shanghai, to mention a few. It became a prominent feature in some of the more dynamic and largest Chinese Christian churches, all of them nonsectarian: Chen Ye-ssu chiao hwei (True Jesus Church), Assembly Hall Church ("Little Flock"), and even the Three Self Church and the underground churches in the People's Republic of China.[100]

Abbreviations

ABCFM	American Board of Commissioners for Foreign Missions
ABS	American Bible Society
AJMR	*Asiatic Journal and Monthly Register*
ATM	*American Tract Magazine*
ATS	American Tract Society
BMM	*Baptist Missionary Magazine*
CR	*The Chinese Repository*
EMMC	*Evangelical Magazine and Missionary Chronicle*
FMC	*Foreign Missionary Chronicle*

MH	*Missionary Herald*
MR	*Missionary Register*
NYO	*New York Observer*
SM	*Spirit of Missions*

Notes

1. Gützlaff, *Journal of Two Voyages along the Coast of China* (New York: J. P. Haven, 1833); "Journal of a residence in Siam and of a voyage along the coast of China to Mantchou Tartary," *CR*, I:16–25, 45–64, 81–99, 122–140 (1832); "Voyages to the north of China," *CR*, I:180–96.

2. ABCFM, *Annual Report* 1833, p. 72.

3. Gützlaff, *Journal of Three Voyages along the Coast of China in 1831, 1832, 1833* (London: F. Westley and A. H. Davis, 1834). Herman Schlyter, *Der China-Missionar Karl Gützlaff und Seine Heimat-basis* (Lund, Sweden: C. W. K Gleerup, 1976), pp. 26–28. Among the periodicals that printed extensive extracts from the journals, the following are typical: *NYO*, 10(48): 189–90 (December 1832); 11(6): 21–22 (February 9, 1833), (7): 28 (February 16, 1833), (13): 50–54 (March 30, 1833); "Review," *BMM*, 15:62–70 (1835); "Voyage of Rev. Charles Gützlaff along the coast of China," *MH*, 29:140–46, 174–78, 213–17, 249–52, 277–82; "Transactions of other societies," *FMC*, 1:158–59 (1834); "Netherlands Missionary Society," *Missionary Record*, 1:109–11, 125–27, 138–40, 155–58 (1833); "China," *EMMC*, 12:208–209, 230–31 (1834); "Review of *Journal of Three Voyages*," *Westminster Review*, 31:119–34 (July 1834); "The journal of the Rev. Charles Gützlaff," *AJMR*, 10:107 (1833), "Attempt to open trade"; *AJMR*, 10: 145–46, "Asiatic intelligence"; *AJMR*, 11:234–36 (1833), "Experimental voyage to the northeast coast of China"; *AJMR*, 12:94–107, 157–73 (1833); "China voyage of the Sylph," *AJMR*, 13: 108–12, 178–81 (1834), 14:24–30; "Review: *Journal of Three Voyages*," *The Athenaeum*, (342):366–69 (May 17, 1834); "Review: *Journal of Three Voyages*," *The London Literary Gazette* (902):305–306 (May 3, 1834); "Netherlands Missionary Society," *MR*: 35–36, 181–84, 276–79, (1833); "Publication of Rev. C. Gützlaff's Three Voyages," *MR*: 268–70, (1834).

4. "Review: *A Sketch of Chinese History, Ancient and Modern* by Rev. Charles Gützlaff," *BMM*, 15:142 (1835); "Extracts from instructions of Prudential Committee to missionaries," *MH*, 29 (274) (August 1833); "ATS, Abstract of 9th annual report," *NYO*, 12(19): 73 (May 10, 1834).

5. "Receipts," *ATM*, 15:46 (April 1840); "Cheering anonymous letter," *ATM*, 12:49 (March 1837); ATS, *Annual Report*, 1841.

6. "Appendix. A Bible every day for China," ABS, *Annual Report*, 1835, pp. 81–82.

7. "Mission to China," *BMM*, 14:94–95 (1834).

8. "Mission to China," *Missionary Record,* 2:150–52 (1834); "Notices of various Christian missions, Church Missionary Society," *EMMC*, 15:191 (1837).

9. "Missionary Intelligence," *FMC*, 2(4): 253 (July 1834).

10. Henry O. Dwight, *The Centennial History of the American Bible Society* (New York: Macmillan, 1916), p. 112; "Foreign appropriations," *ATM*, 11(3): 37 (March 1835).

11. "Mission to China," *Missionary Record* 2:152 (1834).

12. "State of the world," *NYO*, 14(4): 14 (January 23, 1836).

13. ATS, *Ninth Annual Report*, 1834, p. 72.

14. "China. Extent of the missionary field now accessible," *FMC*, 11: 330–31 (October 1843). Also "China opened," *FMC*, 11:53–55 (February 1843). "Appeal to Baptist churches," *BMM*, 23:315–16 (December 1843).

15. "Length of life of Protestant missionaries in China and Chin-India," *BMM*, 27: 385–92 (November 1847). "Of the 63 missionaries in China—39 men and 24 women—the average period of missionary service to the above date was, of males, 5 years and 6 months; and of females, 3 years and 3 months." On the assumption that it took two to three years to learn spoken Chinese, the period of active service was short indeed.

16. "The Million Testament Fund for China," *Report of the British and Foreign Bible Society*, 1854, pp. 74–75; William Canton, *A History of the British and Foreign Bible Society*, 2 vols. (London: John Murray, 1904), vol.1, 447–49.

17. For further biographical details, see Herman Schlyter, *Karl Gützlaff als Missionar in China* (Lund, Sweden: C. W. K. Gleerup, 1946). Though in German the name would be spelled Gützlaff, Gützlaff became so anglicized that he frequently dropped the umlaut and signed himself Charles Gutzlaff rather then Karl.

18. Arthur Waley, *The Opium War through Chinese Eyes* (New York: Macmillan, 1958), p. 233.

19. "Gützlaff's letter of thanks," *ATM*, 12(3): 67 (March 1837).

20. Gützlaff, "An Appeal in Behalf of China," American reprint from *CR* (n.d., n.p.), 12 pp. The *MR*, pointing out that "the spiritual wants of China" were attracting increasing attention, printed a series of articles on China missions: Gützlaff's appeal, brief summaries of Gützlaff's journals, another appeal inspired by Gützlaff's contention that China was open to evangelism, and the report of the London Missionary Society that "the world at this moment presents no object so impressive and attractive" as China. "Survey of Missionary Stations," *MR*: 84–90 (February 1835).

21. Gützlaff, *A Sketch of Chinese History, Ancient and Modern. Comprising a Retrospect of the Foreign Intercourse and Trade with China*, 2 vols. (London: Smith, Elder & Co., 1834); *China Opened, or A Display of the Topography, History, Customs, Manners, etc. of the Chinese Empire*, rev. by Andrew Reed, 2 vols. (London: Smith, Elder & Co., 1838).

22. "Extension of American Missions," *NYO*, 11(52): 206 (December 28, 1833).

23. "Our foreign missionary operations," *Evangelical Review* 5:106–109 (July 1853).

24. "An appeal in behalf of China," *MH*, 30:422–24 (November 1834). Also, Gützlaff, "An Appeal."

25. For further detail, see Fred W. Drake, "Protestant geography in China: E. C. Bridgman's portrayal of the West," in Suzanne W. Barnett and John K. Fairbank, eds., 89–106, *Christianity in China. Early Protestant Missionary Writings* (Cambridge: Harvard University Press, 1985); Elizabeth Malcolm, *"The Chinese Repository* and Western literature on China," *Modern Asian Studies* 7:165–78 (1973).

26. ABCFM, *Annual Report*, 1833, p. 70.

27. ABS Archives, China files, Correspondence.

28. "China—General letter from the missionaries, Canton, March 7, 1838," *MH*, 24: 340–41 (September 1838).

29. ATS, *Ninth Annual Report*, 1834, p. 72.

30. Gützlaff to J. C. Brigham, Macao, December 20, 1834; Gützlaff to Secretary of ABS, Canton, November 10, 1833, ABS Archives.

31. "Letter from Mr. Gützlaff," *NYO*, 11(49): 194 (December 7, 1833); "Open China!—An Appeal, by two friends in behalf of China," *MR*: 87 (February 1835); ABS, *Nineteenth Annual Report*, 1835, p. 57.

32. "Church Missionary Society, Letter from the Rev. C. Gützlaff," *EMMC*, 15:438 (1837); "Evangelization of China. Letter from Rev. Charles Gützlaff," *FMC*, 5:147 (October 1837); Gützlaff, *China Opened*, 2:237.

33. "Visit to the Ankoy tea district," *AJMR*, 16:282–83 (1835).

34. Gützlaff, *Journal of Two Voyages*, pp. 1–2, 148–49, 175–80, 204–205, 210. See also

"ABCFM: Extracts from a letter of Mr. Tracy," *BMM*, 15:115–16 (1835).

35. Gützlaff, *Journal of Two Voyages*, p. 78.

36. Gützlaff, *Journal of Three Voyages*, pp. 421–33.

37. "Visit to Ankoy tea district," *AJMR*, 16:281–89 (1835).

38. Several of the participants in the "Morrison" trip published their journals: Charles W. King and G. T. Lay, *The Claims of Japan and Malaysia upon Christendom Exhibited in Notes of Voyages Made in 1837 from Canton in the Ship "Morrison" and the Brig "Himmaleh,"* 2 vols. (New York: E. French, 1839). Peter Parker, *Journal of an Expedition from Sincapore [sic] to Japan with a visit to Loo-Choo* (London: Smith, Elder & Co., 1838); S. W. Williams, "Narrative of a voyage of the ship 'Morrison,' " *CR*, 6:209–229, 353–80 (September, December 1837).

39. Parkes quoted in Stanley Lane-Poole, *The Life of Sir Harry Parkes*, 2 vols, (London: Macmillan, 1894), vol. 1, pp. 45–47.

40. "Mr. Parker's farewell address," *NYO*, 12 (24): 93 (June 14, 1834).

41. ABCFM, *Annual Report*, 1834, pp. 95–96.

42. Gützlaff, *Sketch of Chinese History*, 1: 472–90; idem., *China Opened*, 1: 472–90; 2: 207; idem, *Journal of Two Voyages*, pp. 142–43, 159, 274–79.

43. ATS, *Tenth Annual Report*, 1835, pp. 87–95.

44. Gützlaff, *Journal of Two Voyages*, pp. 52–53, 318–31; idem., *Journal of Three Voyages*, pp. 441–42; idem., *Sketch of Chinese History*, 2:114–60.

45. Gützlaff to ABS, Canton, November 10, 1833; Gützlaff to ABS, Macao, March 5, 1836, ABS Archives; "Gützlaff letter, Macao, September 16, 1832," *NYO*, 11(25): 99 (June 22, 1833); Gützlaff, "An Appeal on Behalf of China."

46. Gützlaff, *China Opened*, vol. 2, p. 232; Gützlaff, *Journal of Two Voyages*, p. 100.

47. *Gaihan's [Gützlaff's] Chinesische Berichte, von der Mitte des Jahres 1841 bis zum Schluss des Jahres 1846* (Cassel: Chinesische Stiftung, 1850); Letter of August 1842, Nanking, p. 13; "Letter of Mr. Bridgman, Macao, July 1, 1841," *MH*, 28: 100–101 (March 1842); "Survey of Protestant Missionary Stations," *MR*, vol. 3–4, 140–53, 1843.

48. Gützlaff, *Sketch of Chinese History,* 1: 188–99; idem., *China Opened*, vol. 2, pp. 183–184; idem., *Journal of Two Voyages*, pp. 299–304.

49. Gützlaff to Secretary of ABS, Macao, March 5, 1836, ABS Archives; "Gützlaff letter to Dr. Reed," *NYO*, 13(9): 33–34 (February 28, 1835); "Evangelization of China. Letter from Rev. Charles Gützlaff," *FMC*, 5:147 (October 1837); "China and its vicinity; An appeal from Charles Gützlaff," *EMMC*, 15:137–40 (October 1837).

50. "Another letter from China," *NYO*, 11(24): 94–95 (June 14, 1834); "Extracts from letters from Rev. Mr. Gützlaff," *MH*, 30: 309 (August 1834); Gützlaff, *Sketch of Chinese History*, 1:v–vi. See also Gützlaff's presentations to a Chinese audience: "Tung-shang" (Commerce), *Tung-Hsi*, 12:160–62 (1837); "Mou-i" (Trade), *Tung-Hsi*, 1:8–11 (1838); *Mou-i t'ung-che* (Treatise on Commerce) (n.p., 1840), 64 leaves.

51. [Gützlaff]. "Christian missions in China," *CR*, 3:561 (April 1835).

52. For further detail, see Peter W. Fay, *The Opium War, 1840–1842* (Chapel Hill, NC: University of North Carolina Press, 1975), pp. 41–52, 110–27; Michael Greenberg, *British Trade and the Opening of China, 1800–1842* (Cambridge: Cambridge University Press, 1951), pp. 104–142; Jessie G. Lutz, "The Missionary-Diplomat Karl Gützlaff and the Opium War," in *Proceedings of the First International Symposium on Church and State in China: Past and Present*, ed. by Li Ch'i-fang, 215–38 (Taipei, Taiwan, 1987).

53. Jack Beeching, *The Chinese Opium Wars* (New York: Harcourt, Brace, Jovanovich, 1975), p. 61.

54. Chang Hsin-pao, *Commissioner Lin and the Opium War* (Cambridge: Harvard University Press, 1964), pp. 23–29; Gützlaff, *Journal of Three Voyages*, p. 413.

55. Even after accepting the position of Chinese interpreter, Gützlaff did not entirely escape participation in opium affairs. He served as mediator and interpreter for the British in several cases involving opium merchants.

56. Letter of Gützlaff, December 19, 1834, in Appendix, Young Men's New York Bible Society, *Annual Report*, 1835, ABS Archives; "A million Bibles and tracts wanted in China," *NYO*, 13(19): 74 (May 9, 1835).

57. For further information on Gützlaff's secular writings in Chinese, see Lutz, "Karl F. A. Gützlaff," and Drake, "Protestant Geography," in Barnett and Fairbank, *Christianity in China*, pp. 61–88, 95–97. Some of the information in *Tung-Hsi* was paraphrased in the geographies of Wei Yuan and Hsu Chi-yü. The publication of *Tung-Hsi* was somewhat irregular, with no issues during 1836.

58. [Hugh H. Lindsay and K. Gützlaff], *Report of Proceedings on a Voyage to the Northern Ports of China, in the Ship "Lord Amherst,"* 2nd. ed. (London: B. Fellows, 1834), pp. 32–33, 41–42, 58, 93–94; "Attempt to open trade," *AJMR*, 10:145–46 (April 1833); "Experimental voyage to the northeast coast of China," *AJMR*, 11:94–107, 157–73 (August, September 1833); Immanel C. Y. Hsü, "The secret mission of the 'Lord Amherst' on the China coast, 1832," *Harvard Journal of Asiatic Studies*, 17:231–52 (1954).

59. "Another letter from China," *NYO*, 12(24): 94–95 (June 14, 1834); [Lindsay and Gützlaff], *Report*, pp. 21–23, 62–63, 84–86, 177.

60. Quoted in British and Foreign Bible Society, *Twenty-ninth Annual Report*, 1833, p. lxx; "Gützlaff letter," *NYO*, 11(25): 99 (June 22, 1833).

61. "Meeting of gentlemen in N.Y., in behalf of the tract cause," *NYO*, 11(44): 174 (November 2, 1833).

62. See the several edicts translated by Gützlaff in [Lindsay and Gützlaff], *Report*, pp. 19–20, 64–65, 71–73, 78, 179–81; and extracts from the *Peking Gazette* and the *Canton Register* in *AJMR*, 11:75, 124, 231; 12:157–58 (1833).

63. "Journal of occurrences," *CR*, 3:237–38 (September 1834). Napier died in Macao without achieving a resolution of the controversy.

64. "China," *AJMR*, 17:233 (December 1835); "Miscellaneous statement by E. C. Bridgman and J. R. Morrison," *MH*, 21:230–32 (June 1835); "ABCFM, Brief notices," *MH*, 22:161–62 (April 1836).

65. "China," *MR*: 369–74 (1836); G. J. Gordon, "Expedition to the tea district of Fuh-Keen," *AJMR*, 20:130–37 (1835).

66. "ABCFM, Brief Notices," *MH*, 22:161–62 (April 1836); "Letter from Mr. Williams, dated at Canton," *MH*, 22:202–203 (June 1836); "Edict against teaching of the Christian religion," *NYO*, 16(51): 205 (December 24, 1836); "Translation of the edict against Gützlaff's magazine in China," *FMC*, 5:139 (September 1837).

67. Actually, Roman Catholic priests were being smuggled into the interior with some frequency. Most Protestant missionaries either ignored this information or argued that they could not follow suit because they lacked congregations to hide them and they were unwilling to resort to such "subterfuge."

68. "Religious intelligence. Letter from Mr. Gützlaff," *Christian Advocate*, December 1833, pp. 556–57; idem., *China Opened*, vol. 2, p. 79; idem., "An Appeal."

69. Gützlaff to ABS, Macao, March 5, 1836; William S. Plummer to Robert Morrison, November 29, 1834, ABS Archives; "A million Bibles and tracts wanted in China!" *NYO*, 13(19): 74 (May 9, 1835).

70. "Missionary intelligence," *FMC*, 5:120–21 (August 1837); "Appeal in behalf of missions to the Chinese," *MH*, 33:375–78 (September 1837).

71. "Eastern Asia, Mission to China," *MH*, 33:16 (January 1837).

72. ABCFM, *Report*, 1837, pp. 86–89.

73. ATS, *Twelfth Annual Report*, 1837, pp. 107–115.

74. Gützlaff to ABS, Macao, March 5, 1836, ABS Archives.

75. "Church Missionary Society, Letter from the Rev. C. Gützlaff," *EMMC*, 15:438 (1837).

76. "Singapore: Annual report of the mission for 1836," *MH*, 33:336–37 (August 1837); "Journal of the Rev. R. W. Orr, April 6, 1838," *FMC*, 7:121–22 (April 1839); S. Wells Williams, *The Middle Kingdom*, 2 vols. (New York: Charles Scribners & Sons, 1883), vol. 2, p. 332; "Siam. Letter of Mr. [William] Dean," *BMM*, 21:90 (April 1841). For Roman Catholic reports on the uses of tracts, see Peter W. Fay, "The Protestant mission and the Opium War," *Pacific Historical Review*, 40:150–51 (May 1971).

77. Joint letter of W. H. Medhurst, Charles Gützlaff, J. R. Morrison, and E. C. Bridgman to A. Brandam, Secretary to the British and Foreign Bible Society, Canton, December 21, 1835, copy in ABS Archives; Gützlaff to J. C. Brigham, Macao, December 20, 1834; E. C. Bridgman to Brigham, Canton, March 8, 1836; Edwin Stevens to R. Anderson, Canton, May 31, 1836; Bridgman to Brigham, Canton, March 7, 1837, with Document A, "Revision of the Scriptures," all in ABS Archives.

78. See Gützlaff's somewhat defensive letter to the ATS, November 5, 1837, explaining why he was unable to join the "Himmaleh" tour, ATS, *Thirteenth Annual Report*, 1838, pp. 134–35.

79. For details, see King and Lay, *The Claims of Japan and Malaysia*. Also, E. C. Bridgman's lengthy review with excerpts in *CR*, 8: 359–72 (1839). British and Foreign Bible Society, *Thirty-Fifth Annual Report*, 1839, pp. lxxi–lxxiv. A later assessment by a contemporary is in Williams, *Middle Kingdom*, vol. 2, pp. 330–31.

80. Gützlaff letter quoted in Report of O. R. Kingsbury of ATS, January 22, 1839. E. C. Bridgman to J. C. Brigham, Canton, March 18, 1836, ABS Archives. Also, "China, Extracts from the general letter of the mission, dated Sept. 8, 1836," *MH*, 33: 216–63 (January, 1837).

81. "$40,000 proposed foreign appropriations," *ATM*, 14:165 (December 1839); ABS, *Twenty-Second Annual Report*, 1838, p. 59; ABS, *Twenty-Third Annual Report*, 1839, p. 53.

82. "China, general letter of the mission dated at Canton, Oct. 5, 1838," *MH*, 25: 212–13 (June 1839).

83. Hosea B. Morse, *The International Relations of the Chinese Empire*, 3 vols. (London: Longmans Green, 1910–18), vol. 1, p. 694: "a work full of valuable information but requiring some checking on the point of accuracy"; Schlyter, *Karl Gützlaff*, p. 108; John Fairbank called Gützlaff "a well informed contemporary and close student of Peking Gazettes"; "Chinese diplomacy and the Treaty of Nanking, 1842," *Journal of Modern History*, 12:13 (March 1940).

84. Williams, "Review of *China Opened*," *CR*, 8:84–98 (June 1839). See also the review in *The Athenaeum*, no. 569: 695–96 (September 22, 1838). In his *Middle Kingdom*, Williams cited several of Gützlaff's works and commented favorably on Gützlaff's journeys: vol. 1, pp. 100, 193–94; vol. 2, pp. 139, 180, 328–33. Williams' discussion of the early emphasis on tract distribution is balanced and he attempts to answer critics of this methodology.

85. "A letter from Dr. Parker to Dr. Reed," *EMMC*, 15:435–38 (1837).

86. Appendix 3, "Mr. G. T. Lay to the Secretaries," in Church Missionary Society, *Proceedings*, 1838–39, pp. 140–41.

87. "Chinese mission letter from the Rev. Robert W. Orr," *FMC*, 9:310–13 (October 1841). On declining interest, see also "China: From the Rev. W. J. Boone," *SM*, 5: 275–77 (August 1840).

88. Gützlaff to the Secretary of ABS, Macao, November 4, 1838; Gützlaff to the Secretary of the ABS, Hong Kong, December 11, 1845, ABS Archives.

89. For detail, see Lutz, "Karl Gützlaff and the Opium War."

90. British and Foreign Bible Society, *Report*, 1843, p. cviii; "British and Foreign Bible Society: China," *MR*, vol. 126 (1844); "Appeal to Baptist Churches," *BMM*, 23:315–16 (December 1843); "Voice from China," *Christian Intelligencer*, new ser., 3:325–27 (December 1845); ATS, *Eighteenth Annual Report*, 1843, pp. 102–105; *Nineteenth Annual Report*, 1844, pp. 130–34.

91. A. J. Broomhall, *Hudson Taylor and China's Open Century*, 3 vols. (London: Holder and Stoughton and The Overseas Missionary Fellowship, 1981–82), vol. 1, pp. 319–28, 339–47.

92. John K. Fairbank, "Introduction: The place of Protestant writings in China's cultural history," in Barnett and Fairbank, *Christianity in China*, pp. 2–3.

93. Harold R. Isaacs, *Scratches on Our Minds: American Images of China and India* (New York: John Day, 1958).

94. Gützlaff's influence on China is beyond the scope of this essay. For some information on his secular writings, see Drake, "Protestant geography in China" and Lutz, "Karl Gützlaff" in Barnett and Fairbank, *Christianity in China*, pp. 61–106. Also, Suzanne W. Barnett, "Practical Evangelism: Protestant Missions and the Introduction of Western Civilization in China, 1820–50" (Ph.D. dissertation, Harvard University, 1973).

95. The citations of Gützlaff's writings as a source in missionary magazines are too numerous to list. His estimate of the total population of China and his comments on infanticide and the status of Chinese women were, for instance, referred to dozens of times. Some of Gützlaff's papers were printed in the *Journal of the Royal Asiatic Society*: "Remarks on the Yih-Shi, a Historical work of the Chinese," 3:272–82 (1836); "The medical art amongst the Chinese," 4:154–71 (1837); "On the secret Triad Society of China," 8: 361–67 (1846); "Remarks on the present state of Buddhism in China," 16:73–92 (1856). Among the works citing Gützlaff's writings were: John F. Davis, *Sketches of China; Partly during an Inland Journey of Four Months, between Peking, Nanking, and Canton*, 2 vols. (London: Charles Knight, 1841); Charles T. Downing, *The Stranger in China*, 2 vols. (Philadelphia: Lea and Blanchard, 1838); William D. Bernard, *The Nemesis in China, comprising a History of the Late War in that Country*, 2 vols. (London: Henry Colbure, 1844) (1969 reprint); Robert M. Martin, *China: Political, Commercial, and Social, in an Official Report to Her Majesty's Government*, 2 vols. (London: James Madden, 1847).

96. For an excellent discussion, see Michael Hunt, *The Making of a Special Relationship* (New York: Columbia University Press, 1983).

97. See the balanced studies of Schlyter, *Karl Gützlaff als Missionar* and *Der China-Missionar Karl Gützlaff und seine Heimat-basis*. A quite favorable assessment is given in Broomhall, *Hudson Taylor*, esp. vols. 1 and 2.

98. Valentin H. Rabe, *The Home Base of American China Missions, 1880–1920* (Cambridge: Harvard University Press, 1978).

99. Inspired by Gützlaff's publicity, David Livingstone volunteered for the China mission field; he accepted Africa as a second choice because of the uncertainty created during the Opium War. See Broomhall, *Hudson Taylor*, vol. 1, p. 274. For information regarding Gützlaff's influence on Roberts, see "Journal of I. J. Roberts, Missionary to China," *China Mission Advocate*, 1:54–63 (1839); Charles Gützlaff and I. J. Roberts, "Annual Letter, February 17, 1839," *China Mission Advocate*, 1:213–15; ATS, *Fifteenth Annual Report*, 1840, p. 132. For Gützlaff's influence on Taylor, see Broomhall, 1:291–93, 324–25, 344–50, 360–61.

100. For further information, see the articles of Daniel Bays, "Christianity and the Chinese sectarian tradition," *Ch'ing-shih wen-t'i*, 4.7:33–55; Murray Rubinstein, "Pentacostalism becomes Chinese: The Chen Ye-ssu Chiao Hwei (True Jesus Church) and the Sinification of Christianity" (unpublished paper, Columbia University Modern China Seminar, 1985); and Rubinstein, "Born Again in Taiwan," *American Asian Studies*, forthcoming.

4

"HANDS ACROSS THE SEA"
Foreign Missions and Home Support

Lawrence D. Kessler

The American Protestant missionary enterprise in China in the first half of this century has been studied often as a quintessential example of cross-cultural interaction. For the most part, historians have focused on Christian missions as a significant factor in modern Chinese history, providing a Westernizing and modernizing impulse for a people desperately seeking to reclaim their former greatness. Some historians of China missions have turned their sights around, back toward the countries that sent missions, to examine the role the missions played in the formation of American attitudes and policies toward China. Irwin Hyatt, in his marvelous study of Southern Baptists in China, perhaps best summarized the meaning of mission work in these two respects. Protestant missionaries in China, he noted:

> for more than a century were for many Chinese the living face of a new international order. As teachers, as publicists, and simply as privileged foreigners living there, they contributed to the process of modernization and nationalistic self-discovery in that country. As objects of prayerful concern and of money-raising efforts at home, and as indefatigable reporters on the Chinese scene, they also contributed to American opinion and policy regarding China.[1]

Yet, no one has looked carefully at the impact these missions had in shaping the religious life and organizational behavior of American churches themselves. Here is a field of study ripe for investigation and, if my experience is any guide, one that will reward the researcher with immense sets of readily accessible and uniquely valuable data. As part of a larger study of a Southern Presbyterian (PCUS: Presbyterian Church in the United States) missionary community at Jiangyin, I have investigated the connections, both personal and institutional, between the mission station in China and its sponsoring church at home, the First Presbyterian Church of Wilmington, North Carolina.[2]

While one of the smallest churches in size, the Southern Presbyterians assumed a leading role in foreign missions. Their fund-raising strategy took definite shape in 1902 with the establishment of a "Forward Movement," started by three young men who had been recruited to mission work by the Student Volunteer Movement but detained at home for lack of funds. The plan was to have churches, societies, or individuals accept definite responsibility for a particular missionary or station or type of work in the field. By personalizing the relationship in this way, they hoped to raise more funds.[3] In 1907, an interdenominational agreement assigned the Southern Presbyterians responsibility for designated areas in seven countries with a combined population of 25 million.[4] Within a decade, among the nine major American Protestant churches, the Southern Presbyterians ranked first, on a per-member basis, both in the number of missionaries sent abroad (about 9.5 per ten thousand) and in the amount of support for the foreign missions (about $1.50 per member).[5] Most of the PCUS mission force (perhaps two-thirds) and investment were in China, where they had fourteen stations, including the one at Jiangyin, all concentrated in the lower Yangzi province of Jiangsu.

Jiangyin city, with a population in the 1920s of about fifty thousand, lay on the southern bank of the Yangzi about one hundred miles upstream from Shanghai. It was often called the "mouth of the Yangzi" because the great river narrowed down to about one mile at that point. Forts on hills north of the city had trained on the river a twelve-inch cannon that could command traffic and protect the upper reaches of the Yangzi from naval attack. The city's strategic location frequently placed it at the center of fighting between rival combatants in modern Chinese history. The mission station, located just outside the city's East Gate, thus often found itself in danger but also in a position to be of service to the local community.

Mission work at Jiangyin (Kiangyin in missionary accounts) began in 1895 and reached a peak in 1925, just prior to the rise of revolutionary nationalism. In numbers alone, the station had more missionaries assigned to it—twenty-three—than ever before or after. There were four in strictly evangelistic work, nine in education, five at the mission hospital, one accountant, two wives momentarily devoted to raising small children and two on home leave. The foreign staff was aided by about twenty-five native workers: pastors, (male) evangelists, Bible women, and colporteurs. There were about a thousand Christians and almost that number of enquirers (potential converts) at the four organized churches and sixteen chapels throughout the country field. The hospital with ninety cots treated thousands of patients, the two high schools at the central station enrolled over four hundred boys and girls, lower schools run by country chapels taught about three hundred students, and the Bible School trained about forty women.

Funds to maintain such an elaborate undertaking were beyond the reach of the Chinese Christian community served by the station and had to be sought from supporters of foreign missions at home. When the Southern Presbyterians accepted responsibility for specific areas of mission work in 1907, they also adopted a "missionary platform" that included creating the first denominational laymen's missionary movement to raise funds and issuing a call for churches within the denomination to adopt a particular overseas mission field as their special object.

In response to this call, the First Presbyterian Church of Wilmington requested and was assigned the Jiangyin station, where one of its own members, Dr. George Worth, had been working as a medical missionary since 1897. Thereafter, all of the institutional work and most of the salaries of its staff were provided for exclusively either by the church and one of its elders—the great cotton merchant and philanthropist James Sprunt—or by the Woman's Auxiliary of Wilmington Presbytery. Through this "special relationship," about two-thirds of a million dollars flowed from the Wilmington area to the missionaries at Jiangyin until the station was closed in 1951. The congregation of the First Presbyterian Church hailed the Jiangyin church as its "spiritual daughter" and followed its growth with parental pride and concern. They saw the station and its missionaries as extensions of themselves and participated vicariously in mission work through their annual contributions. As one of the Jiangyin missionaries wrote, "We know that your hearts are with us all the times, for 'where your treasure is, there will your hearts be.' "6

Records at the First Presbyterian Church provide a detailed accounting of its annual contributions to Jiangyin. From 1902 until 1951, the church contributed over $560,000 to its special project in China (see Table 1). Support was greatest (ranging from $12,000 to $28,000 annually) in the early years of the Chinese Republic, as station work expanded, but began to decline gradually after the Nanjing Incident of 1927 and the rising doubts about the efficacy and propriety of mission work in China. A precipitous decline in contributions (to about $3,000 a year) came after 1938 due to the cutoff of Sprunt funding.

While such support was obviously of supreme importance to the missionary efforts in China, the missionary efforts also had a profound impact on their supporters at home. The rest of this article will be devoted to a description of the structure of the relationship between Jiangyin and Wilmington and some tentative conclusions about the significance of mission work for American churches.

Missionaries at Jiangyin, like their PCUS colleagues at other stations, were prodigious letter writers. They regularly sent letters to their Mission Board in Nashville for duplication and circulation to a large mailing list that included member churches (such as the First Presbyterian Church), various church agencies, and interested individuals. At the same time, they sent similar reports about their station to PCUS journals in China and the United States (*Bi-Monthly Bulletin, Monthly Messenger, The Missionary, Presbyterian Survey*), and to general missionary publications such as the *Chinese Recorder*. They also kept up personal correspondence with friends, relatives, and financial backers at home (such as James Sprunt). Most important of all, however, in maintaining the "special relationship" with Wilmington, were the semiannual reports Dr. Worth sent to the

Table 1

First Presbyterian Church, Wilmington
Annual Support of Jiangyin Station

1902	$1,342	1919	$13,782	1936	$10,278
1903	626	1920	15,450	1937	13,637
1904	1,387	1921	18,493	1938	13,544
1905	1,602	1922	15,420	1939	3,280
1906	1,610	1923	18,945	1940	2,935
1907	2,216	1924	27,005	1941	2,336
1908	3,381	1925	19,018	1942	2,209
1909	11,483	1926	20,277	1943	2,386
1910	22,009	1927	18,696	1944	3,170
1911	14,448	1928	17,499	1945	3,682
1912	18,279	1929	15,626	1946	4,145
1913	15,459	1930	15,513	1947	3,738
1914	28,654	1931	14,551	1948	7,295
1915	17,341	1932	14,440	1949	4,967
1916	16,769	1933	13,809	1950	5,224
1917	23,855	1934	12,517	1951	4,916
1918	12,044	1935	15,400		

Total $566,688

Notes: Data are taken from the following publications of the First Presbyterian Church: *Handbook, 1892–1913*, p. 20, for 1902–1913; Bulletin of April 30, 1916, in "Scrap-Book of Church History, 1886–1938," for 1914; "Sessional Records," for 1915–51. All figures reflect amount collected as of March 31 in the respective year.

Wilmington Presbyterial Auxiliary, which agreed to underwrite the cost of medical work at Jiangyin, and the weekly station letters sent to the First Presbyterian Church.

The information conveyed through these different avenues of communication provided a wealth of information on the station, all facets of its work (and play), the progress of Christianity in the field, the personal stories of Chinese converts and coworkers, the relationship between the station and the local community, the social and political conditions in the immediate area, and the great events and movements of the time. All this correspondence, in short, provided their recipients (and today's researcher) with a full and intimate picture of the Jiangyin Station and its place in modern Chinese history. It also presented stories about specific individuals who had converted or enrolled as enquirers or with whom they dealt in some other capacity. In this way, these letters replaced American images of hordes of faceless Chinese with real Chinese whose needs could be recognized and alleviated. Missionary correspondence thus was perhaps the most significant way in which mission work was personalized and humanized for the home audiences, giving them a sense of participation and a stake in the great work of evangelization around the world.

As a final comment on the value of this correspondence, it should be noted that missionaries were better situated than any other group of foreigners to observe and report on the activities and attitudes of Chinese. Only missionaries were driven by the nature of their work to move out from the treaty ports into the small towns and villages of China. And, unlike government or business representatives, they were in China to stay. It is estimated that Protestant missionaries in the 1920s and 1930s had an average of thirteen years experience in China, and they usually were able to read and speak the language well.[7] Missionaries, it is fair to say, were the most knowledgeable and perceptive of foreign observers in China. Through them, thousands of ordinary Americans gained their first and probably most lasting impressions of this far away civilization. At a time when public schools had not yet incorporated the study of non-Western cultures into their curricula, churches thus provided a vital educational forum where adults and youth alike received regular lessons on China from their representatives in the field.

The First Presbyterian Church received a station letter from Jiangyin every week, written by different missionaries in turn according to a schedule posted at the station. Lengthy excerpted passages from these letters were printed regularly in the Sunday bulletin, so regularly that the absence of them was cause for comment.[8] Between 1908 and 1921, there was only one year (1913) when fewer than twenty bulletins contained some news item from Jiangyin.[9] Since the bulletin was only issued about eight months of the year (October through May or sometimes June), the congregation could expect to read about the special object of their prayers and support two or three Sundays a month during the active seasons of the church. On some occasions, the station letter would be read at services instead of being printed. Accompanying some of the letters would be photographs of station buildings and of groups of Chinese Christians to "make the work there more real and definite." Special "Jiangyin Nights" were held for presentation and discussion of mission work, and annually curios from China were put on display and offered for sale as a way of raising additional funds.[10] This steady receipt of letters and the other special activities at the church reminded the congregation constantly of their obligations to the mission in China.

On a less frequent basis, but having an equal if not greater impact than station letters, were the personal contacts between missionaries and home congregations during the missionaries' furloughs. On these occasions, the work in China became a palpable reality through the presence of the missionaries. Supporters at home could see and talk to their representatives abroad and learn first hand about the problems and opportunities of the missions. Often, a furlough could be as demanding on a missionary as if he or she were still on the job. In 1921, the father of one

Jiangyin missionary reported that the missionary and her husband (who had come home specifically to recuperate from an illness) "are on the march constantly and have been itinerating almost as much as they do in China."[11]

Whenever Jiangyin missionaries were home on furlough, they made a point to visit the "mother church," as they liked to call it, to maintain the personal ties so important to their fund-raising efforts. Perhaps the most extravagant of these visits came in 1936 when the First Presbyterian Church hosted eight missionaries from the station. During Mission Week, from April 27 to May 3, these missionaries used a variety of platforms to generate interest in and support for their work. Every weekday, one of them presented a ten-minute meditation at the early morning services. George Worth one afternoon addressed the Woman's Auxiliary, which for years tirelessly raised nearly all the funds needed to build and maintain the mission hospital at Jiangyin which he directed. A reception in honor of the missionaries was held in mid-week for the entire congregation. The week culminated in "Foreign Mission Day" on May 3, when Sunday School was entirely devoted to the Jiangyin missionaries.[12]

Missionaries would bring home with them hundreds of photographs and film footage to illustrate their talks. In the late 1930s, for example, a four-reel film was produced at Jiangyin for educational work back home. The footage not only shows mission work at the central station and at a country outstation, but it also records some of the daily activity of Chinese, such as rice cultivation, sericulture, canal traffic, women at work, war relief programs, and street scenes.[13]

The close relationship of the "mother church" in Wilmington and its "spiritual daughter" in Jiangyin contributed to the vitality of both in another way. Sustaining the foreign mission and watching it grow in numbers and importance gave the home church a sense of purpose. The station letters always made a point to give statistics on the number of enquirers in the Jiangyin field and how many new members were added to the church rolls after each examination. These figures were used to challenge the First Presbyterian Church congregation. In a 1909 bulletin, for example, the pastor added the following pointed observations to the latest news from Jiangyin:

> 1st. The work was started there 14 years ago, among heathen, with not a single Christian. Now they have 431 members. This church began in 1817. Now we have 683 members.
> 2nd. They have nine candidates for the ministry. Here at home we have not a single candidate under the care of the Presbytery, though three are about ready to become candidates.[14]

Similarly, missionaries transmitted to Chinese Christians news of the "mother church" (they regularly received the church bulletin at Jiangyin) and spoke of its many achievements and its leadership role within the Southern Presbyterian church. When the East Gate church installed its first pastor in 1918, one of the

Chinese elders urged the congregation "to press on to full self-support and beyond self-support to self-propagation, having as their ideal to be a 'Second Wilmington First Church'."[15]

The Jiangyin connection challenged not only the church as a body but also one of its leading members, James Sprunt, who provided the greatest portion of the church's contributions to missions. Sprunt was Wilmington's most illustrious and prosperous citizen in the early decades of this century. He came to North Carolina from Scotland in 1854 as a young lad and in 1865, then nineteen years old, he entered the cotton trade business with his father, Alexander. When the latter died in 1884, James and a younger brother took over the family business and built it by the turn of the century into the largest cotton exporting house in the United States.[16]

James Sprunt's sustained philanthropic association with the mission movement began in 1908 when he and his exporting company were at the peak of their fortunes. In May of that year, J. Campbell White, the founding general secretary of the Laymen's Missionary Movement, was a guest for three days in the Sprunts' magnificent waterfront home in Wilmington while attending a laymen's convention of all the Protestant churches in the city. White was touring the country seeking to raise a million dollars annually for foreign mission work from prominent businessmen. In the wake of that visit, he asked Sprunt if he would be willing to undertake the annual support of the general secretary's $4,000 salary. One family in Montreal had supprted White for ten years in India as a missionary, and he found such an arrangement "afforded peculiar satisfaction to all concerned. One feels he has in this way the special personal interest and prayers of his supporters, as he cannot do when his support comes out of a general fund."[17] Sprunt readily accepted the challenge, after some quick checking of White's standing among prominent mission leaders, and he even added $1,000 yearly for White's travel expenses.[18]

Through White and his organization, Sprunt, in his own words,[19] began a "career of stewardship," with the notion that man was a lifetime trustee for a portion of God's wealth with the responsibility of using it wisely in support of God's cause. In February 1909, he attended the inaugural convention of PCUS's own Layman's Missionary Movement in Birmingham, Alabama. At the meetings, Sprunt was inspired to pledge $10,000 to foreign missions. White urged his benefactor to direct his contribution to a new station just then opening up in Korea and to make any further donations to the same station. White was particularly concerned that contributions to mission work be centered and used for the thorough cultivation of one field, whether in Korea or elsewhere.[20]

In the end Sprunt accepted White's approach, but he decided to concentrate his efforts not in Korea but in China at the Jiangyin station that the First Presbyterian Church had been supporting for several years and where his friend George Worth had established a hospital. Educational work at Jiangyin was also expanding and there was need for school buildings. On March 31, 1909, Sprunt drew a check for $10,000, payable to the pastor of the First Presbyterian Church as a "special contribution to Foreign Missions, Kiang-Yin.'' In notifying White of this decision, Sprunt assured him that the funds would not go into a general fund but be used exclusively to build a boys' school and girls' school at Jiangyin to train native helpers. Furthermore, he intended to direct all future contributions to the same work, "which will of course be more interesting to me on account of my personal connection with it."[21]

With Sprunt's gift, the station erected two substantial school buildings and named them after Sprunt and his wife. The English names James Sprunt Male Academy and Luola Murchison Sprunt Academy were carved in stone above the entrances, but in Chinese they were known, respectively, as the "Urge to Truth School" and the "Help to Truth Girls School." The donors' portraits were displayed at the schools, and students were read some of the letters Sprunt sent to George Worth and the Littles, who were in charge of educational work at Jiangyin.[22] After the deaths of Mrs. Sprunt and Mrs. Little in 1916, brass memorial plaques were hung in the girls' school auditorium.[23] Here, clearly, was a classic example of the personal relationship in mission funding that the Laymen's Missionary Movement and the Forward Movement had been promoting as the most effective way to expand world evangelization.

Sprunt took an active interest in the work at Jiangyin and was alert to any signs that the station was not being properly supported or managed. In 1921, for example, Sprunt was very critical of the PCUS Executive Committee of Foreign Missions in Nashville for reducing the missionary forces at Jiangyin, rendering that station helpless in his estimation and working its remaining staff to death. In the preceding two years, Sunday bulletins at the First Presbyterian Church had printed a series of letters from Jiangyin that complained of inadequate foreign staff and hospital equipment. George Worth, in one of the letters, was uncharacteristically pessimistic and bitter about the personnel situation:

> Do you know that three years ago the three hospitals of our [Mid-China] mission south of the Yangtze River had a total of six doctors and three nurses, whereas they now have a total of but three doctors and one nurse. What do you think of that for three hospitals? . . . As far as we have any information from home there is not a single doctor nor nurse under appointment for our China field, and that in despite of the fact that thousands of both doctors and nurses have just returned from the war. . . . It is a constant source of wonder to us missionaries why the [PCUS] mission authorities at home do not appear to have made a great effort to win many of these men and women for mission work. . . . The work and responsibilities have increased but the new workers that have joined our ranks do not make up for the actual losses by death, broken health or necessary transfer to other points.[24]

Then, in the winter of 1921, Sprunt received a personal account of the station's problems from a nephew who had just spent two weeks there. The young man noted the lack of personnel—only six left of the normal contingent of fourteen—and, most alarming of all to Sprunt, how overworked and sickly was his host, George Worth, and how handicapped he was in his hospital without an X-ray outfit. "The Chinese," the nephew wrote pointedly, "know that good hospitals have X-Ray equipment, and many go to Shanghai to get the benefit of it." In a letter to his pastor, Sprunt complained that "a hospital without water works, and an operating room without an X-Ray instrument, seem to me a lamentable reflection on our church," and he threatened to "[dis]continue my gift to the cause of foreign missions unless the Kiang-yin Station can be more directly under our control."[25] If Sprunt had read a contemporary study of missionary hospitals in China, he would have realized that the overwhelming proportion of them operated under similar, if not worse, conditions.[26]

After a somewhat encouraging letter from George Worth about station work (despite its depleted condition) and the hope of new appointments there, Sprunt's fears about his mission investment were quieted. His reply to Worth reaffirmed his faith in a God that "can use a few to accomplish the work of many; . . . If the disadvantages which have beset you in the station have been opportunities to show the delivering power of our God, we must thank His great wisdom that answers the intent of our prayers, rather than our actual requests." On a more mundane level, he expressed relief that "you and [Mrs. Worth] have never had to relinquish your hold on the Mission through all the readjustments and the swapping around of workers."[27] Divine will was fine, but some familiar, dear friends in charge were perhaps even more reassuring.

These momentary doubts about mission management did not deflect Sprunt from his commitment to missions, and he remained a generous benefactor for the rest of his life. It was once said that "Santa Claus has no standing at all in Kiang-Yin in comparison with Mr. James Sprunt."[28] After his initial $10,000 gift in 1909, he made an annual subscription through the First Presbyterian Church of $3,000–5,000.[29] He also responded generously to special requests, such as $5,000 for hospital equipment and expansion, and $3,000 for the girls' school and $10,500 for the boys' school when each needed additional space.[30] In 1923, he undertook the support of Charles Worth, son of George, and his new wife when they went out to Jiangyin.[31] In 1924, in one of his last philanthropic acts, Sprunt gave $7,000 to build an additional residence, named after his mother, for the staff at Jiangyin.[32]

James Sprunt died July 9, 1924, but his beneficence continued. The terms of his will stipulated that $10,000 be paid yearly from the Benevolent Trust Fund he set up in 1921 to the Jiangyin Station for a period of twenty years after his death.[33] These contributions continued until 1938 when trustees of the Fund informed the First Presbyterian church that poor performance of the stocks in the Fund precluded any further payments.[34] With the loss of these funds, the amount of church support to Jiangyin decreased significantly (see Table 1). From 1939 to the end of World War II, the annual contribution averaged less than $3,000. After the war, with the prospect of reopening the Jiangyin Station,church support increased to about $5,000 a year, still a far cry from the five-figure contributions during the period 1909 to 1938 when Sprunt money filled the coffers.

In addition to mission work's being a source of information and inspiration to the church and its members, it also had lasting organizational impacts, particularly on the women of the church. Women's support of missions began as soon as the first foreign mission board was formed in 1810, when older charitable societies organized by church women began to divert their funds to that cause. A half-century later, these efforts were promoted more systematically with the organization of women's foreign missionary societies in most of the Protestant denominations. Between 1860 and 1910, forty-four societies had been formed, with local, regional, and national structures.[35] In a journal of one of these denominational societies, an author of a 1869 piece titled "Laborers Wanted" glorified the fund raising work of women at home: "A *few* must go forth to teach, but the *many* must *work* at home . . . to organize praying bands and working circles to earn and raise money. . . . Let every lady, who feels that *she would be a missionary*, go to work at home, and she may, by every dollar raised, teach her heathen sisters."[36] The women who did go abroad as missionaries or as wives of missionaries were a great inspiration to their supporters at home, who by 1910 were raising about four million dollars for mission schools, hospitals, orphanages, asylums and the like.[37]

Through these societies and the vital role they played in expanding mission work, women acquired "a primary source of identification" and expanded their vision of the world and their own lives beyond the roles of wives and mothers.[38] Women became a more active force in their churches, even though they had no representation in policy making. Male leaders were quick to recognize this development and fought to keep them subordinate ("auxiliary") to the church and not an independent force.

The Southern Presbyterians, who were among the last of the major denominations to create a Women's Board, were a case in point. For twenty years, from 1868 to 1888, many PCUS churches formed missionary societies, but there was no uniformity of organization nor cooperation among them nor any higher organization at the regional (presbytery), state (synod), or denominational (assembly) level. In 1884, Miss Jennie Hanna of Kansas City was inspired by the success of the Women's Board of the Northern Presbyterian Church to make a similar attempt to create an integrative structure in the Southern Assembly. The Secretary of Foreign Missions encouraged her to organize on the presbyterial level but not beyond. She attempted to contact mission-minded women in each of the two thousand or so congregations within the denomination and urged them to join with other local churches to form presbyterial unions. The first two were established in 1888 in East Hanover, Virginia, and in Wilmington.

Even this minimal step aroused conservative opposition. Many ministers never replied to Hanna's initial request for the names of women in their churches with whom she could correspond. Knowing of the controversy she was stirring up, the General Assembly polled the presbyteries for their position on this matter. Of sixty-eight presbyteries that responded, only about one-fourth (eighteen) favored women's unions on all levels while over one-half (thirty-nine) urged that they be restricted to the session (individual church) level. The effort to organize was branded by many as "un-Scriptural, un-Presbyterian, unwomanly," and as putting undue emphasis on one phase of church work to the exclusion and detriment of others.

But the women's unions were proving too effective in raising funds to be stopped. By 1910, 78 of the 84 presbyteries and 5 of the 14 synods in the denomination had established unions. Two years later, the General Assembly of PCUS appointed a woman "Superintendent" to coordinate women's unions at all levels and to organize them where they not yet existed, in effect creating a churchwide Women's Auxiliary (the name formally approved by the assembly).[39]

Miss Hanna's urgent call for presbyterial unions reached Mrs. B. F. Hall (Maggie Sprunt, sister of James) of the First Presbyterian Church at the end of 1887. In an enclosed circular, which Hanna asked the recipient to distribute to every church in the Wilmington Presbytery, the author envisioned a quadrupling of women's contributions to foreign missions if only there were a more effective organization. She challenged her readers to come to the aid of their church and its workers in foreign fields: "The constantly recurring debt on our For[eign] Miss[ions] Committee is a terrible witness to inactivity and neglect of opportunity somewhere. The women of the Southern Church are not lacking in the energy, intellect, consecration & ability necessary to organize on a sound basis. Let us try it."[40]

Mrs. Hall turned out to be one of those women of energy and ability that Miss Hanna was seeking; in the next five months she helped organize women's societies in her own and other churches in the presbytery, and by the end of May 1888 the Wilmington Presbyterial Union was formed, the second in the Southern Assembly.[41] In 1890, because of continuing fears about higher levels of organization in women's work, the union was dissolved and replaced by a Women's Foreign Missionary Committee of the Wilmington Presbytery, but the nature of its work did not change and women continued to refer to their group by the earlier name. When the General Assembly approved a Women's Auxiliary in 1912, the name changed again to "Women's Presbyterial Auxiliary."[42]

The Auxiliary's association with Jiangyin, and particularly the medical work of George Worth, began at its second annual convention, held at the First Presbyterian Church in 1889. Worth, who just that spring at a YMCA meeting in Wilmington had announced his decision to be a medical missionary, gave a short address at the convention. His childhood friend and future wife, Emma Chadbourn, made her public commitment to mission work at the same meeting. When they were married in 1895 and went out to China as the first missionaries from the Wilmington

Presbytery, the auxiliary naturally took a lively interest in their work.[43]

It was during the Worths' first furlough in 1901–1903 that the idea of the auxiliary assuming a special responsibility for the development of medical work at Jiangyin took shape. The Worths spoke to the women of the Presbyterial at their annual meetings in 1902 and 1903, laying out the great need and great opportunity for a Christian hospital at Jiangyin.[44] Then, in a 1904 letter to the pastor of the First Presbyterian Church, George Worth wrote of his plans and concluded, "My earnest hope is that our church and Presbytery may undertake this work. It is easily within their means and a work greatly needed."[45] This letter was read at the 1904 annual meeting and the idea fell on fertile ground. The presbyterial women voted to raise the $4,000 needed to build a hospital there for Dr. Worth. They planned to sell eighty shares of $50 each over the next two years, with subscribers receiving special certificates that George Worth had printed in Shanghai containing a photograph of him with Chinese patients in front of the rented building he was using as a clinic.[46]

The campaign for funds was meant to involve as many people as possible so that the stake in the hospital's success and continued growth would be widespread. Eliza Murphy, whom the auxiliary appointed agent of the Hospital Fund, explained that "it is not desired for this fund to be raised by a few, but as many persons from as many churches as possible should have a share in the giving. The consummation of this idea would be reached if when the Hospital is erected at Kiang Yin, its share holders would represent every congregation within our Presbytery." On another occasion, Miss Murphy described the auxiliary's relationship with the Jiangyin Hospital as "yoke-fellows." The two sides were harnessed together in a common effort with equal responsibility and an equal claim to success.[47]

After the hospital opened in 1907, auxiliary women exhibited a proprietary feeling about the institution they built, referring to it always as "our hospital." At every auxiliary meeting, a picture of the facilities was displayed and some report on current medical work and anticipated needs was made. The hospital's claim on the women's attention became so pervasive that each local woman's society in the presbytery was urged to supply its members with a "blessing box" and to ask them to put in a penny a day for the Jiangyin hospital.[48] Through such offerings, thousands of women would be in daily communion with *their* workers at *their* hospital at *their* station in *their* China. Is it any wonder, then, that they were devastated by the news in early 1938 that the Japanese had destroyed the hospital in bombing raids? It was as if their own property in Wilmington had been attacked.

Matching the women in interest and commitment to foreign missions, if not financial resources, were the Young People's societies in the presbytery. The first three were formed in 1888–89, and their work was officially endorsed by the Wilmington Presbyterial Auxiliary in 1902 when it appointed an agent to coordinate their efforts and organize additional "bands," as they were called. As in other presbyterial developments, Wilmington was a pioneer in the Southern Presbyterian Church, being the first to embrace Young People's work. Under presbyterial direction, the Young People's bands grew in number to twelve by the 1903 annual meeting of the auxiliary, and they each adopted as their special object the support of a cot (about $25 a year) at the Jiangyin hospital. Some of the groups began to call themselves "Worth Bands" in recognition of their partnership with the doctor and his work. By 1913 there were thirty-two Young People's bands in the presbytery, and they had raised about $4,000 for cots in the preceding eleven years.[49]

Though the Young People's contributions were modest, they provided another intense, personal link between the work in China and the support base at home. When these bands met, their members would pray for the Worths and for the patients occupying the cots provided by their small change. The young people took particular interest in the plight of their counterparts in China, such as Chin Mei, "Golden Sister." She was a girl about four years old who contracted measles and over a year's time grew weak from a fever, eventually dying after a long struggle. Chin Mei's story was reported to the young people of Wilmington, who included her in their prayers, and one of their number sent her a nursery book, which however only arrived in Jiangyin a few weeks after the Chinese girl's death.[50]

Building the hospital was just the beginning for the women and young people of the auxiliary. As medical work expanded, George Worth turned to them repeatedly for funds to buy equipment, build additional facilities, and maintain the entire plant. Their investment in the medical work continued throughout the life of the station and approached a grand total of $100,000 (see Table 2). The auxiliary was the sole benefactor of the hospital, and a special bond was forged between the two similar to the relationship the First Presbyterian Church had with the station as a whole. In a 1924 communique to the auxiliary, Worth reminded them "that the Kiangyin Hospital is the child of Wilmington Presbyterial, the child of your prayers, you gave it life in 1904 and you have nourished it ever since, and never let it be forgotten that this hospital has no other source from which to draw its support."[51]

Worth nurtured this relationship in every way possible. From the start, he sent at least two letters a year to the auxiliary, one timed to be read to the women at their annual business meeting in the spring (usually April) and the other in time for their fall Day of Prayer. In his letters, Dr. Worth was profuse in his appreciation of auxiliary support. In 1934 he proclaimed its membership of over 2,200 to be "a regiment of hands across the sea" doing "grand, greathearted [work] in God's service."[52] In the last letter he sent to the auxiliary before his death in 1936, Worth professed to "have never tired, and I trust others have never tired of my expression about what a blessing the Wilmington Presbyterial has been to me, and to mine, to the Church at Kiangyin, and to the whole cause in China during the 32 years since the Presbyterial first decided to put a Kiangyin Christian Hospital on the missionary map."[53] After his death, one of the Presbyterial women said of Worth, "He never failed in every letter, at every visit, to express to us his sense of loving obligation" and his "ever-flowing appreciation and gratitude."[54] On their furloughs,

Table 2

**Wilmington Presbyterial Auxiliary
Support for Jiangyin Hospital (Summary)**

1904–1907	$ 4,700	Original building (men's ward)
1908–1911	2,000	Waterworks, two small outbuildings
1908–1913	7,000	Women's ward
1909–1919	3,500	Trained nurse's salary ($350/year)
1913	3,000	Enlarge men's ward
1913–1917	6,000	Second doctor's salary ($1,200/year)
1918–1919	3,600	Doctor and wife's salary ($1,800/year)
1922–1952	37,000	General fund for maintenance
1923	2,200	Residence for Chinese doctors
1924–1928	4,400	Additions to women's ward, waterworks
1929–1934	3,800	Nurses' home
1948	5,000	Rebuilding, from reserve fund
1954	11,000	Transferred to projects in Korea and Africa
	800	Left in reserve fund, Nashville
	$94,000	Grand total

Note: The figures, which are approximate, are based on reports given in the WPA *Minutes,* 1904–1954.

Dr. Worth and his wife not only attended auxiliary meetings but also attempted to visit with each of the several dozen women's societies throughout the Wilmington Presbytery.

For the auxiliary, the commitment to Worth and medical work at Jiangyin was the lifeblood of the organization. Its significance was understood clearly by the woman in charge of the Hospital Fund of the auxiliary. In her 1913 report on their fund-raising efforts, she enumerated four "distinct blessings we have received as a Presbyterial":

[1] In the first place, it has meant the uniting of all the forces and the enlisting of new forces. Perhaps half the people of the presbytery who are interested in missions today have become interested within the last ten years through the definite interest in our definite object.
[2] It has been the inspiration to organization. When the children's bands grew in two years from 3 to 23, the thought shining before those dear young eyes was cot-support in Dr. Worth's hospital.
[3] Figures have shown from year to year the increase in giving—the growth in "this grace also."
[4] Far beyond our taking account is the cultivation of the spirit of definite intercession and faith. We have found the high privilege of working together,

praying together, rejoicing together; not only working together here, but working with those across the seas. A share in the ministry to a million people—a thousand every month.[55]

Inspiration, organizational growth, increased donations, sorority, a sense of responsibility, as well as an enlarged vision of the world—these were the fruits of the auxiliary's lifetime partnership with the Jiangyin mission.

Despite this very personal, exclusive relationship between the Wilmington Presbyterial Auxiliary, on the one hand, and the Worths and the Jiangyin hospital, on the other, all the funds raised were submitted to the Executive Committee of Foreign Missions in the Nashville headquarters of the Southern Presbyterian Church, who had the final authority to approve disbursements to Jiangyin (and all other mission stations) for specific projects or expenses. This arrangement was one of the prices the women's foreign missionary societies had to pay to gain approval in 1912 for a denominational auxiliary. Another was to work not just for foreign missions, as had many of the societies originally, but for home missions as well, and all the other benevolent causes of the Church.

While it was not exactly true, as later claimed, that "the forming of the [Wilmington Presbyterial] Missionary Union (later the Woman's Auxiliary) [was] for the one express purpose of building a hospital in Kiangyin,"[56] still very early in its existence it took on that rationale. In 1911, the women were reminded that other benevolent causes of the church could be helped through regular monthly collections in each congregation, but women's society offerings needed to be concentrated on their special object in China.[57] When the churchwide auxiliary was created in 1912 with its mandate to work for all causes of the church, there had to be some adjustments at lower levels. The solution in the Wilmington Presbyterial was fairly simple: at the 1914 annual convention, it was reported that:

> in answer to a question concerning the distribution of funds, under the sometimes perplexing new order of things, [the superintendent of the denomination's auxiliary] told the body that it would be better to give one dollar to each of the other causes, thereby acknowledging the claim, and give all the rest to our Hospital, than ever at any time to fail in loyal support to our own object already established before the "Auxiliary" days.[58]

As for the redirection of funds through Nashville, this was, of course, true for any of the Sprunts' gifts or monies raised by the First Presbyterian Church and any of its agencies as well as for the Presbyterial auxiliary. The local donors often suspected that Nashville was not properly managing the funds. We have already seen how James Sprunt in 1921 was fuming about not having direct control over the use of funds for the Jiangyin station. George Worth, too, expressed concern in 1932 about the annual maintenance support from the auxiliary. In a letter to its president, he detailed the financial crisis arising from the cut in funds that the Executive Committee had imposed on all mission fields. In the previous fiscal year

(April 1931 through March 1932), the hospital had only received $800, and in the 1932–33 year he expected that to be cut to $450, which would have dire consequences for the hospital, perhaps even resulting in its closing. Worth urged the auxiliary to use whatever means necessary to see that "your Hospital" received at least $800.[59] Prompted by this letter, the auxiliary president reminded the Executive Committee in Nashville of the agreement made in 1922, "that all money sent in for our work at Jiangyin was to be applied to this work; the same not being subject to cut."[60]

The special relationship between Jiangyin and its home base in Wilmington was a mixed blessing for the Executive Committee. While such generous support from the First Presbyterian Church, James Sprunt, and the auxiliary relieved Nashville of much of the financial burden of maintaining its mission station in China, missionaries of independent means or with good personal connections to a home church could be somewhat independent of denominational control. This was particularly true when the support came from trust funds (such as James Sprunt's or the one set up for George Worth by his father[61]) that could only be used for their stated purpose. The generous support given by Wilmington donors exclusively to the Jiangyin station also meant that little or no funds could be expected from them for other foreign mission projects of the Executive Committee.[62]

The tension between the First Presbyterian Church and the larger PCUS foreign mission bureaucracy over management of funds was yet another example of how the missionary enterprise affected churches back home. Further research could undoubtedly uncover other impacts—the sharpening of doctrinal debates between conservative evangelists and proponents of a Social Gospel comes to mind immediately—but enough has been given already to suggest that the study of foreign missions need not be limited to their work abroad.

Long after the Jiangyin Station and its evangelical, educational, and medical enterprises passed from the scene in China, the legacy of mission work in Wilmington persisted. Down to the present day, literature of the First Presbyterian Church still proudly refers to its historic "special concern for overseas missions." In sustaining the Jiangyin mission for over fifty years, a dense network of human connections—"a regiment of hands across the sea," in George Worth's words—was forged that enriched as well as altered the lives and work of all those who participated on both sides of the Pacific.

Notes

1. Irwin T. Hyatt, *Our Ordered Lives Confess: Three Nineteenth-Century American Missionaries in East Shantung* (Cambridge: Harvard University Press, 1976), p. ix.

2. The sources for this study include, most importantly, sessional records and Sunday bulletins of the First Presbyterian Church in Wilmington (FPC/W); the papers of James Sprunt at Duke University in Durham; the minutes of annual meetings of the Woman's Auxiliary of Wilmington Presbytery (WPA) and other files of this organization preserved at the Historical Foundation (HF) in Montreal, which serves as the repository for PCUS

records; and the routine letters sent home for circulation by all Southern Presbyterian missionaries, also found at the Historical Foundation.

3. Samuel H. Chester, *Behind the Scenes: An Administrative History of the Foreign Mission Work of the Presbyterian Church in the United States* (Austin: Von Boeckmann-Jones Press, 1928), p. 39; Ernest Trice Thompson, *Presyterians in the South, 1890–1972, Vol. 3* (Richmond: John Knox Press, 1973), pp. 126–27; John Leighton Stuart, Fifty Years in China* (New York: Random House, 1954), pp. 30–33.

4. G. Thompson Brown, "Overseas Mission Program and Policies of the Presbyterian Church in the U.S., 1861–1983," *American Presbyterians*, 65:2 (Summer 1987), p. 162.

5. These calculations are based on 1916 data found in James Reed, *The Missionary Mind and American East Asia Policy* (Cambridge: Harvard Council on East Asian Relations, 1983), p. 19, Table 2.

6. Bulletin of FPC/W, April 17, 1921.

7. It is remarkable and instructive in this regard that the last conversation George Worth had on his deathbed with his daughter Ruth was mostly in Chinese, not English; see Charles Worth letter, November 26, 1936, reprinted in "Dr. George C. Worth" memorial booklet (Wilmington: Wilmington Presbyterial Auxiliary, [1937]), p. 10. For an assessment of missionary interpretive abilities, see Bruce S. Greenawalt, "Missionary Intelligence From China: American Protestant Reports, 1930–1950" (unpublished Ph.D. dissertation, University of North Carolina, 1974), pp. 12–13.

8. See, for example, the Bulletin of October 25, 1908.

9. In the period indicated, the First Presbyterian Church has almost complete runs of the Bulletin for each year except 1916 and 1917, for which only one or two are available. There are collected sets of Bulletins through 1930, but so far I have examined systematically only those through 1921.

10. Bulletin of FPC/W, November 29, 1908 (curios), January 19, 1913 (photographs), and January 4, 1925 (Jiangyin Night).

11. Alexander Sprunt to James Sprunt, November 21, 1921, in "Alexander Sprunt & Son Papers," Duke University Manuscript Collection (hereafter ASSP).

12. Bulletin of April 26, 1936, in "Scrap-Book of Church History, 1886–1938" of FPC/W.

13. A copy of this film, made in 1939–40, was given to the author by Ruth Worth.

14. Bulletin of June 13, 1909.

15. Bulletin of February 3, 1918.

16. *James Sprunt—A Tribute from the City of Wilmington* (Raleigh, NC:1925), pp. 35, 39–40; James Sprunt to Fred Olds, February 12, 1910, in ASSP. For an account of the firm's business operations, see J. R. Killick, "The Transformation of Cotton Marketing in the Late Nineteenth Century: Alexander Sprunt and Son of Wilmington, N.C., 1884–1956," *Business History Review*, 55:2 (Summer 1981), pp. 143–69.

17. FPC/W, *Handbook, 1892–1913*, p. 17; J. Campbell White to James Sprunt, May 19, 1908, in ASSP.

18. See letters of Robert Speer, May 23, 1908, and D. L. Pierson, May 25, 1908, to Rev. McClure, and letters of J. Campbell White to James Sprunt, May 27, 1908 and March 1, 1909, in ASSP.

19. James Sprunt to Mrs. J. Campbell White, March 1, 1920, in ASSP.

20. See correspondence of James Sprunt with J. Campbell White and with Charles Rowland, dated February 23, February 25, March 2, March 5, March 10, March 13, March 22, and March 29, 1909, in ASSP.

21. Canceled check dated March 31, 1909, and letter of James Sprunt to J. Campbell White, April 2, 1909, in ASSP.

22. *James Sprunt—A Tribute*, pp. 73–74.

23. Kate Moffett, *Bi-Monthly Bulletin*, 9:3 (May–June 1917), p. 946; Miao Quansun, *Jiangyin jinshi lu* (Supplement to 1920 Jiangyin gazetteer; reprinted in Taibei: Chengwen Publishers, 1970), pp. 93–94 (ch. 2:5); "Sessional Records" of FPC/W, April 1, 1917.

24. Bulletin of FPC/W, November 16, 1919; see also Bulletins of January 26, 1919, June 6, 1920, and June 13, 1920.

25. Letter of William H. Sprunt, Jr., January 23, 1921, quoted in Bulletin of FPC/W, February 27, 1921, and in WPA, *Minutes of Annual Meeting* (located at HF), 1921, pp. 18–19; James Sprunt to Dr. Wells, February 28, 1921, and William H. Sprunt, Jr. to James Sprunt, March 4, 1921, in ASSP. Worth got his X-ray machine in 1922, bought while he was in the United States on furlough, with funds provided by Jiangyin gentry (Katheryne Thompson letter, December 15, 1922, *Bi-Monthly Bulletin*, 13:3 [March–April 1923], pp. 1, 462).

26. Harold Balme, *China and Modern Medicine—A Study in Medical Missionary Development* (London: United Council for Missionary Education, 1921), pp. 104–105.

27. Exchange of letters between George Worth and James Sprunt, April 6 and May 9, 1921, in ASSP.

28. Bulletin of FPC/W, March 2, 1913.

29. In 1910 and 1911, he was giving $3,000 a year (see Private Ledgers for those years, in Vol. 2 of ASSP), but by the end of the decade the amount was $5,000 (see Letters of James Sprunt to Edwin F. Willis, December 10, 1919, and of J. C. Williams to James Sprunt, October 21, 1920 and October 4, 1921, in ASSP, and also the Private Ledger for 1922, in Vol. 4 of the same collection).

30. Bulletin of FPC/W, March 10, 1912 and January 25, 1914; Lacy L. Little, "Our Kiangyin Schools" pamphlet, April 15, 1916 (PCUS, Board of World Missions Archives, HF), p. 3; James E. Bear, "The Mission Work of the PCUS in China, 1867–1952" (unpublished manuscript, Union Theological Seminary, Richmond, VA, 1963–1973), Vol. 5, p. 142; *Missionary Letters, China* (PCUS, Board of World Missions, HF; these are mimeographed letters from missionaries in the field); Caroline V. Lee, July 10, 1923.

31. Charles Worth, "Recollections of a Happy Life" (unpublished 1968 manuscript in Charles Worth Papers held by his widow, Hilda Worth of Wilmington), p. 24.

32. *James Sprunt—A Tribute*, pp. 63–64.

33. W. H. Sprunt to Dr. Gilmour, September 12, 1924, filed with "Sessional Records" of FPC/W; "Sessional Letter" to First Presbyterian Church congregation, March 8, 1925, in "Dr. James Sprunt" folder, FPC/W.

34. Correspondence between Walter P. Sprunt and Rev. Gilmour, December 1, December 7, and December 31, 1937, January 14, and February 1, 1938, filed with "Sessional Records" of FPC/W.

35. R. Pierce Beaver, *American Protestant Women in World Mission: History of the First Feminist Movement in North America* (Grand Rapids: William B. Eerdmans, 1980), pp. 25, 87–88; Rosemary S. Keller, "Lay Women in Protestant Tradition," in *Women and Religion in America*, Vol. 1: *The Nineteenth Century*, ed. Rosemary R. Reuther and Rosemary S. Keller (San Francisco: Harper & Row, 1981), pp. 242–43.

36. Keller, "Lay Women," p. 264; emphasis in original.

37. Beaver, *American Protestant Women*, p. 54; Helen B. Montgomery, *Western Women in Eastern Lands* (New York: Macmillan Co., 1910), pp. 243–44.

38. Keller, "Lay Women," p. 245.

39. Thompson, *Presbyterians in the South*, Vol. 3, pp. 384–91; Hallie P. Winsborough, *The Women's Auxiliary, Presbyterian Church, U.S.* (Richmond, VA: Presbyterian Committee of Publication, 1927), pp. 19–26; Lois A. Boyd and R. Douglas Brackenridge, *Presbyterian Women in America* (Westport, CT: Greenwood Press for the Presbyterian Historical Society, 1983), pp. 217–21.

40. Jennie Hanna to Mrs. B. F. Hall, December 28, 1887 and January 18, 1888, in Mrs. B. F. Hall Papers, HF.

41. Mrs. J. A. Brown, *History of Wilmington Presbyterial Auxiliary, 1888–1922* (Raleigh, NC: Edwards and Broughton Printing Co., 1923), pp. 16–19; Mrs. B. F. Hall, "Sketch of Woman's Foreign Missionary Union of Wilmington Presbytery" (typescript, 1911, in "Wilmington Presbyterial [1888]" file, HF), p. 1.

42. *Minutes of Woman's Foreign Missionary Committee*, 1890, in Mrs. B. F. Hall Papers, HF; Brown, *Wilmington Presbyterial Auxiliary*, pp. 22–23, 47.

43. Brown, *Wilmington Presbyterial Auxiliary*, pp. 21, 71–72.

44. Brown, *Wilmington Presbyterial Auxiliary*, pp. 37, 39.

45. George Worth to Dr. Wells, April 5, 1904, in FPC/W, *Manual, 1904*, pp. 28–29.

46. WPA *Minutes*, 1905, pp. 17–18; 1906, p. 18; 1907, pp. 17–20; Eliza Wright Murphy, *The Story of Kiangyin Hospital, China* (Wilmington, NC: Wilmington Presbyterial Auxiliary, [1930]), pp. 3–4; Mrs. B. F. Hall, "Sketch," pp. 5–6.

47. WPA *Minutes*, 1906, p. 18; 1921, p. 18.

48. WPA *Minutes*, 1926, p. 13.

49. WPA *Minutes*, 1903, pp. 13–15; 1913, p. 20.

50. Ryda Jourolman, "Little Golden Sister" (undated pamphlet, in "China Materials" folder, FPC/W).

51. WPA *Minutes*, 1925, p. 21.

52. George Worth to Mrs. Howell, April 26, 1934, in "Memorials and Letters of George Worth" folder, FPC/W.

53. George Worth to Wilmington Presbyterial, August 7, 1936, in "Dr. George C. Worth" memorial booklet, p. 6.

54. Susan Hall, "Memorial Paper," in "Dr. George C. Worth" memorial booklet, p. 33.

55. WPA *Minutes*, 1913, p. 17.

56. Mrs. Walter Sprunt to C. Darby Fulton, March 7, 1953, in Lacy I. Moffett Papers, held by his son, Alexander Moffett of Taylorsville, NC.

57. WPA *Minutes*, 1911, p. 5.

58. Brown, *Wilmington Presbyterial Auxiliary*, p. 55.

59. George Worth to Mrs. W. P. M. Currie, June 9, 1932, in "Memorials and Letters" of George Worth, FPC/W.

60. WPA *Minutes*, 1933, p. 13.

61. *North Carolina Presbyterian*, April 2, 1896, in (untitled) "Binder," FPC/W; "Testimonial to Dr. Worth," in "Histories of Churches" binder, FPC/W.

62. Valentin H. Rabe, *The Home Base of American China Missions, 1880–1920* (Cambridge: Harvard University Press, 1977), pp. 144–45.

5

HAINAN FOR THE HOMEFOLK
Images of the Island in the Missionary and Secular Presses

Kathleen L. Lodwick

Presbyterian missionaries on Hainan island, like missionaries elsewhere in China, wanted to publicize their work. It was essential that they keep the homefolk informed of the progress they were making and to ensure continuing contributions to support the work of the mission. Because they were in a remote part of China, far from the centers of missionary activity on the mainland, they were also mindful of keeping missionaries elsewhere in China informed of the important work they were doing and the progress they were making. With these goals in mind, this paper will examine how two periodicals, the *Hainan News Letter*, and the *Chinese Recorder* conveyed news of the Hainan mission. These were by no means the only publications that covered the work on Hainan, but I will leave the more specialized women's periodicals such as *Women's Work for Women*, the annual reports of the women's and church mission boards, and the miscellaneous publications as well as the coverage of the Hainan mission by the secular press to other papers. These preliminary thoughts on Hainan in the missionary press will be part of a larger study, a history of the Hainan mission from its beginnings in 1883 as part of the Canton mission until the last missionaries departed the island in 1953, on which I am currently working.

In surveying the two periodicals it is important to keep in mind that each had a different audience. The *Chinese Recorder* was the foremost ecumenical publication of the Protestant missionaries in China. Published in Shanghai, first by the Presbyterian Mission Press and later by a Chinese Christian publisher, it served as a communications link among the various mission stations in China, where it also had correspondents. Its circulation probably never surpassed 3,000, but that number certainly belies its readership since it is known that it was common for one member of a station to subscribe to the *Chinese Recorder* and then circulate it to the other members of the station. At home its circulation was primarily to theological schools and mission boards or to individuals who were concerned with the whole of the mission movement in China rather than with one particular denomination. Its articles dealt with the problems, questions, and strategies common to all the Protestant missionaries in China. While seeking to cover the big picture of mission work, the *Chinese Recorder* was less likely to carry the extremely personal news of specific individuals or stations. Although it did list arrivals and departures from China, the missionaries of Hainan were rarely included in this section since they entered China through Hong Kong, not through Shanghai, and often did not send such news to the editors of the *Chinese Recorder*. Although Hainan was mentioned in virtually every issue of the *Chinese Recorder* from 1882 until 1941, only thirteen of the eighty-three missionaries who served on the island appeared in it by name.

The *Hainan News Letter* had quite a different audience than the *Chinese Recorder*. The *Hainan News Letter* was published by the missionaries on the island and was aimed at their supporters at home. It appeared on an irregular basis between 1912 and 1948 and reflected the work of the mission. Margaret Moninger, who arrived in Hainan in 1915, was the long-time editor, but virtually every missionary on the island wrote articles for it. Its circulation would be hard to determine, but it is known to have been sent to all those on each missionary's correspondence list. These would have included ministers of home churches, women active in mission work in the individual churches, teenagers involved in mission bands, the secretaries and other members of the various women's mission boards, and officials of the Board of Foreign Missions in New York, in addition to countless relatives, college classmates, neighbors, friends, and missionaries in other countries.

Although certainly far from a complete listing of all mission publications in China, Rudolph Lowenthal's *The Religious Periodical Press in China* did not list the *Hainan News Letter*. Some of the listings in Lowenthal do suggest that this newsletter was not unique. Publications listed, which were of a similar nature, included the Chung Hua Sheng Kung Hui (Anglican) publications, the *District of Anking Newsletter*, the *Wuhu Newsletter*, the *Hankow* Newsletter, the Church of Christ in China's *Information Service* (about its work in the Kwangtung Synod), and the Honan Mission of the Union Church of Canada's *Honan Quarterly*. A few ecumenical publications such as the *West China Missionary News* published by the West China missions and circulated to missionaries and church workers in the home countries were also similar.[1]

The *Hainan News Letter* generally contained a variety of short news items from the three stations—at Kachek, Nodoa, and Kiungchow-Hoihow. Frequent topics of its articles were women, the numbers and devotion of converts, difficulties with officials, and the political unrest in China.

Because the *Hainan News Letter* was not published until 1912, the earlier articles about work on the island appear in the *Chinese Recorder*. Indeed, the first mention of Hainan in the *Chinese Recorder* was in the November–December 1882 issue. In that issue a short note reported that the Reverend B. C. Henry and Dr. C. C. Jeremiassen had just returned to Canton from a trip through Hainan. "They were everywhere received with great kindness by the inhabitants—both the Hainanese and the native tribes. Jeremiassen had numerous applicants for medical treatment. Books were readily bought and hospitality was everywhere cordially extended to the travellers.''[2]

The editor noted that he hoped to receive an account of Henry's travels, which began appearing in the May–June 1883 issue. (It should be mentioned that the editors of the *Chinese Recorder* frequently requested articles to publish.) Henry's three articles, running twenty, twenty-four, and thirty pages, are extremely long for the *Chinese Recorder*. In the first he writes of traveling about the island and discovering that there were many distinct linguistic groups in Hainan, each maintaining its separate language and customs while constantly intermingling with other peoples. He noted that the Loi dialect of the interior was quite distinct from either the Miao language or Hainanese and that there were also villages of Cantonese speakers.[3]

The second article, in the July–August issue, continued the story of the Reverend B. C. Henry's travels with descriptions of several of the towns and villages he visited. The town of Woshe, he wrote, had one broad street, five temples, two of which were large and showy, and an inn which was ''a long, narrow building with a succession of apartments whose arrangements showed the thrift of the owners. Facing the street was an ordinary shop on one side of which were several counters let out to small traders on market days; the middle and main section was set apart for guests, and the rear was occupied by the family.''[4]

The third article, which appeared as the lead story in the September–October issue, continued the story of the trip and contained a description of the difficulty of travel ranging from leeches to discontent among the carriers:

> Our old Le bearer, who . . . [was a] habitual opium smoker . . . took us to the house of a [Chinese], for our greater comfort he said, but to facilitate his getting a little opium for himself we believed. Our coming to this house was the beginning of disaster. . . . Our first employment as we sat down was to get rid of the leeches which were more abundant this day than ever. From my feet and legs I picked off nearly forty of all sizes, the [Chinese] man's Le wife bringing hot coals to destroy them and exclaiming at the great number.

As they prepared to leave ''he told us the stream was impassible, being at least eight feet deep at the crossing, but the water would subside in the night, and took us down to the bank to prove that he was not deceiving us.''[5]

Stuck in the village for the night more trouble ensued:

> To make matters worse a quarrel broke out between our Le bearers and the Chinese on account of the food. We tried to treat matters lightly, but feared some serious trouble was brewing, especially when our host united with the others in urging us to give up the plan of crossing the hills and take the nearest way out to Lingmun. We feared our host was working against us in an

underhanded way which suspicion was fully confirmed afterwards. When we started the next morning they led us up the stream to a shallow ford, where the water was only waist deep, which could have been crossed as easily the day before. We waded this large stream four times and passed three villages before reaching the residence of the chief.... Our worst fears were realized as the chief informed us that no men were to be had in his village and that he could do nothing to help us forward. Our Le bearers were only engaged to this point and with the exception of the old man, were not willing to go further while our Chinese were in a mutinous frame of mind, and even if they had been willing, were not sufficient to take us through. It took but a few moments to see that our case was hopeless and there was nothing for us to do but yield to the inevitable. There being no accommodation in the chief's village, we retraced our steps, recrossing the broad stream three times, and put up for the night at a small village we had passed in the morning resisting all efforts of the [Chinese man] to take us back to his house.[6]

Unfortunately, Henry ends his account at this point, but it should be noted that he later wrote a book, *Lingnam or interior views of southern China*, so the rest of his journey is recorded.[7]

Two years after Henry's account appeared in the *Chinese Recorder*, the Reverend. H. V. Noyes of the Presbyterian mission at Canton went to Hainan in the company of Jeremiassen. Excerpts of a letter, dated June 17, 1885, from Noyes appeared in the July issue of that year. Noyes reported that he and Jeremiassen had traveled into the interior of Hainan some ninety miles from the treaty port of Hoihow where they visited the market town which was the site of the first Protestant chapel on the island, which had been established by Jeremiassen ten months earlier. Noyes reported that the congregation numbered between forty and sixty and that twenty had applied for baptism and nine had been baptized during their trip. Noyes did not identify the market town, but it was Nodoa, where the first of the three mission stations on the island had been established.[8]

Although Noyes does not mention it, it was certainly evident to missionary readers in China that with his report Noyes was claiming Hainan as a Presbyterian mission field. Indeed the comity agreements which the Protestant missionaries had worked out called for each to actually establish mission stations in the areas they claimed. In an article by Frank P. Gilman a few years later, the claim of the Presbyterians to the island as their mission territory was again laid. Gilman noted that the American Presbyterian Mission was the only one to have regular work on the island, although the Church Missionary Society had had a dispensary at Hoihow for a time and the British and Foreign and American Bible Societies had sent representatives there from time to time.[9]

Frequently information in periodicals published in North China revealed how little foreigners there knew about Hainan. The *Chinese Recorder* repeatedly referred to Hainan separately from Kwangtung province and sometimes even called it another province. In 1898 the *Chinese Recorder* reprinted from the *North China Daily* News a story of an uprising among the aborigines in Hainan. Indicating the ignorance of the island on the part of personnel of both periodicals, the article stated that the uprising was eighty miles southwest of Kiungchow, but went on to say that another dispatch received from Hoihow "not very far distant from the scene of the insurrections" reported the deserters and disbanded soldiers were among the aborigines causing the troubles.[10] Hoihow was in fact immediately adjacent to Kiungchow.

The *Chinese Recorder* was also sometimes used by the missionaries on Hainan to report that they were still there, still at work, and that the latest rumors about the island were untrue. Such was the case of a short note by Frank P. Gilman dated Hoihow, July 3, which appeared in the August 1901 issue. "You will be pleased to be assured that the work of the missionaries in Hainan is progressing very favorably and that though there are rumors of the coming of the French to take the island, that none of the rumors have any proof as far as the French activity in Hainan is concerned."[11]

The complicated communications between Hainan and Shanghai were evident in the July 1886 issue of the *Chinese Recorder* which published news of Hainan under the category "Echoes from Other Lands." There was reprinted an article from the *New York Evangelist* which was written by the Reverend B. C. Henry. He reported that at Nodoa nine people had been baptized in 1885 and there were fifty inquirers on the rolls:

> A chapel has been requested at Namfung, twelve miles further inland, and in many other places the people are anxious for the missionary to come. The coast and the northern half of the island are occupied by Chinese, while the uncivilized aborigines of Malay origin occupy the southern interior. These aborigines "are exceedingly friendly, treating the missionary with great consideration, and urging him to open schools in their towns."[12]

The importance of medical work to the missionaries was clearly demonstrated in a short article about Hainan which appeared in 1889. Noting that medical work had helped missionaries make progress "in almost all parts of the heathen and Mohammedan world," the article mentioned that

> Dr. Jeremiassen, an American missionary physician, has lately been greatly occupied with the soldiers of the garrison at his interior station in the great island of Hainan, off the South-west coast of China. He had been successful during the prevalence of a fatal epidemic, and General Feng, the commanding officer, has telegraphed to the Viceroy at Canton that "but for Dr. Jeremiassen he would have had no soldiers left." The General has authorized the missionary physician to have two buildings for hospital use erected at the government's expense, and after the present military inmates have sufficiently recovered to be able to leave them, they are to be made over to the mission. The prestige thus gained for the recently established American Presbyterian Mission in the interior of Hainan is very great.[13]

Unfortunately, the author of that article did not realize what an entangled series of events were to ensue from Jeremiassen treating the soldiers of General Feng.

The first lengthy article specifically about mission work in Hainan appeared in the *Chinese Recorder* in June 1890. It was written by Frank P. Gilman, the first Presbyterian missionary sent by the board to the island. He wrote that while in Nodoa Jeremiassen had treated the soldiers who were suffering from the epidemic of fever and thus had gained the respect of General Feng. The general agreed to have two buildings built and he told Jeremiassen that he would give $600 for the hospital and assured Jeremiassen that he could have the property as soon as the rebellion the general had been sent to suppress was put down. One of the buildings was constructed, but the general left for Kiungchow before settling the matter. Jeremiassen followed him and asked for a paper stating the general's commitment. Unfortunately for the missionaries, the general had been instructed by his superiors in Canton to have nothing to do with the foreigners and the district magistrate was ordered to report within three days that the buildings at Nodoa had been destroyed or the magistrate would be dismissed. "The building was not destroyed, and it was afterwards reported that the order was sent to the local mandarin in Nodoa, whose life Jeremiassen had saved during the epidemic, and that he destroyed the order instead of destroying the hospital."[14]

At the same time that these difficulties occurred in Nodoa, the missionaries were also engaged in a dispute over title to their land in Kiungchow and they were unaware that they were being attacked by the antiforeign gentry at Kiungchow who had reported to officials in Canton that General Feng was building a large chapel for the missionaries.

The issue became more complicated when General Feng, who had aided in building the hospital, returned to Nodoa and decided to destroy the building since it was the only fault the viceroy had found with his conduct of affairs in Nodoa. "A petition (asking for the destruction of the hospital) was prepared, to which the names of the most prominent men of Nodoa were attached, and it was presented to General Feng."[15]

Jeremiassen was in Kiungchow when the petition was drawn up, but returned to Nodoa before any action had been taken. "On his arrival he was presented with the cards of several of the most prominent men of the place, stating that they had nothing to do with sending a petition to General Feng concerning the hospital, and if their names were attached to such a petition it was without their consent."[16]

But this was not the end of the matter. Jeremiassen still believed General Feng to be friendly to him and so gave the gentry's cards to General Feng, who suggested he go to see the district magistrate at Tamchow. Feng told Jeremiassen he was going to see the magistrate that very day and the unsuspecting Jeremiassen asked the general to present his case. Something apparently made Jeremiassen suspicious because he decided to go to see the magistrate on the following day, but in the meantime wrote a report of the entire situation and sent it to General Feng hoping for a written reply which would confirm the general's role in the matter. Receiving no reply Jeremiassen then sent the letter to the magistrate who happened to be meeting with the general at that time. The same evening Jeremiassen received a message from the general asking him, "as a friend, to remove the cheaper of the two buildings" at the hospital. Jeremiassen refused and the messenger said the general was then ready to issue "proclamations telling the people to tear it down." Jeremiassen replied he would not take the building down and if the building was torn down he would hold the general responsible. Gilman concludes his account of the incident by saying, "It is sufficient to add that the building still stands. The magistrate was informed of the threat and advised, since it was for his interest to maintain quiet in his district, that he had better hold a certain hostile graduate in Nodoa responsible for any disorder. This he afterwards did, and quietly notified the military mandarin there to preserve order, and since then everything has been progressing quietly in Nodoa." This article also contained a lengthy account of the difficulties of obtaining a legal deed to the mission property in Kiungchow.[17]

Such difficulties were not limited to the early years of the mission, as the *Hainan News Letter* also contained stories of the trouble the missionaries had in obtaining land and constructing buildings, walls, and gates, which they felt were appropriate, but to which the Chinese objected.

In 1914 the missionaries purchased land adjoining the Pitkin Compound, taking care to get the deed stamped by the local magistrate. When they began to construct a wall,

> there was such an uproar among the adjacent villages that it sounded like an excited mob which sent shivers all over one, and the matter was dropped for a while. The villagers declared that the wall would destroy the idol's power, that if the open spaces on both sides of the Temple were not perfectly even in width, it would make him "dizzy" when taken out in a chair.
>
> Not relishing the prospect of an infuriated mob attacking the whole community here, we willingly returned nearly all of the newly purchased land, valued at about $60. But it was necessary to close in our own Compound. In the meantime three leading men had dragged the original landlady to the Yamen and after an examination, she was released. When we again began excavating, there was another uproar and we were again obliged to cut off just one foot so that the edge of the wall would not be directly opposite the center of a well. If opposite the center, "it would injure the Dragon and spoil the water of the well." This small portion in front is finished. Now, there is an objection made to our closing it in the rear, as the big idol must not catch a glimpse of the wall as he looks out through the Temple door, although it is 150 feet away from his majesty. We promised to round the corner which would greatly please the idol. The case is not yet settled. As fast as we dig they fill in. They assert with all seriousness that ever since the wall enclosing the Boys' Compound near the well was built, bad luck has descended upon the village for nothing but girl babies had been born in it.[18]

Another cause for concern were the Chinese who wanted to join the church to gain the support of the missionaries in their disputes with local officials. In November 1902 the *Chinese Recorder* editorialized about a placard they had received from the Reverend A. E. Street in Hoihow. The editorial noted that the ''very neatly gotten up placard, printed on good red paper with fancy border, the design of which is to set before the people the attitude of the missionaries towards all lawsuits and to warn the people against expecting any help in litigation because of professed church membership.'' Street had reported that in Hainan one man was then in jail for posing for years as a church member. ''He is understood to have been well on the way towards wealth when we stopped him. To meet the misunderstanding that arises from the attitude of the Catholics, we issued the enclosed statement that we have tried to make as attractive as possible, enough to keep it in sight a short time at least.'' The editorial urged others to experiment with similar placards as a ''deterrent effect upon some of the people who wish to come into the church from sordid motives.''[19]

The conversion of the aborigines was the subject of many articles in both periodicals, but one of the most interesting was that written by George D. Byers, ''The Miao Awakening in Hainan,'' which appeared in the December 1917 issue of the *Chinese Recorder*. He reported that a Miao chief by the name of Dang Zit Koang had come to the Kachek mission in the spring of 1916 and was told of the Gospel. Then in November 1916, Byers, Elder Li, and a Chinese servant set off for the Miao country. After an all-night trip up the Kachek river they reached the landing of Lak Hak Kau where there was only one hut and found no carriers available. The owner of the sole house reported that the road into the interior ran for twenty-seven miles and that it was a difficult one to carry goods over. Elder Li went ahead in the company of some traders and after three days three men from the Miao village returned to carry the baggage.

> They brought their own rice and said that our two light loads would have to be divided into three as we would have very difficult roads. One of them looked at my leather shoes and said the water on the road would be very troublesome to one wearing shoes. I assured them I was good on the jump and if the water was too deep my boy could carry me. Our guides led us over this mountain, the steepest trail over which I have ever known men to carry a load. As we passed down the other side of this mountain our carriers pointed out a distant peak, at the foot of which lay the village we were seeking. The sun was disappearing behind the mountains when we finally arrived there.[20]

Byers reported that the Miao used slash-and-burn methods in their agriculture. ''Thus thousands of acres of choice forest trees are almost wantonly destroyed because modern methods of forest conservation have not yet reached Hainan.''[21]

> We presented the chief with a Bible in Chinese character, also a hymn-book. . . .
> He at once began reading and Elder Li assisted him with the more difficult

characters, and explained the meaning as he read. The first three chapters of
Genesis were thus eagerly read twice over. Then turning to me he said: "I have
always wanted to know this but never found a book before that told me. . . ."
Our host and his younger brother were the only two who could read with us and
this they did, but the neighbors came to hear also. While we were there, the two
brothers learned the Lord's Prayer and the Apostle's Creed.

The chief promised to build a school if a Christian teacher were sent, and the teacher
went to the village later.[22]

A chapel was also built in the village and

reports kept coming to Kachek of a wonderful movement among his people. On
Sundays from five hundred to a thousand people would come from their homes
in the forest to hear the new doctrine. Some, indeed, came four and five days'
journey from the most distant districts of the island. Many brought paper and
incense, as they had been accustomed to use such things in the worship of idols
and knew no better way. Our Chinese helper found it difficult to hold a service
with such numbers, many of whom could not understand Hainanese and all of
whom were unaccustomed to listening to instruction. He also reported that many
were seized with a strange shaking and trembling and crying out, which they
ascribed to the power of the Holy Spirit, but which greatly disturbed their
meetings. Some of our helpers who visited them at this time ascribed it to demon
possession. The chief came to Kachek and reported it. He also reported that his
people were hearing noises from heaven in the night and many were coming to
inquire what these things meant.[23]

After consultation in the station meeting at Kachek it was decided that Katherine
Schaeffer would go immediately to the village and that Byers would go later. Miss
Schaeffer spent two Sundays in May 1917 in the village with seven hundred to
eight hundred people attending the services on those days. "She also reported that
several of the women, and one woman in particular, were seized with a strange
trembling, swaying and crying out which was greatly hindering the helpers in their
work of teaching the people. Her observation of these cases led her to believe they
were not caused by the Spirit of God."[24]

Byers again visited the village in June and reported "no disturbance, but a few
cases of the swaying were reported from the women's meeting" at the first
Sunday's service. Then on the second Sunday

as soon as the service began a woman started swaying and attracting attention.
We had her removed a short distance but she resisted those trying to lead her out
and returned. When I began preaching she got directly behind me and began
bowing before the Lord's Prayer which was printed in large Chinese characters
at the back of the chapel. I told the people it was not the work of the Holy Spirit,
as she was distracting their minds from hearing the Word of God. But finding
that I could not persuade any one to take her out, I did so myself. She seemed as
one in a hypnotic sleep. The following day we met the woman in her home village

and found her wearing native charms. We admonished her to put these off and had prayer with her.[25]

The account of Byers' trip which ran six pages in the *Chinese Recorder* was reported in just one page in the *Hainan News Letter* of February 1917 and just over a page in the August issue of that year. These articles mention the shaking episodes, but do not mention that some thought it to be associated with possession by demons.[26]

The *Hainan News Letter* often contained very personal news about the missionaries, which would be of interest to their families and friends at home and which would never have appeared in the *Chinese Recorder*.

For example, the *Hainan News Letter* reported that when Paul Melrose, whose parents had pioneered at the mission in the late nineteenth century, returned to Hainan with his bride Esther Agnew Melrose his mother received many congratulations on her foresight and shrewdness in her choice of a bride for her son.[27]

Often there were articles about the plight of women. For example, one of the earliest issues contained the story of one of the Christian women who was a student at the mission school. When she went to her husband's home for Chinese New Year she encountered trouble.

> Her husband has never supported her since she was married, nearly 15 years ago, nor their little girl. She has worked in the fields for her brothers in order to earn a living for herself and child.
>
> She has accompanied Miss Skinner on some of her trips with the older Bible-woman, and has assisted in instructing the women that came into the chapels. Some of her village people saw her on these trips and told her husband that she was following men. When she went home, he beat her, cutting a gash in her forehead and bruising her in many places. He also threatened to cut off her ears and nose, for this is permitted, when women are thought to be disloyal to their husbands. She was very much frightened and under the pretence of going out into the fields to dig sweet potatoes, ran away and came out to Kiung-chow and is still here. She is an earnest Christian and is in training for a Biblewoman.[28]

The summer 1923 issue carried an article by Luella Tappan recounting the story of a girl, about seven, who had been left for dead near the mission compound. Her family, who lived across the straits on the mainland, had brought her to Hainan and sold her for $60 because their village had been sacked and burned by robbers and the family needed money to buy rice. Her new owner was hesitant to give her away, even though he did not want such a sickly child, but finally consented to allow the missionaries to take her home. In a plea for help and with hope for the future, the article ended, "We have no plan for her yet, no money, no clothes, no name even! But who knows what she may turn out to be? Three of our finest graduates, now teaching, were no more promising ten years ago when the bugs had to be picked out of their dirty little heads for days. Now to see the beautiful accomplished girls they have become makes it almost unbelievable.''[29]

Other topics covered often were the intricacies of twentieth-century Chinese politics and the undisciplined nature of Chinese armies. Readers of the November 1918 issue were told that the island was occupied by General Lung Tsi Koang and his troops who were loyal to the Peking government in the struggle that was then going on between North and South China. Lung's soldiers in Kachek revolted in June declaring themselves independent. When troops loyal to the general arrived from Kiungchow the Kachek faction fled the city after taking about $1,000 from the market. The few missionaries then living in Kachek were besieged with requests to take in refugees or to secrete valuables. It should be noted that the mission compound at this time was not surrounded by a fence, so whatever protection the missionaries might offer was largely based upon the desire of the Chinese army not to move against the foreigners. Although the article reassured readers that the fighting was not directed against the missionaries, it went on to describe the missionaries and their children and the pupils from their schools huddled into the corners of the houses while bullets whizzed by. The girls' school and the mission hospital were hit several time by bullets.

When the fighting subsided, the troops held the town for only a week before fleeing when news arrived that more men were coming from Kiungchow to avenge the loss. The leading merchants of the market then sought the advice of the missionaries on how to deal with the arriving army. Rev. Byers agreed to accompany the merchants out to meet the army, but several days later the merchants reported they could recruit no volunteers to act as emissaries to the troops. Instead, after another five days passed and more consultations were held, it was decided that Byers should send letters to the officers inviting the entire invading army— some six hundred men—to drink tea and meet with the merchants. The reaction of the army to the missionaries and the merchants was mixed. Wounded soldiers were treated at the mission hospital and a few of the men accepted the offered tea, but the rest refused fearing they might be poisoned. The officer in charge was entertained by the head merchant who then took the officer to his place of business, a pawn shop, only to discover it had already been looted by the soldiers! Looting in the market and the surrounding villages continued for several days with Byers reporting that one hospital assistant was robbed of all his clothes only a mile from the hospital, a soldier who was an inpatient at the hospital was robbed of a jade bracelet he had been wearing, and a relative of the mission school's head teacher was stabbed and died of his wounds.[30]

The news of the various stations, which appeared in each issue of the *Hainan News Letter*, was similar to the *Kachek Station Report* in the September 1912 issue. It reported that over four hundred people attended the communion service in July. Bible classes were held at the church following the service where Reverend David Tappan asked the ''converts from heathenism: 'Tell us of Pentecost,' 'Who was

Barnabas?' 'Why was Peter willing to preach to Cornelius?' 'Describe Paul's conversion,' etc.'' The question period was followed by testimony by various church leaders.

> In Tin-Gou market when I was selling books I was accosted with the greeting, "peace." Said I, "Where does your peace come from?" When I learned that it was the peace of Jesus, I rejoiced and gladly accepted those brethren's invitation to spend a night in their village. The awakening in Bang Khoe region is due to the labors of Seng-dou, a man who is unlettered in Chinese characters, although he knows Romanized; but he has the Holy Spirit in his heart and therefore is successful. Remember that you brethren who cannot read.[31]

Readers at home were thus being told that the numerous converts were quite knowledgeable about very specific aspects of Christianity and that those unlearned in Chinese characters could, through the romanized system of the missionaries, come to learn enough of the religion to become a leader.

The Autumn 1931 issue of the *Hainan News Letter* commemorated fifty years of mission work on the island. This special issue contained a picture of all the foreigners then at the mission and individual pictures of six ordained Chinese who were pastors. These included a former and present pastor of the Nodoa church, the pastor of the Hoihow church, and pastors serving the Kachek, Vangneng, and Limko fields. In a brief introduction to the work on the island, church membership was set at 4,711. The issue also included a brief history of the island and its economic development. Biographies of each of the mission pioneers follow and reveal that while his colleagues had called Rev. Gilman ''the Bishop,'' he referred to himself as ''the Stop-Gap'' since he had taught school, built a number of the mission houses, and served as mission secretary and printer in addition to preaching and training Chinese clergy.

Tracing the developments of the mission under the Ch'ing government, the republic, and the Nationalists, this issue presented some interesting and amusing insights. For example, with the end of the dynasty and the beginning of the republic the men and boys cut their queues; then in 1925, when the First Communist Army arrived in Hainan proclaiming full equality of men and women, it was the women and girls who cut their hair—''the long shining braids of the Chinese schoolgirl and even the smooth coiffuer of the married woman gave way to the bobbed hair of freedom!'' Yet it was more than hairstyles that changed with the arrival of the Communist army, as it was noted that the ''Kachek schools were not open and Nodoa schools not greatly affected, but the Kiungchow schools were veritable laboratories of communism.''[32]

In summary then, one can say that the coverage of Hainan in these two mission periodicals was both similar and different. Coverage was similar in that they both contained news of the difficulties the missionaries were having with Chinese officials and with the warfare that wracked China in this century. This is an periodicals was both similar and different. Coverage was similar in that they both contained news of the difficulties the missionaries were having with Chinese officials and with the warfare that wracked China in this century. This is an educational aspect of the mission movement in China frequently overlooked by scholars. Readers of mission periodicals at home learned a great deal about the complex nature of China in the twentieth century from the news they read of the missions. It would be extremely difficult to judge just how these stories influenced their thinking about China and the problems she faced. The periodicals were also similar in that coverage of the conversion of aborigines and others to Christianity.

Yet the differences between them are greater than one would expect to find because of the differences in audience. The *Chinese Recorder* was never known for publishing lengthy articles, but the *Hainan News Letter* was even more brief in its coverage of any one topic. The *Hainan News Letter*, of course, contains more specific news about the island mission and the people who worked there. To the American at home reading the *Hainan News Letter*, it would be easy to conclude that the island was ready for mass conversion to Christianity and that positive progress was being made among the people who were not opposed to Christianity. The difficulty was quite evidently some Chinese officials who were opposed to Christian missions for reasons never explained by anyone writing for the *Hainan News Letter*.

Any reader of the *Chinese Recorder* would immediately be struck by the similarity of the problems missionaries on Hainan had to the difficulties missionaries elsewhere in China were having. The articles about the aborigines on Hainan were, of course, quite different than what most missionaries in China encountered, but still bear a great likeness to articles about aborigines elsewhere in South China. While readers elsewhere in China would want to be informed about the work in Hainan, it is safe to say they found little that was unique about that missionary work. In many respects Hainan was a microcosm of mission work in China.

Notes

1. Rudolph Lowenthal, *The Religious Periodical Press in China* (Peking: Synodal Commission in China, 1940), appendix of charts.
2. *Chinese Recorder [CR]*, 13:469.
3. *CR*, 13:469.
4. *CR*, 14:302.
5. *CR*, 14:364.
6. *CR*, 14:365.
7. B. C. Henry, *Ling-Nam or Interior Views of Southern China* (London: S. W. Partridge, 1886).
8. *CR*, 16:280.
9. *CR*, 21:280.
10. *CR*, 29:153.
11. *CR*, 32:421.
12. *CR*, 17:275.

16. *CR*, 21:279.
17. *CR*, 21:278–79.
18. *Hainan News Letter [HNL]*(December 1914): 9–10.
19. *CR*, 33:579–80.
20. *CR*, 48:771–72.
21. *CR*, 48:773.
22. *CR*, 48:774.
23. *CR*, 48:775.
24. *CR*, 48:775.
25. *CR*, 48:776.
26. *HNL* (February 1917): 9–10; (August 1917): 12–13.
27. *HNL* (February 1917): 4.
28. *HNL* (July 1914): 2.
29. *HNL* (Summer 1923): 17–18.
30. *HNL* (November 191): 13–15.
31. *HNL* (September 1912): 3.
32. *HNL* (Autumn 1931): 23.

6

FRANK RAWLINSON, CHINA MISSIONARY, 1902–1937
Veteran Deputationist

John Rawlinson

Missionaries on furlough were expected to do "deputation work," that is, give talks to gatherings of the faithful to raise money or recruits. Also, their written reports from the field were often turned into newsletters or read from pulpits of supporting churches. James Reed, in his *The Missionary Mind*, estimates that in a typical year there were 30,000 deputation talks, all across the United States.[1] He builds his case for missionary influence on U.S. policy from 1911 to 1915 on this sort of evidence. I do not pretend to demonstrate that Frank Rawlinson personally had much effect on home-base policy, but he certainly tried to influence his board, and was a leader in the extrality fight in the mid-1920s. His efforts are in any event illustrative of the changes in him as he shuttled back and forth between his home base and his Shanghai station. He worked for two boards: the Southern Baptist Board in Richmond, from 1902 to 1921, and then the Congregationalist American Board in Boston, until his death in the Shanghai fighting of 1937—and that change in sponsorship was also a function of the same personal evolution, which, of course, affected what he had to say. This paper, while making no pretense at psychohistory, will delve into pertinent subjective as well as objective aspects of the subject's life as a reporter (and, not incidentally, editor of the *Chinese Recorder* from 1914 on;[2] that, of course, is another story).

The days when Rawlinson felt his Call—it came at Northfield in 1900—were heady, reverberating with the U.S. Student Volunteer Movement slogan: "Evangelize China in this generation!" Heathen was the "in" term; perhaps the image was necessary for missionaries. Fundamental, of course, was that Christianity was superior to all Asian religions—Protestant Christianity, that is. As Rawlinson embarked on his Great Commission, he was suffused with an urgent desire to save as well as to advance the interests of his denomination; he also had an unquestioned sense of Western superiority and a sense that the mission movement was vital to the life of the church at home.

At the outset, apart from proseletyzing with native evangelists, the newcomer was plunged into his mission's educational work. Although language study brought frustrations, like hitting a wall with the head, as he put it, slowly it brought rewards. His letters to Richmond were very pious, with many deferential references to "the brethren," and plenary invocation of the Deity.[3]

As for the "heathen," he was at first given to jocular gibes about how dirty they were—how astronomical would be the count of *all* the body vermin on *all* of the Chinamen, etc. Chinese customs were diametrically opposed to those of the missionaries. Whether or not the Chinese could be civilized was a question that began to press on his mind, although before long he came to see that the answer was in part a "pocketbook problem." The unhesitating answer: Send more men!

In the meantime, relations with Chinese in the mission's schools were becoming intricate. There was (Richmond was told) the question of control of the schools, which Rawlinson and most of his colleagues felt should rest clearly in missionary hands, the Chinese being unready to take over or to preach the Word. A most delicate situation arose in 1904 when the mission was trying to get a Chinese graduate student in the United States to sign up for a projected new Baptist college. He was even offered the salary of a single missionary! But the insuperable obstacle was that the man had become engaged to an American woman! Rawlinson was not prepared to attack the received racist tradition then.

It was not only the heathen who needed ministering to. In the spring of 1905 Rawlinson wrote Richmond that the wickedness among the foreigners was appalling. He had no hesitation in deploying the word "sin" then. Perhaps the Divine Spirit would "stir the dry bones in Shanghai."

In 1905 the anti-American excitement in Shanghai reached even into the ranks of "our Christians."[4] Missionaries, Richmond was told at the end of the year, were being looked at askance—but it was not the old xenophobia, said Rawlinson, who had become a student of China's rebellions. Something new was afoot. And while the Chinese giant stirred, God would make the native Church even more self-reliant and staunch. The day of the missionary was far from over, but in training natives, they must have a care not to arouse pecuniary motives; Rawlinson could not but report how his graduates preferred commercial jobs in Shanghai, where their English could command more pay than any possible pulpit service. But be of good cheer! Editing out personal parts, the board secretary made the letter into a newsletter titled "Good News From China."

Still, perhaps partly because of the subtleties of the language, which he now knew enough to appreciate, Rawlinson concluded that for conversion, a Chinese should talk to a Chinese.

At home on furlough in 1908, Rawlinson shouldered a heavy burden of deputation work, ranging through Maryland, Virginia, Kentucky, Tennessee, and even Indiana. His sheaf of notes had plenty of simplifications. Never mind that the "erroneous efforts" of the early Nestorians and Catholics had come to naught! In the last century, Protestants had enlarged their foothold until the missionary could buy or build anywhere in the Empire. There were 632 "occupied" places (later he would object to that word) under 3,700 missionaries, and, if out stations were counted, 5,700 places in China now shone where once there had been "only total darkness and spiritual degradation." Counting all the peripherals, the speaker swept 750,000 souls into the fold. After all, Barbarian Europe had needed 1,000 years for its conversion, and it had taken force at that. In China, he went on glibly, overlooking Western actions that he later found inexcusable, there had been "only the campaign of a book, persuasion, persistence, and the Power of God." Let the home-base brethren pray for China's churches, lest they slip into "the clutches of the ever-present *revolutionist!*" and so that the native churches would find their own amalgam of the old and the new, e.g., "a proper respect for their departed with the full elimination of ancestor worship" (hardly a new idea among missionaries, but no doubt, his Christian brew was thickening).

Yet how bright the outlook! The Boxers had ravaged but 10 percent of the huge country;[5] the government's refusal to honor Christian diplomas was not working; Chinese officials were even then using Christian materials. Send men! Send money! Let there be four times the present missionary force, which was still but a tiny band "midst hordes of heathenism." Then came the clarion SVM manifesto, somewhat amended by experience: "China must be evangelized in this generation!"

One should be aware of a new development, double edged. Since Chinese Christians were starting to do their own evangelizing, with a home missionary "army" of seven thousand, the term "native helper" must soon give way to the term "foreign helper," applied to the missionary.

Another canned speech was dubbed "The Achievement of Christianity in China." Had the $80 million invested in China missions in the last century (not as much as the $200 million sunk into the Panama Canal, threw in the speaker, always one for statistics) paid off? Forsooth! See China's "astounding reforms": the promised constitution, which would undercut corruption and nurture the rights of commoners; the dramatic abolition of the old examination system and the springing up everywhere of Western-type schools; the antiopium drive; the fact that natural feet were "rapidly becoming the fashion."[6] Only beginnings, granted, but the influence of Christianity shone through it all, as also in pressures on polygamy, prostitution, etc. "China," he proclaimed for the edification of all, "has a glimpse of better things . . . from the light bearers who follow the Light of the World." Another of his talks bore the self-explanatory title: "Many Gods, No God."

There were other ways to influence the work. Rawlinson persuaded the board not to send a bachelor missionary to a small North China station tenanted thus far only by two single missionary ladies—the Chinese would never understand! Or one could make a personal appeal for money, as, for example, in Rawlinson's success in getting one generous soul to put up $850 for an artesian well for the new Shanghai Baptist College.

Back on station, in 1908, Rawlinson found again that while students in China were extraordinarily respectful of teachers, nonetheless, whether because of family opposition or the lure of commercial pay, his own were not coming into the ministry. He wondered—heretical thought!—if missionaries made the best models. Back home, the corresponding secretary cut out the part about students slipping away and made a newsletter out of what students *would* do: Bible work, prayer meetings, street chapel and tea-shop work, even joining the church. The newsletter was titled: "Religious Work by Students. Missionary Frank Rawlinson Sends Good News Concerning the Students at Shanghai Baptist Academy."

Grappling with such complexities, Rawlinson editorialized in *The New East* (a new Baptist publication he briefly edited) for November 1909 that missionary educators had a right to use pressure to lead men into the ministry. Yet one must not judge Chinese by Western standards. Overwhelming candidates with Western surroundings might encourage materialism. One must differentiate between Westernizing China and Christianizing the Chinese. In time this glib and conservative formula led the man to ponder what in the Word was essentially Christian and what was Western.

He also had to admit that, for him, educational work was overtopping the older evangelistic approach. Another concern was the growing competition with government schools, which might force a dilution of the Christian element. He was confident that the Lord would guide in all such problems, however.

Some of the erstwhile "heathen" lads were learning their lessons well enough, it seemed. One of Rawlinson's student's essays was sent to Richmond in 1908 as an example. The youngster had combined a nautical metaphor with Confucian and patriotic elements, his effusion suggesting how his teacher introduced concepts of Sin, Heaven, and Hell. Thus, ships depend on rudders; so too, humankind, which could be divided into the ignorant and the wise. For all, everything depended on the course set: one led to Hell, which was vigorously described; the other, although it took one through mighty tempests, led to Bliss. Who would be the helmsman? Who was this famous man, this hero? Of course, it was Jesus. The board thought the item was brochure material, giving it the minimalist title "Men Like Ships."

In these years, while Rawlinson served as educator and administrator—he was treasurer, and on the executive committee—his correspondence became almost entirely mundane, businesslike, unadorned with conventional pious cliches. Perhaps one of the reasons was an ineluctable friction with the board—by no means unique to this missionary—in the matter of ultimate control. The December 1911 issue of the *Chinese Recorder* was devoted to the question, and Rawlinson was in the table of contents. Missionaries were not servants, said he; rather, they were brothers, and brothers at the center of the action. The old paternalism would no longer do. One might add here that Rawlinson at least did ruffle some feathers, particularly those of an editor at home base, who later wrote a number of stinging editorials on the temerity of folk on the field in imagining that they could best decide how home-base monies should be used! Or that they could trim the Baptist creed—say, in the matter of union with other missions—to suit field conditions. Another element in the changing self-image of missionaries, at least of this one, was the need for specialists—educators, business agents, and construction men. The Call would demand far more than lofty idealism.

There was no doubt that for Rawlinson and others, field conditions led to the conclusion that only in union with other denominations—minimally, that between Northern and Southern Baptists to set up the new college—could the Great Commission in China be served. This demanded a softening of the old adamantine exclusivity of the Southern Baptist Convention. A corollary was that in time the Chinese must control their own church.

If Rawlinson was not unique in holding these views, he was in some ways clearly in the vanguard. In a 1910 editorial in *The New East*, he wrote of "the welding together of all denominations to make one Christian Church in China, some features of which would certainly be Baptist." Let Baptists make a new formulation of their Fundamentals (he was thinking of the insistence on exclusive communion, which he was not observing in his own Grace Church). And—anathema to many home-base readers—he ventured that *there might be some good in all religions*, even if the forefathers had not found it so.

Yet the man had not slipped his cultural moorings. In an article for the December 1912 *Chinese Recorder*, titled "The Chinese Idea of Truth," he admitted that his study of the Classics had uncovered a fundamental indifference to truth, as understood by Western Christians. To wit: "There is an atmosphere of insincerity about the Classics that I cannot shake off. I have an impression of moral ventriloquism or of marionettes—what is seen only suggests what might have been." Ergo, the over-use of the Classics in missionary school rooms would undermine "the splendid truths" otherwise dispensed therein.

Of course, the "Revolution" (he always used upper case in referring to the 1911 uprising) made a deep impression. In September he called on Richmond for prayer over "disturbing conditions," a phrase which the board used as a caption for a newsletter broadcasting his story of rampaging attacks on Christians near Shanghai, sparked by the famine of 1910 and suspicions that certain modernizers—not only Christians—had disturbed the river gods. At least this was not simple Boxerism! On November 11, he wrote of real change, the Revolution itself, which had caused some missionaries to come downriver. No doubt, the "heart and soul" of China was with it. Again, he asked for prayer that China might move ahead. His reports became more frequent as the Revolution moved "by leaps and bounds," as he put it, albeit still without molestation of foreigners. However, the "hooligan element" might seize the day. As for the mission, it was immune, so no special prayers from the Richmond constituency were called for. But the letter of December 11, also made into a newsletter, was more ominous, opening with, "Your hearts will be more or less uneasy, I assume," a line which the corresponding secretary blue-penciled. While Rawlinson's academy was still open, eight students from the college had joined up, and the faculty out there had been issued guns by the U.S. Consul "as a precaution against robbers simply," Rawlinson explained. Nevertheless, there was more blue-penciling here. From Nanking came "terrible news of indiscriminate slaughtering of anyone caught with a queue."[7] Shanghai's revolutionary leaders were looking for money, and might turn "reckless and restless" or "untoward" toward foreigners.

On May 8, 1912, Rawlinson could tell the board that the patriotic volunteers from the college had come back; things there were quiet, and, indeed, there was "almost a total absence of cigarette smoking and other vices." No doubt heads at home nodded over that bit (Rawlinson, who did not ask whether the tobacco problem was Western or Christian, did not take up the weed for another decade).

None of this affected home-base thinking. Richmond rejected a plan for union in a projected school in Nanking in 1912, though Rawlinson had enthusiastically joined others in the project. But he took solace, way out there in Shanghai, in the convening in 1913 of the China Continuation Committee. Here was the first regular interdenominational organization, all-China, albeit without binding power. At about the same time, however, the home-base convention voted to eschew *all* union work, which cast the FCC under a deep shadow and was to create problems for Rawlinson as editor of the *Chinese Recorder*, which he became in 1914 while continuing full-time in his mission.

World War I was a fundamental challenge to Western complacency, and while not all missionaries were equally upset by it, Rawlinson came to be. How to explain how Christian nations fell into fratricide? What was the *real* Christian message, after all? What was the future of the missionary in a China daily growing more nationalist? In a December 1915 editorial he projected a series of articles on "The Christian Apologetic for China" and another on "The Relation of Missionaries to the Chinese," topics which would not have occurred to him ten years before. He was chairman of a CCC committee on the training and efficiency of missionaries, and started talking in terms of an "ambassadorial" role for them. Home-base true believers did not take well to such talk; in fact, Rawlinson had just tangled with a fellow editor on related questions. One answer to the challenge of the war, increasingly persuasive to Rawlinson, was the social gospel. Of course, that approach was entangled with "the Western impact," a phrase he first used in 1918. Events were clouding the clear Northfield vision!

As it worked out, Rawlinson did relatively little deputation work on furlough in 1916–17. He enrolled at Teachers College and told Richmond that since China was changing so fast, study was essential. Some might object to this seeming indifference to the board's need for fund-raising stump work, "but I have decided to give my life to the uplift of China," he declared, further amending the Northfield formula (which still hypnotized many new missionaries, until culture shock intervened), "and I want to do it in the most efficient way." The courses he took were variations on the theme of religious education.

It may be added that the man passed through a personal crisis on this furlough. His wife of seventeen years, and mother of his six surviving children, died after an accident. What should the widower-father do? Before long he started to court a YWCA worker from India whom the family had met on shipboard. As their understanding grew into an engagement, he conspired with her on the problem of her becoming the wife of a Southern Baptist, a union which, of course, needed Richmond's blessing. The trouble was that she could not in conscience accept the SBC policy on union work, which was the polar opposite of the YM-YW ethos. In their lengthy correspondence in 1917, marked by love talk mixed with bravado on his part in the matter of his relations with his board, he confided that he had gotten plenty of criticism on his editorial and personal positions. He had been specifically warned, indeed, about his work for the nondenominational *Recorder*. Said he to her, "After I get back to China I may say all that is in my heart and let the chips fly. . . . Then too I often think that perhaps it is part of my task to bear this and help these people into a little broader life. While I do not represent the crowd that is in control, yet I do represent many in the Convention." Here was a *really* new definition of the missionary's task! Later, writing to Richmond in the matter of that controversial editorship, he said that he had not publicized his views in the South, particularly in the matter of Christian cooperation on the field, because he had not wished to embarrass the board. Deputation was not so easy now!

Shortly after taking up the Shanghai reins again, Rawlinson reported to his Baltimore supporting church, cataloging his activities, e.g., a speech to the Japanese Club on "What is Democracy?" and weekly talks in his night school on such posers as "What Is The Difference Between a Bad Man and a Good One?" No doubt his remark that "too many of the churches in China have no objective whatever" was most arresting. He also told these distant benefactors that he had volunteered as a special constable for the Shanghai Police Force, whose Caucasian cadre had been sharply cut by wartime enlistments. Rawlinson had been restless, wanting to get into wartime YMCA work in France, but had been dissuaded. Here was an outlet.

The most dramatic evidence that Rawlinson was not ameliorating home-base opinion was the final crisis over his editorship, which he would not surrender. Although it took eighteen months of courtly and legalistic correspondence, he was finally dismissed from the SBC as of the end of 1921. His colleagues in Shanghai had been strongly supportive (save one, who had written privily that the man did not seem to have Baptist beliefs). After much personal trauma, he (his family was now enlarged by two infants) was taken on by the American Board, to give full time to the *Recorder*. Although his editorials fall largely beyond my scope, note that they were increasingly given to the social gospel and to the exigent extraterritoriality question,[8] and were virtually unmarked by piety.

The nerve-wracking search for a new board took its toll. At one point he wrote his new wife from Peking, where he was experimenting with being on the

Yenching faculty, that praying seemed too much like an evasion. Some of his missionary students in the Peking and Nanking Language Schools, where he started an annual stint of lectures, were shocked by his idea that Confucius had had some useful ideas! They prayed for him. This is to say that this lecturer-editor became enmeshed in the fundamentalist-modernist controversy, though he tried to keep the *Recorder* impartial. At one point in 1924, from Nanking, he wrote home that he was "afraid I shall be considered a menace to Christian work in China." More intimately, he wrote to his wife of his growing religious crisis: "In my heart I seem to be peering around the universe. My soul seems to be searching for an outstretched hand, that look in any eye. But in those moments when I am most myself and most honest I have to admit that that hand and that look seem hidden." Save, that is, for the times he was with her, he hastened to add.

Furlough came again in 1924–25. On the way to the United States, the ship lay over at Honolulu, and VIP Rawlinson was asked to talk in various places. One audience was at the Pan-Pacific Conference (no lunch, he griped to his married daughter in the United States). At the Lions Club in Los Angeles, he spoke on interracial relations.

Once again he chose to study, now at Union Theological Seminary, which was showing signs of change itself, offering new courses on social welfare (but none on China per se). Although study and the death of his fourteen-year-old daughter were not conducive to it, he did some writing. The October issue of *Missionary Review of the World* carried his "The New Christian Struggle in China," a frontal attack on home-base stereotypes. Christianity's uphill push in China was not a matter of native racial antipathy: it was a function of poverty, ignorance, and denominationalism. The Christian faith did clash with deep-rooted Chinese traits, to be sure; there was also that new patriotism. How *could* Chinese Christians observe the twenty-fifth anniversary of Christian martyrdom at Boxer hands? A Chinese educator friend, he wrote, had confided to him "with bitterness tempered with pathos, that he disbelieved categorically in the truth of revelation, and was appalled by the disastrous effects, from the standpoint of the Chinese, wrought by Christian missions." But the faith was backed by the Treaty Powers! This was a new brand of deputationizing.

Early in 1925, Rawlinson sat in on a missionary convention in Washington with over five thousand in attendance, keynoted to the ponderous theme, "What Progress Have We Made in Understanding and Making Known the Personal Significance of Christ for the Whole Wide World of Men?" Although he would have tackled that windy question with gusto once, now he had to keep his tongue in his cheek. He told his *Recorder* readers later, "This deponent never passed through such an uninterrupted flow of speechmaking. . . . The programs worked almost as stiffly as a slot-machine [a curious simile, say I]. Hymns, prayers, speeches, tramped after each other with a sort of thumping orderliness . . . a mission board meeting on a continental scale, with a lack of a sense of humor." As for the real problems, e.g., the great religious fissure in the movement, "the spirit of controversy gently slumbered and slept." Above and beyond was "that Christian mirage, detached idealism . . . which shimmered serenely over human contacts instead of *through* them." It was not heartening to this observer to see that most mission financing was American. Only a "distressingly small" portion of the audience (2 percent, he threw in) was Chinese. Yet he had heard some corridor talk: "These young Chinese Christians must not expect to come there and tell us how to run Christianity." Folks at home base must wake up, cried the *Recorder*'s editor. "The day is rapidly drawing to a close" when the Occidental could dub himself "the chosen leader in the evangelization of the world." So much for Northfield! Still, he sensed at the meeting a disillusion with all civilizations, and a stirring of interest in the Oriental version thereof, said he, reflecting a growing tendency in himself. He hoped anyway that this would be the last purely Occidental Christian extravaganza.

In the second semester at UTS Rawlinson gave a course of lectures in the Foreign Department which he called "The Developing Christian Movement in China." Here was a form of deputation work, after all. Much of his syllabus reflected his personal quest for understanding of his adopted country, e.g., he explained China's backwardness in terms recently used by Hu Shih, who traced it back to Wang Yang-ming.[9] In such a poor country, Christianity had a hollow ring; it would take a new psychology to spread the Word now, and he illustrated Chinese psychology in family-system terms. To be sure, they were adopting some Westernisms (e.g., written contracts) and, alas, religious intolerance. Trainees must ingest more of China's spiritual heritage; it was an illusion that the Chinese were "absolutely ignorant" of principles underlying Christianity. Liang Ch'i-ch'ao had said of Mo-tze, "Add but a cross and you have Christ." Rawlinson had long since quit talking of the "heathen."

The new Christian ambassadors must beware the incubus of imperialism and the Chinese suspicion that missionaries were political agents. Could they work under Chinese direction? One must also ponder whether "the Christian dynamic" was detachable from its Western cultural matrix. Take the curse of war, and whether it would be Christianity or economics that would obviate it. He gave considerable attention to the new National Christian Council (1922) and its interest in the social gospel, e.g., the need for a workable, concrete Christian ethic for employers in China.

Perhaps the West's main contribution (he said in another lecture) was "efficiency in the organization of life and economic processes." He had doubts about the viability of Western individualism in China, yet it was the gist, which he linked to Christianity's personal relationship to God, that was such a "tremendous liberalizing force." Yet Christianity must be naturalized in China. Long since it had taken on Judaic, Roman, Greek, and American elements; the Chinese church now must have its turn, eliminating, say, the sermon, and working its own rituals and eldership-type of governance.

Rawlinson's most public and radical deputation piece in this period came in his article "Missionaries at Caesar's Footstool," which he published in the liberal *Christian Century* of April 30, 1925—just a month, as it happened, before another frenzy of resentment swept Shanghai and China.[10] Clearly, extraterritoriality must go, but he blunted the point by the plenary use of rhetorical questions. He admitted that he over-minimized the protective value of the existing system, but, after all, what *real* protection did missionaries living miles from the nearest gunboat enjoy? "Cannot the missionaries who helped to form the present arrangements take the lead in seeking for just ones?" Of course, there were indignant rebuttals from interior missionaries, but the board secretaries at home base came out for "readjustment" in the system, and the editor of *Christian Century* openly attacked it, citing Rawlinson's controversial article.

Still, the man could write, at about this time, for friends alone, a poem on China which was full of hoary cliches, e.g., "Oh! venerable and wrinkled, horny-handed, staid, sedate. Back-wrenched with toil, heart-slowed with sighs, yet face still smiling on thy fate. Lift up thine eyes!" It was as if the May 4 storm had never darkened this sentimental urban vision. Yet he did not rhapsodize on how the missionary would save this lovable old codger.

Although it took some doing by the board, Rawlinson found a new supporting church on this furlough. So that the congregation could assess him, he took the pulpit on a Sunday in March 1925 (one screening committeeman, impressed, noted that the candidate told the truth "without any of the usual wail that is so often used"). Some were concerned that he talked over the heads of the congregation, but they took him on. He also made recruiting talks in Toronto, Vanderbilt University, Rochester Theological Seminary, a SVM gathering, a conference for Chinese students in New York, etc.

Of course, on his return home to Shanghai, Rawlinson resumed his reports to the board, which were entirely political, since he had no mission business to present (some space went to his mounting financial difficulties, however). Writing to his new supporters in Newton, Massachusetts, he compared May 30 to the fall of the Bastille. The Chinese were closely watching the Tariff Conference,[11] and might denounce the treaty system out of hand if the powers were obdurate, yet the Chinese he was associated with personally were friendly. In October, he rejoiced in the stand the board took on the treaties and also in the unequivocal position of his American board missionary colleagues in the push for revision. Still, he said to Boston more than once that he didn't know what the "missionary mind" was on this urgent issue.

Of great personal meaning was a YMCA-organized retreat on Taishan to which Rawlinson was invited in mid-1926. There he supped intellectual and religious fare with a few entirely congenial souls, both missionary and Chinese.

fulminations marred their probings into the divinity of Christ (no one upheld it), and even whether or not one could follow Christ without some cavil—Rawlinson said he could not overlook the fact that He was so much larger than life. It seems that he even forgot to bring his Bible ("Tell it not to the Fundamentalists!" he said, partly in jest, to his wife). Elsewhere he wrote, "I have little difficulty in meeting the needs of a crowd like this but I shall have to imbibe for an eternity in heaven under the shadow of the Fundamentalist seminary there before I can hope to satisfy them. I think that even God will have to speak carefully lest they will tell Him how to run the universe." On the mountain he had an inner experience he could not articulate, even to his wife, save to say the companionship was an essential ingredient. No doubt all this was "red theology!" That mordant humor kept intruding; if the retreat were fully reported, he mused, the story would contain enough dynamite "to blow us all to some retired place in heaven or elsewhere." Rawlinson, it might be added, was assigned by his fellows to the "Smokers" division, a fact which in itself would have been, to some, a proof of perdition.

After a group of missionaries called on U.S. Minister McMurray—this was in the wake of the Wanhsien affair of September 1926,[12] an interview that Rawlinson felt produced only evasion of the official's part—he wrote to his married daughter stateside in a discouraged vein, "I have been in a number of conferences lately and have come out of them with a sense of futility beating in my heart." Missionaries simply could not agree on what was the *Christian* thing to do! Turning to the homefront salient, he wrote to A. L. Warnshuis of the International Missionary Council in November, taxing him for the sort of defeatism which the editor Rawlinson was encountering among missionaries. What sort of people were they sending out, to be so easily disheartened by the real China? Many just could not cope with the idea of Chinese leadership. "You fellows had better get after this situation," he chided, not being entirely jocular.

It may be significant that in his editorial summary for the 1926 *China Christian Year Book* (no longer the *China Mission Year Book*, note), a thirty-page recap of the tumultuous twelve months just passed, Rawlinson made but one reference to the Deity, viz., "God will work out in China the building up of a people who know Him and are re-energized by faith in Him." Perhaps any comparison with the bombastic Northfield credo would be superfluous.

Of course, his reports to the board and the IMC (often identical) were accelerated and intensified by the events of 1927, which brought a flood of missionaries downriver to Shanghai, many doubly upset by having to leave their work in Chinese hands. He was concerned about the probable effect that the mass evacuation would have on the liberal-conservative balance among missionaries, i.e., that the latter, being more insensitive to Chinese feelings, would return in larger numbers than would the former, wanted or not. He wondered if a *real* civil war were not in the making. As for Chiang K'ai-shek's slaughter of Shanghai workers on April 12, [13] he noted, with treaty-port condescension,

> For a while there was a good deal of fighting around Shanghai between detachments of soldiers connected with the moderates, and the communists, mainly in the form of armed laborers. These armed laborers seem to have been effectively suppressed for the time being at least. Labor in Shanghai is therefore more disposed to work and a little less disposed to cavil over its privileges or rights.

Nevertheless, nationalism was a real change, and in it one saw China's response "to the two most prominent aspects of Western life, first, democratic principles, and second, militarism." He hoped the first would prevail, but was not sanguine.

This man's thinking, with roots running far back in his China experience, was reflected in his *The Naturalization of Christianity in China,* which he published in March 1927 in the thick of events. The contents had in fact appeared serially in the *Recorder*, but here he added two chapters, even more radical. Christianity, in China to stay, must rid itself of all excrescences, including the Western superiority complex and the besetting Western sin, "the love of authority," and, thus disencumbered, enter with the Chinese into a joint search for a new individual and social Christian civilization, with but a single tenet: "All those who show *ethical* loyalty to Jesus [italics mine; see there the Chinese influence] should be admitted to Christian fellowship, which means sharing the pulpit and the fellowship table." To the "socialistic revolution," Rawlinson retorted, "The Christian world movement must become the model effort to teach men to *share life* by enabling them everywhere to share their experience and their goods." (Christian socialism, of course.) Contemplating this millenial fusion of many great cultures, Rawlinson's mind "lept with confidence" over all difficulties. Needless to say, he made no attempt to keep this publication out of conservative hands, on the field or at home.

In fact, he was already being pilloried by true believers, lay and religious, for his having written what many Shanghailanders saw as a traitorous piece in a Chinese Christian pamphlet called *Long Live the Nationalist Government,* put out to show that Christians were in the patriotic van. Another response of his to the crisis was to put Chinese on his editorial board. However, there was much to be disheartened about, he told the board: even those favoring abolition of the treaties had had to rely on gunboats; events had overtaken Christian idealism, "completing the disillusionment of the missionaries." Here was the end of an era in Christian work; Chinese control had become a fact. He did have to say, after having interviewed many of the refugees, that the Nanking incident was clearly a scheme to embarrass Chiang with the foreigners, although some said it was a Chinese *suan-chang*, a settling of accounts, for foreign reprisals in the Boxer aftermath. [14]

Again—this in April 1927, to Boston—he wrote that while he expected "the extreme communistic aspect of things" to pass, he did not know how long it would be before the moderates won out. In the short run, too, "it sometimes looks to me as though for missionaries to stay in their stations under present circumstances is simply to make themselves a liability that increases the difficulties of the Chinese Christians."

Editorially he was more upbeat, seeing in the exodus a day of opportunity for the Church, which would perforce be more independent and would become innovative. It would take five years to adjust to the post-Nanking trauma, even if "communist agitators" were eliminated. Many of the current questions, e.g., school registration,[15] would persist. No doubt there would be fewer missionaries in the future, with more of them single, and *all* invited by the Chinese Christians.

In the fall of 1927, perhaps partly because of exhaustion (coupled with having had all of his teeth removed), Rawlinson plunged more deeply into religious disillusion. Writing to his wife, he said he had quite lost the simple faith he inherited from his Plymouth Brethren father. What was God? Only in companionship, he said again, in love—he was quite erotic in this private talk—could he find any sense of God. He admitted, slipping into a sort of pop-psychology mode, that he was in fact two men: the conforming missionary/editor, and an inner creature who frequently growled at being chained up. That was his male ego, he admitted; *he* got "damned little appreciation." But was life only a passing illusion? At times, he sounded like a Buddhist, although he did not go so far as to yearn for obliteration.

Reportage to Boston was, of course, unaffected; there spoke the public persona, who in fact had long since abandoned public piety. He discussed the political scene, e.g., whether Chiang was an autocrat, discrediting the idea; whether the Chinese would not sit still for a military dictatorship; whether they would create a committee government of some sort. On the other hand, disillusion with Nanking was spreading; all that talk about peasants and workers had created expectations which were patently frustrated. But there was a new set in "the Chinese mind," no doubt. As for the NCC, he was becoming ambivalent, seeing that a new system of representation (no longer by missions) would probably give the Chinese conservatives the edge. Anyway, the delayed 1927 meeting had mumbled cliches only. He asked Warnshuis of the IMC not to publish these gloomy asides.

Right after New Year's Day in 1928, Rawlinson wrote again to Warnshuis on the question of the missionary return. He was cautious. Although Communist influence would surely increase, something in the Chinese nature, he was sure, militated against its final triumph. Take Feng Yu-hsiang (there was speculation on whether he was still eligible to be a sort of Exhibit A for the Christian effort): he admired the Communist spirit but deplored their actions.[16] Denying pessimism, Rawlinson still foresaw a life struggle for Christianity over the next decade, hinging "to no small extent" on the way in which it related to "China's older religious and cultural ideals."

In that fluid situation, he was soon saying to Warnshuis ("do not publish, please'') that ''the lid might blow off politically.'' Maybe China was ripe for a Napoleon; he hoped that the widespread suffering did not portend ''general revolution.'' Many missionaries were coming back, but how long would this Thermidor last? In a March letter, Warnshuis read more on the devastating modernism controversy. It would be exceedingly difficult to make anything like ''a mass movement'' out of Christian materials. Still, for his *Christian Century* constituency (he was now their China correspondent) he was more cheerful, offering in April a piece on ''Breaking Down China's Church Fences.''

Coincidentally, reacting to general correspondence, Rawlinson penned a May editorial on ''Telling the Truth.'' Did not missionaries in their deputation talks overdo both the good and the bad in China? A missionary correspondent had brooded on the dire effects that candor had on home-base support. ''Strong medicine!'' cried the editor. It seemed there were furloughing missionaries who avoided deputation work because they did not know how to mix the black and the white. A little later, writing to Boston, Rawlinson confessed that he was ''a little weary over a lot of impractical idealism and over-boasting of the achievement of Christianity in China.'' Yet a home-base reader praised him for his editorials, which stressed the triumph of Chinese Christians under trying situations. ''You have been playing a far more important role than you realize,'' said this reader. Evidently so: Rawlinson got a surprising invitation to speak to an Illinois church on Christians and gunboats.

After the Tsinan incident of May 1928,[17] Rawlinson told Warnshuis that it had accelerated a movement for military training in the schools. Publicly, in an editorial, he deplored it all, saying that the moral of the affair was that ''mutual trust and good will are essential.'' A little later he reported a privy meeting of missionaries and a special British envoy, covering the Tsinan crisis and the proposed People's Conference. All agreed, Boston learned, that Japan was at fault, but did not know what China should do. Another report on the affair enclosed remarks by a prominent Chinese on the actual engagement—the killing of hospital patients, etc.—which was not to be published. In all, Rawlinson felt that Nanking still had general support. What choice had China?

In the meantime, he passed on to Boston favorable impressions of the new government at Nanking, which controlled the country save for Manchuria: its ''reconstructive'' plans were impressive; the U.S. accession to the new tariff treaty was good news everywhere but in Japan; there was the coming of the period of Political Tutelage, as prescribed by Sun Yat-sen himself; there were prominent Christians in the government, and so on.

That November, he lobbed off a twenty-one-page political report to Boston, remarking that the new government rested on an unstable base, which gave full scope to the sagacity of Chiang K'ai-shek. He took a legalistic view of the new basic law, pointing to various checks and balances. He moved on to the fundamentalist challenge, noting here that Boston could use anything save for this last material. Elsewhere he noted a ramification of the Western impact, which was not edifying, i.e., "the rapid development of incidental, morbid, realistic sex literature," as witness a ten-volume sex manual packed with "intimate and even repulsive details." Some blamed it on the Russians; others countered that the Chinese were carrying it beyond the limits marked out even by such infamous mentors.

Early in 1929, Rawlinson could report that missionary numbers had risen back to half the mid-1920s maximum, but that conservatives seemed to be in the ascendancy. Young Chinese were confused about the Message; some wondered if the Church could survive at all. Upcountry missionaries in some stations had come downriver again and, as for reforms, Nanking was slow—but one must remember the United States and prohibition, he added, evenhandedly. Shanghai, with its bandits, was almost as exciting as Chicago! Overall, what with rumors of civil wars, the China situation was so baffling that it was hard for him to get up his monthly quota of editorials. Things had surely changed since his early days! Of course, there was much of the old, and the new had hardly permeated the vast hinterland. But for the first time, the Chinese were not merely passively assimilating, as with Buddhism, but were consciously trying to adjust to outside pressures. Here was a new motif. "It is the psychological root," said he, "from which are now springing all kinds of aims and programs."

In mid-1929, the NCC decided to launch a Christian challenge to China, in the form of a Five-Year Movement to increase membership, a joint effort presented editorially by Rawlinson as a bold plan "to use *all* Protestant forces in *one* movement!" He was less euphoric to the board: modern Chinese were being replaced in the NCC by evangelistic types, who had little sympathy for the social gospel; there was no real progress toward a united Church, although one *could* say that 125 years had at least produced Chinese church leadership. His stress in 1929 reports to Boston was on the divisiveness of the movement. In April, after Japan had at last withdrawn from Tsinan, he had to acknowledge that for most Chinese there was no room for a pacifist organization, which made him reluctant to voice his own preferences in the matter, lest he be charged with trying to keep China weak. By mid-year, he reported that there was little talk of extraterritoriality those days, and indeed that the Church seemed to be enjoying a breather, with Nanking being preoccupied. Washington's decision not to press for an end to the old treaty system was a blow, but missionaries were mostly silent on the issue.

A number of months in 1930 for Rawlinson were given to a special furlough for health, and he left no record of any deputation work.

In mid-1931, the returned reporter was basically optimistic, e.g., Nanking was winning its war on the Communists. But, of course, the tornado struck on September 18 at Muken,[18] and the pace of reporting picked up. Nanking was in a predicament; the League had disappointed everyone, and Washington's vacillations had not helped. Would China turn to Russia? What would the Russians expect by way of payment? He thought that if the two nations did fight Japan, China would become Communist "to a large extent." What then of missions? Gloomily, he asked Boston not to publicize these misgivings.

After the December 1931 student protests, he wrote Boston covering the political front; the student agitation was an unfortunate manifestation of nationalism. But there had been government changes, which showed that while China lacked democratic machinery, no government could stand against public opinion.

Sino-Japanese fighting flared in Shanghai on January 28, 1932, and Rawlinson, whose wife worried over the strain in him, stepped up his writing to Boston. Some of his reports were not for publication, e.g., one enclosing an NCC assessment of changes in the Chinese mind, which had grown more militant, despite Chiang's insistence on nonresistance. Clearly, Japan was at fault. Members of the League of Nations Lytton Commission had called on the *Recorder*'s editor, wanting his assessment of the Japanese charge that China was too chaotic for self-government, and of Chinese antiforeignism. The first idea he dismissed as superficial; as for the second, he countered that they were not "inherently" xenophobic. In April, the situation having quieted, he sent off to Boston a report by a YMCA colleague on the Manchurian situation, where the Japanese were pressuring the associations (not for publication, please).

Furlough in mid-1932 was a release (although Rawlinson and wife agonized over whether the board, in that time of depression, could keep them on).

Back in rural Indiana (Mrs. Rawlinson's folks' place) Rawlinson made deputation talks at the Rotary, in churches, and so on. His son, Alfred, in one audience, had a queasy impression. Was it an off-day? Anyway, the subject was "Why I am Going Back to China." Fifty years later, Alfred wrote, "I couldn't help but feel . . . that he was sort of trying to psych himself up, trying to find some excuse, some reason for going back, other than the motive that had driven him in the beginning. He just sounded like somebody who had lost the feeling of significance in the work he was doing. . . . He never came up with any concrete reason; he was just fanning the breeze as to why he was going back after lo these many years."

However, he could be pungent. Japan's actions smacked of "international racketeering," and the Chinese had fought back "with endurance surprising even to themselves" (nothing on the bitter internal debate over that). Actually, he had little to say about Japan; it moved him too much, he told his wife later.

He did have a great deal to share about China's stage of development, war or no. New laws were taking the country into an era of contracts, but these were in some ways traditional. Modern industry there was: cotton, silk, cars (no China-made engines), canned goods, even silk stockings. T. V. Soong was struggling to hold down the surging military budget. The Communists and Nationalists leaned respectively toward "sovietism and socialized capitalism," both being imported ideas, "but the country seemed to live her own life in a modern way," said this Shanghailander somewhat vaguely. China was an important pawn on a huge Pacific board cornered by Russia, America, and Japan.

He also insisted that missions had an assured future, adumbrating the sort of sharing/learning role for missionaries shortly to be so forcibly presented in the *Laymen's Report*. In one talk, he made an off-hand observation, "Some of us must go and live at numerous points among other peoples in order to release among them the spirit which alone will relieve the political, racial, and commercial strains marking and blighting our time." No Northfield battlecry, that!

Among his talks on that furlough was one on the reaction of the Chinese intelligentsia to the Message. He admitted that he was speaking only of the few, the masses, with their talk of tongues, healings, prayers for crops, etc., being beyond his ken. But as education spread out there, so would critical self-awareness, "which means, if true, that much that is now being built up will perforce have to come down again." A dubious pitch, that! As for the educated, it was Jesus the man, the ethical preceptor, who appealed. Doctrines of Virgin Birth, substitutionary death on the Cross, etc., were unintelligible or repulsive. If Christ were indeed free of sin, what good was he to mortals? asked Rawlinson, rhetorically, although he had put the very same question to himself on Taishan in 1926. To the educated Chinese, salvation was seen as an educational proposition, rather than a theological one. Preaching was of little value, but *teaching*—there was something else.

In these musings, which may have gone over some rural Indiana heads (and pocketbooks), he said also that the Church had had no answer in the matter of the recent Sino-Japanese fighting. One could not just give in to such predators; on the other hand, in the spirit of Christ one could not uphold force. Part of the problem was that Japan was just resorting to methods long used by the West.

Another forum for appealing to home-base opinion was *World Unity*, a visionary postwar publication whose recent contributors included Norman Thomas and Frank Lloyd Wright. Rawlinson wrote a ten-part series for it. In this massive 360-degree survey, the author had much to say on politics, but readers should know that despite the failings of the KMT, China would not go back. The CCP was only in part a Russian product, and only a few of its members really understood Communist principles. The party had suffered "ruthless suppression," he said, going farther than he had in his editorials, but was "far from dead." Neither party had "clear aims and machinery." Perhaps peasant unions were more stable than the urban counterpart, which Nanking had encouraged. But KMT ideas on "party dictatorship" were not hospitable. Although he described the reorganization of the *hsien* (the basic administrative unit), he felt that provincial-central relations were really a carryover of the old viceregal autonomies. Militarism most concerned him; perhaps a free vote could uproot it, but one wondered. He also reviewed legal reforms, distinguishing between theory and practice, and including vignettes on the changing position of women, fragmentary but impressive when placed in close array. China was waking! Here was a change for real "international sharing."

Looking farther back, he dated the Chinese Revolution to 1898. Christianity had been involved in all of its spasms, even if not all Christians had been. Recent anti-Christian attacks, note, were couched in Western terms. The Revolution, centered in the treaty ports, had overtaken the Church in social reform, leaving the latter in an identity crisis. In this "adolescent self-awareness," perforce Christians were showing a greater appreciation of other religions. Christianity had its own share of tangles, being tied to imperialism, the missionary standard-of-living problem, etc. Its chief problem was science, which missionaries themselves had introduced. The Bible was exerting "tremendous influence," he said, warming, marshalling statistics from the Christian Literature Society; it had penetrated the Chinese daily round. Until 1913, Christians tended to accept Chinese society, save for foot-binding. Not so now; see the social gospel, although it lacked an adequate formulation for a "mass attack." But Christians were better organized than most groups, if they would only take up the challenge. Their influence was not always indirect; note that recently "a prominent Nationalist general" (Chiang K'ai-shek, of course) had married a Christian woman and to do so had had to put aside his concubines. Schooling, even though now under Chinese control, still caused tensions in the families of Christian students. These schools exposed students to Western material ways, and "to this extent Christianity has promoted foreign commercial interest in China"; indeed, Westernizing traits had "beclouded the real advantages of Christian education." For all that Christianity had yet to make a unified approach, "a cultural revolution had begun." Would the Church take the lead? None of the sure-fire inerrancy of his 1908 approach here!

In 1932, Rawlinson's keenest interest was in promoting the *Laymen's Report*[19] and he organized discussion groups on it. The central idea was that while Christianity was primary, it must shuck off all Western trappings and blend heartily and humbly with natives in the search for broad, ethical solutions to social questions, rather than limiting itself entirely to individual salvation. Actually, Rawlinson had been urging the Laymen's program piecemeal for years, save for the last point, which was that there should be a supradenominational board, to excite youthful idealism.

He had some reservations. In a report for the *Christian Century*, he objected that the *Report* did not stress the social gospel enough; perhaps also it overplayed the uniqueness of Christianity, which tended to diminish in confrontation with Buddhism and China's own ethical idealism. The *Report* would encourage the progressives, although only a few even of them were ready for its conclusions, and most Chinese Christians were trained to march with the conservatives. But if a break must come, let it! What was most dreadful to contemplate was that after all *nothing* might come of this brave proposal.

In a letter to a Shanghai colleague, Rawlinson was more candid. Some of the sponsors were getting palpitations; as for the superboard, he didn't see how it could work. Anyway, many hackles would rise. But here was the voice of the laity. Welcome it!

As for his influence on home base, note that Rawlinson for about a year kept a box score in the *Recorder* on support for the *Report*, but then he had to drop the tabulation, since indeed nothing was happening.

In the next few years, the tone and detail of Rawlinson's reporting to Boston changed but little, although there were some new topics, e.g., the New Life Movement, which soon enough was a disappointment.[20]

On special furlough in 1936, Rawlinson undertook a heavy schedule of deputation work. One talk was given to his Newton church, but the subject is lost. He did note to his wife, perhaps a bit primly, that at dinner afterwards smoking was general, including by "one or two quite young girls." Later, enroute to Indiana, he spoke at the First Congregational Church in Oberlin, marked for him mainly by his sale of a subscription to the pastor. Writing home to his wife in Shanghai, he recalled visiting the board rooms at Beacon Street, where his sense was that they were "keeping an enterprise going that runs in front of a failing wind." Another tidbit from a liberal: "The old appeal of thousands slipping into hell every minute no longer holds. . . . So far as I can see all the peoples of the world are lost together." Rawlinson's private mood came through in his telling his wife of being unable to advise a man who was running a school for expectant missionaries just what he ought to do. *Pace* Northfield!

In St. Louis (he failed to interest the manufacturer of Purina in the *Recorder*) he addressed four Congregational groups, saying that no one fed him for his pains. Wandering about (the movies were "so much of a muchness," said this veteran Shanghai moviegoer), he listened to a Salvation Army band, but felt that their words were dead. "I wonder sometimes if I regret having wandered so far from that simple faith and that naive use of words. Several times people have said that I give them a new idea about missions. Well, I guess I can't deal in *new* ideas and find meaning in the old ones too."

On the southern trail, headed for his daughter's home in South Carolina, he gave talks on subjects like "Christian World Life Goes On," "The Increasing Fellowship," and "The Future of Christianity in China." As for that, he was reassuring, although missions would no longer be the focal points. The backstage view he shared with his wife: "Fortunately, I do not have to make a new speech each time . . . though that way I do sometimes get tired of hearing myself speak. However, I feel I ought to help the board a little." He confessed that he was getting weary, but not too much to note that his rail fare to one out-of-the-way church just about equaled that group's entire contribution to missions last year.

At Southern Pines, North Carolina, he made a pottage of talks. One day was a real "sockdolager," his wife later read: two morning talks at Durham, then a drive to someplace called Haw River, which was "about the only dud of a meeting I have had. Only four or five people turned out; the afternoon was sultry. The only man present went to sleep before I had gotten started talking." Next, at Burlington, his host did not show, so the not-so-VIP had to hie himself to the church and a bolted supper after his talk. After that, though, at yet another place, he had a good crowd, "but was I tired!" Back at his hotel he asked for a whiskey and soda, but had to settle for hot milk. "What a day!"

Occasionally someone objected to his stress on the social gospel, and once a man "in somewhat sepulchral tone wanted to know if 'souls were being saved.' " But, in general, he found his hearers "liberal and open-minded."

At Greensboro, a mill town, the visitor talked of mill conditions in Shanghai, which "seemed to click." But the round of missed connections, dirty towels, rotten train and bus service, and the famine of mail made him feel "like a highjacker fleeing from justice." Some people asked him if he knew so-and-so in China; of course, he was inveigled into talking Chinese, but he refused to sing! "To some extent I am a curiosity. I have found much interest in missions though I am inclined to decide," he wrote home, "that it is now a sort of waning interest kept up by the inertia of the spirit of the elderly members. . . . After all I just flit into a church and out again . . . a sort of aerial bombardment with little chance for anti-aircraft guns to work on me," he said, unwittingly deploying a figure of speech which foreshadowed his own death within the year.

There were highlights. One pastor was interested to meet the man who wrote for *Christian Century*—and subscribed to the *Recorder*! Rawlinson's statistical recap showed five speeches in St. Louis, then twenty-three days in Virginia with as many stops, reaching twenty-five churches and making thirty-four speeches.

At his daughter's home in Florence, he seemed to be accepted as a Baptist. At a reception he shook hands "with umpteen women some with hands like dry leaves and others with hands cold and fishy and heard them say they were *glad* to see me and I reciprocated. . . . What a whopper! The pastor of the Baptist Church wants me to speak. But I don't know. I cannot talk in Southern Baptist terms. But I may risk it if he insists." The Lions Club held no such lurking dangers. Actually, he talked to Baptists four times, unscathed, which was "pretty good for one kicked out of that fellowship," he gloated to his wife. One Southern Presbyterian invitation, by a man related to one of his most ardent China critics, caused more hesitation, but he toned down an expression or two. The pastor could only bring himself to say, later, "Glad you came!" One or two hearers were more forthcoming, however.

Florence also boasted a burlesque show, but Rawlinson did not go—in fact, he told his wife, he had caught it at Greensboro, characterizing it as "a third-rate leg show. It was not so hot! Advertising placards are much worse than the show," he went on, adding, as one who knows, "as usual."

At last, enroute home to Shanghai and the residue of his family, Rawlinson wrote from the *Empress of Canada* to the larger Stateside contingent of that family:

> I read about four books a day jumping from Oppenheim to Gertrude Atherton without restraint. In these books I have touched the various countries in East and West and most of them deal with the sorrows and perplexities of women. All of

them treat of man's romantic reach after a vision . . . that ever eludes them. When shall we catch up with our dreams? Heaven, I presume, will be made up of the dreams we have caught . . . the worthwhile memories we have accumulated. If we have had neither dreams nor memories, why how can there be any heaven? The last six months have laid up many pleasant memories but all the time I have felt like a wanderer lacking any reason for my wandering.

It is difficult to assess the influence Rawlinson had on home-base opinion, particularly since this account has been based on his own record, with little tracking of published reactions along the trail of talks. Clearly at first, in 1908, he talked in terms consonant with smug stereotypes of his American listeners, although he did soon start to think of missionaries as "foreign helpers," which did not exactly fit the Northfield image. It is significant that the board secretary in Richmond felt it necessary to edit his field reports before making newsletters of them; evidently, some things he said might have the wrong sort of influence. Along this line was the reaction of the editor of the *Western Recorder*, a Southern home-base Baptist paper, alluded to briefly above, who excoriated Rawlinson and his liberal colleagues for supporting the unionist movement for national missionary field organizations—e.g., the China Continuation Committee. A baleful influence that had to be countered!

After the War, Rawlinson was nowhere near so cocksure about Western and/or Christian supremacy or the role of the missionary. In connection with the growing pressure to end extraterritoriality, he was a leader, in his editorials and in the pages of the liberal *Christian Century*, whose China correspondent he became. But, of course, the glacial pace of change in that system hardly augurs that he exercised as much influence as he hoped to. And as for the explosive *Laymen's Report* of 1932, one might say that since he had advocated most of its ideas for years, his editorials and counsel played a significant role in its formulation—but since virtually nothing came of it all, one cannot see here what he wanted to see, at any rate.

In the 1930s, his religious disillusion affected his private outlook and, to some extent, his public comments on furlough, although, of course, there was hardly a one-to-one correlation. His frequent request to the American board not to publish some of his ruminations is suggestive of his own assessment of his influence. His extensive deputationizing in 1936 was orthodox enough, but his wry comments on it to his wife suggest that at times he must have lacked fire. Indeed, China changed him more than he did the home base. Is that surprising?

Notes

1. James Reed, *The Missionary Mind and American East Asian Policy, 1911–1915* (Cambridge: Harvard University Press, 1983), p. 25.
2. The *Chinese Recorder*, a nondenominational English-language monthly, was about fifty years old when Rawlinson (FJR) became editor. See Kathleen Lodwick, Index to *The Chinese Recorder* (Wilmington, DE: Scholarly Resources, Inc., 1986), Introduction.

3. FJR's correspondence with the Southern Baptist Board is preserved in its Jenkins Memorial Library and Archives Center in Richmond; later correspondence with the American Board of Commissioners for Foreign Missions is in the ABCFM papers at the Houghton Library, Harvard; personal letters are kept in the Day Missions Library of the Yale Divinity School. No attempt is made in this paper to document all references, which is, of course, done in my full-scale biography of FJR.

4. A boycott protesting the U.S. Exclusion Act; see Paul A. Varg, *Missionaries, Chinese, and Diplomats: The American Protestant Missionary Movement in China, 1890–1952* (Princeton: Princeton University Press, 1958), p. 135.

5. The Boxer Rebellion of 1900 ravaged North China, but fears of a recurrence were very active in Shanghai's foreign community.

6. See Immanual C. Y. Hsu, *The Rise of Modern China* (New York: Oxford University Press, 1970), ch. 17, "Reform and Constitutionalism at the End of the Ch'ing Period."

7. A reference to the "pigtail" hair style required of all males by the Manchus.

8. Extraterritorial rights for foreigners dated to the so-called "unequal treaties" of the Opium War. The system was increasingly obnoxious to China's new patriots, particularly after May 4, 1919.

9. See Hu Shih, *The Development of Logical Method in Ancient China* (Shanghai: Oriental Book Company, 1922), pp. 4–5. To modern Chinese scholars like Hu, Wang's distortion of the Confucian tradition was at the root of China's evils.

10. The May 30, 1925 explosion followed shootings of Chinese by British-led police in Shanghai. See Hsu, *The Rise of Modern China*, p. 627.

11. To revise the unilateral tariff provision in the "unequal treaties"; see Dorothy Borg, *American Policy and the Chinese Revolution, 1925–1928* (New York: American Institute of Pacific Relations and Macmillan, 1947), ch. 6.

12. An attack by British gunboats on this upriver Yangtze port, producing some 3,000 Chinese casualties. See T. F. Millard, *China, Where It Is Today and Why!* (New York: Harcourt, Brace, 1928), pp. 133–35, for a contemporary account.

13. A watershed in the Nationalist Northern Expedition, in which Chiang K'ai-shek bloodily terminated the shaky alliance with the Chinese Communists. See Hsu, *The Rise of Modern China*, pp. 614–24, for context.

14. March 24, 1927. This attack killed six foreigners and induced panic in the foreign community. See Borg, *American Policy,* ch. 14.

15. Registration of Christian schools involved control of curriculum and installation of Chinese officers.

16. Feng was the so-called "Christian General." See James F. Sheridan, *Chinese Warlord, the Career of Feng Yu-hsiang* (Stanford: Stanford University Press, 1966).

17. A sharp clash between Japanese troops and China's Northern Expedition; Hsu, *The Rise of Modern China*, p. 623, for context.

18. Another step taken by Japanese Kwangtung Army conspirators to start a war with China. See Hsu, *The Rise of Modern China*, pp. 644–45. They succeeded in taking Manchuria.

19. The Laymen were a liberal nondenominational group that advocated a thorough overhaul of the U.S. missionary effort in China. See *Rethinking Missions, a Laymen's Inquiry After 100 Years* (New York: Harper & Brothers, 1932).

20. Chiang K'ai-shek's abortive answer to Communism. For a critical account, see Lloyd Eastman, *China Under Nationalist Rule, 1927–1937* (Cambridge: Harvard University Press, 1974).

7

IDA PRUITT
Heir and Critic of
American Missionary Reform Efforts in China

Marjorie King

Ida Pruitt, best known today as the author of *A Daughter of Han: The Autobiography of a Chinese Working Woman*, was born in 1888 in P'eng-lai, Shantung, the daughter of Southern Baptist missionaries. Her childhood and young adulthood were spent largely within the mission community in North China, where she taught at her parents' school, 1912–18. She subsequently turned from a missionary vocation to professional social work. She founded and directed the Department of Social Service at the Peking Union Medical College (PUMC), 1921–38. After China's occupation by Japan, she organized and eventually became the Executive Secretary of Indusco: The American Committee of the Chinese Industrial Cooperatives, 1939–52. She authored several now-classic books about traditional Chinese women and numerous essays about China.[1] Finally, Pruitt spoke in favor of American recognition of the People's Republic of China after 1949. As an administrator at several China-based American reform institutions, as a writer, and as a political activist, Ida Pruitt was a prominent figure during the century of America's "special relationship" with China.

This chapter, based on the private papers of Ida Pruitt and her mother, Anna Seward Pruitt, on Ida Pruitt's published oral history, essays, and social work articles, and on the archives of the Rockefeller Foundation and the Chinese Industrial Cooperatives, will place Ida Pruitt in the context of Western efforts to help China. It will argue that, although Ida Pruitt worked in China-based Western reform institutions her entire life and translated a number of missionary themes into secular terms, she differed fundamentally in motivation and achievement from other Western reformers, including other children of missionaries ("mish-kids"). The origins and significance of Pruitt's differences will be suggested. Finally, the paper will speculate on Ida Pruitt as a neglected resource for United States policy makers and journalists blind to the development of a revolutionary situation among the Chinese peasantry during the 1930s and 1940s.

The Southern Baptist Mission station in Huang-hsien, Shantung, was the childhood home of Ida Pruitt and her younger brothers. Her father and mother, C. W. and Anna Pruitt, reestablished the mission station in 1887 and were the only Westerners for many years at Huang-hsien. In many ways, Anna Pruitt typified the Western advisers described by Jonathan Spence in *To Change China: Western Advisers in China, 1620–1960*. Anna established a boys' school and a medical clinic and conducted woman's work among Chinese women, assuming that Western scientific education, the English language, and Christian ideals would transform a morally depraved people into a progressive, Western-oriented civilization. As did military officers, political officials, engineers, merchants, physicians, and other missionaries, Anna assumed Western superiority based on moral righteousness and technological advance. Like the others, Anna was seriously disappointed by China's rejection of her efforts. Her confidence in American civilization and in herself blinded Anna to question by what right she had tried to change China.[2]

C. W. Pruitt shared his wife's evangelical and educational commitment but was much less enamored of Western scientific advances and patterns of modernization. He engaged a Chinese tutor, studied the Confucian classics, devoted much of his life to the translation of Christian theology into Chinese, and generally seemed more at home in agrarian villages than did his wife. He adopted Chinese dress and enjoyed evangelizing ("itinerating") widely throughout rural Shantung. He was influenced by the experiences of Lottie Moon, a unique Southern Baptist missionary who lived alone among Chinese villagers during the 1870s and concluded that she and other Western missionaries were no better human beings than the Chinese peasants.[3]

Ida Pruitt identified with her Sinified father and reacted strongly against her mother's zeal to Americanize China. The Chinese "amah" or nanny, whom Ida and her brother John called "Dada," exerted as strong a formative influence on the American children as did their own mother.[4] Ida's relationships with Dada and her Sinified father were nurturing and emotionally satisfying, while her relationships with her mother and the Chinese Christians were conflict ridden and intrusive.[5]

Most of Ida Pruitt's childhood and adolescence were spent in the mission compound rather than at the China Inland Mission boarding school in Chefoo where many "mish-kids" were sent. Pruitt's autobiographical reflections, written in her retirement years, associate the sights of Chinese architectural patterns and the smells of Chinese foods and indigo dye with her earliest and fondest childhood memories.[6] She deeply resented her mother's American menus and failed efforts to transform the Chinese compound into a midwestern American home. As expressed directly in private writings and as portrayed symbolically in her description of the Westernized architectural remodeling of the compound, this early identification with the Chinese people and culture and hostility toward the Western missionaries such as her mother and Westernized Christian converts helped to shape and give conviction to lifelong attitudes and political leanings.

Many missionary children were raised in China by amahs. John S. Service and John Paton Davies are well-known examples of "mish-kids" who, as U.S. Foreign Service officers, devoted their lives to bettering relations between the countries of their birth and their ancestry. Ida's younger brother, John, planned a career in the Foreign Service but died the day before his appointment arrived. It is impossible to know whether or not Ida would have applied for the Foreign Service in China if it had been open to women.[7] Ida Pruitt differed from most "mish-kids," however, in her prolonged isolation from Western culture and, perhaps, in the problematic nature of her relationship with her own mother, both of which deepened her early identification with China.

Ida Pruitt's early career path was a typical one for American daughters of missionaries in her generation. After graduating from Cox College, Georgia, and studying at Columbia Teacher's College, she returned to China, taught at her parents' mission schools in Chefoo, and became the school principal by 1918. She was appointed to a 1917 committee to draft China-wide mission curricula but rejected the chance for advancement in mission education. "I was alarmed. I did not want to dry up into a missionary school teacher." Neither did she accept American consul Julean Arnold's invitation to organize the new American School in Peking.[8]

By the summer of 1918, at the age of twenty-nine, Ida Pruitt was restless to escape the missions and foreign settlements. She resigned from the mission school and worked in the United States for a year as a social worker. In 1919, she eagerly applied for the position of medical social worker at the newly-established Peking Union Medical College (PUMC) because it represented an opportunity to live in Peking, to meet Westerners outside missionary circles, and to work among Chinese of all classes and backgrounds. Her expressed motivation bore none of the religious, reformist, or romantic overtones of most Americans bound for China.

The China Medical Board of the Rockefeller Foundation operated on different assumptions when deciding to hire Pruitt as the social worker for the PUMC. A native Chinese speaker, an experienced social worker, and the daughter of Southern Baptist missionaries, Pruitt appeared to be a religiously motivated "do-gooder."[9]

The PUMC in 1919 stood on the narrow ground between a clinically oriented missionary hospital and a secular research institution. The forces of professionalism soon outweighed those of evangelism, but for many years the Christian mission of the hospital was given token acknowledgment, largely out of respect for John D. Rockefeller, Jr., a devout Baptist.[10] Hiring a professionally trained social worker with proper Southern Baptist credentials helped to forestall the decision to abandon completely the PUMC's missionary origins.[11]

As head of the Social Services Department, Pruitt soon grew as restive in the Western reformist institution as she had in the mission station. The PUMC goal, China's national salvation through medical research, professional training, disease prevention, and institutional care, superseded nineteenth-century mission goals of individual salvation through evangelism and treatment of disease. However, the impulse to change China to a Western model surged through doctor and missionary alike.[12]

Both were anathema to Ida Pruitt. She was appalled by the arrogance and ignorance of the Western physicians and Western-trained Chinese physicians toward the simple peasantry and working people who represented the majority of PUMC patients. Pruitt felt that most of the PUMC professional staff members were motivated by private career ambitions or social reform agendas such as the public health movement initiated by Dr. John Grant, rather than by a desire to promote recovery, alleviate suffering, and restore China's social order, the goals of her department.[13]

Although Pruitt assigned members of her social-work staff to social agencies, she saw the primary purpose of her department as one of mediation, not reform.[14] She and the caseworkers she trained mediated between patients and their families, potential employers, the Western hospital staff, and—all too often—the Westernized Chinese staff. They attempted to bridge differences in language, culture, and class. Agencies created by the Social Service Department all worked toward the same goals of promoting recovery and adjustment of individual patients within the Chinese order.

The divergent premises and goals of the Social Service Department and the larger institution occasioned conflict at the PUMC. Many of the PUMC staff and the China Medical Board administrators failed to understand the purpose of the department as distinct from the Department of Religious and Social Work and public health nursing. Pruitt was pressured to dispense Bibles and offer prayers to patients, to establish an orphanage run by the physicians' wives, and to perform nursing tasks while making home visits. Throughout the eighteen years of Pruitt's tenure as head of social service, reorganization plans sometimes called for the merger of her department with nursing or with religious work.[15]

However, the medical staff and administrators who had personal involvement with the social-service staff invariably defended the department's role at the hospital. The Social Service Department was said to have "unbelievable follow-up results" and performed an essential "mission of friendship" between the PUMC and the Chinese public, according to a 1923 questionnaire.[16] Under Pruitt's tutelage, the department established the model for professional social casework throughout China.[17]

Pruitt's social workers recorded thousands of case histories that documented the individual and family lives of Chinese peasants and urban workers during the convulsive social upheaval of the 1920s and 1930s. Olga Lang's *Chinese Family and Society* was based to a large extent on the Social Service Department records. Karl Wittfogel, aware of the records' uniqueness as a large-scale sociological survey of the Chinese common people in transition, unsuccessfully urged the China Medical Board to ship the patient records to the United States as the Japanese grew nearer to Peking.[18]

Pruitt's patient care, caseworker training, and lectures on social casework at Yenching University involved her directly with Chinese of all walks of life. She instructed urban, Western-educated students in the ways of their own people. Wherever possible, she resolved patient dilemmas according to Chinese custom. Former patients treated her with the affectionate respect of an elder teacher or family member. She utilized the Rockefeller Foundation's material resources to ease patient transition from hospital to community but refused to promote Christianity, Western ideas, or institutional reform.[19]

If Ida Pruitt had no desire to reform Chinese society or shape American institutions, she strongly aspired to influence American attitudes and policy toward China. In 1938 her position at the PUMC was transferred to a Chinese administrator in accordance with the Rockefeller Foundation policy of recruiting Chinese leadership.[20] Pruitt applied widely for other employment. Being a fifty-year-old social worker without the possibility of entering the U.S. Foreign Service, which was available to her brother and to other missionary sons, her options were few.

Pruitt had begun writing about China for professional social service journals and the *Atlantic Monthly* in the late 1920s, and she considered writing to be her true vocation. However she was unable to support herself by writing about China. In light of the noted ignorance about China among American policy makers and journalists, Pruitt's proficient Chinese language skills and lifelong association with the Chinese peasantry would have been an enormous resource. American journalism's failure to utilize Ida Pruitt's knowledge may be explained by the press's attitudes of superficial romanticism, elitism, and adventurism toward China. Sexism against women in journalism played a lesser role in China than elsewhere; about 10 percent of American journalists in China were women, twice the number assigned to Europe.[21]

In the absence of other channels for influencing American policy and attitudes toward China, Ida Pruitt joined the Chinese Industrial Cooperatives. The CIC, initiated in 1938 by Edgar and Helen Foster (Peg) Snow and New Zealander Rewi Alley, offered an alternative to complete Chinese dependence on American aid and relief during the Japanese occupation. Thirty thousand small, decentralized industrial production units, owned and managed by the workers, were to utilize local materials and markets to provide both war and civilian goods, thereby creating much-needed jobs for coastal refugees and local peasants.[22] The industrial cooperatives were a China-aid movement Ida Pruitt could support wholeheartedly. While eschewing dependence on Western charity, expertise, and leadership for Chinese self-help, the industrial cooperatives offered Pruitt a significant role in the Chinese resistance against Japanese encroachment.

Pruitt organized the International Committee for the CIC in Hong Kong, then founded "Indusco," the American Committee in Aid of the Chinese Industrial Cooperatives. Between 1939 and 1952 she engaged in fund-raising and public relations on behalf of the CIC and was the executive secretary of Indusco after 1944.[23]

Pruitt was a consistent proponent of local cooperative control and planning, advocated by the Snows, Rewi Alley, and the International Committee based in Hong Kong. Over and against this strategy was the centralized strategy of H. H. Kung, appointed by Chiang Kai-shek to head the Central Headquarters for the CIC in Chungking, and the Western-trained Chinese Board of Directors of the CIC Institute.[24] United China Relief (UCR), of which Indusco was a part after 1941, sided with the Central Headquarters in Chungking. Pruitt feared that the UCR elements "trying to control all China Aid and get it into the hands of missionaries and of the Kuomintang" would have a stultifying effect upon the movement.[25]

The Kuomintang and others suspected the CIC of Communist leanings because the industrial cooperatives spread throughout both Communist and Nationalist-controlled areas of Free China. Edgar Snow conceived of Pruitt's role as key to channeling some portion of Indusco funds to cooperatives in the Communist-controlled regions of China at a time when the U.S. government was dramatically increasing its wartime aid to China and when Generalissimo and Madam Chiang were championed as China's only legitimate national leaders.[26] Rewi Alley vividly recalled forty years later that Ida Pruitt "was a very tough fighter. . . . She knew a good deal about all these little . . . gangs . . . trying to seize power, . . . push over the top person. . . . She held on like grim death there. . . . It meant a great deal to us to have that support."[27]

According to Peg Snow's recollections, Ida Pruitt walked a fine line between the conservative and left wings of Indusco. Snow believed Pruitt's close association with missionaries paved a "very rocky road" of political faction fighting within Indusco. "All the Protestants trusted Ida Pruitt as compared with any other person." Peg Snow perceived Pruitt's major role to be one of mediating between the Luce/Rockefeller/missionary-controlled UCR, which supported Kung's Central Headquarters, and the International Committee, which favored local control.

Another major focus of Ida Pruitt's Indusco work was the American public. She wrote and spoke widely throughout the United States. Judging from personal notes penned by small Indusco contributors, Pruitt generated sympathy and support among Americans of all walks of life for the Chinese resistance against Japan.[28]

Indusco remained in existence after the end of the Japanese occupation and throughout the Chinese Civil War, sending funds after 1947 directly to Rewi Alley's Sandan Bailie School in Kansu province instead of through the International Committee.[29] After the Communists came to power in 1949, many American supporters of Indusco, disheartened by our "loss" of China, discontinued their financial contributions. Pruitt's lengthy personal letters to dozens of former supporters emphasized the apolitical nature of the Bailie School.

Consistent with Indusco's nonpartisan position during Kuomintang rule,

Pruitt reassured supporters that aid to the school did not imply endorsement of the Communist government.

> Our desire to help the Chinese people help themselves is not conditional on endorsement, or lack of endorsement, of the newly-established government; just as Indusco's aid to the Chinese people in the past did not imply approval or disapproval of the former regime.[30]

If Pruitt's position on Chinese internal politics was muted, she openly voiced her opinion on U.S. China policy. Often referring to Chinese and American history, she strongly supported China's struggle against semicolonial dependence. In an oblique reference to the Korean War and to the U.S. support of Chiang Kai-shek on Taiwan, she asserted,

> there is no evidence that the Chinese want in any way to export their way of life or government. . . . They do not want war. But they want their borders inviolate, and these borders include the minorities that have for many centuries been a part of China.[31]

Pruitt responded to the concerns of former missionaries and other Christians alarmed by reports of Communist persecution of missionaries and the takeover of Christian churches and colleges. She emphasized the development of native leadership in the Chinese Christian churches as a positive consequence of political events. She referred to the "vibrant spirit of service" among Bailie leaders, Chinese and Western, which derived from their Christian upbringing.[32] As Pruitt helped American Christians to understand China's transition from Western reform to Communist revolution, she completed her own transition from missionary reformer to critic of American China policy.

During the 1950s and 1960s, Pruitt spoke about China at public forums and living-room gatherings. She drew as much on anecdotes from her childhood in Huang-hsien and her work at the PUMC as on personal letters from friends remaining in China and her own trip to China in 1959 as an honored guest of the Chinese people.[33] Interweaving descriptions of life in contemporary China with references to Chinese history, geography, philosophy, and economics, she stressed the common humanity behind tremendously different material and cultural foundations.[34] Her political message was a simple one of international relations based on diplomacy and nonintervention.

> It is my faith that if our government in Washington would recognize China is a nation in the world, as we recognize a neighbor even if we don't like the way he runs his family affairs, and talk the whole matter over, that a way of living in the same world can be found.[35]

Pruitt admitted her limited understanding of the current government in China and refrained from commenting on particular policies or leaders. However, her general support of the People's Republic of China and opposition to the United States–imposed "bamboo curtain" was clear. The curtain raised a wall of ignorance about China in America. To one who always considered herself a bridge between the two countries, the U.S. policy was intolerable. "It is not easy to talk to people in this country about China, either to its friends or to those who fear it. It is neither heaven on earth nor a man-made hell."[36]

In this statement, Ida Pruitt expressed her differences from left-leaning American reformers as well as the pro–Chiang Kai-shek majority. Pruitt shared many political views with American liberals and radicals who challenged myths of America's special relationship to China, of Chiang Kai-shek's popularity as a democratic nationalist who remained China's legitimate leader after fleeing to Taiwan, and myths of the Chinese Communists' foreign aggressiveness.[37] She deplored the McCarthy attacks on Foreign Service officers John S. Service and John Paton Davies, on China scholar Owen Lattimore, and on William Holland of the Institute for Pacific Relations. However, her life and work challenged deeper myths often held by Americans across the political spectrum. The vast majority of Westerners, drawn to China by desires to save or reform a backward people, tacitly assumed the superiority of Western institutions and values. They differed only in their institution of preference: Christianity, science, democracy, or revolution.[38] Missionaries and merchants of previous centuries shared with journalists and do-gooders of the twentieth century a personality of risk-taking and a quest for adventure and meaning in the exotic, pitiful East.[39]

In contrast, Pruitt identified with the Chinese people and culture to an unusual degree due to a prolonged immersion in a traditional village, a distant relationship with her mother, and close relationships with her amah, her Sinified father, and Lottie Moon. She respected Chinese civilization as equal (if not superior!) to Western civilization and trusted in the ability of the Chinese people to solve their own problems. She saw her role at the PUMC and in Indusco as a mediator between traditional Chinese and modern Westerners and as a channel for funds from the Rockefeller Foundation and the United China Relief to the Chinese common people.

No doubt the number of Americans who heard Ida Pruitt speak or who read her articles and letters was small. Relatively few understood or agreed with Pruitt's position of noninterference in China's internal affairs and China's formal recognition by the United States and the United Nations. Her impact on American attitudes toward China, though significant, was definitely a part of a minor tradition of anti-imperialism in the United States.[40]

Ida Pruitt probably reached more Americans through her literary writing than through her political talks and articles. Her portrayal of traditional China has left a more enduring legacy than her defense of contemporary China. However, Pruitt's best-known work, *A Daughter of Han: The Autobiography of a Chinese Working*

Woman, received with critical acclaim at the time of publication in 1945, drew wide attention from American students of Asia only with its reissue by Stanford University Press in 1967.[41] *Old Madam Yin: A Memoir of Life in Peking, 1926–1938*, was ignored by publishers until Stanford published it in 1979. Pruitt also wrote many short stories and essays which, like her stories of Madams Ning and Yin, were based on the lives of the Chinese she knew in Peking. Most have never been published.

Judging from the difficulty that Pruitt had in publishing her stories and essays, as well as the comments by the numerous publishers who rejected her manuscripts, the themes and images of Chinese people and culture that Pruitt presented were not popular with American audiences. Most striking of Pruitt's themes were the capability of Chinese women and the meddlesome quality of foreign interference in Chinese civilization.

A Daughter of Han is the narration of Ning Lao T'ai-t'ai's life of hardship and ever declining fortunes from her childhood in P'eng-lai, Shantung, to her marriage to an "opium sot," her years working for Western missionaries and Chinese officials, and her struggles to reunite the family and support her children. Pruitt's book portrays a woman whose "gift of humor and of seeing things as they are" overcame her bitter destiny; her strength of character and dignity in the face of adversity represented the finest of the Chinese spirit.[42] The book's title, itself, honors China's women as heroines, female counterparts of "hao han-tze"—virile sons of the Han race.

In recording Ning's life story, Pruitt let Ning's voice speak throughout the book. Brutality and tenderness, weakness and strength coexist on each page. It is a sympathetic but unsentimental presentation.

In one example of this, Ning told of childhood beatings by her mother. "She broke a broom over me. She broke a stool beating me. I screamed and said that I would not do it any more. She said, 'The more you say you will not, the more I will beat you.'" Ning tempered the brutality of this story with comical descriptions of her own misdemeanors and of the chickens who divulged her misdemeanors to her mother ("the chickens did not give us face"). Ning's presentation was neither a defense nor a condemnation of her mother for the beatings, but simply a comment on the difficulties and heartaches between mother and child.[43]

Likewise, in a passage about foot-binding, Ning's tone is that of recounting to a close friend the love and care which motivated her mother to bind her daughter's feet. Ning felt no need to justify or condemn the painful practice or her mother's role in perpetuating it. Nor did Ida Pruitt, as Ning's biographer, feel any need for editorial comment on the practices of foot-binding and child abuse.

Pruitt's presentation of Madam Ning was a striking departure from writings about Chinese customs such as her mother and other women missionaries wrote.[44] Throughout the nineteenth century, mission societies inspired both financial contributions and calls to overseas service by the publication of lurid stories about Asian women's brutal oppression and victimization. Missionary women's goal was to save the lives and souls of Asian women through Christian conversion, a goal that was furthered by their portrayal of women as oppressed victims to their congregations in America.

Anna Pruitt's reaction to her daughter's treatment of Chinese womanhood in *A Daughter of Han* was to call it a "huge dose of unvarnished heathenism . . . [and] a direct call to increased evangelistic effort."[45] She failed to see the extent to which Madam Ning had succeeded in responding with dignity to her fate, meeting violence and brutality with strength, compassion, and resourcefulness.

Drawing on her Chinese friends, acquaintances, and PUMC patients' lives, Ida Pruitt might well have carried on the themes of victimization, oppression, and sexual submission expressed in other Western literature about China, including her mother's writings. From thousands of hospital cases, she might have chosen Pai Shun-ke who, like Ning, had a husband whose opium addiction had brought the family to ruin. Pai chose the route of a suicide attempt, while Ning chose to work, first as a servant and finally by begging, in order to feed her children.

Both suicide and begging were traditional solutions to women's problems. Missionary women and novelists focused on Chinese women as victims. Ida Pruitt clearly chose to portray a very different sense of the ordinary Chinese woman. Pruitt wrote about women who participated in shaping their fate within Chinese tradition. A feisty soul who rebuilt her life and household after years of servitude and begging, Ning's strength came from within herself and her tradition, rather than by blaming and rejecting that tradition. Pruitt's selection of Ning for her literary model over either the victims of the tradition or the feminist rebels against tradition was her response to the missionaries and reformers who decried traditional Chinese society and sought to change it.

The focus of Pruitt's defense turned from the peasantry and folk culture to the gentry and Chinese civilization with her essay, *Old Madam Yin: A Memoir of Life in Peking, 1926–1938*. True to its subtitle, the essay was a reminiscence of an aristocratic friend told in Pruitt's voice. In the pattern of Yin's dress and speech, her design of courtyards and interior rooms, in every lift of the eyebrow Pruitt found the character of Madam Yin's personality and Chinese civilization at its finest.[46]

Pruitt's presentation of Yin left little room for the problems and weaknesses in Chinese civilization.[47] Pruitt placed Madam Yin above the multiple crises of the historic moment in which she lived, a memorial to China's greatness prior to the onslaught by foreigners who—this time—could not be absorbed.

The memoir of Madam Yin continued themes begun in the biography of Ning and expressed in Pruitt's social and political work. The aristocratic Yin, no less than the earthy Ning, was able to develop personal strength, astute managerial skills, and considerable wisdom within the confines of the traditional Chinese social structure and value system.[48]

Pruitt's disapproval of the missionaries and "do-gooders" reform impulse also emerged in her memoir of Yin. In a revealing passage, Pruitt caught her own critical evaluation of Madam Yin's rental property: "There was something wrong with that black-and-white pattern (of unfinished houses)." The low walls and small, narrow courtyards provided little privacy for the six poor families crowded into the space normally occupied by one "middle-class" family. Pruitt searched for a redeeming quality in the cramped quarters and was relieved to see that her friend-turned-landlady had constructed the houses to withstand the rains of many Peking summers. Madam Yin bore the responsibilities of her position and had not just sought immediate profit. Yin's motive for building the apartments was also one, albeit a modern one, of which Pruitt approved: "I'm building these houses for my granddaughter. They're to put her through college."[49]

Pruitt's account immediately moved beyond criticism and approval of Madam Yin to a reflection on her own reactions to her friend's business affairs:

> Why after all should I expect Lao T'ai-t'ai to go beyond the pattern of the way of life in which she had been brought up and in which she lived? Why should I expect her to think of people outside her family, her own circle? Was not her duty to get all she could for her own family?[50]

In questioning her right to impose her own values onto a Chinese friend, Pruitt questioned all Westerners' rights to judge and attempt to change China.

Although both of Ida Pruitt's works on Chinese women were well received by the scholarly community and represent her lasting contribution to Sino-American relations, Pruitt's writing has not captured the public imagination in the way missionaries and novelists have done.[51] Pruitt eschewed the popular American images of Asians as inscrutable and Asian women as either erotic objects or silent victims. The violence she portrayed was the tragic, inevitable consequence of forces outside the control of individuals. In place of villains and victims were complex personalities whose actions were rarely clear-cut. They challenged the American stereotype of China as "the sick man of Asia" in need of salvation. Through the voices of Chinese women, Pruitt confronted Americans' most cherished national myths—the superiority of our political, economic, social, and religious institutions and our consequent obligation to export these institutions abroad.

Yet, in the self-reflective discussion of Madam Yin's rental property above, Pruitt revealed herself as more of a Western outsider than she generally liked to admit. In fact, she was an effective bridge between Chinese and American culture, especially between missionary do-gooders and their clients, because she straddled both cultures. Although she objected to much that the PUMC represented in China, she was a loyal and effective administrator in the American reform institution for eighteen years. She did not oppose all change in China, rather she directed the Rockefeller resources to ameliorate the worst repercussions of China's inevitable transformation. Her "mission of friendship" to the Chinese public helped to promote PUMC programs.

Pruitt continued to work among Western-oriented reformers during the Indusco years. She worked closely with missionaries and other Americans who devoted their lives to China's salvation, even as she fought for local Chinese control. Her effective fund-raising among American Christians owed much to her identification with the missionaries, as much as she objected to the mission boards' policies and political alliances. To those who mistook her anti-interventionist stance for Communist sympathies, she evoked both biblical and Confucian values in her defense.[52]

Pruitt's writing, while an act of preserving China's tradition against the Western onslaught, also continued missionary efforts to garner American public support for the Chinese cause through the written word. Her mission had become a secular, relativist one of promoting world peace through understanding. But she, like her mother and numerous other missionary women, furthered her mission by recording the lives of Chinese women as she perceived them.

Pruitt was one of the most effective interpreters of Chinese and American cultures to each other, a critical supporter of China's, and arguably the most sensitive American chronicler of Chinese women's lives. Yet, because she implicitly challenged America's deepest myths about ourselves and the Chinese, and perhaps because she was among the first generation of American professional women working abroad, her influence and achievements never moved beyond the personal level. Her perspectives, knowledge, contacts, and even her patient files were ignored as serious resources by the American government, press, and scholarly community.[53]

Notes

1. *A Daughter of Han: The Autobiography of a Chinese Working Woman* (New Haven: Yale University Press, 1964) has become one of the top fifteen best-sellers since Stanford University Press reissued it in 1967. *Old Madam Yin: A Memoir of Peking Life, 1926–1938* (Stanford University Press, 1976) has received equally positive critical reviews although its publishing record has not matched Pruitt's earlier work. Ida Pruitt has also published the following: "Day By Day in Peking," *The Atlantic Monthly* 147 (January–June, 1932), 611–19; "New Year's Eve in Peking," *The Atlantic Monthly* 149 (January–June, 1931), 47–53; "Faith," *The Atlantic Monthly* 150 (July–December, 1932), 782–83; "Husbands and Wives," *Democracy* (Peiping: 22 June 1937), 122–26; "Hospital Social Service in Diagnosis and Treatment," *Chinese Medical Journal* (June 1928), n. pag; "Medical Social Workers: Their Work and Training," *Chinese Medical Journal* 49 (1935), 909–16; "Social Work for Children in a Hospital," *Chinese Medical Journal* 50 (1936), 623–25; "A Study of Sixty-Nine Adopted Children," *Hospital Social Service* (September 1931), 157–83. Pruitt also translated Wu Yung, *The Flight of an Empress*, transcribed by Liu K'un, introduced by Kenneth Scott Latourette (New Haven: Yale University Press, 1936, reissued by Hyperion Press, 1973), and Lau Shaw (Lao She), *Yellow Storm* (New York: Harcourt, Brace and Co., 1951).

2. Anna Pruitt's published articles are part of an extensive collection of papers, private letters, photographs, and other materials of the Pruitt family temporarily in the possession

of Marjorie King, pending deposit in the Arthur and Elizabeth Schlesinger Library on the History of Women in America. For a complete listing of the papers, see Archie R. Crouch, *Christianity in China: A Scholars' Guide to Resources in the Libraries and Archives of the United States* (Armonk, NY: M. E. Sharpe, 1989). Anna Pruitt's evangelical work is described by Marjorie King, "Exporting Femininity, not Feminism: Nineteenth Century U.S. Missionary Women's Efforts to Emancipate Chinese Women," in Leslie A. Flemming, ed., *Woman's Work for Women: Missionaries and Social Change in Asia* (Boulder: Westview Press, 1989).

3. Marjorie King, "A Georgia Evangelist in the Celestial Empire: Cicero Washington Pruitt (1857–1946)," in Jonathan Goldstein, ed., *Georgia's East Asian Connection: Into the Twenty-First Century* (Carrollton, GA: West Georgia College, forthcoming).

4. For an analysis of Ida Pruitt's relationships with her mother and amah, and the literary expression of these relationships in her biographies of traditional Chinese women, see Marjorie King, "Ida Pruitt: Biographer of *A Daughter of Han* and *Old Madam Yin*," presented at the Conference on Autobiography and Biography: Gender, Text and Context, Stanford University, 1986.

5. Ida Pruitt, *A China Childhood* (San Francisco: Chinese Materials Center, 1978).

6. Ida Pruitt, *A China Childhood*. See also deleted autobiographical chapters, Pruitt papers.

7. The first woman sent abroad with the U.S. Foreign Service was Lucile Atcherson who was assigned to Switzerland in 1925. In 1928 the entrance exam for the Foreign Service was opened to all American Citizens, regardless of sex, between the ages of 21 and 35. Ida Pruitt was then 40 years old. Homer L. Calkin, *Women in the Department of State: Their Role in American Foreign Affairs*, Department of State Publication 8951, Department and Foreign Service Series 166, September 1978.

8. Ida Pruitt (Chefoo, 1912–1918), TS, n.p., p. 21. Untitled draft of autobiography, chapter 13, Book 2, TS, p. 217; Book 3, TS, pp. 86–88.

9. Dr. Franklin C. McLean, director, Peking Union Medical College (hereafter PUMC), to Edwin R. Embree, secretary of China Medical Board (hereafter CMB) and PUMC trustees, 6 February 1920; McLean to Dr. Henry S. Houghton, acting director of PUMC, 22 February 1920; Rockefeller Archive Center, Box 143, Folder 1034 (hereafter 143–1034). Pruitt was not the first choice, however. See marginal comment of Roger S. Greene on Edith Shatto letter to him, 3 May 1919 (143–1034).

10. The relationship between the missionary origin of the PUMC and its development into a model for medical research has been explored in Marjorie King, "Saving Souls and Doing Good in China: The Departments of Religion and Social Service at the PUMC, 1917–1941," *Annals* of the Southeast Conference of the Association for Asian Studies, 1987. See also Margery K. Eggleston to Roger S. Greene, 17 June, 1926; George Vincent to John D. Rockefeller, Jr., 18 June, 1929; CMB, Inc., PUMC (137–989), 2 October 1930; Rockefeller family archive (14–130); Mary Brown Bullock, *An American Transplant: The Rockefeller Foundation and the Peking Union Medical College* (Berkeley: University of California Press, 1980), pp. 24, 30, 189.

11. Edwin R. Embree, Secretary, CMB and PUMC Trustees, to R. M. Pearce, 5 February 1921, (142–1032); Ida Cannon to F. C. McLean, 3 February 1920, (142–1032).

12. Medical doctors were "like religious men . . . who believe in their own vision . . . and wish to go among others with a scientific gospel," Robert H. Wiebe, *The Search for Order, 1877–1920* (New York: Hill and Wong, 1967), pp. 113, 115. Charles W. Eliot, President of Harvard University, deplored the Chinese reliance on intuition and meditation. He supported Rockefeller efforts to convert them to the "inductive method of ascertaining truth." See Frank Ninkovick, "The Rockefeller Foundation, China, and Cultural Change," in *Journal of American History* 70: 4 (March 1984), 802.

13. Several successive heads of the Department of Religion as well as a few physicians also expressed this concern. Dr. C. E. Lim complained, "our professors are just thinking about their jobs. The don't love China, and we turn out students who just look for fat jobs." Quoted in Egbert M. Hayes, "Impressions after six months in PUMC," p. 3, Rockefeller family archive (14–130).

14. Ida Pruitt, "The Social Service Department of the PUMC Hospital," TS, p. 4; Louise She, letter to Marjorie King, 25 October 1983, p. 1, Pruitt papers.

15. Ida Pruitt *"Politics at the PUMC,"* p. 2, Pruitt papers."There seems . . . to be a feeling . . . that all of women's work can be done by one group of women." See also E. Cockerill, "Can a Hospital Afford Not To Have a Department of Social Service?" *Transactions of the American Hospital Association* 39 (1937), 734–45; Hayes to JDR, Jr., 8 April 1935, family archive (14–130).

16. Responses to questionnaire sent to all medical department heads by Roger S. Greene, summarized in interoffice memo from Greene to E. R. Embree, 15 May 1923. Andrew Woods to Sloan, 7 March 1923; George Tsou, "A Brief Talk on the Family Welfare Agency," 20 April 1935; Dr. Smyly, excerpts from section on Social Service Department, CMB-PUMC (142–1032).

17. Mary E. Ferguson, *China Medical Board and Peking Union Medical College: A Chronicle of Fruitful Collaboration, 1914–1951* (New York: CMB of NY, Inc., 1970), p. 91.

18. Karl Wittfogel, "Memorandum to the Rockefeller Foundation," 28 March 1939. Rockefeller Archive Center, (143–1034).

19. Pruitt would have opposed the cultural objectives of American liberal reform in China as Akira Iriye defines them, "The China Hands in History: American Diplomacy in Asia," p. 93, in Paul Gordon Lauren, ed., *The China Hands' Legacy: Ethics and Diplomacy.* Liberty, progress, and enlightenment were, in Pruitt's eyes, American institutions which could not be as directly inculcated into Chinese society as Iriye implies was possible. Iriye also calls for two-way communication between Chinese and American cultures. Pruitt would definitely agree with this second goal of mutual understanding between peoples but did not confuse understanding with the transfer of social institutions and cultural values. As a *mediator*, she promoted understanding. Most Americans, however, were primarily interested in *changing* China in our image. Pruitt was not opposed to change, but felt strongly that the Chinese were capable of initiating such changes within their tradition, maintaining *control* of the selective borrowing from Western institutions. In this position, Pruitt was closer to a Chinese reformer than an American reformer.

20. J. Preston Maxwell, acting director, PUMC, 27 April 1937 minutes, CMB-PUMC (143–1034), Rockefeller Archive Center, Tarrytown, NY.

21. Stephen R. MacKinnon and Oris Frieser, *China Reporting: An Oral History of American Journalism in the 1930s and 1940s* (Berkeley: University of California Press, 1987), pp. 3–4, 185ff.

22. Douglas R. Reynolds, "The Chinese Industrial Cooperative Movement and the Political Polarization of Wartime China, 1938–1945," diss. Columbia University 1975, pp. 1, 10–12, 228–33, 240–52, 346–61. Although the Snows and Alley first conceived of the model for rural industrial cooperatives, leadership soon was transferred to a Central Headquarters headed by H. H. Kung and to an International Committee composed of various nationalities.

23. Reynolds, "The Chinese Industrial Cooperative Movement," p. 354. Almost $3 million was raised in the U.S., 1940–1945. Minutes of Indusco Board of Directors, 26 April 1944, Resolution 4/12/44. Indusco Collection, Columbia University, Rare Book and Manuscript Library, Box 132.

24. Reynolds, "The Chinese Industrial Cooperative Movement," pp. 359–60.

25. Reynolds, "The Chinese Industrial Cooperative Movement," p. 363.

26. Michael Schaller, *The U.S. Crusade in China, 1938–1945* (New York: Columbia University Press, 1979), pp. 49–51. In a lengthy letter to Rewi Alley on the eve of Japan's invasion of Pearl Harbor, Snow detailed the factional struggle in the American Committee for Indusco and Pruitt's role in the struggle. "We must next get IP on the Board somehow. And, after that my next task is going to be to educate the committee on guerrindusco." Edgar Snow to Rewi Alley, 3 December 1941, p. 4, Columbia University Rare Book and Manuscript Library, Indusco Collection, Box 177.

27. Rewi Alley to Chris Gilmartin, 6 July 1982, Beijing. Tape of interview in Pruitt papers.

28. Ida Pruitt, "Special letters file," Pruitt papers.

29. Ida Pruitt letter to Indusco supporters, 16 July 1951, "Special letters file," Pruitt papers.

30. Ida Pruit letter to B.A. Garside, United Service to China, 5 June 1951, "Special letters file."

31. Ida Pruitt letter to Sophia Voorhees, 16 January 1952, "Special letters file," Pruitt papers.

32. Ida Pruitt letter to Helen Judson, 17 September 1951, to Helen (no last name), 2 May 1951, "Special letters file."

33. Ida Pruitt files of lecture notes, correspondence, and essays, 1950s and 1960s, Pruitt papers. She traveled to China in 1959, 1972, and 1979.

34. "Very early in my work at the Social Service Department in the Rockefeller hospital in Peking, China, I learned that what all mankind wants is the same but that they often go about it in different ways to get these [sic]." From 1950s "Material on China for lectures" file.

35. Ida Pruitt letter to Sophia Voorhees, 16 January 1951, "Special letters file," Pruitt papers.

36. Ida Pruitt, "Report from China," TS, n.d. (after 1959 trip), Pruitt papers.

37. Robert P. Newman, "Lethal Rhetoric: The Selling of the China Myths," *The Quarterly Journal of Speech* 61: 114–16, enumerates six China myths whose legacy led to the American disaster in Vietnam.

38. Iriye's description of the China Hands of the 1940s is suitable for most China-based American reformers. They perceived "an image of China that would share certain values with American liberalism and that would replicate the reformist features of American democracy. For many of the China Hands, the Communists appeared in this regard to be more deserving of support than the Nationalists, whereas for some others, the latter were truer to American ideals." But both sides assumed China would be closely linked to the U.S. and the non-Soviet Bloc after the war. Iriye in Lauren, p. 91.

39. Spence, *The Memory Palace of Matteo Ricci* (New York: Viking Press, 1984), p. 292, describes the common denominator of Western advisors to China. Behind the desire to help China lay a deeper impetus to help themselves. Their personal character thrived on risk, yearned for radical solutions, and experienced frustrations at home. "China seemed to offer them freedom of maneuver, a chance to influence history by the force of personality, and thus to prove their own significance." MacKinnon and Frieser describe a similar personality in twentieth-century journalists in China.

40. E. Berkeley Tompkins, *Anti-Imperialism in the United States: The Great Debate, 1890–1920* (Philadelphia: University of Pennsylvania Press, 1970).

41. *A Daughter of Han* is one of Stanford University's all-time top fifteen best-sellers.

42. Pruitt, *A Daughter of Han*, p. 2.

43. Pruitt, *A Daughter of Han*, pp. 23, 27–28.

44. Anna Seward Pruitt was a prolific contributor to missionary periodicals and a

frequent correspondent with major American journals. Many of her articles and letters have been collected in family scrapbooks, now in the Pruitt papers. Her major publications include: "California in the Eighties," *California Historical Society Quarterly* 16:4 (December 1937), 291–303, and 17:1, 28–40; *The Day of Small Things* (Richmond, VA: Foreign Mission Board, Southern Baptist Convention, 1929); *Up From Zero in North China* (Nashville, TN: Broadmen Press, 1939); with Nan F. Weeks, *Whirligigs in China: Stories for Juniors* (Nashville, TN: Broadmen Press, 1943).

45. Anna Seward Pruitt letter to Ida Pruitt, 4 December 1945, in Pruitt papers.

46. Pruitt, *Old Madam Yin*, p. 128.

47. In other writings Pruitt attributed China's century of crisis to the convergence of internal corruption such as occurred at the end of every dynastic cycle and unprecedented foreign political and economic interference. See 1960s lecture note file in Pruitt papers.

48. Pruitt's positive presentation of Chinese women within their tradition was insistently restated in later writings and speeches. See notes on the position of women in traditional China in 1959 lecture note file, Pruitt papers.

49. Pruitt, *Old Madam Yin*, pp. 31–32.

50. Pruitt, *Old Madam Yin*, p. 32.

51. Daniel B. Ramsdell, "Asia Askew: U.S. Bestsellers on Asia, 1931–1980," *Bulletin of Concerned Asian Scholars* 15: 4 (1983).

52. Ida Pruitt, "To Those Who Call Me A Communist," Pruitt papers.

53. John K. Fairbank, who knew Ida Pruitt well during those years, commented recently "There was nobody you could talk to, even if you went to the academic research centers, who could really tell you what the situation in the countryside was. . . . We had no way to gain any knowledge of the life of ordinary Chinese people." MacKinnon and Frieser, p. 182.

8

WITNESS TO THE CHINESE MILLENIUM
Southern Baptist Perceptions of
the Chinese Revolution, 1911–1921

Murray A. Rubinstein

Introduction

From the final years of the Old China Trade and continuing to this very moment, Southern Baptists have been involved in attempting to transform the lives of China's millions. These evangelical Protestants[1] have made the Middle Kingdom a core area in their extensive missionary enterprises. They have worked to convert the "heathen Chinese" (as Baptists of the early twentieth century would refer to their all-too-unregenerate flock), to plant their own denominational churches, and to help an emerging Chinese Baptist community to take root and flower;[2] even as the Southern Baptists worked to convert the Chinese they kept watch on an ever changing China and recorded what they saw.

This chapter will cover the crucial years from 1911 to 1921. It will examine how the missionaries of the Southern Baptist Convention, situated as they were in many strategic areas of China, perceived the Republican revolution taking place around them. It will also scrutinize how these observers recorded their perceptions of events and how they communicated these images and impressions to their home board.

I argue that the Baptists can be seen as reluctant, if astute, witnesses of these events: as fishers of men they wished to save Chinese souls, not tamper with the political structure of the often explosive and rapidly changing nation that they thought would become Christian in the decade after the 1911 Revolution. They conveyed many word images of a changing China, images that members of Southern Baptist congregations could read in the SBC's annual reports and its missionary magazines. My thesis is this: The missionaries' writings, as they appeared in edited form in SBC publications, provided the typical Southern Baptist believer with different sets of windows through which he or she could observe and learn about the people of that alien land, half a world away, as they experienced the triumphs and the tragedies that accompanied China's Republican revolution.

The Republican Revolution in
Southern Baptist Eyes: The 1911 Revolution

The revolution that began in the central Changjiang (Yangtse) Valley city of Wuhan in October of 1911 took no one in China by surprise, perhaps because its unfolding had something of the air of a Keystone Cops comedy.[3] In the years before the outbreak of the revolution, on those occasions when they devoted space to the political realm, the Southern Baptist missionaries made the readers of the *Annual Reports* and *Home and Mission Fields* aware that a new age in China was about to dawn. When that day came in the fall of 1911, they felt obliged to show support for the new direction proclaimed by China's new Republican leader. Yet those missionaries writing the reports and magazine articles were careful from the start to temper their sincere praise with notes of caution.

In the *Annual Reports* of 1908, 1909, and 1910, they had talked of the new mood they sensed. In 1909, for example they had written about the movement for educational reform then being promoted by Zhang Zhidong[4] and suggested that Chinese officials had now seen the light.[5] In 1910 the same South China missionaries once again reported their sense that they recognized that China was on the brink of transformation. They also reminded their superiors and the Baptist lay people who read these reports that millions of Chinese still went to bed hungry and that millions more died without ever having heard the Gospel. They implied that China needed religious as well as political change, and they stated that only Southern Baptist missionaries and Chinese Baptist workers could help bring such religious change about. "Unlovely now," the missionaries stated, "she [China] needs but His light to make her shine."[6]

The revolution began in October of 1911. Two months later SBC missionaries were telling Southern Baptist readers about what had happened. The task fell to E. T. Snuggs of the South China Mission. In his article in the Foreign Mission Board's own magazine, the *Foreign Mission Journal*, he wrote that "the rebellion in active progress as these lines are written is the most momentous and far reaching in its effects of all the rebellions that have occurred in that land over the past two and one half centuries for it is not only an outward movement for the overthrow of the usurper. The most vital point is the inward yearning of a mighty people for a better day."[7]

In these lines Snuggs showed both his obvious sympathy for the Republican cause pioneered by Dr. Sun Yat-sen (Song Zhongshan) and the Tongmenghui's anti-Manchu viewpoint. He then went on to give his readers a brief history of rebellion in China since the days of the Taiping Tianguo, and suggested continuities between the goals of the Taiping leadership and those of the new revolutionaries of 1911. He also noted that at the moment he was writing his article, in November of 1911, the extent of the rebellion already equaled that of the Taipings. Of greater significance in his eyes was the fact that all classes seemed to be taking part. "All," he suggested, "seem sick of the old regime and are clamoring for radical changes to bring in new ideals which may broadly be described as the American Spirit of democracy, human rights, fair play and equal opportunity."[8]

The rebellion, he then suggested, was brought about not only by deep-seated opposition to the Manchu rule—opposition that had been manifested over the years by sectarian rebellion—but also by the process of Westernization that the missionaries themselves had begun. This infusion of Western religious, social, and political ideas provided the Chinese with new concepts and theories for defining their future.[9]

The missionary was optimistic for the future of China. For China, he believed, the rebellion meant that "through much tribulation and the shedding of blood she is now finally and fully turning her face from looking backward and breaking away forever from a hoary past to looking forward to all that is brightest, hopeful and good of the present and future."[10]

Snuggs, of course, was not an objective or disinterested observer of the Chinese scene. He was a dedicated missionary with decades of experience in the field—he had come to China in the 1880s and he was writing a report for a Southern Baptist audience. His concluding comments reflected this: "Southern Baptists are now facing one of the greatest privileges, grandest opportunities and most stupendous tasks that ever came to the Children of God."[11] The Baptist message, democratic in its principles, would prove ever more attractive to the Chinese. What were needed were more men and more money for the task.

The missionary had presented his readers with a crisply written and thoughtful analysis of the revolution's background, although one that contained little detail about the Wuhan uprising itself. The months and years that followed would show whether the optimism was warranted. But this article viewed in missiological terms reflects not the brooding doom-ridden sensibility of Dispensationalist pre-Millenarian thought, but instead, the optimism of the "realized eschatology" espoused by William Owen Carver. Carver was considered by many to be the most important Baptist theologian of missions. He was also a man who served as Professor of Missions and World Religions at the Southern Baptist seminary in Lexington, Kentucky, and as such was for over fifty years the theological father to three decades of SBC missionaries. In his classroom lectures and in his essays and texts he defined a Southern Baptist missiology that his students and his peers accepted as their own. Snuggs's article and other pieces reflect the Carver perspective of spiritual reality.

Other missionaries disagreed with Snuggs and his rosy view of the revolution.

Their argument was that the case for saving the perishing heathen had to be made even if political transformation was taking place. As if to balance Snuggs's position, Alice Huey wrote a piece entitled "How Our Young Missionaries Work," describing in detail her work in Laizhoufu and local life there, including the continued strength of force Taoist belief. This China was "old China," bound to ancient superstitions. Her message was that China was still a land in need of missionary help if its people's souls were to be saved.[12]

A third article in the same issue discussed America's role in the country and made the case for a special relationship. An important element in this relationship would be the Southern Baptist's responsibility for "much of the present intellectual awaking," which J. Campbell White suggested "must be attributed to the direct and indirect influence of Christian missions." Thus White reinforced Snuggs's idea that missionaries must share the responsibility for helping to bring about change in China.[13]

The articles in the December 1911 issue of the *Foreign Mission Journal* were but the first of a number of pieces on the revolution. The information flowing into Foreign Mission Board headquarters in Richmond prompted editorials and articles, as well as a series of dispatches from missionaries in various parts of China.

In February of 1912, for example, six pages were devoted to China. The editors first presented an overview of the events and, after reviewing the various movements of the years from 1900 to 1910, suggested that Christian education had helped produce this desire for reform. The writer put it rather bluntly: "This modern learning and the demand for reforms is the direct outcome of Christianity." The next logical step, he suggested, was for China to embrace Christ: "If the revolution now going forward in China results in the overthrow of a corrupt dynasty and the opening of the way to the Kingdom of God, the loss sustained will be compensated for a thousand times."[14] It is interesting to note that in this passage the word revolution is substituted for the word used in earlier pieces, rebellion: the unrest had now spread throughout the whole country. The disruption wreaked upon Western missionary work was described in a series of reports published under the general title of "The Revolution and Our Work," written by the men and women in the field.

Having learned some painful lessons from the Boxer Rebellion, the American Consul urged missionaries to leave the interior for the safer havens of the coastal cities. Even in these coastal enclaves changes were afoot. In Shanghai, for example, Miss Zheng—the head of the Baptist Cantonese Language School (a school for Cantonese Baptists living in the great Central China port) and a trained physician—was recruited to work in Hangzhou as a member of a Red Cross medical society. The language school itself was now supported by funds from Wu Dingfeng, who had been Chinese Consul to the United States. Thus the Baptists, Chinese as well as Western, were beginning to play a role in the unfolding events.[15] In Jinjiang the revolutionary unrest had unsettled Baptist efforts, but here, as in Hangzhou, missionaries and Chinese had the opportunity to help in the medical relief efforts, and Rev. James B. Webster reported that he and the other missionaries were willing to respond to the call. For most others in the city, daily life continued to be quite ordinary even as the larger framework of Chinese life shifted most dramatically.

Those in central China were most affected by the revolution during these early months. Much of the conflict occurred in the Changjiang Valley. Thus missionaries in Yangzhou, just outside of Nanjing, could hear the sound of gunfire and were fearful of the danger. The American consul urged all Westerners to move to Shanghai, yet the missionaries decided to remain and they continued to hold services much as they had always done.[16]

In Canton, for so long the center of Sun Yat-sen's activities, the revolutionary forces took over the city and quickly imposed martial law. According to the reports of the missionaries in Canton, work at the seminary and in the various churches in the city was able to continue, but the missionaries in the out stations were told to come back to the city for reasons of safety.

By March of 1912 things were beginning to sort themselves out as the missionaries attempted to make clear to the people at home. In their coverage of events in the *Foreign Mission Journal*, they followed the format they had introduced in February, first an overview of events and then excerpts from letters of those serving in various parts of China.

One particular article, "Our Missionaries and the Chinese Revolution," had a special power and a sense of authenticity impossible for a simple third-person report. The major note struck in the article was one of optimism. Mention was made, for example, of the Christian faith of Sun Yat-sen. Even Yuan Shikai, then maneuvering to wrest the presidency from Sun, was depicted as a friend and protector of missionaries. The Foreign Mission Board saw the new republic as open to Western religions and as a place where religious liberty would prevail. The editors stated that "the only thing that will stand in the way of making China a mighty Christian empire is the question of whether Christian people can be aroused to take advantage of the Great opportunities."[17]

These opinions expressed by the editor were reinforced by letters from men in the field. Rev. W. Carey Newton, writing from Zhefu, noted general expectation of plague and famine were for Shandong a fact of life in 1911 and 1912, as were the floods that struck the province. Yet the change in the political tide, with its promise of a China more open to Christ, gave the missionary hope even in the midst of this great suffering.[18]

Events in Wuzhou, the Baptist center in the southeastern province of Guangxi, had put missionaries in an even more precarious position. Serving as doctors and nurses at the hospital, they had cared for those wounded in the fighting, but the political chaos forced the evacuation by gunboat of the mission's women, leaving only the men to continue to work with the sick and wounded.[19]

W. E. Crocker, who wrote of the events in Jinjiang, gave the most optimistic assessment of the missionaries' situation. He reported on the coming of the new government and the elections for the new national assembly. He had made contact with some members of this new legislature and saw a chance to win influence and converts even as he offered his advice on political matters. Here we can see that at least some members of the SBC mission saw new opportunities for influence in an area that lay beyond those of religion, education, and medicine, the spheres in which the Baptists were already so heavily involved.

The leaders of the Southern Baptist Convention's Foreign Mission Board realized from such reports that China's revolution presented important new opportunities for them to exploit. In the final days of February 1912, they convened a full-day conference of the FMB leadership and those members of the China mission home on furlough. The participants' optimism was heightened even further when they learned by telegram that China's new president, Yuan Shikai, had proclaimed religious liberty and freedom of conscience and that Sun Yat-sen, a man educated by and not above courting those same missionaries, was proposing that temples be turned into Christian schools. According to this telegram, nearly all the leaders of the revolution had shown themselves to be favorable to Christianity. The masses, too, seemed to demonstrate a new interest, for there were now crowds around the doors of Baptist chapels.[20] One must surmise that the Southern Baptists had been in China and in other foreign fields long enough not to be swept away by feelings of optimism, however these missionaries recognized that political or social crisis in any nation created an environment in which individuals are more receptive to alien creeds, and that such moments of openness—such windows of opportunity—can quickly disappear.

An account of this meeting of Baptist missionaries in China was featured in the April 1912 issue of the *Foreign Mission Journal*. The article reflected the widespread optimism, and accompanying materials helped demonstrate the reason the FMB officials were so hopeful. The magazine published the telegram concerning both Yuan actions and Sun's comments, and also letters from missionaries in the field. One that was particularly relevant discussed an instance in which a temple was turned into a church. But not all the letters were this cheerful. One, from Dr. Charles Hayes in Wuzhou, warned that "it will take some time for China to adjust herself to the new conditions and for the new government to control the situation fully." Hayes did feel, however, that "a brighter day is dawning and we will one day see an advance here that was never thought possible before." The letters concluded with one from Nannie M. Pierce who was working in Yangzhou, a city that had also seen military activity. Many were now attending the chapel services there, she told her audience at home. She was a realist well aware that "a time of great trouble and suffering is now visiting China." But she had hope, as she wrote, "We trust that out of this suffering and tribulation will emerge a new China which will stretch out her hands unto God."[21]

The SBC continued to assess the situation and the opportunities in the months that followed. In June of 1912, a month after the denomination had held its yearly meeting and had discussed the issue of China, the editors of the *Foreign Mission Journal* published an article titled "New China and Southern Baptist." This piece served to sum up what the heads of the various SBC mission stations in China thought about events. Rev. W. H. Tipton, who served in the South China mission, had witnessed the sweeping away of the old government and the formation of a new one. He, for one, voiced great optimism about the changes and advocated a policy of strong Western paternalism: "What these mighty changes shall mean to this fourth of humanity may be determined and directed by the Christian nations of the west. Now is the formative period of this young and rapidly growing republic." He urged that "what is done must be done quickly. The minds and the hearts of the rulers as well as the people are opened to the truth. Never before in the history of missions has the Christian world faced such opportunities and responsibilities as now confront it in the Chinese Republic." Tipton went even further in this same vein, writing that "it is for Christendom to decide whether the Chinese people shall be a nation of atheists corrupted by all the sins and vices of the catalogue and thus become a menace to the rest of the world or whether they shall become our allies in the establishment of the universal reign of the Prince of Peace."[22] As may be noticed, this passage demonstrates not only paternalism but also eschatological sensibilities. Tipton was the missionary as messenger of the Millennium. He was also aware of the radical political—and anti-Western—elements in the new revolutionary China. He thus voiced the first warning about the dangers a secularized China might pose to the West and to the Westerners representing religious, diplomatic, or economic interests in China. But Tipton's overall optimism was by his Baptist coworkers representing the North, Central, and Interior areas. A new dawn was breaking, they agreed, and the Chinese seemed warm and friendly to the bearers of Christianity's message. Furthermore, the government seemed well aware of the missionaries' role in helping to educate the people and thus make them more conscious of the need for change. The missionaries' message for their brethren at home was simple—the Southern Baptists had to press forward and seize the opportunity to Christianize the new China.[23]

By July of 1912 things had settled down considerably, and the missionaries in many areas felt secure enough to return to the field. The letters published in the *Annual Report* for 1913 reflected the new tranquility. The missionaries told their superiors just what they had and had not accomplished during the revolutionary year of 1912. We read about the number of students taught, the number of patients treated, and of tent meetings held. What we do not read about are many of those changes that drastically affected China's future but not the daily lives of the missionaries.

P. H. Anderson of the South China Mission was one missionary who attempted to assess the larger impact of the revolution. In a preliminary analysis he presented the upheaval simply in terms of the narrow question of religious liberty. Anderson's perceptions were colored by his mission's loss of several key figures, men who had helped build the Southern Baptist presence in South China; he reflected on the irony that, at the very moment when opportunity was greatest, the mission was weakened for necessary work.[24]

In a later report Anderson did take time to assess the situation in greater detail. He then focused more on the nature of his Chinese flock than on the larger political and socioeconomic factors. He spoke of the ignorance and spiritual blindness of the people and warned, "Let no one be deceived by thinking that China has suddenly become enlightened and civilized. Though great changes have come and though great strides have been made . . . the fact remains that the great masses of the Chinese people are still in ignorance and superstition." In his opinion, "This spiritual blindness constitutes one of the great hindrances to the preaching of the Gospel." Thus, by 1913 at least one man in the ranks felt that the excitement of revolution had worn thin. He reminded his audience that "the task is a mighty one and it will require much preaching, much praying and much patience before the final victory is won."[25]

Charles G. McDaniel, a member of the Central China mission, remained more optimistic than his brother in the South. He saw his highest expectations exceeded. His analysis of the reasons: "I say without fear of successful contradiction that the great changes which are now taking place in China for her good are the by-products of the Gospel of Christ." And, he argued, just as the Gospel had helped bring about the revolution, the revolution would help advance the spread of the Christianity. He predicted that there would be a geometrical rise in the number of converts, for "even the people of Central China are waking up to their lost condition and are coming to Jesus."[26] Thus for this missionary, the revolution had opened China even further and a new age of evangelization was about to begin.

Those involved in medical work also found that China had changed. After the revolution the Chinese were more willing to make use of Western medical facilities. Dr. A. S. Taylor, working in Yangzhou, noted that "there is a growing belief in things foreign."[27]

The period from the fall of 1911 until end of 1912 saw something like the beginning of a new China. For the Southern Baptists an event symbolized the change: Charlotte Diggs Moon—the respected and revered Lotte Moon—for forty years a missionary in North China, a pioneer in Woman's Work, and a person regarded as the exemplar of the female Southern Baptist missionary, died in Kobe. She was one of those who did much to help the Chinese transform themselves, and yet, like the prophet Moses, she was fated to die just as a new dawn was breaking for her adopted flock.[28]

Miss Moon's death best symbolized the painful process of transition China and the Baptist mission had experienced. The missionaries looked ahead to the expansion of their church yet were not sure just how far the revolution would go or what it would mean for their enterprise. The next decade fulfilled many of their hopes even as it presaged a more disturbing future.

The Years That Were Fat, 1913–1921

By 1913 most Southern Baptist missionaries found themselves able to return to their stations and renew their efforts to win the Chinese to Christ. They spent the next eight years working hard to establish a new and Christian China. The annual reports also suggest that these efforts met with considerable success. Kenneth Scott Latourette and other scholars of the Christian mission enterprise in China have suggested that this was very much the case for the mission enterprise as a whole. In his classic work on China missions, Latourette demonstrates that the years after the revolution were ones of dramatic growth for the both Catholics and Protestants. Chinese seemed more and more responsive to the missionary message, and to the missionary efforts in education, medicine, and humanitarian relief that expanded as did the evangelization effort.[29]

Over these years the missionaries became aware that the China they had become comfortable with was dying, passing into political and social disintegration that would continue on through the 1920s. The missionaries felt more and more that it was somehow their responsibility to try to hold things together; they also were intent upon restoring some sense of normality in their own lives. This latter wish pervaded the reports in the 1914 *Annual Report* and those published in the seven years after that. These same reports suggest that the men and women of the mission also felt they had the obligation to tell their audience at home more about what they were doing and less about what was going on all around them in a changing China where they felt increasingly uncomfortable.

The missionaries sensed that they were holding on to a lost China. At the same time, they worked to build a new Christian China. Both of these feelings are reflected in the missionaries' reports on the details of mission-related activity.

For example, one can trace the steady evolution of Southern Baptist educational facilities. Over these years the Shanghai Baptist College emerged as an increasingly distinguished institution of higher learning. The college also became a showplace of Baptist interdenominationalism, run smoothly and effectively by both American and Southern Baptists. These same years were witness to the steady development of the major Southern Baptist seminaries in North China, in Central China, and in South China. At such institutions as the Graves Seminary, the Baptist readers were told, a new generation of Chinese Baptist leaders were being trained to assume the responsibility for directing the destiny of their emerging national church and the destiny of their now revolutionary and Westernizing nation. Primary and secondary schools were also shown to be developing during these years. The argument was that the missionaries had the obligation to train this new Chinese generation, thus making this generation better able to assume the burdens of leadership of a rapidly changing China. The hope that some among the students would see Christ as their Savior was always alive in the hearts of the missionaries, and those directly involved in the educational effort expressed such a hope in their letters and more formal reports.

One can also see the steady progress those involved in medical work were making. The hospitals in Wuzhou and North China's cities continued to grow, and the Baptists' ability to care for larger numbers of patients increased. Modernizing and upgrading of facilities also went on year after year. Over this same span the doctors and nurses continued in their efforts to train Chinese in Western medicine. More patients treated also meant more people available to hear the Gospel, and the reports suggest that a typical Southern Baptist doctor in his capacity of missionary took full advantage of the opportunities presented to him by this captive audience.

The reports give a sense of a growing Baptist influence in the spiritual life of the Chinese, and revival movements and individual conversions were described in detail. The reports conveyed the sense that these were years of revival: more and more Chinese were making decisions for Christ at these large-scale meetings. Church membership statistics were published as were reports on the evolution of individual churches.

This reading of the *Annual Reports* would suggest that the Baptists had been able to make solid and steady progress in China. These same reports did but little to convey the sense that the China they were working in had itself changed. These years saw the entire span of the early Republic, the rise of military leaders who would come to control entire regions of China, the emergence of a powerful movement for social, cultural, and intellectual change, and the rise of an anti-imperialist sensibility.[30] But the China outside of the mission-compound gates was presented by the missionaries as through a gauze curtain; it was as if the missionaries were unwilling to tell their readers about those things in China that they could not control. Yet this "real China" crept into the reports; the perceptive Baptist reader, one who was interested in China as well as its Christianizing, could glean clues to the political, social, and intellectual environments in China and how the missionaries felt about events.

For example, in the *1914 Annual Report*, which covered the year 1913, the real China can be glimpsed, albeit dimly. In Suzhou, P. W. Hamlett stated that "notwithstanding the interruptions and the general unrest, the year 1913 has been a time of great opportunity for seed sowing both in the city of Suzhou and in the neighboring towns and villages."[31] However, Hamlett was honest enough to admit that the events of the day had hurt his own efforts. His words also suggest a real tension that missionaries felt. On the one hand they praised the many changes they observed, but on a more pragmatic level they made their readers aware that such changes only produced interruptions and disruptions in the pattern of daily life that had come to suit them.

W. E. Crocker and C. C. Marriot, who were working in Jinjiang in the North China zone, made similar comments. In their report for 1913 they stated that "the work of our field was hindered during the summer by the revolution, most of our field being under war conditions for about three months." Hopes of holding evangelistic meetings were put aside "on account of the war." They also added that "many of the members and workers had to flee for their lives but none were killed during the troubles."[32]

Yet there were those missionaries who found that they could be of great service to the general population during these difficult times. Dr. P. S. Evans of the Shanghai station noted that the rebellion had delayed the opening of the college that year, but "a greater part of the summer I was here in Nanjing and so was able to help in the siege, when there was so much distress and alarm among the people."[33]

The revolution had a direct effect on the outlook of those Chinese who had converted to the Baptist faith. This fact was recognized by W. H. Sears who worked in Shandong. As Daniel Bays has recently shown us, Shandong was a hotbed of indigenous Christian development during these years; at least one major independent church, the Zhen Yesu Jiaohui (the True Jesus Church), evolved in the province in the years from 1912 to 1917.[34] Sears, the Baptist on the scene, was sensitive to this emerging current, for he noted that "with the coming of the republic there has arisen an increased desire for independence—independent church movements. By the above plan the Chinese become the employers not the employees." He was in some sympathy with the new feeling, arguing that "it is the mark of a great statesman that when he drops out the state will go on without him. Just so the missionary should continue to train leaders that will early fall in and carry out God's Plan."[35] Certainly the conflict over control of the churches would trouble the Southern Baptists on the mainland for quite some time. Even on Taiwan, where a strong and viable Taiwan Baptist Convention has developed in the past thirty years, the problem of autonomy is still sizable.[36]

The mission in South China had long had a special place in the Baptist pecking order as the pioneer among the missions. Perhaps because of this sense of prestige and because of the simple fact that South China was the country's hotbed of revolution during these decades, the missionaries who worked there demonstrated a marked awareness of the day's political realities. The very least that could be said was that they witnessed the revolution at closer hand than did many of their peers. Thus they were sensitive to the tension that can be seen in the comments of their northern brethren—the tension that missionaries felt in trying to be both the activist and careful observer. J. L. Galloway of the South China Mission demonstrated this in his report for 1913. He summarized the work that the missionaries had done in the region and then discussed the political environment. The revolution, in his view, brought to the surface smoldering antagonisms many felt toward the Western imperialists and against those who stood as symbols of such imperialism. The Chinese were torn by a desire to become more Western and an equally great desire to destroy any influence of Westernization. Inevitably the venting of such passions and the relief of such tensions were painful, but the experience was also healthy—a clearing of the air. Thus, while Galloway recounted the details of the destruction of church property—one chapel had been demolished[37]—he also made sure that he told his readers about the expansion of Baptist press effort that was then taking place.[38] Galloway tried to put the revolution in perspective, recognizing the tragedies and mistakes which were bound to take place, but arguing that the new spirit that could be seen in South China was one that would help the cause of evangelization. As a member of the oldest of the SBC's missions in China, he could expect others to listen.

The *Annual Report* of 1914 contained distinctly contradictory elements, but this was the Baptists' way of being true to themselves. Some saw the revolution as good while others feared it, and both outlooks were openly expressed. The Southern Baptist Convention prided itself on its independence and upon the freedom with which each individual could voice his or her viewpoint. This held true for the *Annual Reports* that were prepared.

The next year, 1915, saw a change in the publication's format. The editors saw the need to give their readers a clear picture of just what China was like and accordingly the order went out to follow a new pattern of presentation in each of the regional segments of the document. An introduction to each region was presented and maps of the work area were printed next to the introduction. The missionaries then gave the readers some sense of how the Southern Baptist work fit into the larger picture of life in that given area. What was lost in this new format was the dialogue that could be seen even a year earlier—some sense of differing opinions and reactions to events. Perhaps this was more a reflection of the fact that the events of that year 1914 demonstrated that the political situation had at least momentarily stabilized. While the new emphasis in the magazine may have been due to the particular emphases of the editors, the absence of "hard news" about China might also be interpreted in this way: those missionaries who were more concerned with describing mission work than with drafting analyses of Chinese political life had won the upper hand.[39]

The calm that existed in 1914 was shattered but two years later, and the *Annual Report*, written and published in 1917, reflected the fact that China was now entering a new and most dangerous stage in its revolution. The format used in the previous two years was followed. The missionaries thus gave accounts of life in their respective areas before discussing their own activities. The tone of the report was generally upbeat, and again diversity of opinion was absent.

However not all missionaries wrote such bland positive reports. George W.

Leavell, a doctor working in Wuzhou and representing the South China Mission, discussed the evolving political and military situation. He told his readers of Yuan Shikai's attempt to become the new emperor and explained the consequences of these efforts. He also told of the beginning of the civil war which would herald the start of the warlord era. However, he suggested that in Canton (Guangzhou) things were a bit better than they were in other parts of China, for a new government was in place. "Thus the advocates of the old form of government were overthrown and the republican form of government at last established. Not only in form, but we hope, in reality; for the new officials with new ideals have won power and one of the greatest obstacles to the work of the lord in South China has been removed. . . . Possibly never before in the history of Canton have our opportunities been greater or our hindrances been fewer."[40] Here Leavell was doing what his compatriots had seemingly been unable to do, at least in this particular year: he linked the work of the mission to the larger flow of Chinese revolutionary history giving readers at least some sense of the political environment the missionaries faced when doing their work in China.

The reports prepared for publication in the last years of the decade suggest that the missionaries were continuing to do what they had in the years following 1912 and were retreating to the confines of their own mission stations. Taken as a whole, the reports must have given the readers little sense of what China was experiencing: the further deterioration of the Beijing-based republic and the rise of the warlords.[41]

There were those missionaries who refused to put on blinders and instead tried to give their American audience a clear picture of just what was going on. In 1919, Margie Shumate of the South China Mission took on this task and wrote about the events that had taken place the year before, summarizing the major political and military trends as seen from her vantage point of Canton. In her report she outlined just how confused the political situation had become by early 1919, and described for her readers the conflict between the northern and southern militarists and the attempts of each faction to claim legitimacy for itself. Mrs. Shumate was optimistic about the chances for reform and for the reestablishment of a viable Republican government. She also held fast to the belief that America's special relationship with China would prove to be of significance in this crisis. She noted that "we rejoice that America is recognized as a true friend of China. We believe this is the most hopeful element in the present situation. China's leaders are willing to give attention to whatever our great president says." She also saw advantages the situation created for the Baptist missionaries. "We believe," she said, "that the day of unparalleled opportunity is dawning in China," and she called upon the board to support China mission efforts.[42]

The Southern Baptists focused upon their own efforts. This, as the 1919 *Annual Report* demonstrated, reflected accelerating success of the SBC enterprise as converts were being gathered in greater and greater numbers in almost every area where work was being done. China was indeed a wartorn land and its people were being victimized by rapacious warlords, but it was precisely such conditions that provided the Baptists with the chance they needed. There were far more Chinese now ready to become Christian, as was clear in the Baptists' reports with their detailed information about mission progress.

In the year 1919, revolutionary China experienced a new phenomenon, the evolution of a widespread movement joining together students, urban intellectuals, industrial workers, and middle-class business people. This May Fourth Movement was a response to the Peking government's failure to prevent the Japanese from gaining the areas that the German Empire had ruled in Shandong province. The betrayal of national sovereignty by those Chinese diplomats present at the Versailles Peace Conference was protested strongly, and the protest soon spread and gained strength. This protest movement then served as the central point for a wide-ranging series of activities. Out of May Fourth came a movement for language reform, the birth of a vernacular literature, a new interest in Western intellectual and scientific trends—as demonstrated by the lecture tours made by Bertrand Russell and John Dewey—and, finally, the creation of a Chinese Communist party by key members of the emerging intelligentsia. The movement also reinvigorated the Guomindang just as its leaders were reaching the nadir of their fortunes.[43]

The members of the Southern Baptist missions were aware of this China-wide movement and reported on it in the 1920 issue of the *Annual Report*. W. W. Stout, who served in the North China Mission, had lived through the birth of May Fourth in the part of China where it had occurred, thus he was the best man on the scene to give the Baptist leaders at home a good idea of just what was going on.

Stout began by describing the movement. He pointed to the decision to give the Japanese the German concession of Chingdao as the precipitating event. He told his readers that "here [in Shandong] where the people are most concerned things have been at a fever pitch." The missionary saw the movement as patriotic in nature. He admitted that he and many of his fellow Westerners had not expected the movement to last long or to become as widespread as it did. "Six or seven months ago most foreigners in China thought the outburst would subside like the rest but the persistence of the movement has been a surprise. The spirit of the people is as determined as it was in the beginning." What was also important about the movement was that students, including those from the Christian universities, were at its center. The students from the mission schools, Stout suggested, had taken an important part in the movement: "It was recognized by all that their work has been most effective."[44]

Stout then shifted focus from events to their causes. He blamed the imperialistic Japanese much less than he did the Chinese government, which had proven so weak in the face of Western and Japanese pressure. He told his readers that "the central government is a body of military leaders who are mortgaging their country for great loans, the bulk of which they keep for themselves or use to pay robber armies by whose help they hold their power.'' He then broadened his condemnation, writing that ''from the high officials of the central government down graft, rapacity, extortion and insensibility are taken for granted.''

The Southern Baptists used to condemn the Qing regime in much the same terms. Thus the words' reoccurrence mark an important shift in SBC perception of the Chinese Revolution. The revolution, Stout suggested here, had been stolen from the people, and now the people—the students, the workers, the merchants—were trying to take the revolution back. This was a time for Baptist action, for the missionaries had to impress upon all Chinese that it was impossible to save a nation whose individual citizens were at heart selfish, corrupt, and sinful, and thus in need of Christ's salvation.[45]

Stout's account was not the usual Baptist rhetoric nor even the brand of optimism others had displayed in discussing revolutionary China. Instead it suggested a new sense of realism about what was going on in China, one that the home audience was probably grateful for.

Stout's words were echoed in the report for the South China Mission written by J. T. Williams. Williams, too, examined the political situation but focused instead upon the diplomatic events that had led to the internal crisis. He, like Stout, was honest and realistic in his account. Though President Woodrow Wilson was not criticized harshly, he was taken to task for the disparity between his words—the Fourteen Points—and his delegates' actions in dealing with the Shantung case at the peace conference. Williams suggested that the students had acted in the only manner they could when they had taken to the streets. He was less sanguine than his brother to the north about the influence of the Chinese Christian students and voiced fears that the Christians would be left out of the national reconstruction that he saw was about to take place.

Williams was more optimistic when he looked at the South China scene, for he felt that Canton was now about to become the modern city it needed to be. The city walls had been destroyed, opening the city up. This had not been done without cost, for an old Baptist church had to be destroyed in the process, but Williams accepted that as small enough price for the gains he felt his mission was now making.[46]

The events of 1919 had clearly made some members of the Southern Baptist mission more aware of the major movements then taking shape throughout China. The reports the missionaries published in the SBC's *Annual Report* of 1921 reflected this increased level of consciousness, but reflected as well the fact that the majority of the missionaries remained more focused upon their own work and felt compelled to show just how much they had accomplished in their own areas of expertise. There were times when the two spheres—the inner sphere of mission work and the outer sphere of events beyond the station wall—would connect. That was when the larger patterns of events would directly affect the work the missionaries were doing.

This was the case in Suzhou in Central China in 1920. Miss Sophie S. Lanneau, the missionary on the scene, made this clear in her report when she stated that "the student movement, national and local, has had a marked effect on our work during the year." She spelled out just what that impact was: "Student propaganda became so political that we had to forbid students from conducting their activities on or from our mission compounds." Here the Baptists' motive was not opposition to the ideals of the new movement—though such opposition would be natural to conservative evangelicals, and many in the SBC fit this description—but rather fear of the local authorities. The Southern Baptists publicly were nonpolitical and were, according to their formal statements, strongly opposed to the church or the mission playing any role in the radicalized political realm. Thus, on the surface they would oppose what their students were doing. However, there is a subtle difference between the public statement and the private action. As the missionaries would later demonstrate on Taiwan in the years from 1949 to 1989, it was quite possible to publicly state one's neutrality and desire to remain above politics while quietly and effectively supporting one or another of the groups contending for power. The missionaries recognized that most of the students were now politically aware and active and were working to arouse the patriotism of their fellow citizens. Thus they gave their support, but they did it in ways that would not gather attention to themselves. Thus Lanneau tells us about the Chinese teacher of a Baptist school who quietly applauded the actions of his students, efforts such as house-to-house visits. He also told these students that once the activities had been concluded they could return to school. The missionaries gained by this subtle support and for these actions of their students that "added no little to the reputation of the school."

Miss Lanneau linked the actions of the students—their support of the May Fourth movement—and the reaction these actions produced in the local community to the growing attitude of acceptance of Christians and their faith. In earlier times, she noted that "the local attitude . . . has proverbially been one of lofty scorn or absolute indifference; that is on the part of the upper classes." However, now there was to be seen a gradual change taking place, for when street or chapel preaching were done "the congregations at street chapels have been wonderfully attentive to the preaching of the gospel." However, Miss Lanneau was still wary about the progress the Baptists had made for she realized full well that "it is still true that joining the church means social ostracism to members of good families in Suzhou."[47]

The May Fourth Movement also helped Chinese Baptists to change their attitudes toward the parent church and its workers. While the attitude of most such Christians was generally one of appreciation for Baptist efforts, this feeling was "tinged with a growing desire to have a larger share in the direction of affairs." Miss Lanneau saw this new desire as important and added that "they are proving their fitness and are assuming more and more of the responsibility—financial and administrative—of our work.''[48]

Other SBC missionaries were less positive about what was going on in this year of 1920. E. F. Tatum of the Yangzhou station noted that the boycott that was a part of the anti-Japanese movement was now becoming more generalized. He noted that "this seems to suggest the further thought that all things foreign were bad and that foreigners were unfriendly. Hence the epithet, 'Foreign devil' has more frequently been heard." The missionaries were not tarred by this same brush but there was still "some disrespect for the average native Chinese Christian, his motive being impugned by the average heathen."[49] On the whole, Tatum was optimistic, as was Alice Huey of the North China mission. Writing the report for North China, she told of her school at Huangxian, near Dengzhou. At this school students had participated in the May Fourth Movement and this much impressed the local citizenry. Here, as in the case of Sophie Lanneau's area, the student movement had proven able to break down some of the barriers.[50]

E. M. Poteat, working in the Interior Mission, did not see much positive in the events of 1920. He noted simply that "during the year our interior mission work has been adversely affected by famine, by the civil war, and our country work, by brigandage." In spite of these very real difficulties, it was his impression that "so far as efforts spent and results noted are concerned, we have had a good year. We have much to rejoice and praise the Lord for."[51] The eternal optimism of the missionary, built upon his own deep and abiding faith and reinforced by the realized eschatology that was a part of the seminary schooling, kept him true to his course and positive in his outlook, even in trying times.

In looking at the *Annual Report* for 1921, we find that the missionaries continued to be affected by the events that had begun the previous year. While the reports the missionaries wrote were generally positive, there was a distinct undertone of tension—a deep sense of wariness about what the near future would bring their way.

Yet the *Annual Report* for 1922, covering the 1921 calendar year, reinforced the positive feelings many SBC missionaries had felt during 1920. As in years past, some of the missionaries were quite conscious of the larger trends, but nothing dramatic enough occurred to suggest that such movements would threaten the work of the Southern Baptist enterprise.

One of the old hands, Sophie Lanneau of the Central China Mission, noted in her remarks that "the year [1921] marked the tenth anniversary of the Chinese Revolution and the resulting establishment of the Chinese Republic. Many forces have been at work ever since in the life of the nation but all seemed to come in the one year, in the veritable tide of new thought that swept all over China." This is a brief but perceptive analysis of the decade. Miss Lanneau then added a personal note that showed how the missionaries themselves were affected: "Some of us felt it more than others. Some who had been plodding along year after year were yet conscious of the sudden change. . . . There was developed in those months a new spirit, a new attitude. It showed itself in social life, in educational life, in national consciousness, and best of all, a new spirit of earnest attention to the message of the gospel.''[52]

Missionaries in the other regions also continued to devote at least some of their time to the study of the political and military scenes and to report on what they had learned as they reported on what they had accomplished over the course of the year. From the Interior Mission, Mrs. Milton L. Braun reported on the problems faced by people in Honan province. While famine and drought were affecting North and Central China, the northwestern provinces, defined by the Baptists as the interior region, were being deluged by floods. Houses were destroyed and crops could not be planted. The people were open to the ravages of famine and were easily preyed upon by bandits. The disintegration of the Chinese institutions that was so much a part of this warlord decade could be seen in this area, and the Southern Baptist missionaries could only try to help by organizing famine relief and by continuing to sponsor other benevolent and self-help activities.[53]

In Northern China, disaster and political turmoil both took their toll. The droughts of one year had become the deluges of the next. Whole villages were swept away in the Qingling area and the Baptists there were busy organizing various types of relief services for the local residents. Other areas in Shandong were more affected by the political events of the day rather than by national phenomena. This was the case of Chingdao, one of the points of dispute at the Versailles conference. The missionaries expected trouble yet none occurred during the year even though over the course of 1921 the city was at the very center of the discussions of the Washington Conference on China. Edgar Morgan, a Southern Baptist missionary in Chingdao, noted that ''the present military government has in no wise molested or hindered us in any way in the gospel work.''[54]

The freedom to labor unhindered was something the Baptists had long sought and now, ten years after the revolution, they felt more secure. They also felt that this meant that the conversion of many more Chinese was at hand. Mention of this feeling of security and of the feeling that a new Christian age was coming into being was expressed by many missionaries in many of the Protestant denominations. These feelings were expressed in the book published by the China Continuation Committee, a large and detailed volume to which they gave the rather unfortunate title, *The Christian Occupation of China*.[55] In this elaborate volume, the Baptists published maps and statistics detailing just how extensive the Protestant presence in China had become. Morgan, writing the report for the North China Mission, pointed with pride to the fact that the Pingtu area that the Baptists had pioneered, was one of the most well developed mission fields of all of China. He praised God for what had been accomplished and looked to the future for even greater progress.[56] Yet the missionaries had unwittingly signed what some would see as almost a death warrant for their cause, for the Chinese intelligentsia would react with violence to this volume and its assumptions of religious domination.

In South China, as in years before, a more detailed and more knowing account of the year's events was written by the missionary assigned to the task, A. R. Gallimore. Gallimore told his audience of Sun Yat-sen's inauguration as president and of the attempts of the southern warlords who supported him to launch their promised Northern Expedition. When the missionary wrote his report for the year the results were not yet certain but Gallimore was optimistic. The missionaries in the South were directly affected by these problematic conditions, for, Gallimore wrote, "These unsettled conditions have given the robbers a free hand." As a result, "a number of our missionaries suffered an attack from these bands as they proceeded up the River Fu at the close of our mission meeting in July." Even under these difficult conditions the missionaries in this area remained optimistic about their efforts, as he noted, "but the doors of opportunity for the preaching of the gospel will bear fruit throughout the years to come."[57]

The year 1921 marked the end of the first decade of Republican China. The country had begun to change in ways that few had expected. The united empire the Qing had ruled was now broken down into zones of warlord influence, and local and regional military leaders controlled counties and provinces and tied themselves, when necessary, into larger systems of alliances. The Beijing government continued to maintain the fiction that it spoke for all of China, but the mistakes its nominal leaders and their warlord masters had made in the field of diplomacy had served to discredit it even further. In this fluid political environment, among the only voices people still listened to were those of the new generation of intellectuals and those they taught.

For the missionaries this decade had proven to be one of opportunity, for the political chaos and social disintegration created openings both for indigenous Christian sects and for Westerners. The progress the SBC missionaries had made was considerable; for them these were truly the years that were fat. The Millennium, at least as far as it meant the conversion of China's millions, seemed close at hand.

The missionaries were less aware than they had to be about the flow of events in the world beyond their walls, and this in the end proved tragic. The older missionaries were sophisticated and generally knowledgeable about the China they lived in, but the newer arrivals seemed to show little concern for learning about this larger world. Instead they preferred to concentrate upon their own efforts, which they then wrote about in exhaustive detail. Carver had called for missionaries to see things in the broadest possible light and to be aware of the total environment in which one worked, but this advice does not seem to have been followed by most Southern Baptists in the China field. This tunnel vision was a flaw that would prove dangerous in a China that was changing so fast.

Conclusions

The Southern Baptist missionaries, reluctant observers though they might have been, were able to draw clear and perceptive word pictures of China as it experienced its Republican revolution. Their superiors at the Foreign Mission Board headquarters in Richmond were then able to make use of the letters and reports of these men and women, as well as their personal observations when they were home on furlough, to give the Southern Baptists public a concrete, if slanted, idea of events in that far-away nation.

Notes

1. The question of whether the Southern Baptists can properly be termed evangelicals is a somewhat controversial one. Based on the literature I have examined and the interviews I have conducted I would suggest that they can be so defined. On this debate see James Leo Garrett et al., *Are the Southern Baptists "Evangelicals"?* (Macon, GA: Mercer University Press, 1983).

2. The Baptists celebrated the hundred and fiftieth anniversary of their work in China in 1986. In honor of that event they published an elaborate memorial volume. *Chinese Baptist Memorial Booklet* (Taibei: Chinese Baptist Convention, June 1986).

3. There is a rich literature on the background and the unfolding of the 1911 Revolution. The most useful essay collection on the subject remains Mary Wright, ed., *China in Revolution* (New Haven: Yale University Press, 1968). Two more detailed studies on the origins of the revolution are Mary Backus Rankin, *Early Chinese Revolutionaries* (Cambridge: Harvard University Press, 1971) and Joseph W. Esherick, *Reform and Revolution in China* (Berkeley: University of California Press, 1976). The sense of comi-tragedy is best gained from a reading of Vidya Prakash Dutt, "The First Week of the Revolution: The Wuchang Uprising" in Wright, *China in Revolution*, pp. 383–415.

4. On Zhang Zhidong's career and his role as modernizer see William Ayers, *Chang Chih-dong and Educational Reform in China* (Cambridge: Harvard University Press, 1971) and Daniel H. Bays, *China Enters the Twentieth Century* (Ann Arbor: University of Michigan Press, 1978).

5. The major sources for this essay are the annual reports of the Southern Baptist Convention. The reports from the various mission stations were published in the larger volume which detailed the work of the denomination over the course of a given year. They will be cited as follows: author's name, type of mission work, mission station, Southern Baptist Convention (SBC) Annual Report (AR) year, pages. "Educational Work," "South China," *SBC AR (1909)*, 156–157

6. "Outlook," "South China," *SBC AR (1910)*, 183.

7. The second major body of sources were the magazines the Foreign Mission Board of the SBC published for the Baptist public. E. T. Snuggs, "The Great Rebellion in China," *Foreign Mission Journal* (December 1911), 162.

8. E. T. Snuggs, "The Great Rebellion in China," *Foreign Mission Journal* (December 1911), 163.

9. Ibid., 163–164.

10. Ibid., 164.

11. Ibid., 164.

12. Alice Huey, "How Our Young Missionaries Work," *Foreign Mission Journal* (December 1911), 167–171.

13. J. Campbell White, "Important Facts Concerning China," *Foreign Mission Journal* (December 1911), 171–172.

14. "Revolution in China," *Foreign Mission Journal* (February 1912), 239–240.

15. "Report from China," *Foreign Mission Journal* (February 1912), 241.

16. A. J. Crocker in "Report," *Foreign Mission Journal* (February 1912), 242.

17. "Our Missionaries and the Chinese Revolution," *Foreign Mission Journal* (March 1912), 260.

18. W. Carey Newton, "A Religious Revolution Impending," in "Our Missionaries and the Chinese Revolution," *Foreign Mission Journal* (March 1912), 260–261.

19. Dr. Charles A. Hayes, "Red Cross Work by Missionaries," "Our Missionaries and the Chinese Revolution," *Foreign Mission Journal* (March 1912), 261.

20. Yuan's years as president are examined in detail in Ernest P. Young, *The Presidency of Yuan Shih-k'ai* (Ann Arbor: University of Michigan Press, 1977).

21. "The Situation in China," *Foreign Mission Journal* (April 1912), 293, 306–307.

22. W. H. Tipton in "New China and Southern Baptist," *Foreign Mission Journal* (June 1912), 356–357.

23. "New China and Southern Baptist," *Foreign Mission Journal* (June 1912), 357–360.

24. P. H. Anderson, "South China," *SBC AR (1913)*, 186–187.

25. Ibid., 192–193.

26. Charles G. McDaniel, "Central China," *SBC AR (1913)*, 204.

27. Dr. A. S. Taylor, "Yangchow," "Central China," *SBC AR (1913)*, 226.

28. On Lotte Moon see the sophisticated and most unhagiographic portrait in Irwin T. Hyatt, Jr., *Our Ordered Lives Confess* (Cambridge: Harvard University Press, 1976), pp. 65–136.

29. Kenneth Scott Latourette, *A History of Christian Missions in China* (New York: Macmillan Company, 1929), pp. 743–822.

30. For a useful overview of this period see James E. Sheridan, *China in Disintegration* (New York: The Free Press, 1975).

31. P. W. Hamlett, "Soochow," "Central China," *SBC AR (1914)*, 210.

32. C. C. Marriot, "Evangelistic Work," "Chinkiang," "Central China," *SBC AR (1914)*, 212.

33. Dr. P. S. Evans, "Shanghai," "Central China," *SBC AR (1914)*, 217–218.

34. Daniel H. Bays, "Western Missionary Sectarianism and the Origins of Chinese Pentecostalism in the 20th Century" (unpublished paper prepared for the 39th Annual Meeting of the Association of Asian Studies, Boston, MA, April 10–12, 1987).

35. W. H. Sears, Missionary to the Shantung Baptist Association, "North China," *SBC AR (1914)*, 232–233.

36. On the Taiwan Baptist Church and its evolution, see Murray A. Rubinstein, "American Evangelicalism in the Chinese Environment," *American Baptist Quarterly*, vol. 2:3 (September 1983), 269–289.

37. J. L. Galloway, "South China," *SBC AR (1914)*, 250–251.

38. J. L. Galloway, "South China," *SBC AR (1914)*, 260.

39. "China Mission," *SBC AR (1915)*, 175–229.

40. George W. Leavell, "South China," *SBC AR (1916)*, 226.

41. The best study of the complex process of the politics in the capital is Andrew J. Nathan, *Peking Politics, 1918–1923* (Ann Arbor: University of Michigan Press, 1976).

42. Margie Shumate, "The South China Mission" *SBC AR (1919)*, 284–285.

43. The best comprehensive treatment we have is still Chow Tse-tung, *The May Fourth Movement* (Cambridge: Harvard University Press, 1960). A major new study is Vera Schwarcz, *The Chinese Enlightenment* (Berkeley: University of California Press, 1986).

44. W. W. Stout, "North China" *SBC AR (1920)*, 78.

45. W. W. Stout, "North China" *SBC AR (1920)*, 79.

46. J. T. Williams, "South China" *SBC AR (1920)*, 99.

47. S. S. Lanneau, "Central China," *SBC AR (1921)*, 295.

48. S. S. Lanneau, "Central China," *SBC AR (1921)*, 295–296.

49. E. F. Tatum, "Yangchou," "Central China ," *SBC AR (1921)*, 302.

50. Alice Huey, "North China," *SBC AR (1921)*, 313.

51. E. M. Poteat, "Interior China," *SBC AR (1921)*, 305.

52. S. S. Lanneau, "Central China," *SBC AR (1922)*, 246.

53. Mrs. Milton L. Braun, "Interior China," *SBC AR (1922)*, 258.

54. Edgar L. Morgan, "Tsingtao," North China, *SBC AR (1922)*, 266.

55. Milton Stauffer, ed., *The Christian Occupation of China* (Shanghai: The China Continuation Committee, 1922).

56. Edgar L. Morgan, "Pingtu," "North China," *SBC AR (1922)*, 269.

57. A. R. Gallimore, "South China," *SBC AR (1922)*, 283–284.

9

CHINA AS PORTRAYED TO AMERICAN CATHOLICS BY MARYKNOLL MISSIONARIES, 1918–1953

Jean-Paul Wiest

Early in the twentieth century, a group of men and women banded together to realize their common dream: to send American Catholics to the foreign missions. In the fall of 1912, this pioneer group established its headquarters outside of Ossining, New York, on a hillside above the Hudson River. The hillside was dedicated to the Mother of God and named "Maryknoll."[1]

The organizers, Fathers James A. Walsh and Thomas F. Price, were convinced that, to survive, an American foreign mission society needed the widespread support of mission-minded Catholics. Therefore, from its earliest days, one of Maryknoll's clearly defined goals has been the education of American Catholics about foreign missions.

Characterized by a bold and imaginative use of mass media, Maryknoll has relentlessly sought better ways of reaching American Catholics and has been quick to make use of new forms of mass communication. By far, its most successful means of spreading mission information has been the magazine *Maryknoll*, started by James A. Walsh in 1907 under the title *The Field Afar*.

This magazine immediately emerged as the main vehicle to draw the attention and the generosity of American Catholics toward China. By 1923, in less than twenty years, the magazine had more than 100,000 subscribers throughout the United States. With half a million cover-to-cover readers, it had a larger circulation than the then-popular *New York Evening Telegram*. By 1941, the Maryknoll magazine had an average circulation of 216,000 and continued to climb to more than 600,000 copies distributed monthly in 1951, when most foreigners left China.[2]

A study of the thousands of stories and articles published in this magazine between 1918 and 1953 reveals that the Maryknoll Fathers, Brothers, and Sisters painted a highly favorable, but not always accurate, picture of China.

A Great Civilization and a Great People

Perhaps the most prevalent theme found in the magazine was one which extolled the qualities of the Chinese and their civilization, trying to rid American readers of silly misconceptions or sheer ignorance about China. *The Field Afar* presented this list of "don'ts" in 1918:

> Don't say "Chink," unless you are trying to make enemies.
>
> Don't imagine that all Chinese women bind their feet or that all Chinese men wear queues. Modern Chinese are discarding these things, just as modern American women are ceasing to wear "hobble skirts" and American men to wear "peg-top" trousers.
>
> Don't ask your Chinese friend whether he eats rats and dogs. It will please him just about as much as it would please an American to ask him if he ate snakes and toads.
>
> Don't try to make persons believe you know all about China just because you have visited Chinatown in San Francisco, Shanghai or Hongkong. They are no more like the real China than the East Side of New York is like America.
>
> Don't think that because one or two Chinese in your city operate laundries all Chinese in China are engaged in the same kind of business.
>
> Don't try to purchase "chop suey" in China. It's a dish prepared by Chinese in America for American consumption and is unknown in China.[3]

Maryknollers liked to instill in their readers respect toward China by reminding them of its ancient civilization. The following opening remarks to an article on education in China are typical:

> Chinese civilization was hoary with age when our own European ancestors were barbarians. Her greatest philosophers . . . preceded by generations Socrates, Plato, and Aristotle, as well as the Egyptian [sic] Euclid. . . . China traces her ancestry far back of any Western written record. . . . She developed independently of the West, and when Western empires crashed and were consumed by succeeding waves of civilizations, China rode the storm.[4]

Francis X. Ford, one of the first four Maryknollers to set foot in China in 1918, was without a doubt the most enthusiastic. In presenting the basic differences between Chinese and American civilizations, he had no qualms about tilting the balance in favor of China:

> China has much that we have lost in culture. . . . The modern world bases its life on "the survival of the fittest" with the hasty conclusion, as a background, that "every day in every way we are growing better." Chinese life has its roots in the command, "Honor thy father and thy mother," and includes in this the members of the family and the clan, besides ancestors dead or deified. This inculcates reverence and obedience and worship and sinking of self for family solidarity, and reacts on the minute details of daily life. . . . There is, I think, less danger of abnormalities in acting as a family unit than as an individual. Certainly there is less danger of forgetting principles, of losing control of patience, when the restlessness of the individual is checked by tradition.[5]

Ford and other Maryknollers wrote many articles to illustrate this point of view. Ford struck at the core of American life-styles by claiming that life on the farm and in the city were much more human in China than in the United States. He drew a bleak picture of the lonely and isolated life on American farms and the migration of the rural people to the city. In the American city, according to Ford, most people still lived in isolation despite the physical crowding because of a lack of common interests and family ties. Moreover, he predicted that the "uncrowding" of the cities by spacing homes farther apart would only bring the disadvantages of country isolation to the city. Ford claimed that China, on the contrary, had none of these problems, neither among its huge farming population nor in its large and centuries-old cities.

Naturally his advice was to look to China for a solution to America's problems. In his opinion, the backbone of the Chinese countryside was the village, which pulled together common yet diverse interests:

> The Chinese population is still eighty percent farmers and a nation that can keep its farmers has solved a problem that has stumped the West. . . . Chinese farmers build, it is true, in the valleys near their crops, but they group houses into a village surrounded on all sides by common fields for grazing grounds and hills to supply firewood. . . . The village is alive and a unit and a hive of mutual service. . . . Every inhabitant of an average village is related to all his neighbors at least by marriage, usually on the father's side, so there is found the strongest bond of common interests that reconciles at once the privacy of family life and the need of companionships outside the immediate family.[6]

Ford also blamed rural decline in America on the lack of character of American farmhouses. To him, these box-like structures of unpainted wood and tar-paper roofing did not deserve the name of home. By comparison, the Chinese farm was a building made of several courtyards and rooms clustered around large guest-rooms with patios and cool corners. Built and enlarged by its inhabitants as the family grew over several years, it housed several generations under one roof. Ford reported:

> Such construction if adopted more generally in America would solve many problems. It would beget a pride in our homes, to counter a restless urge to move; it would focus and thereby intensify the natural instinct in all of us to own something permanent; it would localize and color childhood memories, now dissipated over a dozen dwellings; it would be the expression of a family's united aim and harmonious labor. Morally, it would be a bond between the present and future generations; it would be the loadstone for the restless youth and a safeguard of its communion with parents. Economically, it would prove the solution of financial difficulties for pioneering couples; it would abolish the numerous middlemen who now control house shortage. It is an investment that enhances the land and the stability of its dwellers.[7]

As for the Chinese cities, they were also extremely livable, according to Ford, because every Chinese was a farmer of one sort or another and kept close to the soil even in the city. "A block or two away the country begins—not a dump of discarded scrap iron but in genuine fields where each householder grows his daily vegetables."[8] Explaining that the Chinese word for family was composed of two characters signifying a pig under a roof, Ford asserted that this was still a reality almost everywhere in China. Even in the city, the Chinese house was a miniature replica of village life, which avoided many of the evils found in American cities.[9]

Although Maryknollers were aware that China was undergoing drastic changes and entering a new modern order, they did not seem to have understood the depth of the transformation until the early 1930s. They considered the changes merely as a veil over the older civilization; the older civilization was permanent and the modern a veneer. In 1933, Father Thomas Kiernan was the first Maryknoller to explain that China's transformation was fundamental. In an article in *The Field Afar* entitled "A Matter of Education," Kiernan raised the question of whether or not China, which had always assimilated her conquerors while remaining fundamentally Chinese, would be able to do the same with modern Western learning and culture. His analysis of the situation was that Christian schools, educational reforms, and "returned Chinese students" from universities in America and Europe had irreversibly altered China. His hope was that China would not lose her old way of life while adopting modern Western learning but instead blend the best of the two together into a more nearly perfect civilization:

> We are inclined to think that at last "East and West will meet" and will blend into one common civilization—at least in China—the good of the old supplying what is wanting to the new. . . . Our prophecy is not without suspicion that modernity in China will have its typical and essential dress.[10]

Other Maryknollers followed suit, presenting a very optimistic picture of the transformation of China. In October 1935, Ford likened the change to a spiritual renaissance rather than a mere imitation of Western culture. By importing the best from the West and banning the bad, China held firm to its ancient natural virtue:

> This is a spiritual renaissance that must be sensed rather than it can be proved in black and white—yet recent, continued legislation forbidding cabarets, extravagant banquets, birth control propaganda and certain cinema productions seems to point to serious underlying motives.[11]

Two months later, Father Joseph Ryan pointed out the difference between civilization and modernization: China could not be called uncivilized because it had passed that point centuries before any European nation; by borrowing Western learning and technology, China was becoming modernized. Ryan rejoiced that while retaining certain national traits and customs, Chinese were becoming more and more like foreigners. He dared to predict that "before long a traveler in China will find only minor differences such as he would find in any European country."[12]

To counter the muddled mental image of a baffling Confucius and an even more mysterious Fu Manchu so common among Westerners, Maryknoll's writings presented the ordinary human side of the Chinese. In a short article displaying pictures of smiling Chinese children and toddlers and a mother with her baby, *The Field Afar* asked:

> Have you ever stopped to consider that however "queer" the Chinese may appear to us, with their slant eyes, their yellow skin, and their odd clothes, they are after all like ourselves, "just folks." People who joy and suffer, who marry, who bear children, and who, like every one of us, at the end go out alone into eternity. Souls for whom Jesus suffered the death of the Cross.[13]

In many instances, the qualities of the Chinese people were upheld as examples for the West to emulate. Maryknollers described the spartan simplicity of Chinese furnishings and meals as a sign of fortitude. They maintained that these sparse living conditions did not result from poverty but from a conscious choice made by very contented people who knew how to differentiate the important from the superfluous. Describing an average Chinese middle-class home, Ford said:

> On entering it, one does not receive an impression of poverty, much less of unhappiness. It looks planned and balanced with deliberate avoidance of a frill or frippery. The Chinese enjoyment of life is in human beings, not in incidentals.[14]

During the hardship of the Sino-Japanese War, Maryknollers regularly emphasized Chinese endurance and discipline. In 1943, Ford wrote:

> It is stamina that has enabled China to thrive on a six-year invasion exhausting to her enemy. . . . This stamina is inbred in the Chinese through generations of hard living. . . . It has that good-humored element in it of the Poverello: smiling hunger, nonchalance in pain, endurance unconscious of heroism. It retains zest for adventure even in prosaic daily happenings, and keeps the nation supple.[15]

At the end of the war, two years later, Bishop James E. Walsh, superior general of the Maryknoll Society, made a very similar remark:

> My sadness at the sight of war privation and hardship was tempered by the cheerfulness and courage of the Chinese people in breasting their sea of troubles. Not even eight years of warfare could daunt them. There was misery, everywhere, but there were the same smiles, patience, industry, energy. That is China. . . . Its people are surely the most durable human beings in all God's creation.[16]

A Country Ready for Christianity

The overwhelmingly positive picture of China and its people presented in the Maryknoll magazine led easily to the conclusion that Christianity was bound to succeed in such a naturally virtuous civilization. Early articles in *The Field Afar* intended to alarm readers—the Catholic Church could miss wonderful opportunities in China because of *its* lack of missionary spirit. The magazine warned that Catholic Europe, weakened by World War I, lacked the manpower and financial resources to sustain mission work in a China ready for Christianity, and that American Protestants were pouring into China while American Catholics remained unconcerned. In a diary published in *The Field Afar* in May 1919, Father Bernard Meyer referred to the good results of Protestant work and to its terrible consequences for the Catholic Church:

> Not only have Protestant missionaries established hospitals and brought over doctors who are the same time engaged in propaganda, but they are training the natives, men and women, and having them trained in America as doctors and, at the same time, disseminators of Protestant teaching. . . . In their education work, the Protestants instill into the minds of thousands and hundreds of thousands of Chinese children, who are bound to be a power, perhaps the power, in the next generation, a deep contempt for the Catholic Church as an out of date institution, a bar to progress.[17]

In later years, appeals to counter the Protestant efforts gave way to the theme of China as a place naturally prepared to receive the Catholic faith. In the 1933 article ''Holy Week in the Orient,'' Ford showed that life in China, which greatly resembled the Palestine of Jesus' time, made the gospel's parables more easily understood:

> [It is] a land devoted to simple agriculture with a barefoot people who walk, not ride, who bear the heat of the day and the burdens, who gather the crops by hand and winnow the chaff in the wind, who draw water from the pool, who make bricks with straw and burn the grass of the field; a land whose temples have porticos, and whose cities are girthed with walls, whose blind and lame sit begging at the city gate, and whose lepers are a common sight.[18]

In looking at Chinese civilization, Ford also saw in it traces of the four signs—one, holy, catholic, and apostolic—which characterized the Catholic Church as a perfect society:

> Chinese civilization is one—a unified force, evolved from and revolving around filial piety which permeates each action of life. . . . Chinese civilization is holy in that it is rooted in reverence. Its ethics have molded the minds of the youth to uphold the dignity of age. . . . It is catholic, extending to all Chinese, embracing an area twice the size of the United States. . . . And finally it is a traditional civilization above all. Its very essence is derived from ancestry.[19]

The proper attitude of American Catholics toward China was indicated by James A. Walsh, Maryknoll's first superior general, in the following quote from a counsel he had received from Cardinal Camillus Laurenti, a long-time friend in the Roman Curia: "Warn your missioners not to impose on their converts in Asia the customs of the West. Leave these people as they are so long as what they have and what they like is not harmful to soul or body."[20] This admonition was a reminder of the solemn instruction given by the Propaganda Fide to its first vicars apostolic in 1659, some three hundred years earlier: "Do not attempt for any reason whatever to persuade the people to change their rites, customs, and manners, provided they are not openly contrary to religion and good morals."[21] Walsh affirmed that he had never failed to pass on Laurenti's admonition to young Maryknollers.

In contrast to the positive articles on Chinese civilization in general, Maryknoll literature had no words of praise for Chinese religious beliefs until the late 1930s. In accordance with the Catholic soteriology of the time, non-Christian beliefs were superstitious or pagan. An article by Father Ryan on Chinese civilization and modernization was very representative of that attitude. While upholding the greatness of Chinese civilization, the article called, in fact, for its demise by advocating not only material modernization, but also spiritual modernization to replace the "ancient superstitions of China." Without using the word "Westernization," Ryan pointed out that modernization, meaning the adoption of modern methods of life from Westerners, would eventually result in accepting their scientific, political, and of course religious doctrines:

> The substitution of Catholicity for the ancient superstitions of China is not now a difficult matter for the individual, since the nation as a whole is ready to accept what is foreign, and side by side the material and the spiritual change goes on to form a new China.[22]

Looking into the future, Ryan saw the possibility for China "to become the great central power of the world—the Central Kingdom" and imagined how comforting it would be for the world to find "China [as] a Catholic nation governed by Catholic principles, and carrying on her international relations on the same Catholic principles."[23]

It is important to note, however, that in spite of its disparaging tone toward Chinese beliefs, Maryknoll literature did not convey a negative image of the Chinese people. Rather, it stressed how unfortunate it was for a race endowed with so many beautiful natural virtues to remain ignorant of the Gospel.

In late 1939, *The Field Afar* printed an article entitled "China's Three 'Isms,' " which reflected Rome's changing attitude toward the Confucian rites. In this very positive presentation, Father Meyer referred to each of China's three great "teachings" as a path that paved the way for Christianity, rather than dismissing them as superstitious:

We have the Confucian ethics, the Taoist philosophy, and the Buddhist religion, each developed by earnest seekers after the truth, and each contributing to one of the best natural foundations on which to build Christianity. To Confucianism it owes the idea of a personal God, as well as social and family virtues; to Taoism, the concept that man is akin to the infinite and that the highest good is found in mystical contemplation and union with the infinite; to Buddhism, an appreciation of the value of meditation, prayer, and fasting, and a well-developed theory of moral responsibility.[24]

The Faith of Chinese Catholics

The wonders of Catholic faith among "naturally virtuous Chinese" composed another favorite theme of the Maryknoll publication. *The Field Afar* abounded with descriptions and photographs of zealous new converts, exemplary old Catholics, apostolic catechists, and stories of their steadfastness in the midst of war, isolation, and persecutions.

In 1939, Father Aloysius Rechsteiner answered the question, "What kind of Christians do the Chinese make?" with a narrative of his first experience as a young curate just out of language school. He arrived in the parish of Kochow and volunteered to spend the Feast of the Assumption among new Catholics in a small outstation called Ch'eung Paan:

> I went, saw, and heard, and returned, thanking God for the opportunity of having seen the depth of faith which people can reach. . . . Their eagerness to learn more about God and the doctrine of the Catholic Church has certainly been an inspiration. . . . Ch'eung Paan's faith and good example has spread. A village nearby has caught its spirit and already has laid foundations for its own chapel.[25]

Maryknoll knew that Catholics in America would be moved by such manifestations of faith and highlighted some of these narratives to generate financial contributions. To replenish the catechists' fund, there was the story of Ahman, a native catechist assigned to prepare a little group of catechumens in a distant mountain village of a bandit-infested region:

> Ahman, the catechist chosen by Monsignor Ford, accepted the post gladly, though he knew perfectly the dangers to which he would expose himself. When he had been in the village awhile, the bandits came and ordered Ahman to point out the houses where they could find money. This he refused to do. He was then backed against a wall and nailed there with outstretched hands, while the houses were being searched. He died from the treatment. Greater love than this no man hath that he lay down his life for his friends.[26]

To persuade more American Catholics to give the one dollar necessary to sustain a missioner for a day, the magazine printed the story of a visit by two Maryknollers to a remote Catholic village in the wooded mountains of Manchuria—a village where no priest had gone for twenty years:

These poor people were overjoyed at the unhoped opportunity of again receiving the sacraments and assisting at Holy Mass. When the Maryknollers started on the long homeward trek, the Christians followed them to the outskirts of the forest, gazing after them with tear-dimmed eyes and calling out, "Come back to us! Do not abandon our souls!"[27]

Besides the lives of exemplary rural Catholics, *The Field Afar* also gave visibility to contributions by the Church and the Chinese Catholic elite to the building of modern China. In the twelve years following the opening of the Catholic University of Peking in 1925, *The Field Afar* had no fewer than fifteen articles on that institution, which almost always mentioned its older sister, Jesuit Aurora University in Shanghai. It was also routinely mentioned that Maryknoll's South China missions traditionally supplied students to both universities.[28]

If a local Chinese official or businessman happened to have been educated in a Catholic institution or, better yet, was Catholic, articles always stressed his contributions to social progress and the improvement of relations with the Church. Prominent Catholic laymen, however, were still unusual in China, and *The Field Afar* does not mention many. Among those introduced to Americans was Vincent Ying, cofounder and editor-in-chief of the Tientsin progressive newspaper, *Ta Kung Pao*. In 1912 he became the first Chinese scholar to advocate the idea of a Catholic university in Peking and in 1925 became its first dean.

Also introduced as a "model Catholic layman" was Timothy Yin, a banker from Antung in Manchuria:

> His position brought him in contact with pagans and pagan practices but his faith and personality—especially his gracious smile—touched many hearts. There was no class distinction with Timothy. He was a friend of the lowly coolies as well as the highest official. . . . He was valuable to the Church in his secular position; his charity toward the poor made him a God-given asset to the parish.[29]

He was also described as a man of prayer. His circle of friends reached into the heavens to the company of saints, whose help he counted on to remain a good Catholic and a successful businessman: "I ask the Little Flower [St. Thérèse of Lisieux] to keep me in God's grace, and beg St. Jude to keep me from going broke."[30]

However, the Catholic layman who was given by far the most prominence in *The Field Afar* was Lo Pa-hong, the famous Shanghai entrepreneur and benefactor. Between 1918 and 1938, when he was assassinated, twenty-four articles in the magazine focused on Mr. Lo, with many others mentioning his name. Lo's impressive titles convinced American readers of his outstanding business acumen: he was director of a Shanghai tramway company and general manager of the China Electric Power Company of Shanghai, the Chapei Electricity and Water Works Company, the Shanghai Inland Water Works Company, and the Tatung Zung Kee Steam Navigation Company.

These businesses, however, were only part of his activities. His tremendous energy raised funds for the poorest people of Shanghai. On his initiative three important establishments were built for the least privileged. With two thousand inmates, St. Joseph's Hospice was the largest Catholic charitable institution in China. It sheltered sick people, penniless old folks, wayward girls, orphans, and the sick from the city prisons. Lo also built Sacred Heart Hospital, a three-hundred-bed facility providing free treatment for the poor. Free clinics at the two hospitals treated up to one thousand outpatients daily. Lo Pa-hong not only built these institutions but also visited them regularly to spend time with the patients. His third outstanding accomplishment was the construction of Mercy Hospital for the mentally ill, the first of its kind in China. He also visited frequently at the Shanghai Municipal Prison, bringing blankets and clothing to prisoners, teaching them doctrine, and baptizing and comforting those about to be executed. In addition to his business titles, Mr. Lo acquired others which better reflected his Christian charity. He liked to refer to himself as the "coolie of St. Joseph," while others called him the "Vincent de Paul of China" and the "chaplain of the brigands."[31]

The Rise of a Patriotic Catholic Church

When Maryknollers arrived in China in 1918, the country was in turmoil. The Chinese Revolution of 1911 had not brought peace or unity. For all practical purposes, the country had no government. Warlords still fought each other, bandits were frequently encountered in the hills of South China and in the forests of Manchuria, and pirates made travel perilous along the coast. Maryknollers did not attempt to hide these facts. They gave an accurate portrait of "poor old China" with its "all jumbled political situation." However, they stressed that this "awful muddle" was not the fault of the Chinese—"the most patient people in the world"—but the result of the greed of a few men:

> When it is recalled that the great masses of China's people are peace-loving and industrious, intelligent, and at heart religious, there is every reason to look for changed conditions soon. . . . We hope and pray that in their country law and order will soon be established, and the wolves, large and small, who prey upon and scatter these helpless human beings, may soon be exterminated.[32]

Maryknollers asked their readers to abstain from passing derogatory judgment on China. They reminded them that the ratification of the Constitution had not changed the United States into a peaceful democratic nation overnight; rather, democratization had been a long process which had included—as in China—the cruel test of civil war.[33]

When antiforeign agitation flared up in the mid-1920s, *The Field Afar* asserted that these manifestations were not antireligious but political. The Soviet Union, it said, was fanning the anger of the Chinese people, and the Western nations were paying the price for their arrogance and their mistreatment of China:

> It is being recognized gradually that China has not had a "square deal" from some of the Powers, and that Soviet Russia has taken advantage of this fact to strengthen herself and to embitter Chinese, especially those of the student class, against the Westerners generally.[34]

Following the Northern Expedition and the Nationalist victory, Maryknollers in China welcomed quieter times and emphasized how the unhampered and rapid transformation of the country into a great modern power went hand in hand with the growth of the Catholic Church. China's economic progress in the fields of communication, industry, and education were continuously described. For instance, *The Field Afar* described how the Chinese Ministry of Education realized the usefulness of private educational institutions and accordingly relaxed some of its policies toward Christian schools. Also mentioned was the Ministry's decision to recognize and extend subsidies to private institutions of higher learning, benefiting the two Catholic universities in Peking and Shanghai and the Industrial and Commercial College in Tientsin.

When the government promoted the New Life Movement in 1934 to revitalize the moral fiber of the people, *The Field Afar* explained its meaning: "Invented by statesmen, conscious of their country's needs, it seeks to inculcate lessons of order, industry, hygiene, civic pride, and mutual charity."[35] Maryknollers backed the movement as a worthwhile enterprise, although they felt that unless it was grafted onto Christianity, it could never bring the real "new life" to China.[36]

During the decade of 1927–37, the overall message was that China was making progress, but that China's economy of scarcity was so characteristic of old agricultural conditions and practices that it could not be changed overnight. There was no suggestion that the Nationalist government was not coping with rural problems or not implementing a comprehensive social and economic plan. The Soviets were blamed for trying to discredit the Nationalist government and for fomenting rural discontent rather than helping implement the government's reforms.

In 1937, the widening of the Sino-Japanese War severely disrupted China's development. Railway lines were bombed, bridges blown up, roads cut open, and many factories and universities removed into unoccupied China. In fact, as described by missioners, the China of the late 1930s and the mid-1940s was much like the China they had found in the early 1920s, with shortages of food, displaced people, and lack of communication and electricity. The war had eliminated most of the progress of the previous twenty-five years.

For several years *Maryknoll—The Field Afar* refrained from anti-Japanese statements. China was fighting a faceless invader because articles sent by Maryknollers in China and Manchuria were carefully edited in order to not reflect any negative judgment on Japan. It was only in the summer of 1942, when

Maryknoll headquarters received word that most interned Maryknollers would soon be repatriated, that the magazine began to develop the theme of a patriotic Chinese Church rallying behind the Christian figures of Generalissimo and Madame Chiang Kai-shek to free China of Japanese invaders. Chinese Catholics were praised for their active participation and leadership in the national war effort. The presidential couple was presented as God's blessing for China. According to *Maryknoll—The Field Afar*, Chiang had grown to understand and respect the Catholic Church and its members, Chinese and foreign. He told his army officers at the Whampoa Academy to model themselves after the Catholic missioners in China. He was, said Francis Ford, "the world's only silent dictator [who] played on no emotions, stirred no throngs with hysterical harangues, [and] appealed to no race hatreds or mob action." Chiang was like Lincoln because "he sensed in this moment of China's crisis the need of moral principles to found a new nation," and by his integrity "won the reverence of his people."[37]

By 1946, Bishop James E. Walsh had become even more enthusiastic than Ford in his praise of the Generalissimo:

> We have almost reached the halfway mark of the twentieth century, and it is safe to predict now that, when the history of our age shall be finally assessed and written, the present leader of China and her people will stand revealed as one of its greatest men. . . . Among the great war leaders, Generalissimo Chiang Kai-shek stands out above all his contemporaries, President Roosevelt and Prime Minister Churchill not excepted.[38]

Maryknoll—The Field Afar also acknowledged Madame Chiang as "the only one person in public life in the world" who matched Chiang's accomplishments and high moral standards. The magazine proudly reprinted one of her speeches praising missionary contributions to China:

> Large numbers of Catholic missioners at the risk of their own lives have protected refugees and preserved the honor of terrified and helpless women. . . . Others devoted themselves to the rescue and care of innocent and bewildered children caught in the whirlwind of war. Others continued educational work among the stricken and the destitute. Their lives of self-denial and inner discipline has proved to be a source of inspiring courage to all those they serve and with whom they suffer.[39]

Articles hailed her as the perfect combination of "the Christianity of the Western world with the age-long wisdom, beauty, and graciousness of the Orient."[40]

The magazine also presented other Chinese Christian officials who led in the defense and reconstruction of the country. Among them was H. H. Kung, the self-proclaimed seventy-fifth lineal descendant of Confucius, who served as finance minister and vice-president of China's cabinet, the Executive Yuan, under

Chiang Kai-shek (and who happened to be his brother-in-law). Today his graft and corruption have been well documented. At the time, however, Maryknollers seemed unaware of Kung's unscrupulous dealings or unwilling to believe they really took place. Instead, *Maryknoll—The Field Afar* praised Kung for modernizing China's fiscal system and quoted his call to the country's 270 million Confucians to become followers of Christ:

> Confucianism is proposed as an ethic, not a religious system. In my study of religion, I discovered that God is a loving and kindly heavenly father. The Confucianist masses should embrace Christianity in order to perfect their Confucian principles.[41]

Kung proudly announced that in the missioners' preaching of Christian brotherhood he had found the achievement of his ancestor's ideals that "within the four seas, all men are brothers":

> Through the evangelical activities and scientific and literary pursuits of Christian missionaries, the East and West were brought to each other, and humanity moved closer to the Christian ideal of universal brotherhood.[42]

Another prominent person who often appeared in the pages of the Maryknoll magazine was Bishop Yü Pin, vicar apostolic of Nanking, national director of the Catholic Action, and a member of the Legislative Yuan, China's parliament. As a prelate, he was presented as "a pillar of the Catholic Church in China"; as a Chinese citizen he was depicted as "an ardent patriot [and] a pillar of his nation."[43] His message to American Catholics explained that World War II had helped to reveal the true nature of the Church to the Chinese and especially to its leadership:

> The Catholic Church in China has a rising popularity with the whole nation. The leaders of China, in the past, felt that the Church was too far from national interests. The war has changed all this. . . . [Chinese] Catholics have helped to build homes for the wounded soldiers. We work in military hospitals. We have organized Red Cross groups to go to the front lines and take care of the wounded. We have opened homes to shelter refugee students while they continue their studies. . . . The Catholic people apply their Catholic philosophy to their own lives and environment. This philosophy is simply loyalty to God and country.[44]

A Country Touched by Christian Charity

It was not by pure chance that the Catholic Church assumed an important role in social welfare during the Sino-Japanese War. The reliance of the Catholic Church on works of mercy was at the core of missionary work. From the days of their arrival in China, Maryknollers were convinced that, with the Chinese in particular, good example could be more persuasive than reason. As far back as January 1919, a page of Meyer's diary reprinted in *The Field Afar* introduced that idea: "The Chinese are a people who can be appealed to only by practical examples set before their eyes and affecting them directly. . . . They are not going to be reasoned into the Church." Then, with the disparaging tone so typical of that time toward nonwhite races, he added:

> Even among races more highly gifted, the "beginnings of faith," the channels of the first graces, have been an act of charity, a good example, a simple devotion that appealed not so much to the intellect as to the heart.[45]

As Maryknoll used works of charity to reach the Chinese, so did Maryknoll's publications use descriptions of them to reach American Catholics. Readers were presented with a thousand and one ways to participate in the works of mercy of Maryknollers in China. Abandoned infants and lepers received the largest coverage. From the beginning, the "saving of Chinese babies" was the charitable work with the most visibility. In the 1930s, a combination of these articles with the presentation of leper work formed a compelling image of China that no reader could forget. The poignant pictures of dying babies and distorted bodies, the happy faces of cared for babies and lepers and the vivid narratives of Maryknollers about their orphanages and their leper colony were skillfully presented to touch both the heart and the wallet of American Catholics.

Monetary appeals for saving Chinese babies, mostly girls, were routinely run. The initial cost was estimated at five dollars and covered the donation made to women who found the children—five cents per child. If the child died, it also defrayed the burial expenses of about thirty-five cents. Because healthy babies were entrusted to outside "wet nurses" at the cost of one dollar a month, the original offering was spent in less than half a year if a child survived. Although the plea for Chinese babies appealed to the readership of the magazine as a whole, a special emphasis was made in the "Juniors" and "Crusaders" pages to galvanize American youth to donate money for their less fortunate Chinese sisters. Mission activities of many school groups centered on raising funds for Chinese babies; "save a pagan baby" became their slogan.[46]

With the widening of the Sino-Japanese War in the late 1930s, the Maryknoll magazine shifted its readers' attention from the abandoned babies to the drama of the multitude of Chinese "warphans." These children were left alone to fend for themselves. Some had been separated from their relatives in moments of panic and flight and had not been able to find them again. Others had seen their parents killed. All were traumatized children whom readers were asked to help through Maryknoll's programs such as orphanages and boys' towns:

> Imagine that you are six years old, that you live in a good section of a Chinese city, with kindly and wealthy parents. Then imagine that men with guns and planes and tanks come to wreck the city. . . . At night crying, frightened, hungry,

you creep out of the ruins. Playmates are lying dead in the streets. All around are fires. Other children join you. . . . Begging, sleeping in ditches, living like animals, you children make your way across country. . . . At last you come to a town where tall, white-faced men in black robes give you food and shelter. . . . You do not understand, but you know they are good people, and you feel sure that their America and their God must be good, too.[47]

The magazine also printed pictures of these children who were not easily forgotten by well-fed and well-dressed Americans. In a five-page photo story on "China's Desperate Millions," focusing mainly on orphans of the war, American Catholics were told, "Look at the faces of these Chinese. Study them well. Then turn away if you are able. Then try to forget their grief."[48]

The rapid growth of Maryknoll's leper colony in South China showed that American Catholics were moved by the reports of such work and gave it their seal of approval with generous financial backing. Between 1933 and 1943, the number of lepers sheltered by Maryknollers increased from twenty to five hundred. The accommodations improved from a few clusters of ramshackle huts to a modern leprosarium.

Although during and after the war the emphasis shifted to the problems of war orphans and refugees in general, the magazine still continued to present the plight of the lepers as one of the biggest needs. The cry was even raised in poetry:

> *Forced to roam*   *Lepers, too*
> *Far from here*   *(Not a few)*
> *Almost nude,*   *At Ngai Moon*
> *Without food.*   *Need rice soon,*
> *Refugees—*   *In Christ's name,*
> *Help them, please?*   *Feed these same?*[49]

At other times the appeal was a lengthy article, such as one by Father John Joyce in November 1947, which retraced fifteen years of Maryknoll's work among lepers. The most commonly used form was a short moving entry in the "Want Ads" section of the magazine: "To be a leper anywhere is pitiful. To be one in torn, bleeding, starving China represents about the limit of human misery. Can you spare $5—the price of a month's life—for a Chinese leper?"[50]

After the surrender of Japan, Maryknollers thought the time was ideal to launch an all-out campaign of charitable works. They hoped to capitalize on the good reputation earned during the war by Chinese Catholics and missioners alike. The magazine reiterated that financial support had become even more important and valuable:

Out of the evil of the war in China, one good thing has come. Many thousands of Chinese, young and old, are ready to accept Christianity. Homeless, ragged, sick and starving, guided by rumor or chance, the Chinese came thronging to the

Maryknoll missions through all the years of war. And there they were helped and kept alive by the food and medicine, the clothing and shelter, which American friends of Maryknoll had provided. . . . Chinese understand self-interest but they could not understand why foreign priests were devoted unselfishly to them. . . . Many Chinese are grateful, their hearts are touched, they are curious. If Maryknollers can instruct them now, they will become Catholics. If not, they may be lost to the Church of Christ.[51]

The readers were told that they could participate in the reconstruction of China through the missioners. Most important was to help the estimated 84 million people (in a country of 440 million) who needed relief—food, clothing, shelter, and education.

In one article entitled "The Greatest Opportunity in History," the magazine pointed to the results that could be expected from helping war orphans. "If we can feed them, care for them, keep them alive, bring them somehow through this time of trial, they may be Christians—they, and their children, and other descendants, forever!"[52]

A Country Threatened by Communism

Starting in 1945, the magazine also stressed that there was much more at stake than just seizing or missing an opportunity. It prophesied that if the Church lost that opportunity, the Communists would seize it and capitalize on it. Concerning the care and education of war orphans, the magazine warned American Catholics:

If these youngsters and others like them are sheltered and fed and trained by Maryknoll missioners, they will grow up as friends; powerful friends in years to come for our country, our Church, our God. If we neglect them—be assured the International Communists will not![53]

In 1946, Bishop James E. Walsh wrote an article calling for "true friends of China" not to be deceived by reports from the press vilifying the Nationalist government. Walsh readily acknowledged that the Chinese government was not perfect and had not been elected by popular vote. On the other hand, however, he described it as

a well-intentioned government, one full of plans and reforms for the welfare of the Chinese people . . . [which] respects the rights and preserves the liberties of the people and is the only one that is wanted by the people.[54]

Walsh recognized that the Nationalist party contained "petty despots, unprincipled opportunists, inefficient officials, and dishonest grafters," but he maintained that its percentage of bad elements was not larger than that of any other political party in the world. On the contrary, he said, the Nationalist party, especially its top leadership, had a "preponderance of patriots and statesmen who set the standard and determine the policies to further the welfare of the people and the nation as a whole."[55]

In conclusion, Walsh lashed out at the Communists for not supporting the war effort and for sabotaging national reconstruction:

> The Communist group took advantage of their own people's misery and their own country's extremity, to impose themselves on great sections of the population who despised and feared them, establish a separate state, divide the nation, sabotage the war effort, abstain carefully from fighting the Japanese invaders; and finally, to broadcast around the world the claim that they represent a spontaneous movement of the Chinese people. . . . China has a good government and will set its house in order; and all true friends of China will be known by their support of that constructive program.[56]

Recent studies on Chiang Kai-shek and his entourage have been critical of Chiang, H. H. Kung, the Soong family, and other prominent Nationalist officials of the government and the military.[57] In the light of these findings, Walsh's article and others written in the same vein appear to have been naive and to have misled the Catholic readership of *Maryknoll—The Field Afar*. Not all Maryknollers, however, were so uncritical of the Nationalists. Some raised serious reservations about their unscrupulous methods and corruption, but these views were never published. These Maryknollers eventually concluded that, as bad as the Nationalist régime was, it was to be supported because, in the eyes of the Church, communism was no alternative.[58]

Obviously, the course of events did not turn out as Maryknollers had expected. Between 1947 and 1951, the Maryknoll magazine opted to remain silent on the changing political situation in China and concentrated instead on the rapid growth of the Catholic Church. Only when Maryknollers themselves were forced by the Communists to leave China did the magazine suddenly explode with numerous stories on the plight of the Chinese Catholics and the missioners at the hands of the "Reds" or "Commies." By the peak of the missionary exodus in 1952 and 1953, twenty-seven articles had been printed on the Communist persecution.

At the same time, Maryknoll published several popular books with accounts of life under the Communist regime in Maryknoll's mission territories. *Nun in Red China* by Sister Mary Victoria retraced the appalling experiences of Sister Paulita Hoffman and Sister Edith Rietz. *No Secret Is Safe* was the prison diary of Father Mark Tennien. *Calvary in China* told of the jailing, trial, and sentencing of Father Robert Greene. *Bird of Sorrow* by Monsignor John Romaniello depicted the patient endurance, loyalty, and witnessing to the faith of Chinese Catholics.[59]

All these books told stories of arrests on trumped-up charges; of horror-filled months of imprisonment and shocking treatment; of cells that crawled with vermin and were so overcrowded that sleeping space was often only two feet wide. Screams issued from torture rooms all night long. Often missioners were awakened in the middle of the night, bound painfully, and subjected to incessant and bullying questioning. The threat of execution always hung over their heads until the Communists finally released them at the Hong Kong border.

However, Maryknoll did not concentrate for long on lamenting the evils of communism; instead Maryknoll began to reflect on the lessons learned by the Catholic Church in China. Already in 1952 in a very perceptive editorial entitled "Failure in Asia," Father John Donovan attempted to explain why the Christian West had failed in China. Donovan opened his analysis of the historical steps that led to the Communist victory in China by quoting the French Catholic philosopher Jacques Maritain:

> The complaints and curses which the East utters against us are inspired not only by hatred but also by profound disillusion. We cannot hear that outcry without quivering for sorrow and shame. . . . Before becoming indignant with our accusers, let us first admit we have sinned against them.[60]

Donovan then proceeded to explain how the Christian West had failed the Chinese through its traders and statesmen, as well as its missioners. In their relentless search for profit, Western traders had introduced nefarious traffic in opium and Western nations supported unjust treaties with gunboats. As for Western missioners, Donovan wrote:

> They too blindly and too complacently accepted the benefits conferred by imperialistic and unjust treaty rights. Today we see the ethical absurdity of gunboat support for Christian missionary endeavors. Today our missioners suffer in silence the horrors of unjust prison terms or house confinement.[61]

If China had turned to communism, said Donovan, it was in great measure the fault of the Christians from the West with whom the Chinese had come in contact. However, his conclusion was quite hopeful. He believed that the abiding faith of Chinese Catholics under persecution would reveal the true face of Catholicism and become an unshakable foundation on which the future Church of China would be built.

Conclusion

The overall characteristic of Maryknollers portrayed in the magazine and other Maryknoll publications was that they had a deep love for the Chinese people and a great admiration for their civilization. Francis X. Ford, by the number and length of his contributions, appeared as Maryknoll's main spokesman for Chinese culture and human qualities. The Chinese were not strange creatures, but ordinary human beings. Their philosophy of life revolved around filial piety—the reverence for older generations—and upheld the good of the family and the country above the needs of the individual. This discipline was behind the simplicity of their life and their virtues of patience, industry, energy, and endurance against all odds.

In their enthusiasm, however, the missioners, particularly Ford, often gave a portrait of China and its people that lacked balance and bordered at times on fiction. According to Ford, the Chinese simplicity of living was a matter of choice; in times of war and famine it made them bear suffering and hunger with a lightheartedness and a good humor which reminded him of St. Francis of Assisi. Although Ford was from the city and had not experienced farm life, he wrote extensively on the subject. Ford's disparaging description of the American farmhouse as a styleless ugly wooden structure, compared to its idealized Chinese counterpart, showed that his knowledge of the American countryside was very limited. Even the Chinese farmhouse he described, with its several courtyards, rooms, patios, and cool corners, was not a common sight in South China. Most villagers were too poor to maintain such a home. Instead, they lived in small one- or two-room houses that were so dark and humid that tuberculosis was endemic. This "reality" of Chinese life, well depicted in Maryknollers' diaries and letters, was rarely allowed to surface in Maryknoll publications.

In their attempts to prove that Westerners were not morally and culturally superior to the Chinese, Maryknollers often described China as a nearly perfect society nourishing a naturally virtuous people with ancient wisdom. The Maryknoll magazine conveyed a sense of a Chinese state of natural goodness somewhat reminiscent of Rousseau's philosophy or Chateaubriand's writings in *Le génie du Christianisme*.

Maryknollers claimed that China was ideally prepared for Christianity and needed but an introduction. Christianity would incorporate all the goodness of Chinese society and, at the same time, bring about the demise of its superstitions and imperfections—such as the abandoning of baby girls—which were considered marks of the devil. As proof, missioners pointed to the steadfastness and rapid growth of the Chinese Catholic Church with its own priests, Sisters, Brothers, and even its own bishops. Chinese lay people were leaving their mark not only in the countryside but also in the cities and in higher levels of government, business, and education. Maryknollers envisioned a modern China that would enrich and regenerate the splendid wisdom of its ancient civilization by borrowing Christian faith and scientific progress from the West.

Looking into the future, Maryknoll presented American readers with a vision of a great Catholic Chinese nation. All this was but a dream. Certainly the Chinese were rapidly adopting Western methods and discoveries. In the realm of spiritual values, however, most Chinese clung to their own values and viewed Christianity as a foreign and unneeded product of the West.

Most Maryknollers seemed to have been aware of some of these difficulties. Their efforts at adapting the Catholic message, their training of the native clergy and sisterhood, and their development of an apostolic laity were signs that they did realize that China would become Christian only when Christianism became Chinese. By the end of the Sino-Japanese War, Maryknollers saw some signs that efforts of the Catholic Church to become more Chinese were having results. They felt that the strong patriotism displayed by Chinese Catholics during the war helped to wash away the foreign stigma that Catholicism had always carried in China.

It is ironic to note, however, that at the precise moment when the Chinese Church was being recognized as patriotic, its leadership—both foreign and Chinese—endorsed the Nationalist regime and linked their destinies in the years ahead. This attitude was clearly reflected in the Maryknoll magazine's blind praise of the Nationalist leadership. Because communism was no acceptable alternative in the eyes of the Church, the Communist victory left the Church in the camp of the defeated Nationalist government. As the Communists exposed the widespread corruption of the Western-supported Nationalist government, the entire Chinese Catholic Church also appeared unpatriotic.

Nonetheless, if the Catholic Church had not been so closely linked with the Nationalist government and had limited itself to showing its love for China by relieving misery and helping reconstruction, it still would have faced persecution for religious reasons. However, it would not have had to reestablish its patriotism, and it is also probable that some of the current tension between the Chinese Catholic Church and the Vatican might not exist.

In the wake of the religious persecutions and expulsion of the missioners during the 1950s, the Maryknoll magazine quite naturally published many articles that depicted communism as the worst of all evils. Nonetheless, the Chinese people themselves were always portrayed in a favorable light. Bad attitudes and deeds were attributed to "the Reds," as if, by turning Communist, they had lost the admirable traits and virtues of their race and culture.

Since 1972, America's fascination with China is being rekindled by a political rapprochement most visible in the cultural and economic sectors. From a religious point of view, the dream of a Catholic Chinese nation has proven to be an illusion, although the existence of a Chinese Church has become a reality.

Notes

1. The group evolved into two closely linked, but separate, organizations: the Maryknoll Fathers and Brothers, officially known as the Catholic Foreign Mission Society of America; and the Maryknoll Sisters, officially known as the Foreign Mission Sisters of St. Dominic.

2. The magazine was known as *The Field Afar* between 1907 and 1939, then *Maryknoll—The Field Afar* between 1939 and 1957, when the title was changed to *Maryknoll*. Its present circulation is about one million.

3. *The Field Afar*, May 1918, p. 68.

4. *The Field Afar*, September 1933, p. 234.

5. *The Field Afar*, March 1925, p. 81.

6. *Maryknoll—The Field Afar*, February 1942, pp. 5–6.
7. *Maryknoll—The Field Afar*, September 1942, p. 23.
8. Ibid., p. 5.
9. *Maryknoll—The Field Afar*, February 1942, p. 6.
10. *The Field Afar*, September 1933, p. 235.
11. *The Field Afar*, October 1935, p. 228.
12. *The Field Afar*, December 1935, p. 344.
13. *The Field Afar*, June 1933, p. 192.
14. *Maryknoll—The Field Afar*, July–August 1943, p. 30.
15. Ibid., pp. 30, 32.
16. *Maryknoll—The Field Afar*, September 1945, p. 2.
17. *The Field Afar*, May 1919, p. 95.
18. *The Field Afar*, April 1933, pp. 99–100.
19. *The Field Afar*, April 1925, p. 103.
20. *The Field Afar*, May 1933, p. 133.
21. For entire text, see *Collectanea Sacrae Congregatio de Propaganda Fide* (Rome: Typis Polyglottis Vaticanis, 1907), 1:135, "Instruction of the Sacred Congregation of Propaganda Fide, A.D. 1659."
22. *The Field Afar*, December 1935, p. 345.
23. Ibid.
24. *Maryknoll—The Field Afar*, September 1939, p. 241.
25. *Maryknoll—The Field Afar*, November 1939, p. 301.
26. *The Field Afar*, January 1933, p. 32.
27. *The Field Afar*, February 1933, p. 64.
28. *The Field Afar*, January 1926, p. 24; June 1927, p. 157.
29. *Maryknoll—The Field Afar*, September 1939, p. 246.
30. Ibid.
31. *The Field Afar*, May 1933, p. 132.
32. *The Field Afar*, May 1919, p. 86; June 1919, p. 111. See also *The Field Afar*, June 1918, p. 81; August 1918, p. 117; August 1919, p. 163; October 1919, pp. 206–207; March 1921, p. 52.
33. *The Field Afar*, May 1918, p. 68.
34. *The Field Afar*, November 1925, p. 311. See also *The Field Afar*, July–August 1923, p. 196; October 1925, p. 284; February 1926, p. 40; March 1926, p. 68.
35. *The Field Afar*, December 1934, p. 355. See also May 1933, p. 131; January 1937, p. 26.
36. *The Field Afar*, December 1934, p. 355.
37. *Maryknoll—The Field Afar*, June 1943, p. 25. See also July–August 1942, pp. 15–16; October 1943, p. 2.
38. *Maryknoll—The Field Afar*, April 1946, p. 36.
39. *Maryknoll—The Field Afar*, July–August 1942, p. 16. See also April 1946, pp. 36–37.
40. *Maryknoll—The Field Afar*, June 1943, inside front cover.
41. *Maryknoll—The Field Afar*, May 1943, p. 2.
42. *Maryknoll—The Field Afar*, January–February 1945, inside front cover.
43. *The Field Afar*, January 1937, p. 26.
44. *Maryknoll—The Field Afar*, June 1943, p. 32. See also October 1943, pp. 2–3.
45. *The Field Afar*, May 1919, p. 95.
46. *The Field Afar*, June 1930, p. 189; November 1930, p. 321; *Maryknoll—The Field Afar*, November 1945, p. 48.
47. *Maryknoll—The Field Afar*, December 1945, p. 21.

48. *Maryknoll—The Field Afar*, November 1947, pp. 23–27. See also November 1943, pp. 14–16; January–February 1945, p. 20; June 1945, p. 48; March 1946, p. 48; February 1947, pp. 34–35; April 1947, p. 48.

49. *Maryknoll—The Field Afar*, September 1943, p. 48.

50. *Maryknoll—The Field Afar*, July–August 1945, p. 48; November 1947, pp. 18–21. See also January–February 1945, p. 48; June 1945, p. 48; October 1945, p. 48; November 1945, p. 48; June 1946, p. 48; October 1947, p. 48; December 1947, p. 48; February 1948, p. 48.

51. *Maryknoll—The Field Afar*, July–August 1946, p. 45.

52. *Maryknoll—The Field Afar*, December 1945, p. 21. See also March 1945, pp. 3–5.

53. *Maryknoll—The Field Afar*, January–February 1945, p. 20.

54. *Maryknoll—The Field Afar*, April 1946, p. 35.

55. Ibid., p. 36.

56. Ibid., p. 37.

57. Jean Chesneaux, Françoise Le Barbier, Marie-Claire Bergère, *China, From the 1911 Revolution to Liberation* (New York: Pantheon Library, 1977), pp. 198–99, 269–70, 272, 325. Brian Crozier, *The Man Who Lost China* (New York: Scribners, 1976), pp. 242–44, 258–59, 279, 394–95. William Morwood, *Duel for the Middle Kingdom* (New York: Everest House, 1980), pp. 308, 310, 355–58. See also Sterling Seagrave, *The Soong Dynasty* (New York: Harper & Row, 1985).

58. Maryknoll Fathers' Archives, TF04, Father Francis Daubert, pp. 36–39; TS65, Sister Irene Fogarty, p. 34.

59. Sister Maria Victoria [Maria Del Rey Danforth], *Nun in Red China* (New York: McGraw-Hill, 1953). Mark Tennien, *No Secret Is Safe* (New York: Farrar, Straus & Young, 1952). Robert W. Greene, *Calvary in China* (New York: G. P. Putnam's Sons, 1953). John Romaniello, *Bird of Sorrow* (New York: P. J. Kenedy, 1956).

60. *Maryknoll—The Field Afar*, October 1952, p. 52.

61. Ibid., p. 53.

Part II

Missionary Roles in Diplomacy

10

AMERICAN MISSIONARIES AND THE POLITICS OF FAMINE RELIEF TO CHINA

Arline T. Golkin

The American role in providing famine relief to China derived from humanitarian, evangelical, and commercial concerns as well as from American national policy goals. Americans did not respond consistently to Chinese famines. Popular donations rose when conditions appeared promising in terms of various objectives in China, and fell when political disunity, social unrest, and civil war discouraged efforts to sustain involvement in China's internal problems. The American public usually provided emergency financial support in response to missionary appeals, but American official attitudes had overriding importance in determining the final results of fund-raising campaigns. Neither the American public nor American officials displayed enthusiasm for the work-relief programs advocated by missionaries in China. American contributions for emergency relief were not matched by support for long-term famine prevention projects. Chinese official response to American intervention further influenced the nature and extent of relief; Chinese officials, who did not want physical improvements controlled by foreigners, rejected plans for change. By the late 1920s, American official views on diminished possibilities for relief began to supersede missionary appeals on behalf of the Chinese people. Missionary influence on the general public and among the individuals who shaped American policy in China diminished steadily during the 1930s and throughout the World War II years as the U.S. government played a growing role in delivering aid to the Chinese government.

Famine-relief efforts carried out during the late nineteenth and early twentieth centuries represented a spectrum of issues, appeals, and programs that were set forth in tandem with the growth of missionary endeavors in education, medicine, and rural reconstruction and with the growth of American political interest in China's internal affairs.

Timothy Richard, a Welsh Baptist minister, appealed for outside funding and carried out famine relief in China during the late 1870s. His activities helped to focus international attention on the plight of Chinese famine victims and to create

a legacy of ideas for famine relief and for famine prevention.[1] American missionaries took part in some small-scale independent relief operations during the late
nineteenth century, but did not embark on major campaigns until the beginning of
the twentieth.

American programs for famine relief to China originated with the missionary
community, which generated appeals for aid within the United States. While
donations from the American public supported emergency relief measures, the
success or failure of popular fund-raising campaigns was influenced by American
official response.

The importance of official support for famine intervention became obvious
when Secretary of State John Hay gave personal and financial assistance to missionary relief work after the Boxer Uprising of 1900, and when Minister Conger
offered to facilitate distributions.[2] Missionaries used relief donations to operate
gruel kitchens in famine-stricken areas. Some of them devised small-scale work-
relief projects and proposed additional, major improvements which might improve physical and economic conditions enough to prevent recurrent famines.
However, limited outside funding and Chinese resistance to foreign controls held
them back.[3]

In 1906, President Theodore Roosevelt responded to missionary and consular
appeals by appointing the American Red Cross as the agency in charge of funds
that were donated in response to his national request on behalf of famine relief to
China. In addition, he obtained congressional approval for the Red Cross to
transport food donations on military vessels. Roosevelt acted at a time when
boycotts had damaged American interests in China. His action was designed to
generate good will and to emphasize America's political, religious, and economic
opportunities in China.[4] Some one and a half million people received some form
of aid as a result of combined missionary, government, and popular responses.
Timothy Richard urged postfamine investigations into its causes and into methods
for prevention. However, Chinese officials halted minor work-relief projects
undertaken by missionaries during 1906–1907, insisting that such works constituted a government responsibility, the Red Cross program supported only "disaster
relief," and missionaries wanted to finish famine operations and return to the tasks
of education and evangelism.[5]

When civil strife worsened the effects of widespread flooding during 1910–11,
total American relief donations were less than twenty thousand dollars. President
Taft did not issue a call for funds because of what Consul Amos Wilder referred
to as American "disgust with Chinese officialdom for failing to prevent recurrent
disasters." A relatively small amount of aid was provided only after the new
Chinese government assured official cooperation with American relief agents and
agencies.[6]

In spite of physical and financial difficulties, 1911 marked an important change
in missionary perception of their role in alleviating popular misery in China. A

group of missionaries who had been active participants in relief work determined that, in the case of a famine or other calamity, it was the "duty of the missionary body . . . to take part in the work of relief." In addition, they determined that a majority of relief work should be devoted to public works projects. Supplementary proposals addressed medical needs among famine victims and the need for agricultural improvements, educational programs for farmers, and the development of small local industries.[7]

During 1914, Americans turned their attention and their support to civilian war needs in Europe. Limited relief efforts were initiated in 1917, but only after State Department officials announced that the Chinese government had promised to send two divisions of troops to France and noted that it would be "wise and helpful for the Red Cross to assist in relief work at this time."[8]

In addition to efforts made in the provision of food relief, missionaries joined the American Red Cross in a road-building project. It failed because of insufficient donations from America and because Chinese officials refused to cooperate in the endeavor.[9]

The decade of the 1920s marked both the height and the nadir of American official support for private relief efforts. During 1920–21, a favorable international climate and relative political stability within China prompted the largest and most successful famine-relief campaign of the first half of the twentieth century. A dramatic shift occurred during the years 1928–30, when American officials refused to support China relief. Their objections derived from questions regarding the correct form for famine intervention, the opportunity to carry out relief, and even the definition of famine. In the end, official opposition governed the American response to popular misery in China. Missionary voices could not sway foreign policy.

Millions of people in China's northern provinces subsisted on scant food supplies in 1920. Their condition resulted from the cumulative effects of poor recovery from floods in 1917, poor harvests in 1918–19, and widespread drought-related crop failures in 1920. The combination created a situation in which the populace "survived more than it lived."[10] Several factors governed American response. Many Americans living in China sympathized with nationalist feelings that had emerged during and after the May Fourth Movement. The demands of World War I had improved China's urban economy and businessmen were optimistic about their future. Missionaries had begun to perceive solutions to China's rural poverty in terms of educational and agricultural improvements. Most members of the foreign diplomatic body approved of the government formed under Wu P'ei-fu in July 1920, and they were anxious to mitigate the threat of Soviet overtures to their status in China.[11] As a result, direct action, massive financial assistance, and unusually good cooperation among diverse Chinese and foreign groups helped to hold famine-related deaths to about five hundred thousand under conditions which might otherwise have claimed between three and four million lives.[12]

American missionaries spoke of famine conditions to John Earl Baker during July and August in 1920. Baker, who served as railway adviser to the Chinese Ministry of Communications and as chairman of the Peking Chapter of the American Red Cross, responded by transmitting their reports to American Minister Charles Crane. At the same time, Crane began to receive similar reports from consular officials. He and Baker agreed that conditions justified immediate action by the foreign community in China. Americans who attended a September meeting of the Peking Chapter of the American Red Cross voted to request aid from Washington, to launch a drive for contributions from Americans in China, and to have Minister Crane ask his colleagues in the diplomatic corps to adopt similar measures. Crane believed that famine relief would be a "wonderful addition" to the "fine story" of America's sympathetic attitude toward China and that it would help to "reconcile political elements" within China.[13]

The American Red Cross released contingency funds for China relief, but did not launch an appeal for public donations for China because of a primary focus upon postwar relief work in Europe. In addition, the decision not to call for public donations for China permitted Red Cross officials to control the distribution of their funds and to stipulate the nature and extent of their relief operations in China. In accordance with Red Cross instructions, John Earl Baker used the funds to begin an independent relief program, which provided famine victims in specified areas with food payments in exchange for labor on road-building projects. The combined effects of international cooperation and good local management yielded results. Under Baker's direction, some 160,000 workers built more than eight hundred miles of highways, dug wells, and planted trees. The Red Cross later estimated that nearly ninety thousand people had benefited from the program.[14]

While the Red Cross conducted independent relief operations, a major fund-raising program was undertaken in the United States. In December 1920, President Woodrow Wilson appointed businessman Thomas Lamont director of the American Committee for China Famine Fund. Wilson simultaneously appointed Under Secretary of State Norman Davis to serve as treasurer, and he assigned American Red Cross Chairman Livingston Farrand the task of coordinating activities in order to avoid duplication of effort and funding in the famine zone. Presidential support and intensive publicity campaigns enabled Lamont to raise more than $8 million in the United States. An American Advisory Committee, formed in China by Minister Crane, distributed the funds.[15]

While Lamont's committee carried out fund-raising activities, representatives of several foreign, Sino-foreign, and Chinese relief societies voted to merge their activities. As a result, the Peking United International Famine Relief Committee (PUIFRC) was established during the summer of 1921. The PUIFRC had an Administrative Council of eight Chinese and eight foreigners who were given full authority over the mechanisms for conducting famine relief.[16] The Chinese government enhanced PUIFRC efforts by appropriating $1 million for immediate relief work, by reducing official salaries 20 percent, by appointing special famine commissioners to assist the PUIFRC, and by granting free railway transport for relief supplies and relief workers. A four million dollar loan helped to support relief programs; a 10 percent customs surtax provided security on the loan. China's railway minister reduced freight charges by 25 percent on food transported into famine areas. He increased them by the same amount on food moving in the opposite direction. The result was a flow of grain from areas with good crops into places which had none. Hoarding stopped and food prices maintained a steady rate or declined.[17] A majority of PUIFRC funds paid for direct food distributions, but some were invested in programs to buy seeds, establish schools, and initiate small-scale industries. PUIFRC technical volunteers helped to supervise road construction, irrigation, and tree-planting projects. Various missionary groups formed subsidiaries of the PUIFRC. They cooperated fully with the central organization and, in many cases, set forth programs designed to provide for famine-prevention as well as for famine relief.[18]

When the PUIFRC distributed questionnaires designed to evaluate relief efforts, respondents praised the concept of work relief and recommended PUIFRC expansion into the realm of famine prevention.[19] In the autumn of 1921, the PUIFRC responded to growing support for work relief as a means to control famine by organizing a permanent international committee, the China International Famine Relief Commission (CIFRC), which was made up of both Chinese and foreigners, and which was assigned the tasks of providing emergency relief and of carrying out programs for famine prevention.[20] The goals and operations of the CIFRC opened a fresh chapter in famine intervention. Under more favorable circumstances, the commission might have utilized accumulated experience and expertise to carry out long-range projects without impinging on Chinese nationalist sentiments.

Unfortunately, the CIFRC began operations in the face of multiple handicaps. First, the commission depended on private donations for support. As a result, plans for famine-prevention projects could not be instituted until the committee had adequate funds on hand. Second, the committee had difficulty attracting funds from foreign donors who perceived famine relief as a form of pure succor and who did not want to support work relief programs. Third, the CIFRC confined relief efforts to suffering from "natural causes" such as flood or drought. Commission members believed that donors would not want to give aid to bandit-ridden or war-torn districts because it might be misused. As a result, famine conditions associated with military combat or with economic collapse could not be relieved. CIFRC responded in 1925 by expanding its definition of famine to include human causes and to extend relief where distress resulted, in part, from "causes of a political nature."[21]

The Washington Conference of 1921–22 was carried out in an atmosphere of relative amity, but the years that followed were characterized by the spread of banditry and civil war in China and by growing American distrust of Chinese political and military leaders. American officials in China became disillusioned by Chinese neglect of internal disorders. American private donors grew reluctant to contribute for famine relief, and all concerned parties experienced growing disenchantment in light of scandalous reports on the misappropriation of famine funds.[22] American officials began to discourage relief efforts, foreign press representatives in China refused to support relief campaigns, and the American Red Cross devoted efforts and funds to relief work elsewhere in the world. CIFRC appeals for funds to dig wells or build roads in China brought few results.[23]

Ninety-three districts sought CIFRC aid in 1923. Available funds permitted assistance to only forty-five of them. Widespread flooding caused destitution among an estimated 10 million Chinese in 1924, but appeals did not generate adequate relief. Political, economic, and social conditions worsened steadily over the next three years. Antiforeign outbursts occurred in many parts of China during 1925. In 1926, military struggles threatened American interests in China, and American officials had to grapple with demands for treaty revisions. By 1927, grave social, political, and military confusion contributed to the dire effects of widespread drought. American diplomats reacted with dismay and fear when confronted by a rising tide of Chinese nationalism, demands for treaty revisions, and antiforeign demonstrations. Foreigners' escape from Nanking under protective gunfire and consular orders for missionaries to leave the interior added to a generalized sense of apprehension and confusion.

When the CIFRC estimated that some 50 million people faced starvation in 1928, famine relief was least among American official concerns. American missionaries who remained in China's interior appealed for funds to alleviate popular misery in eight northern provinces. The American Legation transmitted their communications to the Red Cross, but neither Legation nor Red Cross officials supported the idea of initiating a campaign for contributions. Consular personnel argued that outside relief was impossible in light of existing conditions. Red Cross officials, calling upon a 1925 policy statement, declared that they would "wholly avoid intervention in cases of civil war."[24]

Lines of disagreement formed among American officials and missionary groups, and a private movement to overcome official opposition to famine intervention was undertaken in the United States. The Foreign Missions Conference of North America helped to form the organization known as China Famine Relief (CFR), which could raise funds from the American public, transmit them to China, and support CIFRC work-relief programs. Henry T. Hodgkin addressed the conference in January 1928: "China needs help from the west and that need will remain for many a long day." Hodgkin acknowledged that the missionary body in China had been "badly shaken and confused" by anti-Christian acts but, he announced, most workers were eager to return. He asked American churches to make large contributions for China.[25] American Red Cross officials provided counterpoint by reporting that famine areas were infested with bandits and roving military bands, that a medical missionary had been killed, and that Americans were seeking shelter in China's treaty ports.[26]

CFR began to campaign despite lack of official sanction, Red Cross support, or strong representation in China's interior. Committee members William Johnson and John Earl Baker asked Thomas Lamont to release funds that remained in trust from the 1920–21 relief campaign, but Lamont refused. According to Baker, he "courteously informed us that if the President of the United States requested him to undertake a campaign . . . he would be willing to serve."[27] Persistent pressure eventually induced Lamont to release $25,000 but he informed CFR that no additional funds would be made available unless a "national figure" headed their campaign. CFR response was immediate. Dr. S. Parkes Cadman, president of the Federal Council of Churches, agreed to serve as chairman. David A. Brown, chairman of the United Jewish Campaign, accepted the position of board chairman, and James Thomas, founder of the British-American Tobacco Company, left retirement to become treasurer. Lamont was obliged to release $75,000 in trust funds to serve as a nucleus for CFR work.[28]

CFR executives realized that they could not approach President Coolidge without State Department and Red Cross approval. Johnson visited Stanley Hornbeck at department headquarters. Hornbeck supported the views of China-based officials and offered neither support nor assistance. Baker asked Red Cross leaders to help CFR raise $5 million dollars for work-relief projects similar to the ones carried out with Red Cross funds in 1920–21. The chairman of the American Red Cross, Judge John Barton Payne, refused to launch an appeal. He wrote to Johnson, "Conditions in China are such that we must all deeply regret the impracticality of taking strong measures to relieve them." A memo to Red Cross Service Heads and Area Managers stated, "It is not enough that help is needed. Opportunity to give help is no less essential."[29]

When CFR officers expressed concern that failure to provide aid might damage America's reputation as a friend to China, Hornbeck replied that any responsibility for damage to American prestige would belong to CFR and that he would "make every effort to refute any imputation of blame which may be directed toward the Department of State." Red Cross officials reiterated their policy of noninterference in cases of civil war.[30] Other potential supporters, including some missionary groups, shared State Department and Red Cross concerns with reports on civil war and political and social chaos in China. The National Information Bureau refused to approve CFR publicity work. Big business representatives turned down appeals because they were convinced that widespread disorder contributed to famine conditions and that donations would be misused. Editors of the New York–based *Christian Herald,* who had collected large sums in response to earlier appeals for China, refused to support CFR because they would not support the concept of work relief as a substitute for free cash and food distributions. Some missionary organizations were divided regarding the role that they should take in political activities and in terms of their attitudes toward Kuomintang leadership. Others issued sympathetic statements, while a few remained "in conference."[31] As a result, work relief, which was the only form of intervention supported by the American Red Cross in 1921, and which served as the primary focus for CIFRC programs, could not provide a practical basis for fund-raising appeals in 1928. Neither work-relief proposals nor appeals for food and cash donations generated a positive response from the American public, which accepted newspaper accounts and official reports on conditions in China rather than appeals from the missionary community.

John Earl Baker decided to go to China and seek ways to overcome what he called the "gospel of hopelessness" preached by State Department and Red Cross officials. His reports confirmed that several million people needed assistance and predicted that conditions would worsen, but his attempts to find support for famine relief proved discouraging. Baker described meetings with press representatives who seemed to hold the opinion that "the . . . missionaries are putting over another fast one on the American people in their effort to curry favor with the damn Chinks." American businessmen in Shanghai concurred, "The Chinese don't deserve anything from America."[32] To make matters worse, Chinese officials rejected aid that would give Americans decision-making powers over relief projects. China's Minister of Foreign Affairs C. T. Wang (Wang Cheng-t'ing) told Baker, "When China wants roads built, she will do it herself, and if she needs money for the purpose, she will borrow it on the market."[33] Wang later elaborated in a conversation with journalist George Sokolsky, "I do not believe that my Government would care to confuse constructive work with charity." He added, "We should welcome out and out charity . . . but I do not believe that we should care to have . . . road building undertaken as part of famine relief."[34]

Baker's efforts were undermined further when the American Commercial Attache Julean Arnold reported that "one of the best crops in years" was being harvested in Shantung province, and that wheat crops in Central China would be "the largest in years."[35] The CIFRC published a contradictory report, but continuing American official opposition diminished possibilities for a successful CFR campaign. CIFRC announcements and appeals were ignored. In 1928, total foreign contributions for famine-relief work amounted to little more than $30,000.[36]

In January 1929, American Minister J. V. A. MacMurray acknowledged that destitution was "worse than usual" in several places because of military operations and political chaos. However, he added, conditions did not fulfill the CIFRC definition of famine as a failure of food supply due primarily to "natural causes" and therefore did not justify outside assistance. The American Advisory Committee in Peking supported MacMurray's conclusions and observed that "only" four million people faced starvation.[37]

The CIFRC responded, "What fundamentally is a famine?" Should the term be used to cover "severe destitution" without reference to its causes or should it be limited to "destruction due exclusively to natural causes?" Should existing conditions be treated as a "crisis" or as a "chronic state of affairs, an attempt to relieve which would be like pouring water into a bottomless well?''[38] The commission acknowledged human causes of widespread destitution, but chose to distinguish existing conditions from chronic misery, to declare a crisis, and thereby to justify continued fund-raising appeals.

Chiang Kai-shek's nominal unification of China took place against a backdrop of domestic disorder, economic chaos, and widespread popular misery. Missionary reports for early 1929 described sales of women and children, deaths from typhus and plague, and cannibalism. A single statement summarized conditions in Kansu: ''Nothing reaped, thousands gone, nothing sown.'' The CIFRC estimated that 57 million Chinese were affected by famine during early 1929, but American officials chose to treat conditions like a ''bottomless well'' and to maintain that they did not match the CIFRC original definition of famine.[39]

Within a matter of months, relative political stability in China, along with government promises of official assistance, gave CIFRC officers hope for improved fund-raising opportunities. They appealed for $12 million. During spring 1929, CFR renewed efforts to get American official approval for aid to China. They did not achieve their goal. Secretary of State Kellogg stated that he had no objection to CFR fund-raising efforts, but that he would not give them his official support. Red Cross officials remained firm in their refusal to launch an appeal. The most that they offered to CFR was their ''best wishes.''[40]

In March 1929, CFR officers issued a statement in response to America's official refusal to support or to engage in relief efforts for China. They declared that they were ''not concerned with the causes of the frightful suffering,'' but with the ''single humanitarian objective of saving as many as possible . . . who have been brought face to face with death from hunger largely through no fault of their own.''[41]

Herbert Hoover received multiple requests for American government aid to China immediately following his election. His experience with famine and refugee relief in Europe and the Soviet Union, and his new authority as president of the United States, made him a potential champion for CFR. Furthermore, he was the only person who could resolve the differences between CFR and State Department and Red Cross officials. Hoover agreed to investigate possibilities for aid. He ordered the State Department to provide him with a full account on conditions in China and with an explanation of the Red Cross position. Secretary of State Henry Stimson summarized department reports for 1928, Red Cross views, and consular reports from China. They all expressed negative views.[42]

Hoover did not doubt that China was experiencing famine conditions, but he was not convinced that American efforts could succeed in arresting them. Before making a final decision regarding America's role, he wanted to have an ''authoritative statement'' made by a ''public body.'' To that end, Hoover ordered the Red Cross to carry out a first-hand investigation of conditions in China on the grounds that Red Cross status could be ''endangered'' by having independent actions going on under agencies of ''lesser responsibility'' whose failings might diminish American prestige in China and elsewhere in the world. Hoover added that, if the Red Cross decided to carry out a relief campaign for China, he would ask CFR to discontinue their activities.[43]

A three-man American Red Cross Commission spent ten weeks investigating conditions in China during the summer of 1929. Their report, published in October 1929, stated that prevalent distress could not be classified as famine because failures of food supplies did not result primarily from "natural causes" such as drought or flood. The Red Cross Commission criticized Chinese official failures to direct relief operations or to coordinate activities carried out by private Chinese agencies. Their report went on to declare that the Chinese people would "give more thought" to the underlying causes of famine if they were "obliged to assume responsibility for the resulting relief needs." In other words, if the United States refused to provide relief, China would be forced to act independently.[44]

CFR and CIFRC personnel reviewed Red Cross findings with dismay and anger. John Earl Baker stated that the report read as if it had been prepared by the American Legation: "The whole Legation assumption is that bad government in China is the result of deliberate intention on the part of the people." CIFRC Chairman M. T. Liang called the report a "diatribe" filled with "pernicious criticism."[45] An article in the *China Critic* asked, "Does charity work depend on political stability?" An editorial stated, "Only by shoving the responsibility . . . onto warlords, bandits and taxation could the (Red Cross) Society crawl out of its . . . cold-blooded and superior attitude."[46] Missionaries in America expressed outrage. A writer for the *Congregationalist* asked, "What has happened to the soul of the Red Cross?" Logan Roots, bishop of the Protestant Episcopal Church for the district of Hankow, declared, "I believe it is up to us now to show that the (Red Cross) report does not represent the opinion or the feelings of well-informed Americans."[47] Roots and other famine-relief supporters refused to believe that the absence of a strong central government constituted grounds for denying relief to people who, he insisted, were not responsible for the disorders which had produced famine conditions. The CIFRC announced that it felt entirely justified in appealing to the American people because "those who are starving are human beings and victims of natural and human circumstances over which they have no control."[48]

Renewed fund-raising efforts, and American public displeasure with Red Cross attitudes, enabled the CIFRC to distribute about $3.5 million in aid by the end of 1930.[49] The funds were too few and they arrived too late to help the six to eight million Chinese who died of starvation and disease during the course of a famine which the American Red Cross and the United States Department of State insisted did not exist because it did not result from purely "natural" causes.

Although conditions seemed better at the beginning of 1931, some one million deaths and almost $2 billion in economic losses resulted from what some observers called "the greatest flood in the history of China." American consular officials blamed the Chinese government for the severity of flood damage and they did not want to participate in relief work.[50]

Private relief efforts played a secondary role to official responses, which were based on American economic and foreign policy concerns. President Hoover approved surplus wheat sales to China in 1931 because they benefited American farmers, the U.S. government, and the Chinese government under Chiang Kai-shek. President Franklin D. Roosevelt's arrangement for a $50 million reconstruction loan further aided Chiang's regime in 1932. United States official wartime and immediate postwar assistance to the Chinese government amounted to billions of dollars.[51]

Missionary groups continued to advocate private American aid to China throughout the 1930s and during World War II but, despite ongoing campaigns, direct donations never reached earlier levels. Furthermore, neither private nor official American relief efforts generated lasting good will. The Chinese were well aware of being trapped in a vicious cycle of economic deprivation and precarious food supply, which produced recurrent famine conditions and necessitated repeated appeals for foreign assistance. Some of them blamed foreigners for contributing to economic decline, imposing burdensome debts, and otherwise inhibiting internal reforms which were directed toward goals of self-sufficiency. Others had little faith in combined Sino-foreign relief committees whose members did not have the authority or the ability to carry out effective famine-intervention measures. The Chinese who made strenuous efforts to provide internal relief resented foreign criticisms of their work, refusals to permit Chinese control over donated funds, and allegations that most Chinese administrators were incompetent, corrupt, or both. Foreign reports seldom acknowledged that, despite political and social disintegration, Chinese official and private relief agencies made significant contributions for famine relief. At least 62 percent of total relief funds derived from Chinese sources during the 1920–21 famine. The figure reached 85 percent during the years 1928–29. The CIFRC received only about 15 percent of its total funding from foreign sources between 1920 and 1933. The majority of support was provided by the Chinese people.[52] Dr. C. Y. Wu summarized long-standing Chinese frustrations in 1938 when he wrote, "My candid opinion . . . is that too little trust (and hence too little support) is given to purely Chinese efforts." He went on to state, "Too much importance is attached to relief work . . . by so-called international committees (really controlled by foreign big-business interests and missionaries), leaving our purely Chinese organizations to take the crumbs." Wu concluded, "It is this obsession on the part of certain influential foreign interests that leaves such a bad taste in the mouth."[53]

A major problem of American relief efforts in China was the absence of a single relief organization that had reliable funding and could function independently. The CIFRC made splendid attempts to fill the need for centralization of relief programs, but could not do so in light of financial problems and because of operational difficulties related to political chaos and civil war. A second problem was the absence of a strong Chinese government that could help to unify and supervise foreign-relief donations as part of cooperative efforts. Although the traditional Chinese state had assumed full responsibility for popular welfare, government leaders of the late 1920s had neither the national unity nor the economic means to function on behalf of famine victims or to cooperate with either missionary agencies or American government officials to accomplish effective relief operations. A third problem derived from public and private reluctance to support long-term famine-prevention projects that might have both relieved and averted recurrent famine conditions. A final problem stemmed from the failure of American officials to acknowledge that famine conditions had multiple human as well as natural causes. Their stance derived from concern for the safety of relief workers and for the uses to which relief supplies might be put in strife-ridden famine zones.

It was, however, a difficult position to justify among missionary critics and their supporters who had field experience in China and who insisted that innumerable lives could be saved through funds and aid to the CIFRC. Controversies rather than solutions resulted.

Similar problems still plague famine-relief efforts in different parts of the world. Private organizations, with little publicity and limited funding, have great difficulty functioning abroad without official sanction and support. The false dichotomy between natural and man-made crises influences famine-relief appeals. Emphasis on emergency needs overwhelms programs that advocate the importance of long-term approaches. While millions of dollars and tons of food have been poured into emergency efforts to halt starvation, relatively little has been devoted to famine prevention projects or to programs that permit some recipient control over relief distributions or that make allowances for nationalist sentiments. Organizations like the American Red Cross must still cope with questions regarding the need for aid and evaluations of the opportunity to provide aid. The logical and unfortunate results ultimately may resemble the problems and the divisions that characterized efforts in China during the late 1920s and may prompt similar negative responses from potential donors and from needy recipients.

List of Abbreviations

ABCFM   American Board of Commissioners for Foreign Missions. Houghton Library, Harvard University, Cambridge, MA. Reports and letters are cited according to catalog numbers, volume numbers, and, for lengthy reports, page numbers.

ARC   Records of the American Red Cross, on file at the National Archives Building, Washington, DC. Red Cross materials are cited according to record group numbers and file numbers.

CFR   China Famine Relief. Established in New York, 1928.

CIFRC   China International Famine Relief Commission. Founded in China, 1921.

HI   Hoover Institution on War, Revolution and Peace, Stanford University, Stanford, CA.

NA   National Archives and Records Service. Records of the United States Department of State, on file at the National Archives Building, Washington, DC. Records of the Department of State Relating to the Internal Affairs of China. Citations to records reproduced in National Archives Microfilm publications include publication, record, and frame numbers.

PUIFRC   Peking United International Famine Relief Commission, formed in Peking, 1920.

Yale Div.   Day Missions Library, Yale Divinity School, Yale University, New Haven, CT.

Notes

1. Paul Richard Bohr, *Famine in China and the Missionary: Timothy Richard as Relief Administrator and Advocate of National Reform, 1876–1884* (Cambridge, MA: Harvard University Press, 1972), pp. 113–14, 146–55. Richard set forth some one hundred proposals for long-term reforms designed to produce lasting material progress in China. Several pertained to the issue of famine, such as facilities for weather prediction, new farming techniques, mining and industrial development, communication, transport, and scientific and technical education.

2. "Editorial Forum," *Christian Herald* (May 8, 1901), p. 428. Hay made a personal contribution of $100. "Editorial Forum," *Christian Herald* (May 15, 1901), p. 460.

3. Report of the Shansi Mission for 1902; Atwood to Smith, January 31, 1903, ABCFM: 16.3.15/5 and 16.3.15/145.

4. President Roosevelt's Speech, December 24, 1906, ARC RG1 898.5/7.

5. "Famine Relief" (December 4, 1906), p. 630; "Rain, Relief, and Reflexions" (February 8, 1907), pp. 298–300, *North China Herald*. Enclosed in Rogers to Bacon, March 25, 1907, NA M862,318,3441/67–80; Report by Commanding Officer, USS Villalobos, Nanking, May 6, 1907, NA M862,307 3142/118; Klopsch to Bacon, January 26, 1907, ARC RG1 898.5/02.

6. Central China Famine Relief Committee, *Report and Accounts from October 1, 1911 to June 30, 1912* (Shanghai: North China Daily News and Herald, Ltd., 1912), pp. 5–10 (hereafter CCFRC, *Report, 1912*); "The Central China Famine," *North China Herald* (February 24, 1911), p. 424; Calhoun to State, December 23, 1910, ARC to Amlegation, December 26, 1910, Wilder to State, February 13, 1911, NA M329, 130, 893.48b/1–3 and 104.

7. CCFRC, *Report, 1912*, pp. 7–11 and 37–38; Lobenstine to Wilder, August 29, 1911. Enclosed in Wilder to State, September 11, 1911, NA M329,130,893.48 b 2/127; Lobenstine to Boardman, November 7, 1911; Ferguson to ARC, April 10, 1911, ARC RG1 898.5/438; Lobenstine to Sun Yat-sen, January 18, 1912, ARC RG1 898.5/08.

8. Persons to Davison, interoffice memo, October 18, 1917, ARC RG2 898.5/08.

9. Greene to Davison, December 7, 1917, ARC RG2 898.5.

10. Peking United International Famine Relief Committee, *International Cooperation in Famine Relief 1920–1921* (Peking: n.p., September, 1921), p. 7 (hereafter PUIFRC, *Interna-*

tional Cooperation). Marie Claire Bergère, "Une crise de subsistence en Chine (1920–1922)," *Annales: Économies, Sociétés, Civilisations* (November–December 1973), p. 1346.

11. Baker to ARC, November 30, 1920, ARC RG2 898.5/08; W. S. A. Pott, "The Economics of the Famine," *Millards Review* (February 5, 1921), p. 528; Merle Curti, *American Philanthropy Abroad: A History* (New Brunswick: Rutgers University Press, 1963). Curti explains the American role in providing relief to China in different parts of the study; Warren I. Cohen, *America's Response to China*, 2nd ed. (New York: John Wiley and Sons, 1980), pp. 101, 107–108; C. Martin Wilbur, "The Nationalist Revolution" in *The Cambridge History of China*, ed. John K. Fairbank, Vol. 12, Part 1, 531–32 (Cambridge: Cambridge University Press, 1983).

12. Peking United International Famine Relief Committee, *The North China Famine of 1920–1921, With Special Reference to the West Chihli Area* (Peking: Commercial Press Works, 1922), pp. 14–15 (hereafter PUIFRC, *North China Famine*). The report acknowledges: "There are no reliable statistics on this matter and any statement is merely a guess."

13. John Earl Baker, "Fighting China's Famines," 1943, Rare Book Dept. Memorial Library, University of Wisconsin, (typewritten), p. 4; Warren Cohen, *The Chinese Connection* (New York: Columbia University Press, 1978), p. 241; Crane to State, September 22 and 23, 1920, NA M329, 131 893.48g/1–2.

14. American Red Cross, *Report of the China Famine Relief, October 1920–September 1921* (Shanghai: Commercial Press Ltd., n.d.) pp. 14, 228–30 (hereafter, ARC, *Report, 1920–1921*). The total figure is an estimate. Personnel shortages did not permit an actual count of how many people were fed.

15. Baker, "Fighting China's Famines," pp. 20–22; Tinsley to State, November 8, 1920; Adee to Keppel, November 12, 1920, NA M329, 130 893.48g/27; Baker to ARC, November 30, 1920; White to Farrand, Confidential Report, December 15, 1920, ARC RG2, Insular and Foreign Affairs 800.08. A full account of Red Cross relief operations 1920–21 is in ARC, *Report, 1920–21;* President Wilson's Proclamation, December 10, 1920, ARC RG2 898.5/71; Thomas Lamont, *Across World Frontiers* (New York: Harcourt Brace and Co., 1921), pp. 25–26.

16. PUIFRC, *North China Famine*, pp. 1–3; Baker, "Fighting China's Famines," p. 10.

17. PUIFRC, *North China Famine*, pp. 167–68; Baker, "Fighting China's Famines," p. 13.

18. PUIFRC, *North China Famine*, pp. 1–3. Baker; "Fighting China's Famines," p. 10.

19. PUIFRC, *International Cooperation*, pp. 16–17, 22.

20. Andrew James Nathan, *A History of the China International Famine Relief Commission* (Cambridge: Harvard University Press, 1965), pp. 11–13, 25–26. (hereafter Nathan, *CIFRC*). Most foreign members were missionaries or YMCA secretaries; the remainder were chiefly medical and technical personnel.

21. PUIFRC, *North China Famine*, p. 53; Nathan, *CIFRC*, pp. 45–46. The CIFRC modified the definition of famine in 1925, and extended relief in a number of districts where "the severity of the distress was due in part to causes of a political nature."

22. *Peking and Tientsin Times*, March 8, 1922. The PUIFRC charged officers of the Yu Feng Commercial Bank in Shanghai with abstracting more than $94,000 in famine relief funds destined for Shensi Province.

23. Bergère, "Une crise," pp. 1391–92; CIFRC, *Annual Report, 1926*, Ser. A, No. 19 (Peking: May 1927), p. 1; CIFRC, *Annual Report, 1927*, Ser. A, No. 123 (Peiping: 1929), pp. 33, 35, 41, 50–51; Cunningham to State, March 3, 1926; Meinhardt to State, May 26, 1926; Simpson to Lockhart, August 15, 1927; Lockhart to State, August 15, 1927, NA M329, 129 893.48/177, 186, 191; Amlegation to ARC, December 16, 1927; Gulick to Hornbeck, October 30, 1928, NA 329, 132 898.48L/56.

24. Cunningham to State, May 26, 1927; Reverend W. W. Simpson, Kansu, to

Lockhart, August 15, 1927; NA M329 129 893.48/177,191; M329,132 893.48L–. During 1927–28, famine conditions were reported from Anhwei, Hupeh, Hunan, Szechwan, Shantung, Chihli, Suiyuan, Chahar, Shensi, Shansi, Kansu, and Honan. Gaus to Amlegation, December 29, 1928; MacMurray to State, February 10 and 28, 1929; Huston to State, January 6, 1928; State to Huston, January 16, 1928; NA M329 132 893.48/1,6,192–194; Payne to Moss, March 2, 1928; Bicknell to Johnson, March 6, 1928; NA M329 131 893.48/11,24. Resolution adopted by the Red Cross Central Committee, May 13, 1925, ARC RG2 898.5/01.

25. Henry Hodgkin, "The Missionary Situation in China," an address delivered at the Foreign Missions Conference of North America in Atlantic City, NJ, January 10–13, 1928, pp. 6–7 and 10–13.

26. ARC, RG2, File 985, Hist. Monograph 74, p. 18; Feiser to Service Heads and Office Managers, ARC RG2 898.5/01; Miss Alice C. Reed, "Excerpts From Letters From China, 1916–1948," printed for Private and Limited Circulation (Claremont, CA: 1966), typewritten, p. 86; Dorothy Borg, *American Policy and the Chinese Revolution, 1925–1928* (New York: Octagon Books, Inc., 1968), reprint ed., p. 361, n. 74. Among the eight thousand or so American missionaries who lived in China's interior, only about three thousand remained after spring 1927.

27. Baker, "Fighting China's Famines, pp. 192–93.

28. Ibid., p. 193; Amlegation to State, February 28, 1929; Johnson to CFR, April 20, 1928, NA M329 132 893.48L/14; Feiser to ARC Service Heads and Managers, May 1, 1928, ARC RG2 898.5/01.

29. Baker to Bicknell, n.d. Enclosed in Payne to Committee of Reference and Counsel, March 6, 1928; Payne to Moss, March 2, 1929; Bicknell to Johnson, March 6, 1928; NA M329 132 893.48L/11–12.

30. Hornbeck to Baker, April 28, 1928, HI, Stanley Hornbeck Papers, Box 24.

31. Ibid.; Baker, "Fighting China's Famines," pp. 194–95; Johnson to Todd, July 6 and 14, 1928, HI Todd Papers, Box 13.

32. Baker, "Fighting China's Famines," p. 204.

33. Ibid., p. 209.

34. Sokolsky to Cunningham, Confidential, July 22, 1928; Cunningham to State, July 25, 1928, NA M329 129 893.48L/202.

35. Report enclosed in Bennett to Johnson, November 7, 1928, Yale Div. William R. Johnson Papers, 6/14/232.

36. CIFRC, *Annual Report, 1928*, p. 9.

37. MacMurray to State, December 1 and December 20, 1928, NA M132 893.48L/68,97. Dispatch number 97 contains 30 reports on investigations ordered by MacMurray.

38. CIFRC, *Bulletin* (December 1928), p. 1.

39. Fang Fu-an, "Economic Problems," *China Mission Year Book*, 1932–33, p. 29; *North China Herald*, January–March 1929, passim; Tucker to ABCFM, October 23, 1928, ABCFM 16.3.7/2/202; Reverend John Shields, English Baptist Mission, Shensi, to Dear Friends, December 12, 1928, Yale Div., William R. Johnson Papers, 6/14/320; Elmer Galt, Fenchow, Shansi, to Mr. Charles Bates, January 25, 1929, ABCFM, 16.5.12/38/59; Reverend W. W. Simpson, Assemblies of God, Kansu, to Lockhart, August 23, 1928. Enclosed in Lockhart to Amlegation, August 23, 1928, NA M329 129 893.48/203.

40. Kellogg to Lively, November 23, 1928; Payne to Lively, November 22, 1928. Enclosed in Payne to Chapter Chairmen, December 10, 1928, NA M329 132 893.48L/63-a.

41. Declaration approved by CFR Board of Directors, March 5, 1929. Enclosed in Lively to Kellogg, March 15, 1929, NA M329 132 893.48L/113.

42. Hoover to State, April 7, 1929; Stimson to Hoover, April 11, 1929, NA M329 131 893.48L/123.

43. Hoover to Bicknell, April 12 and 13, 1928, NA M329 131 893.48L/123; Bicknell, Memorandum to Central Committee, ARC, April 22, 1929, ARC RG2 898.5/01.

44. American Red Cross, *The Report of the American Red Cross Commission to China* (Washington, DC: American National Red Cross, 1929), pp. 14–19, 23–25.

45. Baker to Johnson, October 23, 1929, Yale Div., William R. Johnson Papers, 6/14/234; Nathan, *CIFRC*, p. 23.

46. "The American Red Cross" and "The American Red Cross Report," *China Critic*, October 3 and 4, 1929.

47. "Has the Red Cross Lost Its Soul?" *The Congregationalist*, October 1929. Enclosed in Gulick to "Dear Friend," Confidential, n.d., ARC RG2 898.5/04.

48. CIFRC, *Famine in China's Northwest, American Red Cross Commission's Findings and Rejoinders Thereto*, Ser. B, No. 41 (Peiping, June 1930), pp. 18–22.

49. "Statistics on Various Calamities in China, 1929–1930," *Nankai Weekly Statistical Report*, 1929, p. 3; Grover Clark, *The Great Wall Crumbles* (New York: Macmillan, 1935), p. 169; Lindsay Hoben, "The Scourge of Famine in China," *Current History* (April 1937), p. 67; L. F. H. "Editorial," *West China Missionary News*, 32:7–8 (July–August 1930), p. 6. Mortality reports are estimates. The sources noted above agree that famine-related deaths in China ranged from six to eight million from 1927 to 1930.

50. Edmund Clubb, "Floods of China, A National Disaster," *Journal of Geography* 3:15 (May 1932), pp. 201–202; Adams to State, August 6, 1931; Johnson to State, August 14, 1931, NA 893.48/265 and 268. Nathan, *CIFRC*, pp. 60–61; Republic of China, *Report of the National Flood Relief Commission, 1931–1932* (Shanghai: Comacrib Press, 1933), pp. i–ii, 1, 150–51; Dwight Edwards, "The Missionary and Famine Relief," *Chinese Recorder* (November 1932), pp. 690–91.

51. John Morton Blum, *Roosevelt and Morgenthau* (Boston: Houghton Mifflin Co., 1972), p. 468; John King Fairbank, *The United States and China*, 4th ed. (Cambridge, MA: Harvard University Press, 1979), p. 327; Ross Y. Koen, *The China Lobby and American Politics* (New York: Octagon Books, 1974), p. 30; Michael Hunt, *Ideology and U.S. Foreign Policy* (New Haven: Yale University Press, 1987), p. 169.

52. Ch'en Tsui-yun, "Chiu-tsai cheng-ts'e yu kung-ts'ang chi-tu" (A scheme for disaster relief using an official granary system), *Wen-hua Ch'ien-she Yueh-k'an* 2:6 (March 1936), pp. 62–63, 66–68; Yu Shu-te, *Nung-huang yu fang-tse* (Famine prevention policy) (Shanghai: Commercial Press Ltd., 1923), pp. 94–95; Chi-yuan, pseud. "Chung-kuo nung-min chi chih-huang chi ch'i-pu chiu-fa" (Starvation among Chinese farmers and methods of aiding them), in *I-ko hsin-nung ts'un*, ed. by Sun Chi-yuan, 33 (Honan: Chung-hua nung-ts'un ts'u-chin hui, 1931). Total funds for famine relief are estimates. Partial figures for both Chinese and foreign sources are listed in the following: American Red Cross Expenditures in China, 1907–1937, ARC, RG3, 895.5; Dwight W. Edwards, "Fifteen Years of Famine Relief Cooperation," CIFRC, *News Bulletin* (April 1, 1935), pp. 2–4; Francois Godement, "La Famine de 1928 à 1930 en Chine du Nord et du Centre." Thesis, Université de Paris: 7, 1970, p. 55; Reverend William F. Junkin, "Famine Conditions in North Anhwei and North Kiangsu," *Chinese Recorder* (February 1912), pp. 75–81; Nathan, *CIFRC*, p. 44, Table 2.

53. Dr. C. Y. Wu to Co Tui, August 17, 1938, ARC RG3 FDR 115.8.

11

THE AMERICAN MISSIONARY AND
U.S. CHINA POLICY DURING WORLD WAR II

Margaret B. Denning

The American missionary played a fundamental role in shaping U.S. attitudes toward China throughout the history of U.S.-China relations. Because of their language ability and proximity to events, missionaries commanded a depth of knowledge and experience that were otherwise inaccessible to most Americans. Due to the large audience of Christian Americans at their disposal, the American evangelists' capacity for reaching a considerable and influential segment of the U.S. voting public heightened their importance in Sino-American relations.[1] Although their work was complicated by wartime conditions, missionary influence continued throughout World War II.[2]

The missionary impact on the formulation of official U.S. policy, however, depended to a critical extent on the assessments made by State Department officials of the data gathered from or submitted by American missions personnel. In order for the missionary to affect U.S. policy on China, a certain receptivity on the part of policy-making professionals was required. The larger issue of the views such officials held of missionaries in wartime China merits investigation from a number of perspectives. This chapter will deal with State Department documents, which offer the clearest, most contemporaneous picture of the diplomats' view of the missionaries as a reference point on the China scene in World War II. Because they constituted one of the largest categories of Americans in China, missionaries are mentioned in a variety of contexts in these documents. It is in reference to them as sources of information, however, that missionaries commanded the greatest potential for influencing policy. Within this category, allusions to missionaries fall into three basic groups: in general, missionaries emerged either as (1) unofficial mediators between Americans and Japanese in the China conflict, (2) eyewitnesses of events in China, or (3) experts in evaluating Chinese domestic developments.

Mediation

American missionaries mediated between the United States and Japan before the outbreak of hostilities and then again during the months that preceded the Japanese surrender. Of the prewar settlement efforts, four are particularly instructive in assessing the views of State Department officials regarding missionaries. These are the Walsh/Drought mediation, the negotiations of John Leighton Stuart, Stanley E. Jones's intercession, and the Mills/Bates conversation with Japanese officials in China.

In January 1941, the Reverend Bishop James E. Walsh, superior general of the Catholic Foreign Missionary Society of America,[3] wrote the U.S. Postmaster General Frank C. Walker to suggest that Father James Drought, vicar general in Walsh's society, remain in Washington "on call" during talks between Washington and Tokyo. In recommending the vicar general, Walsh pointed to Drought's knowledge of the Japanese government's plans and his ability to interpret day-to-day developments as assets that would facilitate the talks.[4] Walsh's letter was forwarded to the State Department for consideration.

In making this suggestion, the bishop exploited the opportunity to register his own views on the negotiations. In a January memorandum to FDR (also sent to the department), Walsh assessed the Japanese as "despairing" of much-needed American friendship, a condition that was generally agreed to be the U.S. trump card in obtaining cooperation from Japan.[5] The bishop had received a cable, presumably from the Japanese, that stated that the "remitting" party was prepared to send a representative to discuss the terms of an accord.[6] In a subsequent letter to Walker, Walsh proffered a scheme whereby American-Japanese tensions might be resolved. Walsh recommended an arrangement that would excise Germany as a close ally of the Japanese. He believed that by guaranteeing reinstituted economic cooperation the United States could win Japan's abandonment of claims in China. This plan would also circumvent Japan's need to rely on Nazi economic support and fulfill the U.S. requirement that Japan withdraw from China. Walsh also suggested a Far Eastern Monroe Doctrine be announced, giving Japan the right to intervene in cases of foreign aggression against Asian states. Such a doctrine was intended to allay Japanese fears of possible Soviet intervention and to provide the Japanese with a tool to thwart the advancement of communism in Asia.[7]

Considerable official doubt existed in the State Department about whether Father Drought's assistance could enhance negotiations or whether a plan on the order of the one recommended by Walsh could bear fruit. A memorandum drafted by Far Eastern Division Chief Maxwell Hamilton, signed by Stanley Hornbeck, political adviser, and sent to FDR by the secretary of state cited four factors which portended an inevitable clash between America and Japan and rendered a settlement questionable. The Far Eastern Division considered that (1) the militaristic orientation of Japan, (2) the United States' determination to assist Great Britain, (3) the efforts of the Chinese to thwart Japanese adventurism, and (4) the resulting steady rearmament of the United States were determinative elements in the current situation that made peace unlikely. Pursuance of the Walsh plan was not recommended,[8] and the imminent arrival of a new Japanese ambassador in Washington provided a substantive reason to temporize.[9] The missionaries, however, continued to lobby for their plan.

As the year progressed, official disenchantment with the Walsh/Drought effort extended from the plan itself to the persona of Father Drought. In March of 1941, Joseph Ballantine, assistant chief of the Far Eastern Division, had already indicated that he did not share Drought's optimism about the possibilities of success in reaching an agreement.[10] In June, Hornbeck opined to the secretary of state:

> Father Drought has taken upon himself and is playing the role of promoter and salesman . . . the proposed agreement is in my opinion something which neither the Japanese nation nor the people of the U.S. want.[11]

Then, in mid-July, the chief of the Far Eastern Division delivered an unequivocal call for a conclusion to the Walsh/Drought mediation, citing the need to transfer the matter to the official level.[12]

By the fall of 1941, the two Catholic missions' representatives exceeded acceptable limits as unofficial go-betweens in their efforts to resolve the Japanese-American conflict. Their mediation had assisted in confirming fundamental issues bearing on that conflict. Even their suggestions for ameliorating the situation had received attention. However, when their mediation pursued policies considered untenable by officials, support for their efforts was withdrawn.

The prewar mediation of John Leighton Stuart encountered more enduring interest at the official level. Stuart, then president of Yenching University, was a missionary-educator of considerable experience in China. In his capacity as president of one of the most prestigious mission universities in China, Stuart had cultivated the confidence and support of numerous Americans, Chinese, and Japanese who were consequential in Asian affairs.[13] A February 1941 letter from the first secretary of the embassy in China outlined Stuart's account of recent conversations in which he had participated with the Japanese. According to Stuart, the Japanese had begun efforts to convince Chiang Kai-shek that China and Japan shared a common cause in seeking to suppress communism, and had proposed that the two countries cease fighting each other and unite to quell the encroaching tide of communism.[14] In the first secretary's evaluation, these discussions signaled a new development in negotiations.

The following week, the American consul in Shanghai notified the State Department of information Stuart had received from a high-ranking Japanese military official. According to the Stuart report, eighteen Japanese commanding officers stationed in China were unanimous in desiring a conclusion to conflict with the Chinese. These military officials were prepared to recognize Chiang Kai-shek as leader of China and guarantee China's national independence.[15]

When the Japanese attack on Pearl Harbor precipitated a U.S. declaration of war against Japan, the Japanese detained Stuart in Peiping for the duration of the war.[16] Despite his detention, the missionary-educator's name continued to appear in State

Department documents as a potential negotiator with the Japanese. On January 14, 1944, Ambassador to China Clarence Gauss wrote the department that the embassy had received information that Stuart had attempted to induce Chinese authorities to close a peace agreement with the Japanese. Stuart, who negotiated for the Japanese in the exchange, had been told by Japanese representatives that the motivation to achieve a settlement with China derived from the need to release troops to attack the Soviet Union. Gauss's information further indicated that, since those negotiations had failed, Stuart had been excluded from the deliberations by the Japanese.[17] Then, in April of 1944, Second Secretary of the Embassy Everett Drumright wrote from Sian that his information suggested the Japanese still hoped Stuart would act as a mediator between the United States and Japan. Drumright's informant indicated, however, that the Chinese chairman of the North China Political Council doubted whether Stuart commanded sufficient influence to assume the task.[18]

Stuart, unlike Walsh and Drought, did not attempt to postulate or promote a particular U.S. policy. Indeed, he was a go-between for the Japanese in their negotiations with the Chinese. Also, in contrast to Walsh and Drought, Stuart suffered no expressed disapproval of negative assessment on the part of those officials who transmitted his remarks. By avoiding partisan attitudes toward specific policies or solutions, Stuart remained a valued mediator.

The mediation of Methodist missionary Dr. E. Stanley Jones, however, foundered on his advocacy of a specific scheme. Jones conversed in Washington with Chinese and Japanese embassy officials and communicated directly with the State Department. Jones's efforts gained attention through the support of Congressman John M. Vorys, representative from Ohio. Vorys directed a letter to FDR in July 1941 informing the president that Jones possessed contacts in high places in Japan and China and had discovered an "astoundingly wide area of agreement" between the two sides.[19] Jones paid a visit to Chief of Far Eastern Affairs Division Hamilton in September, at which time he indicated that the Japanese situation had become critical, according to his sources. In addition to providing information and mediation, Jones tendered his own assessment of how the conflict should be settled. In his estimation, three factors bore on the U.S.-Japanese mediation: (1) the fact that the United States did not want to sacrifice China, (2) the Japanese need to "save face," and (3) the importance of Japan's abandoning its association with Axis powers and turning to the United States, the Netherlands, and Great Britain. As a means of resolving differences and acknowledging these factors, Jones suggested that New Guinea be transferred to Japan in return for Japan's withdrawal from China.

Hamilton apprised Jones of the difficulties that would confound such proposals, especially the New Guinea issue,[20] but Jones continued developing his plan, keeping Hamilton informed about his activities during the ensuing months.[21] The missionary also directed his suggestions to FDR in a letter that developed The New

Guinea Plan in considerable detail and echoed the well-advertised premise that peace with Japan would require some guarantee against Soviet encroachment in Asia.[22] Shortly thereafter, Jones discussed the New Guinea proposal with Joseph W. Ballantine of the Far Eastern Affairs Division. Like Hamilton, Ballantine expressed the view that such a plan was unworkable. He took a firmer line with the missionary, however, calling the plan "blackmail" and stating that he considered Jones's discussion of proposals with representatives of foreign governments to be a source of "misapprehension" on all sides. From this meeting on, contact between Jones and the State Department personnel demonstrated a polite but strained atmosphere.[23] Jones had, in short, made himself unpopular by espousing a particular policy and testing it on the Japanese.

The activity of two additional missionaries in Nanking during May of 1941 also promoted a peaceful settlement to U.S.-Japanese-Chinese differences. The Reverend W. P. Mills forwarded a brief of a conversation he and Dr. M. S. Bates had held with Japanese officials concerning a possible settlement. These discussions shed light on the likelihood of a Japanese withdrawal from China. The Japanese Central Army Command indicated to Mills and Bates their willingness to withdraw from their area, but observed that it remained unlikely that the North China Command would agree to do the same. Mills promoted a hard line with the Japanese and recommended firmness on all points. He supported conciliation only where it would produce results and encouraged continued and increasing aid to the Chinese in their opposition to the Japanese.[24] Of all missionary views offered on the Japanese problem, Mills's approached the mood of the State Department in 1941 most closely. The missionary shunned all material concessions, adopting the view that Japan would have to relinquish all foreign territory before amenable relations with the United States could be resumed. Mills's policy advocacy escaped official criticism because it corresponded to the approach supported by policy makers.

Most American missionaries involved in negotiations assumed a strong commitment on the part of the U.S. State Department to achieve a peaceful settlement. By 1941, however, the United States had charted a course aimed at armed conflict in response to foreign aggression in all corners of the world. Missionary input in negotiations was not unwelcomed when it confined itself to information concerning the domestic situation in Japan and to messengering. The formulation of definite policies and insistence that they be executed ultimately encountered decided opposition, however, especially when such proposals ran counter to the official trend.

Eyewitness Reports

Subsequent to the attack on Pearl Harbor, missionaries figured increasingly in the accumulation of data about the Asian war. Foreign Service personnel routinely referred to missionaries in gathering information on conditions in both occupied and unoccupied China. Mission settlements frequently lay in the path of the invading Japanese, and, because such compounds were theoretically inviolate, Chinese refugees sought protection there. Thus, missionaries either witnessed first-hand the atrocities and devastation committed by Japanese soldiers or provided relief for the victims.[25] Much of the gruesome but authentic picture painted of Japanese behavior in China during the 1930s and early 1940s by journalists and Foreign Service officers derived from the accounts of missionaries.[26] Such accounts commonly dealt with incidents on mission property.

In an August 1941 report to the American consul at Kwangtung, Bishop A. J. Paschang of the Maryknoll Mission detailed acts of Japanese violence against American missions property, against male and female missionaries, and against Chinese citizens.[27] Brother Michael Hogan, also of the Maryknoll Mission, reported the story of an English nurse in Hong Kong who witnessed a "locust-like" sweep of Japanese soldiers through St. Paul's hospital in search of young girls. The soldiers were dissuaded in this case by a priest, but not all instances turned out so well. Other cases were reported in which rapes and bayonetting of Chinese girls and foreign nurses had accompanied the Japanese advance.[28]

Such accounts, factual and believable, carried no source evaluation in transmittal. The informants' backgrounds were not explained, except to note their status as missionaries, where they were stationed, and what missionary organization employed them. This view of Japanese violence corresponded neatly to the existing policy vis-à-vis the Japanese, and therefore the bearer of such evidence evoked no criticism.

Testimony to Japanese brutality was the most compelling, though by no means the only, type of missionary report of the war years. Documents demonstrate a wide range of topics on which missionaries provided information. The State Department regularly obtained particulars from missionaries on such topics as Japanese troop movements,[29] the treatment of Americans by Japanese and Chinese nationals in China,[30] the impact of Chinese inflation and economic policy on American interests in China,[31] famine conditions,[32] Russian influence on the Chinese domestic situation,[33] and the conditions in Communist-controlled areas.[34] Among these, the most prevalent references were to the situation in CCP areas.

A January 1944 military attaché report entitled *Leading Men Of The Chinese Communists* cited Stanton Lautenschlager, Canadian missionary with the Presbyterian board of foreign missions, as one of two sources used in developing the vignettes on CCP luminaries. Lautenschlager had traveled in northwest China in 1941, a trip which left him with favorable impressions of certain members of the CCP leadership. During the visit, Chu Teh, Eighth Route Army commander-in-chief, fielded to the missionary's interests by inviting him back to establish a parish in CCP territory. Chou En-lai told Lautenschlager there would be no civil war in China as long as Chiang lived, an assertion which also won Chou the missionary's admiration. The report contains no critique of Lautenschlager's interpretation of his experience with the Communists. In sharper contrast to cautious evaluations submitted by State Department personnel on the opinions of most missionary negotiators, the report on Lautenschlager refrains entirely from comment about his judgments. Unlike several of his negotiator counterparts, Lautenschlager espoused no specific policy. Consequently, he provoked no opposition. The sketches that derived from Lautenschlager's accounts of Chu and Chou were positive, but reflected a factual, nonpartisan approach. Indeed, Lautenschlager never compared the Communists with the Kuomintang.[35]

Bishop Thomas Megan, an American Catholic missionary in Honan, also furnished information on KMT-CCP relations.[36] Megan, whose breadth of activity was considerable, led a Chinese youth organization called the To Tao Tuan. This group operated largely in Japanese-occupied areas in North China and exposed Megan to data sought not only by U.S. officials but also by the National Government. In March 1944, General Tai Li, the KMT's secret service leader, summoned the priest to Sian to discuss the youth organization. Subsequent to that meeting, Megan reported to U.S. officials that Tai Li's main function in the North centered on establishing National Government authority and regaining territory lost to the Communists. He believed Tai Li's power and influence on Chinese politics continued unabated and suggested that CKS leaned on him increasingly. Megan stated that the general considered the Communist question of greater consequence than the Japanese problem.

Megan reported on other topics as well. He provided significant information about the famine in Honan, negotiated with Tai Li for radio devices to be used in the North to transmit American intelligence, and reported on Chinese Communist troop movements. Megan, like Lautenschlager, offered evaluations, but did not attempt to mold policy. His discretion earned him freedom from critical review by those State Department officials who referred to him.

A more undetached informant emerged in the person of Father Cormac Shanahan, an Irish-American Roman Catholic priest who had served in China since 1926.[37] Overtly anti-Communist, Shanahan edited the *China Correspondent*, an English Catholic monthly in China that received support from the Central Government[38] and was designed to accommodate Catholic American troops in China. Shanahan visited Yenan with the now famous party of American journalists, Foreign Service personnel, and military officials who journeyed to the region in 1944.[39] His stated purpose in visiting the area was to gather information and obtain concessions for Catholic communicants in CCP territory. Shanahan, like other members of the party, supplied detailed information about the trip to U.S. officials, including his own assessment of possible outcomes to the KMT-CCP dispute. Unlike the others, Shanahan returned unimpressed with the Communists. The missionary believed that the possibility of a peaceful settlement still existed, but predicted that a postwar showdown would most likely ensue at the cessation of Japanese hostilities. He was convinced that the Communists would never agree to relinquish their army, a position that rendered reconciled relations with the KMT impossible.[40] Although the priest presented the dissenting view on an issue about which most eyewitnesses agreed, his opinions and observations received either neutral or positive treatment. A transmittal letter forwarded from Second Secretary of the Embassy Edward Rice noted that, although Shanahan presented himself as avowedly anti-Communist, the priest had not hesitated to acknowledge those accomplishments of the CCP which he deemed praiseworthy.[41] Key to the receptivity Shanahan enjoyed was his avoidance of policy recommendations.

Experts

A third category among the "missionary as source of input" documents transmits information gathered from certain missionaries to whom the author of the document ascribes authoritative status.

In 1941, John Davies forwarded papers written by John Leighton Stuart, which contained the missionary-educator's prewar evaluation of the existing Japanese political situation. Stuart maintained that Japan's only hope lay in the possibility that the United States might refrain from interfering in the Asian situation and expressed the view that the United States should demand that Japan make a definite decision to abandon its course of aggression. Davies, in transmitting the papers, appraised Stuart's evaluation as "a particularly penetrating and significant contribution."[42] Despite an unmistakable "should do" regarding U.S. policy, Stuart's evaluation came highly praised. Determinative, however, was the policy he supported. The missionary-educator's views coincided neatly with the approach that had been adopted by U.S. policy makers.

Ambassador Gauss registered his respect for the expertise of the missionary-educator community as a whole. In 1942, the State Department conceived a plan to dispatch a "cultural" mission of experts from the United States to China and queried Gauss on the scheme. The ambassador advised against it, warning that the overuse of so-called experts vis-à-vis the Chinese would be offensive, and reminded his superiors that American specialists connected with American mission universities had been carrying out such work for years.[43]

Later Gauss also voiced the opinion that the United States had failed to exploit the plentiful reserve of talent that it possessed among former China missionaries. The Chinese Central Government, however, had not overlooked the value of those one-time China missionaries who had returned to the United States as a result of the war, and had recruited among them for special tasks during the war years. Using such individuals as American missionary Frank Price, Chiang, and Madame Chiang enlisted the skills of qualified American missionaries to serve in China with the Chinese War Area Service corps, an organization that provided hostel and mess-hall services for U.S. troops in China. Gauss suggested to the State Department that the U.S. Army in China give thought to the "recruitment and intelligent use in China of American missionaries and businessmen who had a knowledge and understanding of China,'' in conception a scheme much along the lines of the Chinese government's. For Gauss, the erstwhile missionaries represented an untapped reservoir that had been underrated and ignored.[44]

Later Price himself received high marks from State Department personnel. In the 1945 memorandum of a conversation between Everett Drumright of the Division of Chinese Affairs and Price, Drumright described the missionary as ''unquestionably a man of integrity and (who) is believed to maintain an objective point of view.'' Drumright alluded to the fact that Price had been in close contact with Chiang for about ten years and had repeatedly rejected the generalissimo's invitation to become his personal advisor during the three years preceding 1945. Price had ultimately agreed to advise Chiang, but Drumright was careful to note that Price said he would remain in Chiang's service only as long as the Chinese leader avoided reactionary measures.[45] Price's commitment to a judicious approach to the Asian situation and his avoidance of a ''crusading'' spirit toward KMT-CCP relations won him the respect of State Department officials.

William R. Johnson, long-time American missionary in Kiangsu Province, was also evaluated by State Department officials in positive terms. Johnson lived in Kiangsu during the period of the Communist ascendancy there, 1928–34, and had gained considerable experience with the CCP. Writing a paper on the threat of postwar Soviet supremacy in the East, the missionary held that the United States had been subjected to an intense pro-Communist propaganda campaign. He also offered his assessment of the implications for U.S. foreign policy. Johnson believed that the CCP would accede territory to the Soviet Union and encouraged a policy of full U.S. support of the National Government as one component of halting Russian intentions in the East. John C. Vincent of the Division of Chinese Affairs considered Johnson to be sincere, thoughtful, and in command of considerable knowledge and experience, and deemed his paper worthy of consideration and study. Vincent took issue, however, with the missionary's contention that the CCP would alienate Chinese territory and he countered Johnson's approach to U.S. policy on China.[46]

Conclusions

A review of State Department documents demonstrates receptivity on the part of officials to the information and evaluations provided by American missionaries in China during World War II. Because they enjoyed often exclusive and frequently eyewitness access to events, missionaries provided determinative information in the molding of U.S.-China policy. Their input was both encouraged and relied upon at this critical period in Sino-American relations.

Before the outbreak of hostilities, missionary input was particularly critical in confirming Japan's concern over the spread of communism as well as its perception of a significant Soviet threat. Information from mission personnel also provided insights into the price that would have to be paid to bring about a peaceful withdrawal of Japanese soldiers from China.

During the war, missionaries were relied upon for information about an array of political, economic, and social issues in both occupied and unoccupied China. The details provided by them as well as their interpretations of that data received thoughtful consideration from policy makers.

It was on the level of policy making, however, that the line of competence was drawn. For the average official, missionaries, like other political "amateurs," were discouraged from formulating or promoting U.S. policies, particularly those which countered the current drift among policy-making professionals. Regarded as reliable go-betweens, eyewitnesses, or experts on the significance of events in China, their input was well-received as long as they avoided propagating a particular plan of action.

Notes

1. The historical record of American religious proselytization conditioned the Chinese image of missionaries, as did the fluctuations in Sino-American relations. American evangelists brought Christianity to China for the first time in 1807. See Chao Fu-san, "The Definition of the Chinese Church in a Socialist Society," in *Christian Missions in China: Evangelists of What? (CMIC)*, Jesse Gregory Lutz, ed. (Boston: Heath, 1965), p. 71. Throughout the nineteenth century, their heavy reliance on home governments for protection, in supporting demands for reparations when attacked, and in obtaining indemnities placed them in bad stead with many Chinese. See Paul Varg, "A Survey of Changing Mission Goals and Methods," in *CMIC*, pp. 2, 4. Varg also cites the relatively luxurious lifestyle missionaries enjoyed as a factor that exposed them to critique. Edgar Snow, *Random Notes on China* (Cambridge, MA: East Asian Research Center, 1957), describes the experience of Liu Hsiao, one-time chairman of the political department of the Communist First Front Army, who told Snow about an instance that occurred when he was attending Hunan Normal School (run by missionaries). A friend came to visit him but would not go onto the campus because he considered it imperialist territory.The friend was instrumental in making Liu begin to see "the connection between missions and imperialism." Subsequently, Liu decided to oppose the obligatory chapel for students on Sunday. He was dismissed. Andre Chih, a Chinese Christian and clergyman who rejected Communist ideology, maintains that Western Civilization is in the process of becoming universal, that traditional China inevitably had to change, and that communism constitutes one of the Western elements that China would have to deal with. See Andre Chih, "Chinese Tradition and Christianity Newly Reconciled," in *CMIC*, p. 82. Joseph R. Levenson echoes Chih, saying that the Chinese rejection of Christianity was related to their acceptance of communism. Levenson, however, does not necessarily ascribe to the premise that rejection derived from missionary methods. See Joseph R. Levenson, "The Changing Character of Chinese Opposition Christianity," in *CMIC*, pp. 83ff. Chao Fu-san suggests that the failure of Christianity to achieve widespread appeal lay in part with Chinese Christians. Chao notes that not only did non-Christians look upon the church as imperium in imperio, but also Christians did not take the church as their own. Chinese Christians failed to learn to communicate evangelistic concepts intelligibly to their own countrymen in their own mother tongue. They, in Chao's estimation, were not sufficiently caught up in the love of Christ to be concerned about social welfare.

The missionaries' alliance with foreign legations readily called up associations of foreign domination, which gradually developed into one of the main sore spots of China's foreign affairs. Charity played a significant role in evangelistic techniques in China, and missionaries dealt principally with China's lower classes. This produced considerable suspicion on the part of Chinese officials about the political potential of the American evangelist in regard to Chinese domestic issues. See James E. Walsh, *The Church's World Wide Mission* (New York: Benziger Brothers, 1948), pp. 114, 117, 127, 287. Also Varg, "Survey," p. 4. The Christian denunciation of the long-standing Chinese ethical value system reinforced these concerns, and the doctrine of salvation beyond the clan attacked not only the very roots of Chinese political philosophy but also China's political infrastructure. See Varg, "Survey," p. 4. From the traditional Chinese perspective, the missionary brought little that seemed useful to China, while seeking to remove the precious fundamentals of Chinese life. Despite these considerable differences, good works on the part of missionaries combined with the limitless tolerance that distinguishes the Chinese to minimize violence, and missionaries persevered as a fact of the Chinese political and social landscape. Paul Cohen, in his "The Roots of the Anti-Christian Tradition in China," in *CMIC*, p. 40, notes that as Chinese intellectuals in the twentieth century became increasingly more attuned to Western thought, their arguments against Christianity became more varied and Western oriented. They considered Christianity superstitious, like other religions, and Cohen believed it therefore had no place in a modern world ruled by science. In the same vein, Charles Fitzgerald's "Opposing Cultural Traditions, Barriers to Communication," in *CMIC*, p. 102, points out that missions achieved some unintended things in China: they broke into the closed world of China sowing seeds of scientific knowledge and providing the basis for a new kind of thought. Chiang Kai-shek in his *China's Destiny* (Westport, CT: Greenwood Press, 1985; reprint of the 1943 original, Chungking) claims that China had never adopted an antipathetic attitude toward foreign religions and cultures, which he believed accounted for the complete absence of religious wars in China. Chiang and Fitzgerald are united in the contention that Christianity exerted a salutary influence on the development of scientific knowledge and the reform of social life in China.

The anti-imperialistic mood that produced World War I changed the face of Christian missions in China during the twentieth century; see Varg, "Survey," pp. 7ff. The Nationalist revolution of the 1920s brought changes in the missionary enterprise. It generated a movement toward Chinese control of Christian institutions. Additionally, the decade of the 1920s, with its economic and social problems, left the Chinese with little time to devote to nonessential issues. The "social gospel" group among China missionaries attempted to adapt the gospel to conditions in China. Most missionaries, however, tried to say that the root of China's problems was spiritual. Neither group enjoyed much success. (The lack of success derived from the failure to meet any generally recognized needs and the continuance of a paternalistic approach toward the Chinese. Varg suggests that the Russians succeeded because they tailored their message to meet Chinese felt needs.) Fundamentalists and conservatives persisted in a strictly nonpolitical mode, devoting themselves to the task of evangelism. Searle M. Bates, "The Theology of American Missionaries in China, 1900–1950," in *The Missionary Enterprise in China and America*, John K. Fairbank, ed. (Cambridge: Harvard University Press, 1974), pp. 135–58, cites a general scene of cooperation among the various missions organizations during the period 1922–50. Various nationalities cooperated as well in the several organizations doing social work in China. Bates attributes the amenable relations to the practice of leaving doctrine out of joint efforts. By the 1920s, educational projects had become the central feature of missionary activity, and in the interwar years Christian missionaries founded increased numbers of educational institutions. See Varg, "Survey," pp. 10ff. The support for such projects came primarily from contributions from the United States. The University of Nanking, Cheeloo University, and Yenching

University all had rural extension projects aimed at educating rural people, exposing urban Chinese to rural conditions, and church growth. William A. Brown, "The Protestant Rural Movement in China," in *American Missionaries In China* (*AMIC*), Kwang Ching Liu, ed. (Cambridge, MA: East Asian Research Center, 1966), pp. 232ff., refers to Nanking's Shunhuachen Project, a church-centered rural reconstruction program in which the Seminary and the College of Agriculture cooperated, developing a five-year plan of economic development in which the education emphasis supplemented rather than competed with local education. Nanking became the forerunner in agricultural research.

The geographic emphasis moved away from the cities and into the countryside, where most Chinese lived, stressing strong social programs in rural areas. Thus, when the Japanese menace spread through rural China in the 1930s, missionaries were in an ideal position to serve as sources of information about wartime China and to play an important role in providing humanitarian aid to the Chinese. Brown, *American Missionaries,* p. 220, states that 71 percent of Protestant Church members resided in several coastal areas in the 1920s. Eighty percent of the churches were located either on the coast or in the Yangtze valley. Brown also states (pp. 222ff) that the National Christian Council was established in 1922 to emphasize rural and agricultural needs. The NCC stressed strong social programs in rural areas as well, and a number of agencies were spawned to aid in agricultural education. Stuart Gelder, *The Chinese Communists* (Boulder, CO: The University of Colorado, 1946), pp. 253–55, reported that by the 1940s the Catholics had extended their work into the more remote villages of the interior, carrying with them hospitals as well as churches. Frank Price, missionary for many years in China, investigated Protestant churches in 1936–37. In a series of surveys, he contacted missionary and Chinese Christian workers by letter. According to Price, two-thirds of the then 15,000 churches, chapels, and other places of worship were in rural communities or places where agriculture was the main occupation. He found a great majority to be of the middle and lower socioeconomic class, and that at least 65 percent were farmers, in some churches 80 percent. Although the Chinese shared the leadership of groups with missionaries in most cases, the majority still believed that missionary supervision and assistance were necessary. About half of the rural church's budget was paid by outside aid, and about half of the rural churches studied had primary schools connected with them. See Frank Price, *The Rural Church in China: A Survey* (New York: Agricultural Missions, 1948). The war years in twentieth-century China saw a demise in the number of American missionaries (see table on facing page).

Mission organizations offered the framework through which material aid to those Chinese affected by Japanese hostilities could be organized and distributed. Chao Fu-san, p. 73, indicates that the war years made it impossible for the Church to plan a program because many rural parishes had to suspend work. He cites the general poverty and financial stringency as factors resulting in fewer ordinands and thus fewer workers. Chao says this was a time of sharp criticism of the Church as an instrument of imperialism. Earl H. Ballou, "In North China," in *Christians in Action: A Record of Work in War-Time China by Seven Missionaries* (London: Longmans, Green and Co., 1939) *CIA:RWWC*, p. 12, considered work *more* possible because of the conditions created by the war. The function of the missionaries in providing relief work and restoring confidence enhanced their work, according to Ballou. Christian missions' medical work played an important role in caring for wounded soldiers as well as in assisting the civilian population. See Minnie Bautrin, "In Nanking," in *CIA:RWWC*, p. 35; and Winifred I. Coxon, "In Central China: Hankow," in *CIA:RWWC*, p. 74.

Missions relief work was a function that won the favor of Chinese of all political persuasions and, as a result, missionaries enjoyed heightened respect and confidence during the war. See Brown, *American Missionaries,* p. 221. The early National Government persecuted Christians, as did the pre-Yenan Communists. The early Chinese Communists

Note 1 Table

Year	Churches	Missionaries	Converts
Protestant Churches			
1922			402,539[a]
1924		7,663[b]	402,539[b]
1926		8,200[c]	
1929		4,750[d]	
1935			1 percent of total Chinese population: over 500,000
1947		2.536[e]	
		2,246[f]	
1949	19,493[g]	6,204[h]	823,506[i]
1950			800,000+[j]
1952		nearly all had left China[k]	
Catholic Churches			
1950		400,000[l]	4 million[l]

[a]Leonard M. Outerbridge: *Lost Churches of China* (Philadelphia: Westminster Press, 1952), p. 156.

[b]Alan Gates, *Think China* (Pasadena, CA: William Carey Library, 1979), p. 43. Notice that Gates gives the same figure as Outerbridge does for 1922.

[c]Outerbridge, *Lost Churches*, p. 155.

[d]Gunther Stein, *The Challenge of Red China* (New York: Whittlesey House, McGraw-Hill, 1945), p. 240, gives the percentage. Ronald Rees, ''The General Scene,'' in *CIA:RWWC*, p. 4, gives the figures.

[e]Outerbridge, *Lost Churches*, p. 155.

[f]Paul Varg, *Missionaries, Chinese and Diplomats (MCD)* (Princeton: Princeton University Press, 1958), p. 278.

[g]Gates, *Think China*, p. 45.

[h]Gates, ibid., p. 43.

[i]Gates, ibid., p. 43.

[j]Outerbridge, *Lost Churches*, p. 156.

[k]Gates, *Think China*, p. 46.

[l]Gates, ibid., p. 156. The civil strife of the 1920s accounts for the decline of the number of missionaries in that period.

had contact with Christian outposts, which they treated as imperialistic, harrying mission-aries, putting Catholics to death and driving others away. In time they saw the usefulness of missionaries who fed the hungry and cared for orphans. See Fitzgerald, "Opposing Cultural Conditions," p. 102. As the war intensified, Madame Chiang Kai-shek praised the work of missionaries in helping the distressed and refugees, and Chu Teh did likewise. See Rees, "The General Scene," pp. 10–11, resp. Dr. Richard Brown, a Canadian medical missionary, had assisted Dr. Norman Bethune with the Eighth Route Army in the summer of 1938. Such aid was much needed by the Communists. See Kenneth Shewmaker, *The Americans and the Chinese Communists* (Ithaca, NY, and London: Cornell University Press, 1971), p. 92. During the early years of the war, the CCP gave invitations to missions and other foreign-supported organizations to set up in Yenan. CKS gave approval in 1942, but harassment by officials caused missionaries to demur. Most missions organizations endeavored to avoid conflict with Chungking, although they rarely supported KMT denunciation of the CCP. Chou En-lai told one reporter that he would like to see missionaries return to Yenan. See Stein, *Challenge of Red China*, pp. 237–39. Gelder, *Chinese Communists*, p. 255, reports that in the spring of 1938, Chu Teh and his wife attended a Sunday service at a Catholic church in southeastern Shansi. When asked to speak at the close of the service, Chu stressed freedom of religion and appealed to all Catholics to fight against Japanese fascism. Chou En-lai told Theodore White in 1940 that, if the Communists came to power, "all forms of worship" would be permitted in China. See Theodore White, *In Search of History* (New York: Harper and Row, 1978), p. 118. As the war progressed, the National Government became suspicious of the opinions and information of missionaries and other foreigners traveling in China. All foreigners were instructed to refrain from visiting missionaries in their homes. State Department officials believed that it was aimed at keeping foreign newcomers to China from indoctrination by their countrymen. See *Foreign Relations of the United States* (*FRUS*), 1944, Vol. VI (Washington, DC: U.S. Government Printing Office, 1967), p. 25.

2. Missionaries were usually the last to leave an area when hostilities began and the first to return afterward. Although this presence in dangerous areas precipitated problems for governing boards of missions organizations and for the embassy, their proximity to events was invaluable. Warren I. Cohen, *America's Response to China* (New York: Wiley, 1971), p. 146, refers to such behavior as "foolish." In the occupied areas in which missionaries had remained or returned, the impact of the missionary contribution was often eclipsed by the influence of the Eighth Route Army. See Ballou, "In North China," p. 15; also a report entitled *Information About General Fang Chien (Hsien)-Chueh*, written at Kunming on January 8, 1945, in The Subcommittee to Investigate the Administration of the Internal Security Act and other Internal Security Laws of the Committee of the Judiciary of the United States Senate, *The Amerasia Papers* (*Amerasia*) (Washington, DC: U.S. Government Printing Office), p. 1328: The mission as refuge for persons of all political persuasions exposed missionaries to considerable danger. John Paton Davies, Jr., *Dragon by the Tail* (New York: Norton, 1972), p. 206. The tendency to wait until the last possible moment to leave a hostile area sometimes resulted in arduous retreat. Davies also tells of an American Baptist missionary and several British Quakers who, according to Jack Belden, walked out of Burma with Stilwell (p. 240). The status of missions as inviolate disintegrated in wartime. Considerable destruction, looting, etc., was seen. See Ballou, "In North China," pp. 123–25. The problem was complicated by the fact that Chinese guilty of a serious crime sometimes joined the Christians in hope of obtaining missionary protection. See Varg, "Surveys," p. 3. According to Stein, *Challenge of Red China*, pp. 31, 45, those missionaries who had been visited by foreigners were thoroughly questioned. The Japanese shared the suspicious attitude toward missionaries. See *FRUS*, 1942, Vol. I, pp. 835–36. Missionaries applied to the embassy for assistance in matters of evacuation, protection of their persons and rights,

and, in the later war years, the problem of Chinese inflation and the black market. See *Protection*, 893.111/488, n. 1064, 7–23–41; *FRUS*, 1941, Vol. V, p. 885. 393.1163 AM 3/626, n. 293, 8–18–41; *FRUS*, 1941, Vol. V. 393.115 m/19, n. 79, 9–11–41; *FRUS*, 1941, Vol. V, pp. 895–96. 393.1121/104, 11–7–41; *FRUS*, 1941, Vol. V, pp. 898–99. 393.1121/98, 11–17–41, 393/11121/97, 11–27–41, 393.1115/5039, n. 743, 11–15–41, 393.1115/5072, n. 232, 12–6–41, 393.1163, m 56/358, n. 6011, 1–12–41, 393.1115/1223, n. 347, 11–11–41; *FRUS*, 1941, Vol. V, pp. 898–905. 840.51/frozen credits/4070, n. 148, 9–26–41, 390.1115A/430b n. 100, 2–11–41; *FRUS*, 1941, Vol. V, pp. 796 & 400, resp. See also 125.0090/17, 10–26–42; *FRUS*, 1942: China, p. 688. These items deal with Japanese-U.S. relations relative to the China problem: instances such as Japanese soldiers ransacking missions property, the striking of a nun by a Japanese national, the questioning and arrest of American missionaries by Japanese authorities, the problems of restrictions on travel by missionaries, and the case of missionaries held incommunicado by the Japanese, were all problems dealt with by the embassy. *Evacuation*, 393.1163/1041, n. 106, 2–13–41, 393.1163/n. 38, 2–19–41, 390.1115A/356a, 2–20–41, 390.1115A/357, n. 1, 2–22–41; *FRUS*, 1941, Vol. V, pp. 873, 402, 403, 404, 405–406, resp. 123 Hurley, Patrick J./12–17–44, n. 2031, 12–17–44, 740.0011 PW/3944, n. 116, 4/25/44; *FRUS*, 1944: Vol. VI, pp. 310, 83–84, resp. According to Varg, *MCD*, pp. 274, 724, missionaries were interned in occupied China at the start of the war and were later sent back to the U.S. *Finances*, 393.1163/1053, n. 309, 2–26–41; *FRUS*, 1941, Vol. V, p. 374. 893.5151/905, 11–30–42, 893.5151/900 n. 947, 8–18–42, 892.5151/905 1/2, 11–19–42; *FRUS*, 1942, China, pp. 551–52, 536, 548–49, resp. 893.5151/927, n. 826, 6–1–43, 811.42793/1409, n. 1692, 10–18–43; *FRUS*, 1943, China, pp. 454–55, 544–45, 549, 753, resp. See also pp. 451–52. Arthur Young, *China and the Helping Hand* (Cambridge: Harvard University Press, 1963), pp. 260, 292. Missionaries were not always cooperative with embassy advice: *Evacuation*, 390.1115A/414, n. 373, 3–7–41, 893.0146/896 1/2, 8–20–41; *FRUS*, 1941 Vol. V, pp. 409–10, 557, resp. 740.0011/PW/3558, n. 1681, 12–10–43; *FRUS*, 1943, China, p. 182. 390.1115A/12–1344, n. 2012, 12–13–44; 893.00/1202844, 12–6–44; *FRUS*, 1944, Vol. VI, pp. 209, 201, resp.

3. Or Maryknoll, founded in 1911. See FN, *FRUS*, 1941, Vol. IV, p. 14. Walsh also taught at Georgetown University's School of Foreign Service. See *Amerasia Papers*, p. 1721.

4. 711.94/1973 1/2, 1–27–41; *FRUS*, 1941, Vol. IV, pp. 17–18.

5. 894.00/1033, transmitted from FDR to the secretary of state, January 26, 1941; *FRUS*, 1941, Vol. IV, p. 14.

6. 711.94/1973 1/2, 1–27–41, see note 3, this chapter.

7. Walsh believed that American economic assistance would ultimately create an economic order in the Far East that was so unlike that of Germany that the latter would not be able to do business in Asia. Likewise, Chinese and Japanese reliance on the United States in maintaining this high standard would discourage failure to comply with political agreements and treaties with the United States. 894/00–1033, see note 5, this chapter. Additionally, Walsh traveled to Japan for the ostensible purpose of investigating the impact of Japanese religious legislation on Catholic Christian education during the period. While on the journey, he met with Japanese foreign minister Matsuoka. Walsh carried a message from Matsuoka back to FDR in which the foreign minister expressed his desire for good relations with the United States. 711.94/2005 13/14; *FRUS*, 1941, Vol. IV, pp. 113ff. Aside from the peace proposal, Drought and Walsh drafted several memoranda over Walker's name which contained information on the current Japanese political situation and their own opinions on courses of action. One such memorandum included a promise by the Japanese to turn from their Axis policy. Both Drought and Walsh supported measures that would facilitate Japan's extricating itself from that policy and designed their proposals to entice the Japanese away from European fascism. 711.94/2005 7/14, 711.94/2005 8/14, 711.94/2005 10/14; *FRUS*,

1941, Vol. IV, pp. 95, 96, and 97, resp. Walsh also drafted another memorandum in March over Walker's name, encouraging an acceleration of negotiations, for he believed that assassinations of Japanese leaders could be expected soon. 711.94/2005 11/14, 711.94/2066½, *FRUS*, 1941,Vol. IV, pp. 111–12 and 119–20, resp.

8. 894.00/1033, see note 5, this chapter.

9. In an April 7, 1941 conversation with Joseph W. Ballantine, assistant chief of the Division of Far Eastern Affairs, Drought indicated that the Japanese were fearful of a leak which might lead to their assassinations. Drought believed that, because of this, they might decline to discuss plans with him. On April 9 and May 17, 1941, Drought delivered various plans to the State Department. 711.94/2066 4/9; *FRUS*, 1941, Vol. IV, pp. 132ff. This was one in a series of drafts and was not deemed to reflect the previously more multilateral attitude of the Japanese. See also 711.94/2066 6/9m 4–10–41, 711.94/2133 4/18; *FRUS*, 1941, Vol. IV, pp. 126, 200–201, resp.

10. 711.94/2005 13/14; *FRUS*, 1941, Vol. IV, pp. 113ff.

11. 711.94/2162 5/14; *FRUS*, 1941, Vol. IV, pp. 263ff.

12. 711.94/2178 8/18; *FRUS*, 1941, Vol. IV, pp. 314ff. Walsh, however, continued to register himself. In November he left a document with the secretary of state in which he posited that the Japanese military favored successful negotiations because it would simplify their task. He also evaluated the political position of Prince Konoye, whose advisers he had spoken with personally, as that of a weak man in a strong position. Walsh believed the Japanese suspected that the United States was drawing out negotiations to gain time. He doubted Japan's abilities to carry out an agreement acceptable to the United States, but believed that the situation in the Far East would find a suitable reconciliation. 711.94/2540 10/35; *FRUS*, 1941, Vol. IV, pp. 524ff.

13. Stuart's parents had long been Presbyterian missionaries in Hangchow where Stuart was born. See John Leighton Stuart, *Fifty Years in China* (New York: Random House, 1954), pp. 13, 14. Stuart had lived there until he was eleven. He was educated in the United States at Pantops Academy, Hampden-Sydney College, and Union Theological Seminary (pp. 19, 21, 26). He had personal contact with Henry Luce and FDR (pp. 58ff., 92–93) and maintained contact with important Asians (pp. 105–125, 130, 132ff.) and Americans (pp. 94, 95, 117) in China. His facility with fund-raising began during his year at Union. See John Leighton Stuart, *The Forgotten Ambassador* (Boulder, CO: Westview Press, 1981), Kenneth W. Rea and John C. Brewer, eds., p. xix.

14. 740.0011 PW/79, 2–6–41; *FRUS*, 1941, Vol. IV, pp. 30–31.

15. 793.94119/730, 2–14–41; *FRUS*, 1941, Vol. IV, pp. 36–37.

16. Stuart, *Fifty Years*, pp. 127ff. The Japanese took Stuart while on a trip to visit the Tientsin Alumni Association in early December 1941. Initially he was detained in Peiping along with several hundred U.S. Marines and a number of his colleagues. Stuart was released on August 17, 1945 (p. 154) after an incarceration of "three years, 8 1/3 months" (p. 153). According to Stuart, already in 1937, he had been sending highly confidential reports to Yenching University's trustees about the Japanese (p. 138).

17. *FRUS*, 1944, Vol. VI, pp. 4–5.

18. 740.00119, PW/41, 4–16–44; *FRUS*, 1944, Vol. VI, pp. 53–54. Drumright's informant believed that Stuart had been detained by the Japanese precisely for the purpose of mediation. She also described a November 1943 peace plan drawn up by the Japanese, which Stuart was supposed to convey to American authorities. The scheme envisaged escorting Stuart to unoccupied Chinese territory, where he would be released and proceed to Chungking to contact American officials. The informant did not know why the plan had been scuttled. She had seen the text of Japan's peace proposals which, she said, provided for the return of territory and rights to China but made no mention of Manchuria. These proposals included retention of certain territory by the Japanese.

19. 740.001, PW/517; *FRUS*, 1941, Vol. IV, pp. 306ff. Vorys referred to Jones as "our most famous Methodist missionary." Jones had, at that point, been in contact with Dr. Miao, secretary of the National Christian Council of China (see footnote 1, this chapter) and Dr. Kagawa, a "well-known" Japanese author. Jones believed the situation was ripe for American mediation, and the assistant secretary of state indicated willingness to hear Jones's case.

20. 740.0011 PW/540, 9–17–41; *FRUS*, 1941, Vol. IV, p. 455ff.

21. 793.94/16884, 9–18–41; *FRUS*, 1941, Vol. IV, p. 459. Jones had discussed the proposal with the Japanese ambassador, who indicated that, although he personally found the plan for Japan to withdraw from China potentially agreeable, he did not know how Tokyo would respond. 740.0011 PW/619,10–26–41; *FRUS*, 1941, Vol. IV, p. 555. Here Jones reiterates the New Guinea proposal for the third time.

22. 740.0011 PW/620, 10–27–41, transferred from FDR to the secretary of state on October 30, 1941; *FRUS*, 1941, Vol. IV, p. 557.

23. Jones was received by staff of the Division of Far Eastern Affairs again in November (711.94/2544, 11–22–41). Then, and in a subsequent letter, he reported on conversations with the Chinese and Japanese ambassadors (793.94119/770½, 12–1–41), *FRUS*, 1941, Vol. IV, pp. 641, 702, resp.

24. 739.94119/756, n. 168, 5–31–41; *FRUS*, 1941, Vol. IV, p. 242.

25. Davies, *Dragon by the Tail*, p. 199. Because they were characteristically slow to abandon their posts, missionaries sometimes found themselves among the fleeing refugees. See also footnote 2, this chapter. They composed part of the company of Americans which left Wuhan in October 1938 as the Japanese approached the city.

26. Davies, *Dragon by the Tail*, pp. 202–203. Davies reports the consistency and immediacy with which Chinese women opted for suicide when faced with Japanese soldiers. See also Roy S. Lautenschlager, missionary in Hangchow and Shanghai, for an eyewitness account in his *On the Dragon Hills* (Philadelphia: Westminster Press, 1970), pp. 115, 116, 124, 128. Civilians were not the only Chinese to seek refuge in missions. In July 1943 John Service wrote, "every missionary had had experiences with runaway soldiers appealing for protection and help, requests which the missionaries are forced to refuse." Service also reported that some missionaries had had experiences with deserters of rank as high as lieutenant. 892.22/49, 7–2–43, John S. Service, "Along the Road from Chungking to Lanchow" in *Lost Chance in China*, John Esherick, ed., p. 37 (New York: Random House 1974). Japanese, because of the special status afforded missions and the fact that their representatives remained in dangerous areas despite the peril, often considered missionaries to be spies. The delicacy of the situation presented mission boards with considerable concern. 393.1163 Am3/641, 11–26–41; *FRUS*, 1941, Vol. V, p. 901; 740.0011 PW/260, 7–15–41; *FRUS*, 1941, Vol. IV, pp. 322–33. 393.1163/1053, n. 309, 2–26–41; 393.1163, n. 293, 8–18–41; *FRUS*, 1941, Vol. V, pp. 874, 891, resp. 793.94/16861, 9–17–41; 793.94/16862, 9–19–41; *FRUS*, 1941, Vol. IV, pp. 461ff.

27. Report No. 20, pp. 217–18, *The Amerasia Papers*.

28. See also Davies, *Dragon by the Tail,* p. 199. Davies was a wartime Foreign Service officer in China and was, like his colleague John Service, the child of missionary parents in China. Both wrote memoirs. Davies's reflect a more negative view of missionary impact on China. He cites "the missionary compulsion to persuade the Chinese of the error of their ways," and the fact that "in World War II" missionary dedication had spread to political and military proselytization, "as chief problems of missions at the outset of the war" (p. 339). For him, missionaries had done much to "shatter a civilization that had endured for millennia." Davies grew up in China and attended Yenching University (pp. 443ff.). According to Service's editor, John Esherick, Service displayed greater confidence in missionaries as sources. See Service, *Lost Chance*, p. 8.

29. Missionaries reported on Japanese troop movements and alterations. 740.0011 PW/3219, 4–24–43; *FRUS*, 1943, China, p. 51.

30. 893.00/15033, n. 1201; *FRUS*, 1943, China, pp. 238ff., 269, 717: two American missionaries in Kansu were attacked by "bandits," part of a Chinese and Chinese Moslem group. The missionaries estimated the band to consist of four hundred armed men with rifles and horses and surmised that such groups arose from the worsening economic situation in China, perhaps as an offshoot of secret societies. Not only foreign travelers but also local inhabitants were afflicted by the "bandits": 893.00/15074, n. 1310. During 1944, after the United States and China had agreed to abolition of all unequal treaties, some Chinese apparently considered missionary property fair game for appropriation. 893.00/1530, n. 2234, 2–26–44; *FRUS*, 1944, Vol. VI, p. 354. The OWI official making the report was the son of missionary parents.

31. Missions organizations sought to counterbalance the impact of "Chinese economics" in several ways, among them exemption from taxation and a special exchange rate. 393.1163/1284, n. 2333, 3–21–44; 893.48/11–44, n. 3144,11–2–44; *FRUS*, 1944, Vol. VI, pp. 903, 186, resp.

32. 893.48/3069, 11–5–42; Service, *Lost Chance*, p. 9: Bishop Thomas Megan of the Catholic Church and Elmer Wampler of the American Brethren became sources of information on the famine in Honan during 1942. Wampler thought the famine less widespread than the one which had occurred during the years of 1921–22, but more extensive than that of 1928–29. Wampler had considerable experience in famine-relief work in China. Another missionary in Chengchow told Service that many of the farms had already been abandoned before the famine (p. 14). When Service suggested to Megan that the suffering in Honan might give rise to antiwar discontent among the otherwise uninterested peasants, Megan remarked that no other people in the world would have stood for what the Honan peasant had tolerated (p. 19). Megan came from Eldora, Iowa, and was, according to Ted White's account, a cheerful, healthy, and devout Catholic and American. Megan escorted White through the famine devastated area because he thought White should see the people dying (White, pp. 146–47). For more on Megan, refer to 893.105/97, n. 2494, 4–26–44; *FRUS*, 1944, Vol. VI, pp. 398–99. 893.00/7–1044, n. 3, 7–10–44; *FRUS*, 1944, Vol. VI, pp. 468–69. 740.0011 PW/3–1745, 3–17–45; *FRUS*, 1945, Vol. VI, p. 287.

33. 761.93/1735, n. 53, 8–28–43; *FRUS*, 1943, China, p. 342. Missionaries reported that there had been Russian military advisers at Sian for four years in 1943. They believed that the personnel was rotated every year.

34. When the National Government instituted tight travel restrictions on foreigners late in 1943, some considered it a product of KMT-CCP tensions. When asked why travel visas had been denied, KMT officials responded that robberies along the highways were the cause. 893.00/15275, n. 12, 1–5–44; *FRUS*, 1944, Vol. VI, p. 301. The desire of United States officials and news people to obtain information about Communist-controlled areas met head on with these Chinese measures. Missionaries had been a key source of data for U.S. Foreign Service officers since long before the war. See Fox Butterfield,"A Missionary View of the Chinese Communists," in *American Missionaries in China*, Kwang Ching Liu, ed., 251 (*AMIC*), (Cambridge, MA: East Asian Research Center 1966). Fox notes a SD Archives circular of 1935, 893.00/12990,which refers to a Hangchow consulate request that a large group of missionaries keep it informed. For the September 1944 recollection of Communist figures the late 1930s by a missionary Reverend Herman Swenson, see *Amerasia Papers*, pp. 879ff., no. 1680, 9–18–44. Hugh Hubbard had been the first American missionary to meet with Communist guerrillas, about whom little was known at the time. He reported that CCP troops helped the peasants, worked on roads, conducted relief work, and furthered rural education (Butterfield, "Missionary View," pp. 270–74). Hubbard offered the view that the Chinese Communists came off "quite different from the Russian brand" (ibid., p. 277), thus

inaugurating the role of missionary as political assessor of the CCP.

35. "Military Attache Report: Leading Men of the Chinese Communists," n. 44, in: Service, *Lost Chance*, pp. 330ff. Shewmaker, *Americans and Chinese Communists*, pp. 129ff., records that Lautenschlager traveled the Shen-Kan-Ning Border Region in 1940, making him the last foreigner to visit that region until 1944. He (Lautenschlager) published a book about his sojourn in 1941 called *With the Communists 1941* (London: Edinburgh House, 1941), or *Far West in China 1941* (New York: Friendship Press, 1941). Shewmaker refers to additional information on the trip under 893.00/14680, 3–16–41. Lautenschlager termed himself a "political missionary," although, as Shewmaker observes (p. 337), he did not posit comparisons of the CCP and the National Government.

36. N. 101, 3–28–44, in *Amerasia, p. 472*.

37. Shewmaker, *Americans and Chinese Communists*, p. 169; Harrison Forman, *Report from Red China* (New York: H. Holt and Co., 1945, 1975), pp. 44, 91, 162.

38. Communication from Edward E. Rice, 2d secretary on detail at Sian, to secretary of state on Information in Regard to Conditions in Communist Territory Near Yenan Supplied by Father Shanahan, n. 115, 7–22–44, *Amerasia*, p. 668. According to 2596, 5–22–44 in the same volume, the magazine was made available at no charge.

39. Shewmaker, *Americans and Chinese Communists*, pp. 169, 270. See Rice's report in *Amerasia Papers*, n. 115, 7–22–44, p. 668 (note 38, this chapter). Shanahan obtained permission to reopen the Catholic mission in the Border Region in the Art College at Yenan University, which had been housed in the old Catholic mission previously stationed there. However, Chou En-lai refused to ratify the treaty (Stein, *Challenge of Red China*, p. 91). When the Communists complained that the KMT "Blockade" had resulted in a serious lack of medicines, Shanahan commented that Chinese soldiers elsewhere suffered similar shortages. He promised, however, to draw the Yenan hospital situation to the attention of Chungking officials (Forman, *Report from Red China*, p. 44).

40. 893/7/224, n. 4, 7–22–44; *FRUS*, 1944, Vol. VI, pp. 482–83. Shanahan left Yenan before other members of the group. See Watts's report, 8–14–44, *Amerasia*, p. 746. Under his editorship, the *China Correspondent* became so offensively anti-Communist and pro-KMT that Shanahan was removed as editor. Despatch n. 2596, 5–22–44, p. 497; n. 115, 7–22–44, p. 667.

41. 893.00/7/2244, n. 4, 7–22–44; *FRUS*, 1944, Vol. VI, pp. 482–83.

42. 711.94/2549, 11–3–41; *FRUS*, 1941, Vol. IV, p. 564.

43. 811.42793/535, n. 113, 2–12–42; *FRUS*, 1942, China, p. 700.

44. 1–28–44; *FRUS*, 1944, China, pp. 9–10: Gauss thought those recruited should be commissioned into the army if at all possible and utilized in services of supply, quartermaster corps, security, etc. See also 393.1163/1044, 1–30–41; *FRUS*, 1941, Vol. V, p. 399.

45. 893.00/5–2645, 5–26–45; *FRUS*, 1941, Vol. VII, pp. 392ff. Price considered the situation in China in 1945 as improved over 1944 and reported that the GMO's "mental processes" were becoming more flexible. Price had also been one of the missionaries interviewed by Lauchlin Currie during the latter's visit to China in 1941. 033.1193 Currie, Lauchlin/23, n. 802, 3–3–41; *FRUS*, 1941, Vol. V, p. 606.

46. FE Files, Lot 52–324, 7–16–45; *FRUS*, 1945, Vol. VII, p. 434. Johnson's paper was entitled "Will Russia Supersede Japan as Aggressor in the Orient?"

12

DR. JOHN LEIGHTON STUART AND
U.S. POLICY TOWARD CHINA, 1946–1949

John C. Brewer and Kenneth W. Rea

John Leighton Stuart, the last of the American missionary-diplomats, was seventy and had spent most of his life in China by the time General George Marshall secured his appointment as President Truman's ambassador. For three years, Stuart, an internationally known missionary-educator, sought to influence American policy and change the course of Chinese history. His ambassadorship ended with the collapse of the Nationalist government, and his final return to the United States symbolized the end of a Christian century of Western presence in China.

Taunted by the Communists abroad and shunted aside by the administration at home, Stuart suffered a paralytic stroke in the autumn of 1949 and soon became a forgotten ambassador. His memoirs, published in 1954, and his death in 1962 attracted little notice. Fittingly, recent scholarly analysis of the origins of the Cold War with China has refocused attention on Stuart and suggested the need for a critical evaluation of his short career as a diplomat.[1]

I

Stuart was surprisingly well-equipped by temperament, training, and experience to advise the makers of American policy and to influence the architects of postwar China. The son of a Presbyterian missionary couple, he had been born in China and educated in America, where he attended a prestigious Virginia preparatory school, Hampden-Sydney College, and Richmond's Union Theological Seminary. A promising scholar, he returned to China to become a prominent Presbyterian missionary-educator. Soon a friend of Henry Luce and an acquaintance of Woodrow Wilson, he became president of Yenching University in 1919 and received an honorary doctorate from Princeton in 1930 in recognition of his role in building Yenching into China's leading Christian educational institution. As a university president with an interest in international affairs, he traveled widely between the wars, broadening his circle of acquaintances to include Americans like Franklin Roosevelt and Chinese like Chiang Kai-shek, Mao Tse-tung, and Chou En-lai. The Japanese unwittingly enhanced his reputation by keeping him mysteriously isolated in close confinement from Pearl Harbor to V-J Day, presumably because of his potential usefulness as an emissary to the Chinese government. After a postwar swing through China and a final fund-raising tour in America, he sought out George Marshall in April 1946, offering to assist in Marshall's attempt to end the long civil war between China's Nationalist government and the Chinese Communist party.[2]

Marshall had been in China since late 1945 on a presidential mission to bring about a peaceful unification of the country. The tenuous truce he secured in January had been the first step and, as it turned out, the easy part. His efforts to form a Nationalist-dominated coalition government had failed almost entirely by the time he met Stuart. The Communists demanded reform, but refused to cooperate; the Nationalists would cooperate, but refused to reform. Frustrated, Marshall eagerly accepted Stuart's offer of assistance and, when conditions worsened by summer, Marshall secured Stuart's appointment as ambassador, a post left vacant since Patrick Hurley's abrupt resignation the year before.[3]

Stuart and Marshall were personally compatible, and their strengths and weaknesses were complementary. They shared the same basic beliefs and, although one was the scholar and the other the soldier, they were both reserved, thoughtful, and determined men. However, unlike Marshall, whose viewpoint was American and whose influence was in Washington, Stuart was thoroughly immersed in Chinese affairs. He knew the top Nationalist and Communist leaders personally and enjoyed a special Chinese teacher-student relationship with many of their subordinates. He could thus approach the Chinese on a different level from Marshall and with a perspective rare among Americans.[4]

Reaction to Stuart's appointment was mixed. Chinese official, public, and editorial opinion was favorable, for the Chinese regarded Stuart as one of them. Paradoxically, American opinion was more skeptical for the same reason. The reservations of the career diplomats in the embassy at Nanking rested mainly on the belief that Stuart was "more Chinese than the Chinese." Embassy staffer John Melby complained that Stuart, who had spent nearly fifty years in China, knew little about America, the government in general, and the State Department in particular. Melby admitted, however, that few Americans and no other ambassador had acquired as deep an understanding of the Chinese or possessed as large a network of personal acquaintances.[5]

The limitations that worried Melby would become troublesome if Stuart's ambassadorship outlived Marshall's mission. Needing help now, however, Marshall was less concerned with the defects of Stuart's virtues than with the virtues themselves. Ambassadorial rank would increase Stuart's effectiveness with the status-conscious Chinese, and he was acceptable to all factions.[6]

II

Ambassador Stuart set out at once to help Marshall achieve the goal which had eluded him. Leaving military matters to Marshall, Stuart sought to break the political deadlock. He soon organized and chaired a small committee composed of two Nationalists and two Communists for the purpose of implementing the plan of the Chinese Political Consultative Conference, which had met earlier in the year. This conference of all parties had agreed on a coalition council to govern under Chiang's leadership until a national assembly could adopt a new constitution. Citing substantive and procedural objections to the plan, Communist leaders had refused to join the governing council. Months of formal meetings between their representatives and the government had no effect on their resolve. Now, although Stuart's conversations with Chou were promising and concessions from Chiang forthcoming, Stuart's first effort in personal diplomacy proved unproductive; his committee never met. The experience, however, persuaded him that the Communists would coalesce on their terms only, and this reinforced his personal and philosophical inclination to favor the Nationalists. Yet the Nationalists, not the Communists, provoked the final crisis of the Marshall Mission and, in so doing, strengthened Marshall's tendency to blame Chiang more than Mao for the failure to reach a settlement.[7]

By early autumn, the government's Kalgan offensive revealed Chiang's determination to end the civil war by military force. Coupled with America's recent sale to the government, at discount prices, of almost $1 billion worth of wartime surplus, the attack on the Communist stronghold of Kalgan put Marshall in an untenable position as a mediator, for it appeared that his government was sustaining the Nationalists in their latest effort to consolidate their position. As Marshall expected, the Communists protested sharply, threatening to break off negotiations unless the Kalgan operation was suspended. When Chiang insisted on dictating terms at the end of what he hoped would be a victorious campaign, Marshall angrily asked to be recalled to Washington. Chastened, Chiang agreed to a temporary truce, which the Communists now rejected. Influenced by Stuart, Marshall cancelled his recall, pressured Chiang for concessions, and appealed to Chou. Yet the capture of Kalgan, which proved to be a hollow victory, and the government's arbitrary decision to convene the National Assembly in November without Communist participation effectively ended Marshall's mediation. For two months more, he and Stuart supported the mediation efforts of the minority party and apolitical leaders, but without success. Persuaded that the government faced ultimate defeat on the battlefield, but unable to influence Chiang at his apogee, Marshall ended his mission, returning to the United States in January 1947 to become secretary of state.[8]

The Truman administration remained committed to the goal of a "united and democratic China," but the extent of its commitment was uncertain. Marshall, whose influence with Truman was unrivaled, had a global perspective, could differentiate between greater and lesser dangers, and possessed a keen appreciation of the limits of American power. Moreover, his year-long experience with the corrupt and ineffectual Nationalist leadership strengthened his resolve against large-scale American support for Chiang's government.[9]

More parochial in outlook, Stuart sought to maintain America's presence in China in one way or another. Confident that he could influence Chinese leaders, he had the missionary's view that China was lost but still could be saved. The principal problem, as he saw it, was how to end the civil war. Marshall had failed to end it by negotiations leading to a Nationalist-dominated coalition. Perhaps a strengthened and reformed Nationalist government could overcome the Communists. In his last meeting with Marshall, he therefore argued for a policy linking the offer of substantial American aid for the Nationalists to the achievement of democratic reforms in the government. Failing this, he said, the United States should withdraw from China entirely, although he knew that this was unlikely. Unless the one or the other were done, he continued, American interest and prestige would suffer greatly. Marshall listened but was noncommittal, saying that he agreed in principle. Although it was not readily apparent, the president's new secretary of state and his ambassador in China favored different policies in practice.[10]

III

Freed from never-ending mediation by Marshall's return to Washington and heartened by the adoption of the new constitution which would go into effect at the end of the year, Stuart now sought meaningful changes in the Chinese government. From his first meeting with Chiang as ambassador, he had stressed the importance of democratic reform, an end to corruption, and an improvement in the welfare of the people as the best means of defeating the Communists. Chiang's attempt to reorganize the government along constitutional lines, which was essential to this end, began in the spring of 1947 and received Stuart's warm support. Sharp conflicts between Kuomintang progressive and reactionary cliques and clashes with China's minority parties slowed the pace. Military reverses and a deepening economic crisis made the process more difficult. Stuart, who was a master of the maze of Chinese politics, kept Marshall informed through long-winded telegrams that confused as much as they clarified. Knowing that the Chinese excelled at charades, Stuart himself was uncertain as to whether the reforms taking place were real or illusory, and even he became impatient for tangible evidence of change that would justify large grants of American assistance to the Nationalists.[11]

Always the educator, Stuart treated Chiang like a promising but wayward student and handled Marshall as if he were an exasperated parent. While lecturing Chiang on the virtues of ''government by law,'' Stuart reminded Marshall of the importance of ''face,'' saying that in ''China what is done is rarely as important as the way . . . it is done.'' Yet, Stuart admitted by the end of April that, despite the appearance of reform, nothing had changed. A month later, worsening conditions led to popular demonstrations and student riots. Seeing these as the ''raw stuff of democracy,'' Stuart urged Chiang to champion the ''popular will,'' secure a negotiated peace, and commit himself publicly ''to the democratic principles,'' which he had often proclaimed but ''failed to put into effect.'' Alarmed by the gloomy outlook in mid-June, Stuart responded to urgent pleas for more American aid with sharpened demands for reform, but without result.[12]

When the government outlawed the Communist party on July 4, hopes for peace disappeared, and Marshall's patience ran out. Complaining that Chiang had ignored good advice, he decided to supplement Stuart's careful diplomacy by sending Albert Wedemeyer back to China on a whirlwind tour. An outspoken lieutenant general who had been Chiang's chief of staff late in the war, Wedemeyer was blunt to a fault, but his sympathies were with the government, and he knew the Nationalist leaders. A month of busy fact-finding ended with Wedemeyer's stinging criticism of the government and loud demands for immediate and sweeping reforms.[13]

This sensational performance assuaged Stuart's anger over Marshall's implied rebuke in sending Wedemeyer without consultation or warning. Saying publicly what Stuart had been saying privately, Wedemeyer shocked the government as Stuart could not have done. Yet Wedemeyer changed nothing in China; democratic reform did not take place.[14]

Back in Washington, Marshall suppressed Wedemeyer's report, which recommended greater economic and military assistance to the Nationalists and United Nations intervention in Manchuria. Mounting public and congressional pressure notwithstanding, Marshall refused to commit the United States to the salvation of Chiang's regime. He was fearful of an escalating Soviet-American rivalry in China when America's first priority was Europe. Moreover, he believed that limited aid would suffice if a reformed Chinese government regained popular support and unlimited aid would be insufficient if it did not. Yet it was apparent that aid would have to be increased enough to prevent the government's collapse.[15]

While the debate continued in Washington over the extent of American aid to China, the Communists went on the offensive throughout the North. As autumn gave way to winter, Communist successes and government failures led to greater repression and growing defeatism throughout Nationalist-controlled China. In the aftermath of the Wedemeyer Mission, embassy staffers reported ''a steady deterioration'' and ''creeping paralysis in administration,'' saying the government was a terminally ill patient whose will to live was lessening.[16]

Recognizing this, Stuart sought to restore confidence by popularizing reform. His faith in Chiang and the Chinese student movement undiminished, he urged a return to Sun Yat-sen's ''Three Principles of the People.'' Sun's principles and student activists, not politicians, he believed, had produced the successful Revolution of 1911 and the heroic resistance against Japan. Accordingly, he looked for a new revolution, led by Chiang, joined by students, and supported by the United States. Knowing that this was a "visionary" solution to China's problems, he nevertheless made an appeal to patriotism in a published personal "Message to the Chinese People." On a more practical level, he sought to stave off defeat by encouraging an accommodation with the Communists.[17]

In mid-winter, desperate government leaders had approached the Soviet embassy exploring new possibilities for a negotiated peace based on a coalition government. Stuart thought that this might be a ploy to secure greater American assistance, and he doubted that the Communists, who were "winning on all sides," were interested. Yet he grasped the opportunity to end the war. In an unfortunate United Press interview granted days after his patriotic appeal, he said that an accommodation with the Communists was "the best possible solution" to China's problems. Unaware of any inherent contradiction in his two statements, he was surprised by the unfavorable reaction, which taught him that the world had changed more than he had in the past two years.[18]

Embarrassed before Congress, which was considering the administration's China aid bill at a time of increasing Soviet-American tension, Truman disavowed Stuart's remarks, saying characteristically that he "did not want any communists in the Government of China or anywhere else." This abrupt reversal of the administration's position on a negotiated peace and the spring passage of the China aid bill, enacting Marshall's policy of limited assistance into law, left Stuart few options in his search for a means to preserve an American presence in an independent China.[19]

IV

While Congress debated and the government's military position crumbled, China's National Assembly convened under constitutional mandate to elect a president and vice-president for the republic. The result was a month of open political maneuvering that revealed both Chiang's determination to retain dictatorial power and a serious rift in Nationalist ranks.

The most significant result of the election, from Stuart's point of view, was the emergence of progressive Marshal Li Tsung-jen as an alternative to Chiang. Military headquarters commander in Peking, Li had been gaining political support since autumn. Unlike Chiang, Li favored democratic reforms and an accommodation with the Communists. Li calculated that Chiang would become president despite an early coyness, but that inevitably Chiang would have to step aside because of his intransigence. The vice-president would then take over. Accordingly, Li decided to seek the vice-presidency. Thus the focus of attention in the assembly was on the vice-presidential contest.[20]

As Li expected, Chiang sought early to outmaneuver him. Flirting with the premiership and denying any interest in the presidency, Chiang insisted that as he, a military man, was not a candidate for president, the military candidates for vice-president should withdraw. When this ploy failed, Chiang reluctantly accepted the largely ceremonial office of president, but not before he had secured emergency powers from the assembly. A bitter contest for the vice-presidency now followed. Coming on the fourth ballot, Li's victory established him as the leader of the progressive opposition and dealt Chiang and the conservative cliques their first major political defeat.[21]

Armed with the assembly's demand for effective government, which Li's election represented, Stuart urged Chiang in May to seize the initiative and implement reforms before it was too late. The results were depressingly familiar. Appearing to agree, Chiang, as usual, refused to act. Why was uncertain. Whether or not he was senile, as Stuart's Chinese secretary Philip Fugh suggested disparagingly, or whether it was because he expected Truman's defeat at the polls in November and an outpouring of aid from Republicans thereafter, Stuart did not know. Growing disillusioned with Chiang at last, Stuart began to shift his hopes to Li, who promised to force reforms, or, failing this, threatened to break with Chiang or replace him altogether. At about the same time, Stuart detected Communist interest in resumed peace negotiations. During a June visit to Yenching, he told their spokesmen that "the door was still open." This new evidence of Communist flexibility, together with Li's emergence, offered a slender chance to end the war, which Stuart was willing to take, but time was running out.[22]

V

By the summer of 1948, American aid, which was not enough to help, began to hurt. The Communists stepped up their timetable after the passage of the China Aid Act in order to forestall its effect. Nationalist army commanders now began reporting all engagements as major battles and, when not surrendering out of hand, were withdrawing into fortified places. While a general collapse was not yet expected, the American embassy prepared a warning to its nationals to evacuate North China. Elsewhere, inflation soared and student rioting, which had resumed in May, continued unabated.[23]

Conditions worsened all summer. Chiang contained Li politically and stymied reform, missed military opportunities, and continued to select his field commanders on the basis of personal loyalty, not ability. As the government's prestige sank, anti-American sentiment surfaced. "We are asked increasingly," said Stuart, "why we adopt [a] policy of perpetuating . . . a government seemingly bent on its own destruction and facile only in paving the way for the Communists." Building his case for a change in policy, he complained that American aid now served only to prop up an unpopular regime and delay its collapse.[24]

By late summer, it appeared that the collapse was not far off. Stuart and the embassy staff now speculated that the government either would have to come terms with the Communists soon or that Nationalist China would break up into autonomous regions. Stuart disagreed sharply with staff members, however, on what future course American policy should take. Arguing that a coalition would lead inexorably to complete Communist control, staffers favored the concept of resistance in autonomous regions and sought continued or increased aid to the Nationalists in order to achieve it. More realistic than the professionals, Stuart doubted the effectiveness of regional resistance and favored a coalition as the best means of preserving American influence. Thus he argued, in effect, for a return to the policy of the Marshall Mission. Scrupulously fair, he cabled both recommendations to Marshall in August.[25]

Unimpressed by either, Marshall responded unequivocally, saying sternly that the United States had "no intention of again offering its good offices as a mediator." Moreover, he ordered an end to any encouragement of a coalition government. Pressured at home to increase aid to the Nationalists and faced with a deepening cold war with Russia, Marshall resisted any change in the administration's established China policy.[26]

VI

Undaunted, Stuart persisted in seeking support for a negotiated peace as the cities of Manchuria and North China fell under Communist control in the autumn. He cabled Marshall in mid-October, reporting Li's plans for a coalition and requests for American aid. Stuart stated the case more strongly now. American assistance had been insufficient for its purpose and its continuation was useful only for arousing anti-American animosity. If a public opinion poll could be taken in China, he said, its results would be overwhelmingly against the government. "We may, therefore, at any moment find ourselves accused of violating the democratic principle of the right of self-determination by aiding a dictatorship which does not represent the popular will." Even massive military and economic aid, he said, anticipating the argument of his staff, could now lead to reforms and economic recovery in only a laboratory-like part of the country. Stuart believed that even if this were successful, the result would still be a negotiated peace. The experiment might be tried, but, if for reasons of global policy, it were not, he warned that the United States would shortly have to decide whether or not to withdraw from China altogether or "attempt to modify the course of events through processes other than those of military force."[27]

Marshall had decided already; he would do neither, nor would he otherwise alter American policy. He sent a withering response to an October 22 staff cable which had urged "all out" aid to the government. He also dismissed as untimely Stuart's request, in a cleverly worded countercable of October 23, for a position statement on a hypothesized Communist-dominated coalition. Refusing to be drawn in, Marshall replied that America's position would be decided upon in the event.[28]

Taking this as license to continue, Stuart reasoned that if the United States would not intervene and would not withdraw, the result would be a negotiated peace or a total Nationalist defeat, with the one preferable to the other as a means of protecting American interests and offering opportunities to influence the Chinese Communists. Seeking to break down resistance to the idea of a Communist-dominated coalition, he reminded Marshall of the forces mitigating against Soviet-type communism in China. Most Chinese, he said, were loyal to their "social patterns and cultural attachments," not to ideologies. Moreover, the Chinese were historically anti-Russian and, like Chiang's government, a Communist-dominated coalition would need economic aid, which only the United States could supply. Having said this, he reported that "the latest indications are that the proposed Coalition will announce itself about New Year, and that before or after that date it will open a vigorous political campaign in the hope of detaching KMT members from their present allegiance."29

The administration was less concerned about this eventuality than it was about Stuart's encouragement of it. Neither Truman nor Marshall shared Stuart's optimistic view of Chinese communism, nor did men like Henry Luce, whose *Time-Life* magazine publications were opposed to a coalition government. Moreover, Walton Butterworth, who had worked with Stuart in the embassy but was now back in the State Department, knew that Stuart and Fugh often operated independently of the staff in what Melby called a personal quest to save China. Suspicious of Stuart's activities, Butterworth now reviewed his communications for the last six months, finding the report of his conversation with Communist spokesmen at Yenching during the summer. Butterworth's superior, Robert Lovett, who was acting secretary during Marshall's illness, cabled saying Stuart's statement that the door for negotiations was still open had been unauthorized. "The door was not open." Moreover, Lovett now changed the August order against encouraging a coalition to an order discouraging one. Stuart should tell local leaders, said Lovett, that the United States opposed Communist participation in governments in China or anywhere else in the world. Thus reprimanded, Stuart carefully avoided the appearance of favoring a Communist-dominated coalition as the long expected military crisis came.30

VII

Meanwhile, Truman won reelection in the United States, and Communist forces invaded China proper in strength. The last major battle north of the Yangtze began in November, and over the next two months many of the government's best divisions defected or were destroyed on the central China plain.

With hope of a change in American policy ended by Thomas Dewey's defeat and Communist armies approaching Nanking, pressure mounted for Chiang to relinquish power. He resisted stubbornly at first, determined to fight on unreformed, but evidence of his declining political support accumulated fast. Sun Fo, Sun Yat-sen's son and Chiang's earlier choice for vice-president, became premier in December but could find no one to join the cabinet. Vice-President Li began negotiating with the Communists, promising a government without Chiang. With most of the army and the secret police still loyal, Chiang's political opponents were reluctant to force the issue. As both sides sought Stuart's support, Lovett cabled strict orders against any participation in "discussions or maneuvers" leading to a Communist-dominated coalition. Stuart complied with the letter of Lovett's order, but managed to encourage Chiang's opponents while discouraging him.[31]

Simultaneously, Stuart made an eloquent plea for a reversal of American policy. In a long cable to Lovett, he observed that "organized institutions" usually feared "progressive movements," especially when they seemed "dangerously radical." He hoped that the American government would not "in its . . . justifiable hatred of international communism, fail to recognize . . . elements of progress and reform in its Chinese variety." Granting that the Communists would dominate a coalition government at the outset, he theorized that for a period of time the limitations inherent in a coalition, together with the chaotic conditions in China, would enable the Nationalists and the United States to exercise "a liberalizing influence" which "might have permanent effects." Conditioned on respect for "the basic freedoms," the U.S. government could provide economic assistance for reconstruction and industrial and agricultural development. Private educational and religious organizations could volunteer their services to the Chinese people. These undertakings would dramatize American support for democratic institutions, Chinese national independence, and open international relationships. If successful, this would prove that virulent communism could be fought and defeated "by means other than military force." He admitted that he might be "naively visionary," but he believed that a modification of Chinese communism would more likely be accomplished with American help than without it, and, in any event, the experiment would be better "than abandoning China to her fate." Scholarly fairness compelled him, however, to report that this view was not shared by the senior members of his staff.[32]

Lovett ignored the message, and events now mooted the question. Between Christmas and New Year's, Chiang decided to resign, changed his mind when the Communists broadcast a "war criminals" list with his name at the top, then agreed to a formula under which he would retire temporarily, leaving Li free to form a coalition if he could. The government then began evacuating its archives and ministries south to Canton and removed its assets to Taiwan. Chiang turned over power at the end of January, and for the next three months Li negotiated unsuccessfully with Communist leaders who would accept nothing less than complete surrender. Peace talks ended on Easter Sunday, and Communist forces crossed the Yangtze into Nanking a week later.[33]

Meanwhile, Stuart began his final effort to preserve an American presence in a

Communist China. Sending most of the embassy staff south at the end of January, he remained in Nanking, first to support Li, and later, when it was apparent that Li would fail, to await an opportunity to approach Communist leaders himself. In March he cabled Dean Acheson, who had succeeded Marshall as secretary of state, seeking permission to discuss future Sino-American relations with them. His goal was the establishment of American influence in a Communist China for the purposes of protecting "the basic freedoms" and offsetting the Soviet Union. He conceded that he might be naive to imagine that he could "influence the Chinese Communist Party to a more broadly tolerant policy," but said, "I should feel deep satisfaction in attempting this final service to my country and the cause of liberalism in China." Failing this, he hoped that his reputation as an advocate of "Chinese . . . independence and democratic progress" would at least enable him to help Chinese and American policy makers achieve "a better mutual understanding." He asked Acheson to leave the timing and method of approach to him.[34]

Despite misgivings, Acheson cabled approval in April but insisted that Stuart act secretly, avoiding any publicity that might lead to the embarrassment of the administration at home or abroad. Like Marshall, Acheson believed that the Nationalist government was doomed, but unlike Marshall, he had no experience with Chinese Communist leaders. Mindful of Tito's example in Yugoslavia, he was willing to explore the possibility of neutralizing Soviet influence in a Communist China.[35]

Stuart's opportunity came in May, when Huang Hua, a Yenching graduate, arrived in Nanking as head of the Communist Alien Affairs Office. The indispensable Philip Fugh made the opening gambit in what turned out to be an elaborate game of "face" played between Stuart and the Communist leaders, who also wanted a meeting. Hua, who may have been sent to Nanking for the purpose, made arrangements for Stuart to meet with Mao and Chou in June while in Peking, ostensibly for a final visit to Yenching University. When Stuart's interest in the trip seemed to lessen, Hua sought to stimulate it, promising to make the necessary transportation arrangements and assuring Stuart of a warm welcome. Chen Ming-shu, another old acquaintance and leader of the Shanghai Kuomintang Revolutionary Committee, who had been in Peking early in June seeking his own accommodation with the Communists, now confirmed Stuart's impression, gained from Hua, that Mao and Chou were eager for a meeting as a means of probing American willingness to abandon the Nationalists, recognize a Communist government, and permit the continuation of Sino-American trade and commerce.[36]

Seeking instructions, Stuart cabled Acheson at the end of June, stating, in a rather detached manner, the advantages and disadvantages of the proposed meeting. It would "strengthen the more liberal anti-Soviet element" in the Chinese Communist party, he said, indicate American open-mindedness toward changing political realities, and affect future Sino-American relations beneficially. It would also enhance Communist prestige, however, and appear as a step toward recognizing a Chinese Communist government.[37]

Lacking now was Stuart's earlier enthusiasm for a meeting with Mao and Chou. Events in the spring had led to his growing disillusionment with the Communists. Their unprovoked attack on the HMS *Amethyst* in the Yangtze below Nanking, their harsh treatment of American Consul General Angus Ward at Mukden, their vitriolic propaganda against the United States, and their "unstinted praise" of the Soviet Union had overcome his liberal "instincts and presuppositions" to a large extent. An April message from a trusted Yenching colleague who was "bitterly disillusioned" with the Communist leadership in Peking completed the process. He was thus not greatly disappointed when Acheson cabled on July 1, that he was "under no circumstances to . . . visit Peking."[38]

Truman himself had issued the order back in Washington. Walton Butterworth, now assistant secretary of state for far eastern affairs, and John P. Davies, the State Department's policy planning staff's China specialist, had been concerned mainly about hostile public and congressional reaction to the meeting, for they were certain that Mao and Chou would make as much political capital as possible out of a Stuart visit. Yet Butterworth and Davies were intrigued, as the department had received confirmation independent of Stuart from Peking Consul General Edmund Clubb that Chou was seeking an opening to the United States. Although Butterworth and Davies concocted a plausible cover story for the proposed meeting between Stuart and the two Communist leaders, Truman was unwilling to risk raising a storm of public criticism at home by appearing ready to abandon the Nationalists and accept a Communist China.[39]

American historians have examined this incident in Stuart's diplomatic career thoroughly, treating it as one of America's "lost chances in China." As the Peking meeting did not take place, its probable results can only be guessed. It is certain, however, that Communist attitudes hardened after Stuart declined what seemed to be an invitation. The consensus among historians who have analyzed this and other aspects of Chinese-American relations at the time is that the imperatives of foreign and domestic politics would have prevented Communist leaders in Peking, as they did American leaders in Washington, from reaching an accommodation in the summer of 1949.[40]

VIII

If Stuart were disillusioned with the Communists by the time he left China for the last time, a month and a day after his refusal to meet with Mao and Chou, he was also saddened by the realization that he had failed. He had failed in his efforts to assist Marshall in arranging a Nationalist-dominated coalition in 1946, failed to persuade Chiang to reform thereafter, failed to obtain administration support of Li's efforts to arrange for a Communist-dominated coalition in 1948, and failed to establish American influence in a Communist China in 1949. From beginning to end, his goal had been the maintenance of an American presence in China, one way or another. He had been surprisingly tenacious in his purpose, if flexible in his tactics. Moreover, his short career as an ambassador revealed that his weakness as a missionary diplomat was also his strength. He was almost entirely Chinese-oriented, while the embassy professionals and the policy makers in Washington were American and global in perspective. His success lay in providing alternatives to the policies adopted by the decision makers back home. That they rejected his advice does not lessen the importance of its giving. Although he failed for the moment, his efforts were remembered when another president at another time achieved an accommodation with Communist China.[41]

Notes

1. See, for example, Ernest R. May, *The Truman Administration and China, 1945–1949* (New York: J. P. Lippincott, 1975); Nancy Bernkopf Tucker, "An Unlikely Peace: American Missionaries and the Chinese Communists, 1948–1950," *Pacific Historical Review* 45 (February 1976): 97–116; Russell D. Buhite, "Missed Opportunities? American Policy and the Chinese Communists, 1949," *Mid-America* 61 (October 1979): 179–88; Dorothy Borg and Waldo Heinrichs, eds., *Uncertain Years: Chinese-American Relations, 1947–1950* (New York: Columbia University Press, 1980); Yu-ming Shaw, "John Leighton Stuart and U.S.-Chinese Communist Rapprochement in 1949: Was There Another 'Lost Chance in China'?" *China Quarterly* 89 (March 1982): 74–96; Nancy Bernkopf Tucker, *Patterns in the Dust: Chinese-American Relations and the Recognition Controversy, 1949–1950* (New York: Columbia University Press, 1983); and June M. Grasso, *Truman's Two-China Policy, 1948–1950* (Armonk, NY: M. E. Sharpe, 1987).

2. John Leighton Stuart, *Fifty Years in China: The Memoirs of John Leighton Stuart, Missionary and Ambassador* (New York: Random House, 1954), pp. 1–164, passim. The first half of the book covers Stuart's career as a missionary-educator before 1946.

3. Kenneth W. Rea and John C. Brewer, eds., *The Forgotten Ambassador: The Reports of John Leighton Stuart, 1946–1949* (Boulder, CO: Westview Press, 1981), pp. xvii–xviii. For a summary of the Marshall Mission up to Stuart's appointment, see U.S. Department of State, *United States Relations with China* (Washington, DC: U.S. Government Printing Office, 1949), pp. 132–74. Hereinafter cited as *China White Paper.* Stuart's attitude toward his appointment appears in *Fifty Years in China*, pp. 165–66.

4. John F. Melby, *The Mandate of Heaven: Record of a Civil War, 1945–1949* (Toronto: University of Toronto Press, 1968), pp. 135–37.

5. Amos Wong, "American Aid to China," *China Weekly Review* 109 (December 20, 1947): 78–79; Stuart, *Fifty Years in China*, pp. 174–75; Melby, *Mandate of Heaven*, pp. 135–38, 181–82.

6. Melby, *Mandate of Heaven*, pp. 135–37.

7. Stuart, *Fifty Years in China*, pp. 167–70; U.S. Department of State, *Foreign Relations of the United States* (hereinafter cited as *FR*), 1946, 9:1466–1468; ibid., 10:113; Melby, *Mandate of Heaven*, pp. 143–45; May, *The Truman Administration and China*, p. 20.

8. *FR*, 1946, 10:308–10, 361–62, 457–60, 535–37, 580; Stuart, *Fifty Years in China*, pp. 169–73; Melby, *Mandate of Heaven*, pp. 144–45, 151–53. See also *China White Paper*, pp. 175–218, 227; and Steven I. Levine, "A New Look at American Mediation in the Chinese Civil War: The Marshall Mission and Manchuria," *Diplomatic History* 3 (Fall 1979): 349–75.

9. *China White Paper*, p. 689. For a succinct statement of Marshall's views, see Warren I. Cohen, "Acheson, His Advisers, and China, 1949–1950," in Borg and Heinrichs,

Uncertain Years, pp. 14–15. A fuller statement of Marshall's views on aid to China appears in May, *The Truman Administration and China*, pp. 12–33.

10. Stuart, *Fifty Years in China*, pp. 178–83.

11. *FR*, 1946, 9:1388–93; idem., 1946, 10:111–12, 665–66; idem., 1947, 7:22–23, 27–28, 34, 50–51, 55–56, 58–60, 69–72, 84–94, 102–104. See also Melby, *Mandate of Heaven*, pp. 178–80.

12. *FR*, 1947, 7:105–11, 131–33, 137–38, 149–51, 154–55, 161–62, 191–92.

13. Rea and Brewer, *The Forgotten Ambassador*, p. 123. See also *China White Paper*, pp. 251–61; and Melby, *Mandate of Heaven*, pp. 222–25.

14. Stuart, *Fifty Years in China*, pp. 185–87; *FR*, 1947, 7:650, 774–75; *China White Paper*, pp. 824–26.

15. May, *The Truman Administration and China*, pp. 20–30, 76–77, 81–82. See also Cohen, "Acheson, His Advisers, and China," pp. 14–15.

16. *FR*, 1947, 7:289–90, 295–97, 315–16, 343–46; Melby, *Mandate of Heaven*, p. 232.

17. *FR*, 1947, 7:191–92, 280, 343–46, 367–68, 371–72, 1234–37; idem., 1948, 8:472–73.

18. Ibid., 1947, 7:289–92, 412–13; idem., 1948, 7:76–78, 107–13; Melby, *Mandate of Heaven*, p. 252.

19. *China White Paper*, pp. 271–73. For a brief analysis of the China aid bill, see John H. Feaver, "The China Aid Bill of 1948: Limited Assistance as a Cold War Strategy," *Diplomatic History* 5 (Spring 1981): 107–20. For a succinct statement of Marshall's position, see May, *The Truman Administration and China*, pp. 28–33, 81–82.

20. *FR*, 1947, 7:280–81; idem., 1948, 7:87–88, 177–78.

21. *China White Paper*, pp. 846, 849–59; *FR*, 1948, 7:187–88, 195, 204–209, 211–12.

22. *FR*, 1948, 7:202–204, 221–23, 225–26, 233–35, 237–38, 292, 328–29.

23. Ibid., 214–16, 242, 300–301, 318, 328–30; Stuart, *Fifty Years in China*, p. 209; Melby, *Mandate of Heaven*, pp. 271–72.

24. *Mandate of Heaven*, pp. 27–72, Rea and Brewer, *The Forgotten Ambassador*, p. 251; *FR*, 1948, 7:344–45, 348–51, 364–65.

25. *FR*, 1948, 7:350–51, 388–90, 405–10.

26. Ibid., 415.

27. Ibid., 492–95.

28. Ibid., 505–508, 510–17.

29. Ibid., 518–20, 525–27.

30. Ibid., 566–67, 597–98, 603; Melby, *Mandate of Heaven*, pp. 181–82, 264–65.

31. *FR*, 1948, 7:651–52, 654–56, 659, 663–66, 693.

32. Ibid., 674–77, 695–97.

33. Stuart, *Fifty Years in China*, pp. 213, 216–17, 228–32; Melby, *Mandate of Heaven*, pp. 273–74; *FR*, 1949, 8:20–22, 72, 86, 108–110, 144–45, 255, 263, 269, 652–53.

34. Philip Fugh, ed., *John Leighton Stuart's Diary* (Palo Alto, CA: Yenching University Alumni Association of USA, Inc., 1980), 21; Stuart, *Fifty Years in China*, pp. 228–29; *FR*, 1949, 8:108–109, 144–45, 173–77, 682.

35. *FR*, 1949, 8:230–31. For a full analysis of Acheson's position, see Cohen, "Acheson, His Advisers, and China," pp. 13–51.

36. *FR*, 1949, 8:745–46, 752–57, 761, 764, 766–67, 771–79.

37. Ibid., 766–67.

38. Ibid., 277–78, 769.

39. Ibid., 768–69.

40. For detailed treatments, see Buhite, "Missed Opportunities?" pp. 179–88; Shaw, "John Leighton Stuart and U.S.-Chinese Communist Rapprochement," pp. 74–96; Cohen, "Acheson, His Advisers, and China," pp. 13–52; Michael H. Hunt, "Mao Tse-tung and the

Issue of Accommodation with the United States, 1948–1950,'' in Borg and Heinrichs, eds., 185–233, *Uncertain Years*; Steven M. Goldstein, ''Chinese Communist Policy Toward the United States: Opportunities and Constraints, 1944–1950,'' in Borg and Heinrichs, eds., 235–78, *Uncertain Years;* Tucker, *Patterns in the Dust*; pp.46–48; and Warren I. Cohen, ''Conversations with Chinese Friends: Zhou En-lai's Associates Reflect on Chinese-American Relations in the 1940's and Korean War,'' *Diplomatic History* 11 (Summer 1987): 283–89. See also Cohen, ''Ambassador Philip D. Sprouse on the Question of Recognition of the People's Republic of China in 1949 and 1950,'' *Diplomatic History* 2 (Spring 1978): 213–17; and Cohen, ''Consul General O. Edmund Clubb on the Inevitability of Conflict Between the United States and the People's Republic of China, 1949–50,'' *Diplomatic History* 5 (Spring 1981): 165–68.

41. U.S. Congress, Senate, Committee on Foreign Relations, *The United States and Communist China in 1949 and 1950: The Question of Rapprochement and Recognition*, 93d Congress, 1st Session (Washington, DC: US Government Printing Office, 1973): pp. 7–12.

13

JOHN LEIGHTON STUART'S ROLE IN THE MARSHALL NEGOTIATIONS
The Kalgan Crisis

Edmund S. Wehrle

On July 10, 1946, John Leighton Stuart became American Ambassador to China. Since he expected to return to his position as president of Yenching University in Peking before the end of the year, his assignment was to be limited in duration.[1] In addition, he was to concentrate on one specific task. He was to work with General George C. Marshall, President Harry Truman's special representative in China, in resolving the conflict that was drawing the Nationalist government and the Communist party toward civil war. Marshall estimated that Stuart was the most respected and knowledgeable American in China.[2] More to the point, he saw him as the individual best suited to induce Generalissimo Chiang Kai-shek to agree to certain concessions to the Communists, concessions that would clear the way for a coalition government.

In fact, the appointment of Stuart introduced an unpredictable element into the negotiations. Initially, the Nationalists voiced their disappointment at the appointment. To Marshall's surprise, Chiang told him that the missionary-educator was "merely a college professor." T. V. Soong, president of the Nationalist Executive Yuan, privately protested that a man of greater "international prestige" might have been selected.[3] However, in the following months of negotiations, the Nationalists undoubtedly revised their opinion since, in Stuart, they found a mediator who could not suppress his heart-felt sympathy for Chiang's government. Marshall, in turn, came to realize that Stuart was not the man to wring concessions from Chiang Kai-shek.

Stuart was to play a central role in the resolution of a crisis that constituted the final episode of the Marshall Mission when Marshall was at the brink of breaking with Chiang Kai-shek and partially disassociating the United States from the Nationalists. This was brought about by Chiang's aggressive military campaign against the Communists in the North of China, which was aimed at the capture of Kalgan, the largest city held by the Communists in China proper. This attack constituted a blatant rejection of the negotiating process. Ultimately, Marshall elected to accept the Nationalist capture of Kalgan and remain in China even though his role as mediator had become largely that of passive observer. Stuart played a vital role in preventing Marshall from disassociating the United States from Chiang's virtual rejection of the negotiating process.

But there were other equally important factors that influenced Marshall's decision, and these involved international politics. The creation of a strong, united, and democratic China was seen as vital to American interests in East Asia and this was a central aspect of Marshall's task. Equally important, however, were his efforts to curb Russian influence in China. Washington regarded Chiang's regime as a strong bulwark against Russia and what it presumed to be its compliant tool, the Chinese Communist party. However distasteful alignment with Chiang might become, the removal of American support was seen as a major risk. While Marshall was not fully convinced by such reasoning, he was aware of an additional consideration. Chiang himself had in the past played the "Russian card," that is, when American pressure had mounted in terms of urging concessions to the Chinese Communists, the Generalissimo had pointed to fact that the Nationalists were currently considering the need of making certain economic or territorial concessions to the Soviets. This was a clear message: if Washington demanded too much from Chiang, he might grant certain favors to the Soviet Union. Accordingly, this aspect of international politics must be blended into an analysis of the Kalgan negotiations.

I

The crisis began on September 29, 1946, when the Nationalists initiated a drive to capture Kalgan, a Communist stronghold that lay about a hundred miles northwest of Peiping, just inside the Great Wall of China. For Marshall, the Kalgan campaign was an intolerable breach by the Nationalists of the restraint necessary for successful negotiation with the Communists. It came at a time when Marshall was becoming increasingly exasperated with Chiang. The General had hoped that with the Generalissimo's return to Nanking on September 26, from his summer residence at Kuling, serious negotiations would commence. Indeed, Marshall and Stuart had gone out of their way in urging Chou En-lai, the chief Communist negotiator, to return to Nanking from Shanghai, to which he had retired when the Nationalists had refused to partake in discussions to resolve the military conflict. The Americans anticipated that, if Chiang would agree to an acceptable framework for negotiations, Chou would return promptly. But, in a series of meetings with Marshall, from September 27 to 30, Chiang rejected the General's call for a total cessation of hostilities. Chiang insisted that, prior to the cease fire, certain political issues must be settled in Stuart's Five Man Committee and that Marshall's Committee of Three must complete its work in repositioning all the Nationalist and Communist armies. Marshall was dismayed when Chiang insisted that settlement of these issues must precede the end of hostilities; the American knew that there would be prolonged debate in the two committees, and that meanwhile warfare would gain momentum. Chiang's recalcitrance along with the government drive on Kalgan, led Marshall to believe that the time may have come to end his mediation.[4]

Early on Tuesday morning, October 1, Marshall and Stuart met to assess the situation. The General stated emphatically that he could not, in good faith, sit in on negotiations while the Nationalists pursued their attack on Kalgan. He was turning over in his mind whether or not this development placed the United States in an untenable position, one that would force his withdrawal from mediation. He felt that in effect he and Dr. Stuart were being made "stooges" by the government. The Generalissimo, he said, must be made aware that the Americans were "adamant." He was inclined to "force" the government to back down on some of its demands. He considered sending Chiang a memorandum declaring that the drive on Kalgan could only be justified on the basis of an all-out war; and that the mediators must be given assurances that Chiang would offer reasonable terms. Otherwise, the General told Stuart, he might request that Washington terminate his mission and suspend the American Executive Headquarters and the Military Advisory Group.[5]

Stuart did his best to moderate Marshall's fury. He agreed that such a memorandum should be sent. But, he suggested that emphasis should be given to the point that it was "upon moral grounds" that America could not continue mediation when no basis for a settlement really existed. He urged Marshall to emphasize this moral consideration, not material factors. Thus he would exclude the threat to end "all aid to China."[6] With respect to resolving what he called the deplorable situation in China, Stuart had a suggestion apparently of his own. Marshall and he should issue a statement calling for the simultaneous meeting of Stuart's committee to solve political problems and Marshall's Committee of Three to deal with military affairs. He would simply ignore the fact that Chiang refused to suspend hostilities. Not only did Marshall indicate that he regarded this proposal as unworkable, but he also pointed out that the exact same proposal had been presented to him by Chiang's representative in yesterday's negotiations.[7] It remains unclear whether or not Stuart had taken the hint from the Nationalist camp in presenting this proposal as his own.

Just before noon, Marshall and Stuart met again. Each had come with ominous news. Marshall had just met with the Communist spokesmen, Tung Pi-Wu and Wang Ping-nan, who had handed him a memorandum from Chou En-lai. Chou's note summarized the main features of the government's summer offensive, dwelling particularly on the Kalgan question. The Communist stand was clear: "If the Kuomintang Government does not instantly cease its military operations against Kalgan and the vicinity areas, the Chinese Communist Party feels forced to presume that the Government is thereby giving public announcement of a total national split.''[8] For his part, Stuart had just returned from a meeting with T. V. Soong, president of the Executive Yuan. Soong frankly affirmed that the government wanted to take Kalgan before opening negotiations. Considering these two developments, Marshall told Stuart that he was more convinced than ever that the time was approaching to terminate his mission. Stuart admitted that it looked that way.[9]

That afternoon Marshall wrote a blunt memorandum to Chiang. The General accused the government of ''utilizing a general offensive campaign to force compliance with the government point of view.'' Marshall brushed aside Chiang's claim that he was responding to Communist provocation. He concluded that unless a way was found ''to terminate the fighting without further delays of proposals and counter-proposals, I will recommend to the President that I be recalled and that the United States terminate its efforts of mediation.''[10] Perhaps no more accusatory note had ever been sent to the Chinese government by a presidential representative.

Early Wednesday morning, October 2, just before Marshall's memorandum was formally delivered, Chiang called Stuart in to sound him out on the gist of the forthcoming message. Immediately after, Stuart reported back to Marshall. The ambassador indicated that he told Chiang that his government's military policy had placed the Americans in the position of ''seeming to favor the Nationalist side.'' In an effort to explain Marshall's basic view, Stuart told Chiang that ''he personally sympathized'' with Marshall's attitude.[11] Yet the ambassador's choice of words is revealing: to sympathize with Marshall's position was not necessarily to agree with it. In fact, as will become clear, Stuart dreaded the consequences of an end to American support for Chiang's government and he quietly maneuvered to prevent such a denouement.

Having completed his report, Stuart listened as Marshall resumed his bitter criticism of Chiang's tactics. The General recalled the period of intense negotiations in June, just before Stuart's appointment.[12] With obvious reference to the Nationalists' summer military offensive, Marshall explained that, at the end of June, he took issue with everything the Generalissimo proposed to do and had since done. The single concession that he had pried from Chiang was to allow Communist possession of Kalgan; now seizure of Kalgan had become a government prerequisite to negotiations. The situation, Marshall exclaimed, had become ''intolerable''; the time had come for a ''show down.''[13] It appeared that unless Chiang halted his Kalgan operation, Marshall would end his mission and very possibly terminate material assistance for Chiang's government.

Sometime that afternoon, Chiang received Marshall's severely worded memorandum. Within a few hours, the Generalissimo's reply reached Marshall. Though it came in the guise of an additional concession, it amounted to a rejection of Marshall's demand. Chiang agreed to issue a cease-fire order, but only after certain conditions had been accepted by the Communists. With respect to the state council, he ''conceded'' that the Communists might appoint (with government approval) one additional independent member. While this would raise the number of seats under Communist influence to thirteen, it was still one short of the number the Communists needed to block legislation that might undermine its power in the proposed coalition government. Chiang also insisted that the Communists must list their delegates to the state council and the National Assembly, and complete agreement for the relocation of the eighteen divisions that the Communists would retain in the agreed military reorganization.[14] These political and military arrangements were clearly unacceptable to the Communists; prolonged negotiations would be required before an agreement could be hammered out. These extreme demands laid down by Chiang in his October 2 memorandum should be borne in mind since it would be a crucial factor in the following week of negotiations. However, at this time, Marshall's attention was focused on the fact that nowhere in the Generalissimo's memorandum did he mention the Kalgan offensive.

The following day, Thursday, October 3, Marshall and Stuart conferred once again. The General's anger and frustration had intensified. Once more he expounded his belief that the Nationalist attack on Kalgan was "so definite" a rejection of the negotiation process that it could not be ignored, and that the government would continue to use American mediation as "a cloak" for military action so long as he let them get away with it. Marshall added, that if he were Chou En-lai, he would respond to Chiang's new terms with a categorical declaration that no government proposal would be considered unless the attack on Kalgan ceased.[15]

Again Stuart sought to mollify Marshall. Without mentioning these criticisms of Chiang, he urged that they press for an arrangement that Chiang might accept. Perhaps the Generalissimo would agree to halt his attack on Kalgan for a few days, Stuart speculated, if the Communists could be persuaded to evacuate Kalgan. One cannot but wonder if Marshall was puzzled by the contradictory nature of Stuart's proposition. At any rate, Marshall patiently reminded Stuart of the history of the Kalgan question. Last June, he noted, Chiang's only concession was to agree to Communist control of Kalgan. At that time, Marshall pointed out, the Communists had shown considerable evidence of good faith. In any case, he reasoned, the Communists could not be expected to evacuate Kalgan; nor could he personally insist they do so. He concluded that the government was so intent on taking the city, that they either could not see or chose to ignore other issues.[16]

If, for reasons of his own, Stuart feared the consequences of an American break from Chiang, officials in Washington also were worried at this turn of events. On October 3, the State Department received Marshall's report proposing his possible recall. Undersecretary of State Dean Acheson and John Carter Vincent, director of the Office of Far Eastern Affairs, discussed the situation in detail. They still thought that there was a fifty-fifty chance that the "jig is not up" and that Marshall would succeed at calling Chiang's "bluff." They appeared to agree that Marshall's personal anger had brought the situation to a head. Vincent observed that Marshall was "obviously mad" and had virtually accused the Nationalist leaders of "duplicity." They agreed that the key factor was Marshall's attitude; still they admitted that "in fairness to General Marshall," the United States must reiterate that no assistance should go to a China engaged in civil war. They assumed that if Marshall came home, U.S. Executive Headquarters would be withdrawn, but they would reserve their decision on the withdrawal of the marines and the Military Advisory Group. The following day Acheson consulted with President Truman. The upshot was a cable to Marshall in which they expressed their confident belief that "you can do the job if it is humanly possible"; but they gave full approval for his recall if the situation required it.[17]

On Friday, October 4, at about the time that Truman and Acheson were conferring, Marshall had one last chance to call Chiang's "bluff." Following dinner at the Generalissimo's residence, Marshall and Stuart entered into a three-hour conference with Chiang. Initially Chiang expressed his deep distress over Marshall's memorandum of October 1, which, he observed, accused him of deceptive practices in appearing to negotiate while his armies pressed their offensive operations. The Generalissimo asserted that such "lack of integrity" on his part was "unthinkable"; in fact, "his conscience as a Christian would forbid it." Chiang went on to defend his policies, justifying them with select quotations from the Bible. As to Marshall's recall, Chiang insisted that his withdrawal was "unthinkable."[18]

In response, Marshall immediately assured Chiang that there was no question concerning the latter's integrity, but that he, Marshall, could not allow negotiations, sponsored by the Americans, to be interpreted as "a cover" for a military campaign. More to the point, Marshall asserted that recent developments had convinced him "that while the Communists were demanding a cessation of fighting, the government was actually pursuing a policy of force." Further, the Generalissimo's proposal that a set of political and military issues be resolved prior to a cease-fire would simply consume time while military operations moved ahead. Worse, Marshall continued, the government's proposals for negotiations were "definitely made at the point of a gun." When the conferees moved on to discussion of the precise issue of the Kalgan attack, Marshall later noted, Chiang did not "concede an inch."[19] Marshall and Chiang had arrived at a total impasse.

By Saturday, October 5, Marshall had time to reflect on his lengthy exchange with the Generalissimo. He concluded that his China mission had failed; reluctantly he dispatched a cable to Truman requesting the termination of his mission. In it he regretfully commented that Chiang's coterie of leaders had played its cards carefully in creating the present situation, believing all the while that "Soviet considerations" would force the Americans to accept the government's military campaign. Marshall explained that it was vital to implement his recall immediately; this would spare him the embarrassment of being in place as mediator when Nationalist forces seized Kalgan. Should the United States find itself in this position, he could not predict the Communist reaction. Marshall then ticked off the reasons that necessitated his recall: "The Communists were demanding a cessation of fighting, [while] the Government was actually pursuing a policy of force"; the government's proposal would require "time consuming" negotiation conducted "at the point of a gun"; and to continue under these conditions would place the United States in a position "where the integrity of its actions as represented by me could be successfully questioned."[20] Always the good soldier, Marshall added that, if Washington thought it necessary, he would "gladly" continue his negotiations. He added that there was still time for Chiang to reverse himself, but clearly he doubted that this would happen.

Early Saturday evening, Marshall and Stuart met to consider Chou En-lai's response to a current American suggestion that the Communists might offer certain specified concessions in order to induce the Nationalists to halt their drive on Kalgan. As anticipated, Chou had certain reservations about these concessions.[21] More importantly, it appeared that Marshall informed Stuart that he had telegraphed Washington requesting his recall.

Stuart was "in a panic," and, according to John Melby, an embassy official, the ambassador set out "on his own" to prevent a rupture between Marshall and Chiang.[22] Returning to his residence, Stuart came upon Peter Pee, Chiang's private secretary. Pee was a graduate of Yenching University or, as Stuart put it, a "Yenching boy." Earlier in the year Stuart had registered his pleasure in observing that Pee had become Chiang's "right-hand man in administrative matters."[23] Apparently without hesitation, Stuart revealed Marshall's plans to Pee who, in turn, darted off to Chiang's headquarters.[24] Within half-an-hour, Stuart was summoned to Chiang's residence to which he hastened, apparently without consulting Marshall.

Later that evening, Marshall received an unexpected visit from Stuart; he had come to report the results of his impromptu interview with the Generalissimo. Chiang had agreed to halt the attack on Kalgan for a five-day period, or longer if Marshall insisted. Meanwhile, Chiang insisted that the Committee of Three and the Five Man Committee be assembled with Kalgan the first issue to be settled. Marshall cautioned that the Communists would never agree to this since this procedure suggested that the government would halt its offensive only to take Kalgan "without a fight."[25] However, in spite of his doubts, Marshall cabled Washington to delay delivery of his recall request.

Thus, on Sunday morning, October 6, as Marshall and Stuart arrived at Chiang's residence, negotiations resumed. Marshall immediately told Chiang that he did not favor a short truce since it entailed the "threat of a resumption of aggressive military action." He urged a total cessation of hostilities followed by negotiations in the political and military committees. When Chiang refused, they shifted to consideration of a limited truce. Marshall managed to persuade Chiang to extend the truce offer to ten days, with a possible additional extension. As the Generalissimo saw it, the purpose of the truce was to complete action on his two point memorandum of October 2. As noted above, this called for the Five Man Committee to settle the composition of the State Council on terms that would prevent the Communists from exercising an effective veto on legislation. Also the Committee of Three was to decide on the location of eighteen Communist divisions specified in the military relocation agreement, but no mention was made of the relocation of Nationalist armies. Marshall was reluctant to accept these stipulations and he reported to Washington that these were "merely the best terms he could secure." But, surprisingly, he agreed to Chiang's insistence that it be presented to the Communists as an American-supported proposal.[26]

Once Marshall adopted Chiang's new terms, Stuart's panic subsided. In fact, he was euphoric over what he saw as a morality play unfolding before him. At least this was the tone of his report to the secretary of state. Stuart depicted the Sunday conference as a meeting of "truly great men." There was Marshall who faced unflinchingly the ethical principle involved; he could not allow a "stain upon our country's honor." Then there was Chiang, "proud and stubbornly determined . . . [who] mastered his earlier impulses and graciously deferred to General Marshall's judgment." As "friendliness" was restored between Marshall and Chiang, Stuart pronounced his "indescribable relief."[27]

II

If, in the first week of October, Marshall's anger with the Nationalists mounted to the point where he all but implemented his recall from China, the second week witnessed a near complete reversal in which he blamed the Communists for blocking a negotiated settlement. Stuart's role was somewhat less prominent in this second week, but, nonetheless, he continued to nurture the Nationalist cause.

On Sunday, October 6, after his conference with Chiang, Marshall cabled Washington to cancel his request for recall.[28] Meanwhile the General hastily dictated a statement of Chiang's conditions for the ten-day halt in the attack on Kalgan. It was in the form of a memorandum addressed to Stuart and approved by him, for presentation to the Communist delegation. That afternoon, Stuart called in Wang Ping-nan and gave him an oral summary of the proposal which, of course, consisted of the terms Marshall had wrung from Chiang.[29] Not until Monday did Wang receive Marshall's written summary.

The prolonged negotiations may have been taking a toll on Marshall. His summary of Chiang's terms inadvertently exaggerated the worst feature of the Generalissimo's already demanding statement. The brief truce would require the Communists "to carry out" the two "conditions" specified by Chiang in his statement of October 2.[30] It is understandable that the Communists would see these conditions as a dictation of peace terms. There is no record of Stuart's oral presentation of these terms, but, in general, Stuart tended to be more unyielding than Marshall in his discussions with the Communists.

By Tuesday, October 8, it was evident that renewed cooperation involving Marshall, Stuart, and Chiang had come at the expense of a trusting relationship with the Communist delegation. Wang Ping-nan, the Communist spokesman, called on Stuart to report Chou En-lai's oral response to the truce proposal. The terms were unacceptable. Chou had made three points: the time limitation vitiated the purpose of the truce; unless Government troops moved back to their original position, the truce might be seen as a "strategy" to enhance the Nationalist military position; and limiting discussions to the two conditions raised by Chiang would force the Communists to negotiate "under military coercion."[31]

Later that morning, when Stuart briefed Marshall on Chou's reply, a curious exchange took place. The General asked Stuart to appraise Chou's response. Stuart complained that Chou had expanded his demands to include an "overall cessation of hostilities" before negotiations could begin, whereas earlier Chou had limited his demands to a halt in the government's drive on Kalgan.[32] Based on the written record this would appear to be a gross misinterpretation of Chou's position. In fact, the memorandum containing Chou's oral response said nothing about an "overall cessation of hostilities."[33] Chou did insist that government forces "withdraw to their original positions." The context of the note suggests that it referred to the positions around Kalgan, not in all of China. Indeed this was the demand expressed by the Communist negotiators later that day. Perhaps influenced by Stuart's overstatement of Chou's position, Marshall reversed his own views. He observed that Chou's response placed him in "a position entirely opposite" from a few days ago when he protested against Chiang's offensive operations: now it was the government which offered a truce which the Communists refused.[34]

Stuart suddenly injected a suggestion of his own. He observed that the time might be right for the two Americans to issue a joint statement that would bring the American public and the Chinese up-to-date on the state of the negotiations. Of course, Stuart noted that it should cast blame on neither side and objectively set forth the situation. Marshall agreed and quickly dictated the necessary press release, asking Stuart to check it prior to publication.[35] Stuart may not have realized it but the publication of the joint statement *at that time* became a major source of irritation to the Communists. This point was to surface in the crucial negotiations that Marshall held with Chou on the following day.

Seeking further clarification of Chou's "oral" response, Marshall and Stuart arranged to meet with the Communist representatives, Tung Pi-wu and Wang Ping-nan, later that afternoon. Marshall set the tone for the meeting in immediately expressing his frustration with the Communists. He confessed to Tung that he was "baffled" by the attitude of the Communists. He had obtained the truce which they sought: "What now do you expect of Doctor Stuart and myself, if anything?"[36]

In fact, the Communists were probably baffled by Marshall's benevolent portrayal of Chiang's proposal. Tung listed its deficiencies. Originally, he recalled, Chou had asked for a complete halt in the Kalgan drive, not a ten-day truce, and

Chou specified that the truce was to apply to the vicinity around the city itself. To make discussions possible, government forces should withdraw from the Kalgan area to "their original positions," as was called for in Chou's oral response. Tung added that both sides should be involved in determining the agenda. Otherwise the negotiations would be reduced to a dictation of the "victor over the vanquished."[37] It is difficult to deny the reasonableness of Tung's assessment. In addition, his statement seemed to make clear that Chou's demand for a pullback of forces pertained to the Kalgan area and was not a demand for a cessation of hostilities throughout China.

As the discussion continued, Stuart made a special plea for Communist understanding of the new proposal. The ambassador insisted that negotiations in the Committee of Five would not involve the dictation of terms; they would strive for a "mutually satisfactory solution." Then, "once the government had evidence of the readiness of the Communists to cooperate" on the issues discussed, the larger question of the cessation of fighting could be successfully negotiated, since the government would then have confidence in Communist goodwill.[38] Of course, the Communists must have seen that their cooperation could only be demonstrated by capitulation on the issues presented in Chiang's fixed agenda. Without being fully conscious of what he was implying, Stuart seemed to be affirming that only Communist agreement to the terms offered would bring about the termination of hostilities.

Marshall was grimly determined to undertake one last effort to convince the Communists that Chiang's truce proposal was acceptable. In the previous months of negotiation a bond of mutual trust had been established between Marshall and Chou En-lai; now the American hoped to bring this personal relationship into play. With time running out, Marshall decided to put aside protocol and, without warning, to confront Chou directly.[39] Leaving Stuart in Nanking, Marshall secretly flew to Shanghai where Chou had been residing since mid-September.

On Wednesday, October 9, Chou had been scheduled to meet with General Alvin Gillem, commander of American forces in China. Once in Gillem's office, Chou was startled as Marshall stepped forth from behind a screen to greet the Communist leader. Marshall explained that the crisis had become so serious that he did not want to leave anything undone in seeking a solution. In fact, this personal exchange was crucial. It was the last meeting between the two in which there was at least some chance of maintaining a serious political and military dialogue with the Communists.

Marshall initiated the discussion by noting that yesterday's conference with Chou's representatives in Nanking was unsatisfactory. Marshall handed Chou the minutes of that meeting so that he might familiarize himself with the points of difference. Immediately thereafter, Chou pointed out that his representatives had based their response on Marshall's memorandum of October 6, which indicated that Chiang's demands of October 2 would be "carried out." This, Chou insisted, was "tantamount to a document of surrender." Furthermore his people had not received the Joint Statement of Marshall and Stuart with its more moderate suggestion that Chiang's terms would be "considered" until after yesterday's conference. Marshall was thrown on the defensive. He insisted that the difference in the two phases was not "of such apparent moment;" the point should not be "my English," he stated, but the Generalissimo's intent in the presentation.[40] It was unusual for Marshall not to admit an error and agree that the misunderstanding was caused by his haste in dictation. That he chose to paper over his egregious misstatement suggests the enormous tension he was under as the possibility of a negotiated settlement was slipping from his grasp.

Following a recess for lunch, Marshall and Chou turned to the substance of Chiang's proposal. Chou pointed out that Chiang's so-called "maximum concessions" actually were composed of demands that were unacceptable to the Communists. On the political side, he observed, the Communists would be required to forfeit veto power in the State Council, which would endanger the fragile political compromises arrived at in the Political Consultative Conference.[41] On the military side, the Generalissimo would have the eighteen Communist divisions withdrawn to specified positions while no parallel demand was imposed on the government forces. Such prearranged terms, Chou acclaimed, were "tantamount to an ultimatum," and, in addition, they constituted concessions that the Generalissimo knew the Communists would never accept. Chou also rejected any thought of a temporary armistice for China. The issue he said was "terminating the fighting or not to terminate it."[42]

In response, Marshall insisted that Chou misunderstood the intent of the proposed discussions. The agenda was limited to avoid prolonged discussions that would delay the cessation of hostilities throughout China.[43] Technically Marshall was correct. But only a mortally wounded Communist party would agree to an agenda limited to concessions by Yenan. If such negotiations succeeded it would be a government victory, but failure would be blamed on Communist refusal to yield.

Having insisted that the initiation of negotiations depended on the complete termination of the Kalgan drive, Chou went on to discuss the "stand" the Communists would assume once political and military discussions were renewed. The party's political position was that there must be an unambiguous acceptance of the resolutions of the Political Consultative Conference agreed to earlier in the year. This meant that the Communists insisted on controlling fourteen seats in the State Council which would provide them with the veto power to sustain their delicate position in the coalition government. On the military side, the Communist stand would be that both sides should return to the positions occupied on January 13 in China proper, and on June 7 in Manchuria.[44] Of course, these were the positions specified in the original cease-fire agreements; but, in its summer offensive, the government had seized control of large areas of north China. The Communists insisted that the Nationalists should forfeit these gains.

Chou presented a tough Communist bargaining position; it was just as rigorous as Chiang's proposal of October 2. Chou, in specifying these terms, referred to it as the Communist "stand" and indicated that "only these conditions will insure the truce."[45] Nowhere in Chou's discussions with Marshall or in his formal written response to Marshall of that day, however, did he insist that the government forces must return to their position of January 13, before discussions could begin. It was clear that the Communist "stand" would be the subject of later negotiations. Of course, Chou insisted that such discussions required an absolute halt in the attack on Kalgan and a withdrawal of these attacking forces to their position on September 29.

In any case, the interview terminated on a rather harsh note. The two leaders exchanged remarks that revealed, at least on Marshall's part, how personal the negotiations had become. Chou could not resist mentioning that the Communist party felt that the Americans had given logistical support to the government in the civil war. Further, he went on to state his distress over the Marshall-Stuart Joint Statement of the previous day. The timing of the release, Chou felt, suggested that it was the Communists who were obstructing negotiations. He pointed out that the Americans seemed to resort to such public statements only when the Communists, not the Nationalists, refused to accept an American proposal.[46] Of course, Chou was largely correct. Stuart had urged Marshall to issue the joint statement; but, the week before, he had been silent in this respect when Chiang refused to halt his attack on Kalgan.

At this point, Marshall's temper reached the boiling point. Apparently looking Chou in the eye, he asserted that "I told you some time ago, that if the Communist Party felt that they could not trust my impartiality, they had merely to say so and I would withdraw. You have now said so."[47] Chou sought to set the record straight as to what his statement implied. He observed that, while he clearly objected to the timing of the joint statement, "I do not refer to your over-all efforts throughout the whole negotiations. I want to make that clear."[48] The meeting concluded abruptly.

The day after this tense meeting, Kalgan fell to Chiang's armies. Immediately after, on October 11, the Generalissimo matched his military achievement with a triumphant political proclamation: the National Assembly would meet, as scheduled, on November 4.[49] This, of course, meant that the political reorganization of China would proceed without Communist participation, and that the compromises agreed to in the March meeting of the Political Consultative Conference would be set aside. The national split, which Chou forecast, had occurred. As described above, it was only last-minute maneuvering by Chiang and his supporters that preserved a working relationship with the United States. Now the Communists, by refusing to accept a humiliating truce proposal, appeared to be committed to continued warfare.

III

It should be clear that Stuart played a pivotal role in drawing Marshall and Chiang back together, which, almost axiomatically, forced the Communists into a position where to concede was to surrender. That Marshall should have been so much influenced by Stuart is surprising. It is likely that Marshall was aware of Stuart's proclivity to see things from the Nationalist point of view. In late September, W. Bradley Connors, a USIS official, had been assigned to keep an eye on Stuart, since the Ambassador had a reputation for talking too much to newspapermen and others.[50] The embassy was especially troubled by the full access to Stuart enjoyed by Philip Fugh. Here was a Chinese national who, as Stuart's Chinese secretary and long-time "confidant," not only knew what Stuart knew, but, according to Foreign Service critics, "did Stuart's thinking for him."[51] Further leaks could occur through Stuart's intimate circle, his "Yenching boys," including Peter Pee, Chiang's private secretary, Pee's own secretary, and David Yu of the Chinese Ministry of Information.[52]

It would appear that sometime after the Kalgan crisis Marshall chose to exclude Stuart from certain high-level conferences. On December 1, when Marshall met with top embassy officials for a policy review, Stuart was conspicuously absent. At the meeting, W. Walton Butterworth, the embassy's chief consular, was free to observe that Marshall's departure from China would be "catastrophic" and "in view of Dr. Stuart's inclinations, would cause the United States . . . to drift toward full support for the Nationalist Government."[53] Such a statement concerning a superior could never be made in Marshall's presence, unless it was known that he shared this view.

Stuart, however, was not alone in seeking to prevent a break between Washington and Nanking. John Beal, an American on leave from *Time* magazine and now attached to the Nationalist Ministry of Information, took seriously his assignment of keeping the Nationalists "out of trouble with the United States."[54] By early October, Beal was deeply upset by the possibility that Marshall might withdraw from China in the face of Chiang's refusal to halt the Kalgan attack. He feared the impact this demarche would have on American public opinion, as well as on American policy. Thus, on October 3, he arranged for a personal interview with Chiang. Addressing the Generalissimo directly, he urged him to recognize that if the Marshall mediation were to terminate, it must appear that the Communists were responsible for the rupture. Beal suggested, "Why not call off the drive to Kalgan, giving the Communists until October 12 . . . to nominate their candidates [to the National Assembly] and participate in the Committee of Three."[55] This, Beal thought, would put the Communists on the spot. Later he speculated that Chiang took his advice, gambling on the odds that the Communists would reject these terms. The American granted that this was a somewhat cynical approach to the negotiations, but perhaps necessary to achieve a worthwhile objective.[56]

Both Stuart and Beal played a role in bringing Chiang to propose his limited truce, but without Marshall's willingness to support Chiang's proposal the mediation would have come to an end. No doubt, Stuart's persistent support of Chiang's position played a significant role in Marshall's willingness to support the truce proposal, but there may have been a more compelling factor at work. On October 3, E. A. Bayne, an American official attached to T. V. Soong's office, made a surprising revelation. In a cable to the American embassy in Nanking, he alerted the Americans that Chiang Kai-shek might bow to Soviet economic claims in Sinkiang province. The Generalissimo would probably appease the Russians and concede to them "all mineral and petroleum rights in the province."[57]

What had this to do with the Kalgan crisis? At least one American official was quick to connect the Chinese government's leak with the current negotiation. On October 3, when W. Walton Butterworth handed Bayne's message to Marshall, he added his own memorandum which contained the following incisive comment:

> I enclose a copy of a TOP SECRET telegram. Bayne is an American Government official lent at Dr. Soong's request to him to assist in reparation matters, and he works hand and glove with him. *Is it chance or is it now leaked to remind us of the larger issue?* [Italics added][58]

Chiang had played the Russian card. In dispatches from China "the larger concern" or "the larger issue" always referred to efforts to prevent Soviet intrusion into China. More often than not the question occurred in terms of a threat by Chiang to accept some Russian proposal. Earlier in the year, Chiang had used this stratagem to block American demands for Nationalist concessions in Manchuria.[59] Facing a possible rebuff from Marshall, it is not surprising that the Generalissimo resorted once again to a hint of cooperation with the Russians. The mere suggestion of a possible, though limited, understanding with the Russians in Sinkiang Province unquestionably weighed heavily on Marshall's mind. It may have made him more receptive to Stuart's pleas in favor of Chiang's restrictive negotiating package.

It was quite possible that an additional consideration led Marshall to accept the Generalissimo's terms for a settlement. This entails a brief recollection of Washington's attitude in response to Marshall's signal that he might ask to be recalled from China. It will be recalled that Acheson and Vincent reluctantly had agreed that they must support Marshall's request, and with Truman's approval Marshall was so informed. On Saturday, October 5, having received Acheson's response, Marshall formally cabled Washington requesting his recall; of course, later that evening Stuart's initiative led Marshall to request that action be delayed on his recall request. This may have allowed Marshall time to weight the gist of Acheson's telegram, the crucial portion of which read as follows: "While he [the president] and I maintained confidence that you can do the job if it is humanly possible, he fully approves your memorandum to Chiang and will request you to return to Washington if you indicate that it is advisable for you to do so."[60] It must have been extraordinarily difficult for a man with Marshall's sense of duty and pride in his own ability to admit that he could not humanly fulfill his assignment. He was disappointing his president and his country. Would he not be willing to grasp any opportunity to renew his effort? Later that evening Stuart, as we have seen, supplied him with that opening, and on the following day the General accepted Chiang's highly questionable proposition for a limited truce.

Quite possibly little would have changed with respect to America's long-run relationship with China, be it Nationalist or Communist, had Marshall followed through on his decision to withdraw from negotiations at a time when Chiang had reaffirmed his decision to seek victory by military conquest. But, Marshall's withdrawal, even if Washington elected to maintain minimal support for Chiang, would have emphasized Washington's desire to avoid involvement in China's civil war. By demonstrating that, come what may, the United States would *not* stand by the Nationalists, Chiang might have been forced to deal more realistically with the Communists or at least not extend his military campaign in such a reckless fashion. As for the Communists, their deep-seated distrust of Washington would have been somewhat diluted. Once they emerged as victors in the civil war, acceptable relations with the United States would have been a less distasteful option for the Communist leadership. At any rate, Stuart's role in this potential turning point in America's China policy was of considerable significance; however, in the final analysis, he provided the means rather than the driving force which led to continued American support for the Nationalists.

Notes

1. Stuart to Yenching University Community, [Nanking], July 17, 1946. John Leighton Stuart Papers in United Board for Christian Higher Education Collection, Yale Divinity School Archives, Record Group No. 11, Box 68, Folder 1824. Henceforth referred to as JLS Papers. See also John Leighton Stuart, *Fifty Years in China* (New York: Random House, 1954), pp. 165–66.

2. Marshall to Acheson, [Nanking], July 5, 1946. *Foreign Relations of the United States, 1946,* 10 (Washington, DC: Government Printing Office, 1972), pp. 1297–99. Henceforth Referred to as *FRUS*. It had been anticipated that General Albert C. Wedemeyer would return to China as ambassador. However Marshall realized that to appoint Wedemeyer, who in the immediate postwar period had given Chiang his full support, might lead the Communists to suspect American impartiality at a particularily sensitive point in the negotiations.

3. Minutes of meeting, Marshall and General Yu Ta-Wei, July 31, 1946, *FRUS, 1946,* 10, 1422. Also see John Robertson Beal, *Marshall in China* (New York: Doubleday, 1970), p. 124.

4. Marshall's notes of meeting with Chiang Kai-shek [Nanking], Sept 2, 1946, *FRUS, 1946,* 10, 256–57.

5. Notes of meeting, Marshall and Stuart [Nanking], October 1, 1946, *FRUS, 1946,* 10, 260–62.

6. Ibid.

7. Ibid.; and Marshall to Acheson [Nanking], October 2, 1946, *FRUS, 1946*, 10, 271–74.

8. Chou En-lai to Marshall [Shanghai], September 30, 1946, *FRUS, 1946*, 10, 258–59.

9. Notes of meeting Marshall and Stuart [Nanking], October 1, 1946, 11:45 a.m., *FRUS, 1946*, 10, 266–67.

10. Memo, Marshall to Chiang Kai-shek [Nanking], October 1, 1946, *FRUS, 1946*, 10, 267–68.

11. Minutes of meeting, Marshall and Stuart [Nanking], October 2, 1946, *FRUS, 1946*, 10, 268–70.

12. Ibid. For full documentation of these negotiations see *FRUS, 1946*, 9, 985–1307. The magnitude of these crucial negotiations in late June and early July 1946 has not yet been adequately treated.

13. Ibid.

14. Memo, Chiang Kai-shek to Marshall [Nanking], October 2, 1946, *FRUS, 1946*, 10, 270–71.

15. Notes of meeting, Marshall and Stuart [Nanking], October 3, 1946, 10 a.m., *FRUS, 1946*, 10, 274–76.

16. Ibid.

17. Memo, Vincent to Acheson [Washington, DC], October 3, 1946, *FRUS, 1946*, 10, 276–77; and Carter to Marshall [Washington, DC], October 4, 1946, *FRUS, 1946*, 10, 289.

18. Marshall's notes of meeting with Chiang Kai-shek [Nanking], October 4, 1946, 7:15 p.m., *FRUS, 1946*, 10, 287–89. Also see Beal, *Marshall in China*, p. 246.

19. Marshall to Truman [Nanking], October 5, 1946, *FRUS, 1946*, 10, 289–92.

20. Ibid.

21. Notes of meeting, Marshall and Stuart [Nanking], October 5, 1946, *FRUS, 1946*, 10, 295–96.

22. John F. Melby, *Mandate of Heaven: Record of a Civil War, China 1945–1949* (Toronto: University of Toronto Press, 1968), p. 155.

23. John Leighton Stuart, "A Post-Script on My Favorite Topic, May 23, 1946." Box 68, File 1824, JLS papers.

24. Marshall's notes of meeting with Chiang Kai-shek [Nanking], October 4, 1946, 7:15 p.m., *FRUS, 1946*, 10, 287–88. Also see Forrest C. Pogue, *George C. Marshall: Statesman, 1945–1959* (New York: Viking, 1987), p. 128.

25. Notes of meeting, Marshall and Stuart [Nanking], October 5, 1946, 9 p.m., *FRUS, 1946*, 10, 297.

26. Notes of meeting with Chiang Kai-shek, October 6, 1946, 11 a.m., *FRUS, 1946*, 10, 300–301. For Chiang's October 2 proposal see *FRUS, 1946*, 10, 270–71.

27. Stuart to secretary of state [Nanking], October 7, 1946, *FRUS, 1946*, 10, 308–10.

28. Marshall to Carter [Nanking], October 6, 1946, *FRUS, 1946*, 10, 298–99.

29. Marshall to Truman [Nanking], October 10, 1946, *FRUS, 1946*, 10, 349–54.

30. Marshall to Stuart [Nanking], October 6, 1946, *FRUS, 1946*, 10, 299–300.

31. Oral Statement by Chou En-lai for Stuart [Shanghai], October 8, 1946, *FRUS, 1946*, 10, 310–11.

32. Minutes of meeting, Marshall and Stuart [Nanking], October 8, 1946, 11:45 a.m. *FRUS, 1946*, 10, 311–12.

33. Oral statement by Chou En-lai for Stuart [Shanghai], October 8, 1946, *FRUS, 1946*, 10, 310–11.

34. Minutes of meeting, Marshall and Stuart [Nanking], October 8, 1946, 11:45 a.m. *FRUS, 1946*, 10, 311–12.

35. Ibid.

36. Minutes of meeting, Marshall, Stuart, Tung Pi-wu, and Wang Ping-nan [Nanking], October 8, 1946, *FRUS, 1946*, 10, 314–19.

37. Ibid.

38. Ibid.

39. Marshall to Truman [Nanking], October 10, 1946, *FRUS, 1946,* 10, 349–54.

40. Minutes of meeting, Marshall and Chou En-lai [Shanghai], October 9, 1946, 11:30 a.m., *FRUS, 1946,* 10, 332–41.

41. Ibid.

42. Ibid.

43. Ibid.

44. Ibid.

45. Ibid. One must assume that Marshall was aware of the exact negotiating position staked out by Chou En-lai. If there was some confusion in the oral exchange, which took place during an emotionally charged session, he had Chou's written statement to rely on. See Memo, Chou En-lai to Marshall [Shanghai], October 9, 1946, *FRUS, 1946,* 10, 345–48. In addition, Carson Chang, a well-known moderate who opposed the Communists, wrote to Marshall on October 8, observing that "the Communists do not continue to insist in [on] their previous idea of a cessation of fighting in the whole front. What they demand is a promise to stop the Kalgan drive, and, on their part, they are ready to participate in any political negotiation." See Carson Chang to Marshall [Nanking], October 8, 1946. The Marshall Papers, Box 122, 13 ff. The George C. Marshall Research Library, Lexington, Virginia. Henceforth referred to as ML. It should be noted that there is a common misunderstanding on this question. Even Forrest C. Pogue's recent masterly account of Marshall's years as statesman suggests that Chou insisted that it was absolutely necessary for government forces return to their positions as of January 13 in China and June 7 in Manchuria. See Pogue, *Marshall,* p. 128. John Melby, who was second secretary at the embassy, was deceived by inaccurate information that was current in the embassy. He recorded that Chou En-lai "stiffened up his position" and would accept no truce unless the Nationalist forces returned to the lines of January 13 in China and June 7 in Manchuria. See Melby, *Mandate of Heaven,* p. 155. The *China White Paper,* in summing up Chou's position, provides no clear evidence on this question, and can be read as straddling the issue. See *United States Relations with China with Special Reference to the Period 1944–1949* (Washington, DC: Government Printing Office, 1949), pp. 95–96.

46. Ibid.

47. Ibid.

48. Ibid.

49. Stuart to secretary of state [Nanking], October 12, 1946, *FRUS, 1946,* 10, 361–62. Also see Pogue, *Marshall,* p. 129.

50. Beal, *Marshall in China,* pp. 206–07.

51. Ibid., pp. 129, 203. Also see Melby, *Mandate of Heaven,* p. 181.

52. Stuart, "A Post-script On My Favorite Topic," to secretary of state [Nanking], October 12, 1946, *FRUS, 1946,* 10, 361–62; and Beal, *Marshall in China,* p. 122. Referring to the period just after Marshall left China, in January 1947, John F. Melby recorded that the embassy has become a "sieve" as far as confidential information was concerned. "Everything he [Stuart] knows Philip [Fugh] knows. Everything Philip knows is funneled directly to the Generalissimo." See Melby, *Mandate of Heaven,* p. 181. It would appear that this was also the situation in the fall months of 1946.

53. Minutes of meeting, Marshall and Butterworth [Nanking], December 1, 1946, *FRUS, 1946,* 10, 573–75.

54. Beal, *Marshall in China,* pp. 3–5, 232.

55. Ibid., p. 223.

56. Ibid., pp. 223, 232.

57. Stuart to secretary of state [Nanking], October 3, 1946, *FRUS, 1946,* 10, 1209–10.

58. Memorandum for General Marshall by W. Walton Butterworth [Nanking], October 3, 1946, W. Walton Butterworth Papers, Box 1, Folder 7, ML.

59. This is a reference to Chiang's prolonged dealings with the Soviet Union over added economic concessions in Manchuria. Not until Marsh 5, 1946 did Chiang terminate these discussions with the Russians. Washington had objected to these negotiations, and, it can be argued that Chiang agreed to terminate them, at least in part, in exchange for American economic support and a less demanding attitude on questions such as the dispatch of truce teams to Manchuria. For Chiang's rejection of economic cooperation with the Soviets in Manchuria see *FRUS, 1946*, 10, 1099–1129, especially 1113–14.

60. Carter to Marshall [Washington, DC], October 4, 1946, *FRUS, 1946*, 10, 289.

14

MISSION TO CAPITOL HILL
A Study of the Impact of Missionary Idealism on the Congressional Career of Walter H. Judd

Tony Ladd

The Missionary Impulse in American Society

When six thousand members of the Student Volunteer Movement (SVM), an organization of college students committed to Christian missionary philosophy and action, gathered in Kansas City in 1924 under Walter Judd's leadership, they echoed the words of a nineteenth-century missionary hymn:

> *In Christ there is no East or West*
> *In Him no South or North*
> *But one great fellowship of love*
> *Throughout the whole wide world.*[1]

Feeling that all men were brothers through Christ, those young collegians felt impelled as Christians to attempt "to evangelize the world in this generation."

Of all the students this organization touched in its half century of existence (1888–1940), few were as captivated by its ideals of missionary service as was Walter Henry Judd. That missionary idealism provided Judd with a touchstone for his personal life and a foundation for his social philosophy in his career as a medical missionary and congressman.

This examination of missionary motivation in the career of Walter H. Judd is a study of religious idealism interacting with national and international politics. His life stands at center stage for those who saw the twentieth century not only as the American century but also as the era that would develop through Christian love a unity of mind and spirit among men of all nations. Finally, and perhaps of most significance, is analysis of Judd's clarion call to recognize the special significance of China to the interests of the United States.

The impact of his home upon the development of Walter Judd was foundational.

Every night, Judd recalled later, at least one of his parents remained at home caring for the children. A cohesive bond developed within the family as they united to survive the hazards of post-frontier America. Survival itself was often difficult, as demonstrated by the fact that three of the seven Judd children died in childhood.[2]

Particularly important in the young lad's development was the family's acceptance and promotion of a self-help work ethic. By the time Walter was ten years old he had begun to work at assorted odd jobs by herding cattle and selling magazine subscriptions. In two years he acquired enough money to purchase a second-hand cornet. From that time until after his first year in university he hired out as a farm laborer. His pay was limited but it provided nurture in the philosophy of rudimentary self-help economics. The American dream for Walter Judd was the opportunity for the individual to reach success through initiative and perserverance. In that sense his childhood compared with heroes of the Horatio Alger novels.

Besides the emphasis on a work experience in the Judd home, family life provided a base for a pervasive education. His mother always insisted that any visiting minister, missionary, lecturer, or campaigning congressman stay at the house. As a youngster, a world of potential mission broke into his consciousness as he listened to tales of these travelers and read books and pamphlets from the Congregational Church about its missionary heroes. Amplifying this exposure were the prayers and encouragement of his mother, who asked the Spirit of God to fall upon her family and give to each member a vision of the world.[3] The result was salutory: he later remembered that these family guests awakened his interest in medicine. They also fixed in his mind a precept with which he reckoned in committing himself to public service, "work where the need is greatest and the workers fewest."[4]

Familial rural experience and religious training molded Walter Judd's vision of Christian service as he grew into manhood. At the age of seventeen, while attending a YMCA camp, he underwent a religious conversion. Later, he believed that this decision catalyzed all of these influences into a direct commitment to serve as a medical missionary.[5] To act upon that commitment, Judd enrolled in the University of Nebraska immediately after his high school graduation and worked his way through college by playing a trumpet on the Chautauqua circuit. Later he served in World War I and overcame a severe bout with skin cancer. But it was his involvement in the Student Volunteer Movement (SVM) that had the most impact on his career.

The SVM exerted a pervasive influence upon many Christian young people at the turn of the century.[6] According to John Mott, Judd's spiritual father and head of SVM, God was calling "missionary statesmen as prophets to widen the realm of human understanding."[7] Mott related to the Student Volunteer Convention of 1920 that the group had assembled "to take the wide view, the view or vision of a new world . . . (and) to receive a challenge—a fresh commission." In relating this message to practical means, Mott urged students to attack industry, commerce, and finance, "to apply the principles of Jesus Christ to these great energies and to wield them in the interests of His kingdom." In national and international politics, he continued, Student Volunteers should attempt "to Christianize the impact of our Western civilization upon the non-Christian world."[8]

While some volunteers held to the idea of placing emphasis on both social and personal evangelism, a considerable number at the 1924 Convention where Judd served as chairman advocated exerting most of their efforts for social reform.[9] Taking the latter view, Paul Blanchard offered that the problems of modern industrialism were "a vital part of the whole Christian problem." The church had been too slow, he argued, in realizing that there was such a thing in the world as a "social system which could damn men's souls before they were born."[10] John Mott attempted to moderate the tensions between the two groups. He said he had come to appreciate "both the social and individual aspects of the Christian gospel and likewise their essential unity." They were not exclusive positions for the Christian. Rather, both were necessary to build the Kingdom of God. For him, that Kingdom was present and future; it was to be ushered in by striving to improve the social environment by bringing the individual to a personal commitment to Christ.[11] Walter Judd followed a philosophy similar to Mott's, which incorporated much from both views. As he coupled his idealism for Christian mission work with his rising enthusiasm for medical and educational assistance to underdeveloped lands, he was demonstrating his desire not only "to preach the gospel of healing the sick" but also "to preach the gospel of religion through medicine."[12]

Related to the controversy regarding the implementation of social and personal aspects of the Gospel, another debate emerged at the convention of 1924 in regard to pursuing domestic missions as opposed to foreign ones.[13] Although Judd had previously decided to carry out his mission on the foreign field, as student chairman he emerged as the mediator to encourage the 6,500 students and leaders to shape their approach to domestic and foreign issues into a unified thrust aimed at converting the world for Christ. In his keynote address before these delegates, he argued that "the world could not be divided geographically or religiously into water-tight compartments. No portion of it could be considered honestly without all the rest of the world as a background." There was, of course, "a natural division between evangelized and unevangelized," and the convention's purpose was to discuss the unevangelized portions of the world. We should consider these, he continued, "not in opposition to the needs at home but as one part of the whole." There was "one field, the world."[14] The Student Volunteers' endorsement of the League of Nations[15] and Judd's work later for the establishment of the United Nations sprang from a solid philosophical view of the world as all of one piece.

In cognizance of the goal to bring to earth the Kingdom of God, Judd concurred in efforts to produce a supranational and supraracial spiritual fellowship. He acknowledged that "races, nations, classes and religions were all divisive forces," insisting rather that Christian brotherhood was the unifying element allowing the best opportunity to produce that world order. As a doctor he wanted to transform the world through humanitarian efforts, yet as a Christian his hopes for the regeneration of the world rested ultimately not on human institutions but on the "love of God."[16]

In the summer of 1925, after Judd had concluded a year of recruiting other Student Volunteers, he sailed to China. Yet, as this chapter of his life closed behind him, the forces of earlier days continued to interact upon him, establishing a pattern from which his career as missionary and congressman would follow. The family life in rural Nebraska had given him a heritage, as he described it, of holding to the earthy values of life. Congregationalism had produced a sense of uncompromising individuality. But most crucial of all was his commitment to an ideal, developed through religious and nationalistic ideology, that the world could be changed through application on earth of the principles of Jesus Christ.

The Missionary to China

Fukien Province in southern China, where the young doctor arrived in 1925, was a place so far from Nebraska, yet so close to the heart and mind of Walter Judd. After a short orientation period at the Toochaw language school in Nanking, Judd departed for the interior where the mission board had commissioned him to establish a medical clinic at Shaowu. There he opened a thirty-eight bed infirmary, which later handled as many as eighteen thousand cases a year. Fees were charged when possible, making the clinic practically self-supporting, yet Judd turned no one away.[17]

As weeks and months passed between the times when he saw other Americans, he began to feel at home among the Chinese. One local mother of a family of twelve compelled the young missionary to join her family as an adopted son. He accepted readily, and for the next two years spent much of his time with them. His interaction with the family gave him the opportunity not only to expand his knowledge of the language, but also to broaden his understanding of the people. He suffered disease (malaria), arrest, and testing before firing squads, but these challenges only heightened his passion for working in China. During this period he began to comprehend, he said later, that differences among human beings were trivial. Certainly, "there were differences of color, or language, or custom; but the loves and hates, the likes and the dislikes, and the passions and desires and hungers and aspirations and sorrows and disappointments were all the same." He sensed a kinship with the Chinese, which he felt bridged the external differences between himself and those around him. Reflecting this relationship, Judd asserted, after attending the state funeral of Dr. Sun Yat-sen in June 1929, that he "was welded as never before with the heart of the Chinese people."[18]

While Judd was meeting success serving his first term in China, many problems had arisen in the United States. The stock market crash of 1929 had plunged his homeland into a grave economic and spiritual crisis. When Judd returned on furlough in 1931, he encountered a land and a people differing markedly from that which he had known six years earlier when he had launched his missionary career. When he had left for China in 1925, the nation was riding the crest of Coolidge contentment. But in 1931 the heat of discontent and despair stifled the land. The idealism of the 1920s had faded into the uncertainty of the 1930s. Within Christian organizations the Depression had done much to quiet the controversy between those who had promoted foreign missions and those who were active in domestic concerns. Most Christians at that time immersed themselves in efforts for political, social, and educational betterment in the United States.[19] Yet home as well as foreign missions had felt the pinch of declining interest and diminishing funds.[20] Even before the Wall Street debacle, Reinhold Niebuhr had observed that religion was not in a "state of good health." Indeed, the missionary flame, which had burned so brightly in the hearts of thousands of zealous youths in the early twentieth century, only flickered in the wake of a spiritual depression. Neibuhr wondered if this was the sickness of faith, "the senility which preceded death."[21]

Uncertainty was evident when the Student Volunteers met in their quadrennial session at Buffalo during the Christmas holidays of 1931 where Judd gave the keynote address.[22] For the first time since the inception of the organization, the watchword of the movement, "the evangelization of the world in this generation," was conspicuous by its absence. In its place the organization accepted the social action theme, "the living Christ in the world of today." In viewing this change, Kenneth S. Latourette, the foremost missionary historian of that era, acknowledged that young people sought "to rid the world of war, to solve race conflicts, and to discover an escape from some of the nation's industrial ills" rather than to commit their lives to winning the world to Christ.[23]

But Judd's perspective, as indicated in his passionate speech on that occasion, differed considerably from many of those around him. The confident missionary had met difficulties in China, yet he had overcome challenges that he had encountered—a firing squad, malaria, and numerous arrests. He returned on furlough as a victor reappearing in a defeated land, a foreigner among his own people.[24] The internal problems of his homeland were hardly comprehensible to him, for his unique experiences as a missionary had conditioned his outlook. Even his relations with people in the United States were different. During this period of reentry he asserted that he found it difficult to live abroad for six years and return to the United States as a "good hundred percenter" in regard to domestic affairs.[25] Moreover, while most Americans seemed pessimistic, he was optimistic. The possibility of "brighter days" lured him and other missionaries who served in the field to the "Eastern glow of promise." Free from the futility that possessed many, Judd held a sense of accomplishment through his faith. He felt that he was part of a larger whole with whom he shared a noble responsibility to "bequeath to coming generations a worthier world." The problems of America in the 1930s were not the problems of Walter Judd.[26]

Even though the ardent missionary had planned to return to China in 1932 to continue his medical work there, several factors intervened to alter those plans. After a period of recuperation at the home of his parents in Nebraska, he embarked upon another speaking tour to various Eastern and Midwestern churches and religious groups.[27] During one such speaking engagement in 1932 in Montclair, New Jersey, he met the woman who later became his wife, Mariam Barber. They were married that same year.[28] Then, in April of 1932, instead of returning to China as he had planned, he accepted a fellowship in surgery at the Mayo Graduate School of Medicine of the University of Minnesota.[29]

After Judd completed his research study at the Mayo Clinic in 1934, the Mission Board commissioned him to direct another hospital at Fenchow in Shansi province of North China. Because of his previous encounter with malaria in the semitropical South, he had requested such a reassignment. Rowland Cross, American secretary of the North China Mission during Judd's second assignment there, commended him as an able doctor and hospital administrator. Judd, he acknowledged, had acquired an excellent working knowledge of the Chinese language, enabling him to express his Christian faith to those to whom he ministered. Others described Judd the missionary as independent and strong willed, and apparently sometimes he did not agree with his American colleagues with whom he worked. Nevertheless, the board considered him a valuable man at the mission station. It was only later, after his return to the United States, that many of his North China colleagues differed with him on various aspects of the China question.[30]

Events, however, shortened the time of his work in the North. The countryside blazed into war as the Japanese army advanced on the land mass of China. Less than two years after he had returned to China he moved his pregnant wife and two daughters temporarily to Taiku and then later to Hong Kong. In 1937, heavy fighting erupted around Fenchow as the Japanese conducted the first air raid on the area. The decisive battle for the city, however, did not occur until the early months of 1938 when, in hand-to-hand combat, the Japanese captured the city.[31]

During the period when the Japanese were shelling Fenchow, Judd began to entertain second thoughts regarding the value of his medical mission to China. How could he continue to work effectively in a land torn apart by war? How could the United States, his own country, continue to trade and supply an aggressor he perceived was destroying the work that he felt called to do? One day, while operating upon a wounded victim from Japanese bombing, he extracted a piece of shrapnel that bore the stamp of "Erie, Pa. USA." That small piece of steel, which evidently had originated as scrap steel in the United States, represented to him the lack of understanding in America about what was happening in the Far East.[32] He decided at that point to resign his medical post in China and personally to address this issue with his fellow countrymen. This new mission, to warn of the dangers of Japanese militarism in the Far East, was one that he felt impelled to fulfill.

Furthermore, he thought his medical and missionary work in North China benefited no one unless some stability existed there. Resigning from active foreign work was a drastic measure, yet he felt he had to try "to get at peace" with his conscience. Although he talked of his immediate return to China after he had delivered his message to America, and he undoubtedly thought he would return, nevertheless, that step closed his active missionary career in China.[33]

The Missionary to the United States

Walter Judd returned to the United States with his family in the spring of 1938, embarking immediately upon a pilgrimage throughout the country. The range of his itinerary was grueling as he addressed over fourteen hundred groups in forty-six states.[34] His reputation as a speaker, established as a Chautauqua entertainer, as a recruiter for the Student Volunteer Movement, and also as a missionary speaker while on furlough in 1931–32, had given him a readily accessible audience. He became an electrifying voice, affirming with vigor the positive values of Christianity, the essential worth of the Chinese, and the possible future for Christianity in China, while at the same time condemning the aggression of Japan.[35] Gripped with passion aroused by his recent experiences in China he pointed out in vivid terms the dangers of Japanese militarism and explained that this people even then were a "peril to our Main Street." The government of Japan was a ruthless military machine, he proclaimed, using war materials of which half were derived from American supplies. "Everywhere one saw Chinese troops on foot and Japanese soldiers on American wheels," he reiterated.[36]

Judd cast out his words as verbal barbs to challenge the isolationist sentiment throughout the nation. In an appearance before the Senate Foreign Relations Committee in 1938, he spelled out his view on how the United States could halt the Japanese in the Far East. In highly emotional language, which resembled a "yellow peril" speech, he asserted that, if these steps were not taken, "war with Japan was almost inevitable."[37] Many speeches concluded with his famous baseball caricature. Judd would appear to be in agony as he argued that the United States was in a great baseball game, and that by political ineptness the nation's leaders had allowed the Japanese to get to first base and then to advance to second. Soon she would be at third. Then he would conclude, pounding his fist to the podium, "what shall keep her from striking home?"[38]

The effect of these speeches upon his listeners is difficult to measure. Although most audiences were sympathetic and visibly moved by his passionate oratory, his message did not secure an active response.[39] Although many groups received him politely and often enthusiastically, few responded to his call for action against the Japanese. To some he was a fanatic.[40] Judd himself felt that he had been a "voice crying in the wilderness."[41]

Disillusioned, exhausted, and broke, Judd decided to relinquish his self-declared role as a twentieth-century Paul Revere. When the opportunity arose for him to enter a medical office in Minneapolis, he accepted, not necessarily because medicine was his chosen profession, but rather because he sensed the futility of his mission in its present form.[42]

Nevertheless, his efforts were not completely fruitless. Appearances on national radio[43] and testimony before the Senate Foreign Relations Committee and the House Foreign Affairs Committee, besides his numerous speaking engagements, had aroused interest in the man, if not the message. After his appearance before the Senate committee, one *New York Times* correspondent speculated that the event might herald the beginning of a new political career.[44] Moreover, through his medical work in Minneapolis he developed a wide following. Aside from his competence as a physician, he had a keen sense of the spiritual and emotional needs of his patients. They loved him not only as a doctor but also as a friend. To them, he was a fellow human being—a counselor with whom they could relate. Whether this sensitivity to humanity came as a result of his experiences in China or developed from his nature as a compassionate Christian is not crucial: what is essential is that in his medical work he held relationships with others on a high level. And this sensitivity to the worth of human beings contributed much to the esteem with which he was received in and out of his medical office in 1940.[45]

While working at his medical practice, he continued a speaking schedule of four or five local engagements per week in which he continued to warn of a Japanese menace. Many churchmen were eager to hear the former missionary and the service groups felt that he exemplified in action their own philosophy of humanitarianism. In Minneapolis, at least, he retained his visibility in regard to issues concerning the Far East.[46]

When the attack upon Pearl Harbor came, the young doctor's friends thought it proved him a prophet. A group of young businessmen active in the Junior Chamber of Commerce decided that Dr. Judd was their man and began to urge him to run for Oscar Youngdahl's seat in the United States House of Representatives. Harlan Nygaard and Thomas vonKuster, both presidents of the JayCees during the 1940s, were prime movers in that initial effort. Significantly, these men, as well as many others who later would come to support Judd, had met him first in one of these church talks.[47]

At first, Judd declined to submit himself to the world of politics since, he said, he had no money to finance a campaign. To bypass this difficulty, members of a self-declared Judd-for-Congress Committee headed by Nygaard assured the popular doctor that he would never have to work to finance his own campaigns. They promised that the committee would produce the funds with no strings attached. This promise proved to be precise during that first campaign and each subsequent one, as Judd always remained free to speak wherever he wanted without the drawbacks of attending to fund-raising.[48]

As a final capstone to overcome the fear that he was deserting his calling to the field of medicine, the committee persuaded Judd that it was his duty to serve when called upon. The former missionary was perplexed, for although it appeared that a new mission was unfolding before him, he held many doubts about what he could accomplish within the political system. When his father urged that it was his civic duty as well as his spiritual duty to become a candidate for Congress if a substantial group of responsible citizens wanted him to do so, Judd assented to his candidacy.[49]

Judd's pro-China and anti-Japan campaign theme grew out of his public speaking tours. His campaign workers pointed continually to the isolationist position of incumbent Republican, Oscar Youngdahl, noting particularly his prewar votes against preparedness. This, they contrasted to the suggested foresight of the missionary doctor who had warned citizens three years before Pearl Harbor of the dangers of Japan in the Far East.[50] By the time of the primary election on September 9, Judd had rallied considerable support within the city of Minneapolis. The verdict was never in doubt as the Republicans gave Judd a ten thousand vote plurality out of sixty thousand votes cast. With the primary victory in hand, Judd's election to a seat in the U.S. Congress was a mere formality, since in the fifth district the Republicans held a large majority in registered voters and the opposition was split into two equal camps of Farmer Laborites and Democrats. On November 4, 1942, Judd emerged with a forty-five thousand vote advantage over his closest opponent and a seat in the U.S. Congress.[51]

In 1943, when the forty-three-year-old doctor exchanged his medical bag for a legislative briefcase, he believed that he had simply altered the mode of his missionary role. He hoped that he could initiate legislation to help alleviate some of the "social ills of the day." Through medicine, he remarked later when reflecting upon this turning point in his career, he had helped men "wracked with diverse diseases and malfunctions" of the human body; in Congress he wanted to deal with wider problems. What good did it do, he offered, to "patch up a few bones" when instead one could make the more basic effort to prevent destruction.[52] To those who felt that he had deserted his original calling, he recalled that at that particular moment he felt that he "could do China more good in the Congress of the United States than anywhere else."[53] He accepted the offer to run for Congress not because his missionary vision had declined but in order to enlarge the scope of his mission.[54]

If his varied career as doctor, missionary, and representative were "all of one piece," as he claimed, how was that "one piece" reflected in his congressional career?[55] How would this single missionary impact American attitudes and foreign policy toward China? Also, was the major theme of his life, the striving for a Kingdom of God on earth, translated into action in Congress? I have examined what Judd did and said publicly during his twenty-year tenure in Congress. Published papers were employed for analysis. Examination of the internal consistency of Judd's action as a congressman will await another article.

The Missionary in Congress

Throughout his career as a student and a missionary, Judd had held the view that Christianity and the political structure of the United States offered unique contributions for the formation of a new world order. His work as a foreign missionary had revealed his commitment to the former. Then, by abandoning his foreign mission work to run for political office, he was demonstrating his faith that Christian principles could direct political action. He clearly enunciated this dual focus shortly before traveling to Washington when he asserted that the active practice of the "Christian religion with its primary emphasis on the value of the individual was the only hope" for a world of war and hate. Furthermore, he declared, this nation "must commit itself to the task of rebuilding the world" along lines that would ensure an opportunity for each individual to "play on the team together."[56] In his mind, therefore, the new world order would contain "the extension of the basic principles of the American Federal Union to a global structure."[57] When Judd came to Congress, then, he carried with him a philosophy of internationalism encased within a zealous nationalism.

Yet, aside from this philosophical undergirding, Judd came to Washington in 1943 as a naive politician with only a limited idea of what he could accomplish. His campaign pledges to do all that he could for China and to "get to the bottom of the State Department business" reflects the narrowness of his goals.[58] In the early years especially, Judd did not become involved in committee work or in legislative procedures in the House. During his first year, for instance, he introduced only one bill into the congressional hopper and served quietly on the rather insignificant Insular Affairs Committee. He remained for the most part a speaker for the cause of China and world brotherhood.

What had changed was the respectability that his position in the House gave to him. Congress provided a national platform from which he could proclaim his ideas. For, unlike many other legislators who had to struggle through the seniority system before they could make themselves heard in the House, Judd possessed a quality of immediate cash value. His reputation as a prophet regarding affairs in the Far East preceded him to Washington.

Therefore, in the first eighteen weeks of his initial session in Congress he delivered three major addresses reflecting his emerging role in that body. These speeches are important not only because of their impact on his audience at that particular time, but also because they seem to have set the agenda for his congressional career. In what later became known as his standard "autopsy" speech, Judd used medical terminology and symbolism in his first address to depict his perception of a failed American foreign policy in the Far East and to point to new directions for the United States in assisting the establishment of a new world order. In one of those early speeches he promoted his position as an authority in affairs of China and Japan:

If those Americans who have been privileged to live for some years in the Far East have any particular contribution to make to our country's thinking in a time like this, it is, I believe, primarily because of the simple fact that they have had the opportunity to come to know something of the psychology of the peoples who live there. . . . If we are going to win this war and try to work out a decent peace afterward we must deal with them utterly realistically, on the basis of what it is they really want, what they think, what they feel, what they are after. Unfortunately, we cannot find that out from the Department of Commerce reports or even from the World Almanac. We can find that out, as a rule, only from those persons who have been privileged to live there long and intimately, and have dealt with them and discussed these things with them over a period of years. It is only because of such a background that I presume to stand before you this afternoon to try to discuss our situation in the Pacific exactly as a doctor studies the body of a patient at the autopsy table.[59]

Earnestly he agonized over America's policy of overt racial discrimination. On an international scale, he asserted, "we do not have a right to insult friendly peoples because of their race or color." In America, he continued, "no matter what a man's or a woman's ability may be, or education, or culture, or charm, or professional skill, if the pigment in his or her skin is different from ours, he or she is, because of that fact, automatically and inescapably branded as inferior, forever condemned to a level below us—officially stigmatized."[60]

Besides improving international and national relations through recognizing each individual as a person, Judd also concluded that the United States should assess other nations as they existed rather than as they were seen by Americans. "The autopsy reveals that we went into this war without much real knowledge of our enemy or of ourselves." Judd's candor was remarkable as he pointed out in the midst of the war that the causes of such conflicts were not one-sided. Moreover, if the United States were to have any positive effect upon a postwar world, it could not survive by defending yesterday. We must boldly move ahead, he added, "true to our country's noblest traditions."[61]

The response to his oratory was electric. His colleagues thundered approval by a standing ovation. Editors throughout the nation lauded the congressman's insights. The media focused on Judd, the authority on the Far East and the one to whom they could look in the future for answers to the complicated problems of Asian politics.[62]

When, therefore, he again addressed the House several weeks later, he spoke with such powerful imagery that his words would help frame American foreign policy for an entire generation.

Some weeks ago when I spoke here on the Pacific situation, I said that one of the most important procedures doctors have for learning is the autopsy. Well, there is another procedure equally valuable, and that is the "biopsy." A new growth is developing and we do not know exactly what it is. We do not let it go until it has grown into something that anybody on the street can diagnose. We try to take care of it before it gets to that point, because the thing that makes a cancer bad is not its size or its location. It is just as bad when it is the size of a peanut as when the size of a grapefruit. The thing that makes it bad is the lawless way in which it encroaches on neighboring tissues that do not belong to it. So we do a "biopsy"; we take out a tiny piece and examine it under the microscope to observe how its cells behave. If they are lawless, we do not need to examine the rest; we know the whole thing is vicious and we dare not temporize.[63]

Quite dramatically, Judd had changed the focus from international cooperation to one of containment. In his first address he had asserted that one party alone did not create an atmosphere for war. But in the latter, he placed the blame completely upon the Japanese, claiming that their expansion was comparable to a cancerous growth. By such an analogy Judd had established a mental picture easily understood by most Americans. In his own mind, he had constructed the cancer analogy "so that we could learn from the past and not make the same sort of mistake again." Ominously for the future, he concluded, "when tomorrow comes, if we win this war, which we must, and lawlessness breaks out anywhere in the world, Americans, in their own self-interest, must see that it is checked early, because if we do not check it early by preventive means, as was possible in the case of Japan, then we have no other means ultimately except rivers of American blood."[64]

Before Judd could finish his speech he was interrupted and asked to elaborate upon that idea. He had particularly impressed House Speaker John McCormack. The following exchange is informative:

MR. MCCORMACK. I am very much interested in the gentleman's cancer reference. I think it is a very powerful contribution. I would like to say, if I understand the gentleman correctly, if we and England, for instance, as well as other nations, had stepped in and stopped the invasion of Manchuria, do I infer that the gentleman feels we could have prevented the growth of this cancer which has enveloped the world?

MR. JUDD. That is my judgment.

MR. MCCORMACK. And the same thing in Ethiopia?

MR. JUDD. Yes, sir.

MR. MCCORMACK. And the same thing in the Ruhr?

MR. JUDD. Right.

MR. MCCORMACK. The gentleman has made a great contribution. In other words, under the policy that we adopted for the past 20 years, thinking it was one of peace, it was nothing but an inverted warlike policy, unknowingly and unintentionally, which has contributed to this tremendous catastrophe that confronts us today.

MR. JUDD. Yes; we did not want war, and we assumed that to do nothing, to wait and see, was the way to keep out of it, was playing safe, was being conservative. But a doctor knows that when you are dealing with a lawlessly growing cancer, even if it is only in the toe—or far-away Manchuria or Czechoslovakia—to do nothing, to wait and see, is not really playing safe. It is, in fact, the most dangerous policy, the most radical policy that can be followed. Yet that is what we mistakenly did for 10 years. I am not saying this to condemn. I am saying this to try to understand what we are up against today.

MR. MCCORMACK. I understand. As we look back we can see. I congratulate the gentleman on making that contribution. It certainly has taken away the mist from my eyes, because the gentleman has made it clear that if we all had done the things we could have done, we would have averted this catastrophe, and not doing them has contributed toward the world being in the great pain it is today.[65]

One member of Congress immediately saw the logical conclusion to Judd's suggested course of action. Such a policy would mean, she asserted, that "America must always be strong in all branches of our armed services." In reply Judd readily agreed, "That is one of the conclusions that it seems to me must come from it, unless we are able now and after the war to evolve with other peace-loving nations other methods that will give us even greater security."[66] Thus Judd identified the idea that the United States would have to develop an overpowering military capacity to contain perceived outlaw nations until peaceful nations created a new world order. Thus, the basic post–World War II foreign policy framework of containment was identified and popularized by Judd. The stage was set for the development of the military-industrial complex.

Political Reality and the Stagnation of Vision

The war years saw little change in Judd's participation on Capitol Hill. He continued to avoid involvement in the nuts-and-bolts work of legislation, as his main focus rested upon his speaking efforts.[67] Nevertheless, a variation in the themes of his speeches did emerge. At the same time that he was lauding the causes of world peace through an international body dedicated to world order, he was expanding his concept of defensive preparedness to include condemnation not only of the Axis powers, but of Communists as well. Drawing a connection between the conflict that was in process and the one to come, he commented that "the Japanese were in sympathy with Chinese Reds." Chiang, he related, made his greatest mistake when "he didn't clean out the nest of Communists in his country. He tried to be a Christian as the Americans had taught him." Such anti-Communist oratory was also pointed toward a distrust of the Soviet Union. Dismissing that nation's role in the war, he complained that "Russia will come to the aid of the allies, throwing her strength and resources against the Japs because that is what will benefit the USSR most in the long run."[68] From this position it was but a short step to his early declaration of a domino theory of monolithic communism, arguing that "the Chinese and other Asiatics together with the Russians can be an uncontrollable bloc that can go anywhere it pleases."[69] This message, frozen in concept, became the dominant theme of the rest of his congressional career.

As the war drew to an end Judd became disenchanted with his role as a national orator, especially that aspect that had kept him continually on the road away from Washington making four or five major speeches each week. To one friendly editor he confided, "I wish that my Christian friends would realize that I can help them far more by making a success as a legislator in Washington than by making speeches all over the country."[70]

By the end of the war, a slight change occurred in Judd's activities in the House. The will to make political machinery work would have to come, he thought, from men with "religious motives."[71] Also emergent in Judd's action was a strong thread of independence. In 1945, he led several other party members in bolting Republican leadership to form an independent Republican caucus on foreign affairs.[72] In 1947, he received appointment to a seat on the Foreign Affairs Committee from which he worked to implement legislation in sympathy with his philosophy of world brotherhood.[73] There he attained his greatest success as a congressman.

More than most Americans, Walter Judd sensed the injustice that immigration policies such as the Chinese Exclusion Acts and the Johnson Reed Act of 1924 fostered. By living with the Chinese, he had observed how such laws implied a second-class status to whole nationality groups.[74] He had indicated earlier that these groups were rejecting the old colonial order as they determined to free themselves from "the white man's burden." The nonwhite races formed a block, he asserted, that was twice as large as that of the whites. Against it, the United States could win the military battles for a time, but in the long run that bloc "could out-endure us and out-suffer us and out-breed us."[75] Although Judd used powerful pragmatic reasons to suggest changing restrictive immigration policies, the bottom line was framed by his Christian philosophy of justice. To him, discrimination of any kind was immoral.[76]

In the legislative process, however, Judd had few successes. The Walter-McCarron Immigration Bill, which he had helped formulate, passed through Congress in 1952. Yet, it was still inadequate, he felt, since it did not change the basis of figuring quotas, and those quotas continued to reflect the predominance and preference for Western Europeans. Nevertheless, Judd felt confident that recognition of the problem was a step toward equalization between East and West.[77] In all this work he was an ardent advocate for the Chinese.

In other areas of legislation, one-third of all the bills which he introduced in twenty years on Capitol Hill dealt with some form of health benefits such as the World Health Organization.[78] He had prodded the United States to join this international group and had continued to support funding.[79]

But investigating Judd's congressional activities one finds that few of the congressman's proposals for legislative action were comprehensive. Only the Judd Immigration Bill, modified later as part of the Walter-McCarron Bill, could be classified as a major piece of legislation. Moreover, seldom did he follow through legislative channels to cause implementation of his ideals, even though one might consider his pervasive work for the United Nations and for China as exhibiting that determination. In the legislative process, Judd could diagnose problems and call for immediate remedies, as he concluded many "autopsies" in his congressional addresses, but seldom could he work out legislative details in the House.[80]

When considering Walter Judd's active career in Congress, one must note that many of his efforts were tied to his loyalty to Chiang and the Nationalist Chinese government. The one overriding theme in his work rested upon his efforts to save or salvage what he could for that regime. Since many differed with him over this matter, his overbearing focus in this area appears to have modified his many positive efforts in the House. He could not compromise on the Chinese question and keep his soul. Then, when he failed to demonstrate to a broad section of his colleagues the efficacy of continuing such support, he appears to have become isolated from other members of Congress. He became a voice of alarm and fear during the McCarthy era focusing more and more on an anti-Communist crusade, which used defense of Chiang and the Nationalist Chinese as the keystone. That narrowness was certainly at odds with the broad internationalism that he had accepted from his earliest missionary days.

At the outset of his career in Congress, Walter Judd had worked to implement a new world order by attempting to weld his Christian idealism of establishing a Kingdom of God on earth to the political structure that had emerged as the United Nations. Yet, very early it became apparent that the spiritual fulfillment of brotherhood would not rest within that body. Thus, the United Nations, to Judd, became a tool for keeping peace until a new approach to the Kingdom of God could be built.[81]

Within this perspective he continued to offer in Congress consistent, overt support of that world body. He conceded that practicality ruled idealism. Rational thought dictated that the major world forces could not continue indefinitely on divergent paths, for they were "too interdependent and the planet too small to omit cooperation." He assured his associates in Congress that war waited in the wings if the United States could not get together with Russia. Moreover, if such a war did erupt, the American system could never survive even if the United States won that war. Therefore, "the two worlds had to become one" insofar as having one set of rules for carrying on relations between themselves.[82] In a dynamic address in the late 1940s Judd emphasized this by asserting that mankind had "to get order based on justice with a publicly controlled force so that a nation would not go to war if it could and could not if it would."[83] Then, in time, exchanges of ideas, commodities, and personalities, accompanied by a long-range program of education, would gradually change people's minds and hearts. It was possible "to get along with Russia," he added, it would "just take time to purge out weaknesses."[84] In conceptualizing a new world order he was still at heart the idealistic youth infused with religious enthusiasm.

Yet, Judd's singular focus on resolving the Chinese question through the Nationalist frame took its toll. With the emergence of Mao, Judd was faced with growing disillusionment with the legislative process. He disagreed with many China specialists who were emerging from the McCarthy cloud. By 1958, he had decided to relinquish his legislative post and return to private life. And, even though he changed his mind and decided to run for reelection that year, his decision did not reflect a determination to continue his mission to Capitol Hill. Rather it was a concession to his campaign associates who had worked loyally for him in the past and who had compelled him to continue to serve in Washington.[85] Somewhat later he acknowledged publicly his growing distaste for political work. "I don't enjoy politics," he related, "but its just like going to war; you still do it if it's your duty."[86]

He had lost enthusiasm not only for what he could accomplish in Congress but also for the idealism that he had reflected in previous years about helping China and developing a new world order. In his mind no relationships with communism were possible. In 1959, he protested the visit of Premier Khrushchev to the United States. Also, he himself would not meet with a group of touring Communist diplomats.[87]

Instead of cultural exchanges he turned to policies of containment and isolation. Addressing a Republican committee during that party's national convention in 1960, he asserted that communism could be stopped most effectively by "cutting off its blood supply. . . . Don't trade with it, don't recognize it, don't give it prestige by taking its word for anything." Through that isolation on one hand and America's moral power and military strength on the other, he felt that one day the "scourge of Communism would be removed, by the providence of God."[88] His ideas on containment helped shape American foreign policy during the 1960s through the 1980s in Viet Nam, Grenada, and Nicaragua.

His keynote address at the 1960 Republican National Convention reflected this change in emphasis. Buttressed by rhetoric and passion rather than by a presentation of new ideas, Judd defended Eisenhower's foreign policies of containment against Russia in particular and communism in general. It was not possible, he said, to allow any interaction with the Communists since "overshadowing everything else was the hard fact that a powerful enemy threatened America on every front." Yet, in regard to that "strategy of holding," Judd could offer no evidence that such a position would lead to world peace or in any way establish a new world order. At that time he could offer only the rhetoric of his nationalism, "We must let loose in the world the dynamic forces of freedom in our day as our forefathers did in theirs, causing people everywhere to look toward the American dream."[89]

Judd's gradual shift away from working through political organizations whether national or international led him to a personal approach through volunteer service programs such as the Peace Corps and YMCA. These provided opportunities for implementing on a smaller scale what he had hoped to accomplish in the United

Nations. He fought for the Peace Corps, for example, as a fulfillment of his own missionary efforts in China. It was a necessary outlet for the demonstration of individual idealism.[90] It was one way people could ultimately impact nations like China.

His disillusionment with governments, either national or international, led him to an examination of why a country like the United States was so ineffective in influencing the world about her. In tying together ideas of God and country he believed that Christian allegiance would "outwork, outsuffer, and outwin any other cause."[91] Taken to the extreme, this meant that Christians would need "to demonstrate as strong and deep a faith in their fundamental tenets as the Communists have in theirs, and they would have to work as hard and as skillfully to spread the truth as the Communists worked to spread their falsehoods."[92] Carried one step further such thinking was to lead him in 1961 into the camp of the Swarz Christian-Anti-Communist Crusade, an avowedly arch-conservative group dedicated to "educating Americans about the dangers of Communism."[93] Thereafter, Judd became a familiar speaker at many organizations like the Omaha Chamber of Commerce Cold War Seminar, where he advocated an extreme containment viewpoint.[94] He even gave an unintended compliment to Communists when he said that "what we need in America today is to recapture a faith in our heritage and our faith comparable to the faith the Communists have in theirs."[95]

All of his life Judd had searched for an avenue to the Kingdom of God on earth. And through his years in and out of Congress he had focused on the Christian faith as the means to accomplish that goal, but he could not put it together. Instead of the world copying Christianity, Judd had to plead for Christians to copy the methods of the Communists. Christian love when institutionalized in political spheres did not bring unity among people of one nation, let alone the world. Yet, although the complexity of implementing spiritual principles through secular means tore at the heart of Judd's drive for a world order and for fair treatment to China, he never lost sight of his aim to bring to pass a spiritual kingdom and a spiritual relationship among people. He did lose faith in the efficacy of implementing spiritual goals through the particular institution of the United Nations. With the acceptance of that reality and with an inability to impact directly the political situation of China, his sense of mission to work in Congress faded. His defeat in a realigned district in 1962 released Judd from the commitments that had shaped his life so forcefully a generation before.

What Judd could not foresee was the reemergence of his ideas a generation later. The future president for whom he gave the keynote address at the 1960 Republican Convention would open the door again to China. Others would follow and tear down some walls that Judd had helped construct. In so doing they were using a frame of reference for fairness to China that Judd had preached from the 1920s on. The mission of Walter Judd to help China would be accomplished not through rhetoric and idealism in Congress but through the political process.

Notes

1. Kenneth S. Latourette, *Missions and the American Mind* (Indianapolis: National Foundation Press, 1949), p. 36.

2. Unless noted otherwise, the material for this section on Judd's childhood is derived from reminiscences given in writing to the researcher by Walter Judd through personal correspondence.

3. Walter H. Judd, "I Believe in Teenagers," *Youth For Christ* (July 1960): 26.

4. Minneapolis *Tribune* (September 26, 1955): 18.

5. Judd, "I Believe": 27.

6. David M. Howard, *Student Power in World Evangelism* (Downers Grove: Intervarsity Press, 1970); William H. Beahm, "Factors in the Development of the Student Volunteer Movement for Foreign Missions" (unpublished Ph.D. dissertation, University of Chicago, 1941).

7. Robert J. Cole, ed., *Students and the Present Mission Crisis* (New York: Student Volunteer Movement for Foreign Missions, 1910), p. 173.

8. Burton St. John, ed., *North American Students and World Advance* (New York, 1920), p. 76.

9. David M. Howard, "The Rise and Fall of SVM," *Christianity Today* (November 6, 1970): 15ff.

10. Milton T. Stauffer, ed., *Christian Students and World Problems* (New York: Student Volunteer Movement for Foreign Missions, 1924), p. 87.

11. Ibid., p. 64.

12. St. Paul *Dispatch* (May 20, 1925): 4.

13. Howard, "The Rise and Fall of SVM": 17.

14. Stauffer, *Christian Students*, p. 8.

15. Ibid., p. 261.

16. This theme is recurrent throughout Judd's life; cf. St. Paul *Dispatch* (May 20, 1925): 4; Stauffer, ed., *Christian Students*, pp. 6ff.; "Walter Judd: Congressman," *Advance* (June 1945): 4; Judd, "I Believe": 27.

17. Rowland Cross to Tony Ladd, January 30, 1972, written interview. Cross served as secretary for the Congregational Mission Board in China during the time of Judd's work there. For a description of the work in the clinic, see Omaha *World Herald* (September 27, 1931): A-10; and Stauffer, ed., *Christian Students*, pp. 16–29.

18. Stauffer, *Christian Students*, p. 16.

19. Latourette, *Missions and the American Mind*, p. 36.

20. See R. T. Handy, "The American Religious Depression," *Church History* 29:1 (March 1960): 3, for an incisive description of this downturn in all phases of church life.

21. Reinhold Niebuhr, *Does Civilization Need Religion?* (New York: Macmillan, 1927), p. 1.

22. Ibid., pp. 1–3.

23. Latourette, *Missions and the American Mind*, p. 37.

24. Stauffer, ed., *Christian Students*, p. 19. For editorial comment on the impact of Judd's appearance, see "The Way of Love in China," *World Tomorrow* (March 1932): 84; and *The Missionary Review of the World* (February 1932): 67.

25. Stauffer, *Christian Students*, p. 20.

26. Archibald G. Baker, *Christian Missions and a New World Culture* (New York: Willett Clark and Company, 1934), p. 10.

27. Omaha *World Herald* (September 27, 1931): 1.

28. Dick Basoco, "Rep. Walter Judd: A Nixon Spokesman," Nebraska *Alumnus* (October 1960).

29. James Eckman to Tony Ladd, December 29, 1971. Eckman is a researcher for the Mayo Clinic.

30. Cross to Ladd, January 30, 1972.

31. Ibid.

32. Ibid.

33. Ibid. See also the *New York Times* (August 10, 1938): 11; (September 1, 1938): 11; (April 21, 1938): 1.

34. Cross to Ladd.

35. There is general agreement from everyone whom the author interviewed that Judd was a powerful speaker, even though many personally did not respond immediately to his message.

36. Lincoln *Evening-Star* (November 29, 1938): 1.

37. *New York Times* (April 21, 1939): 8.

38. Personal interview with Kay Lonning in Minneapolis, February 12, 1968. Ms. Lonning was Dr. Judd's head nurse in the clinic. She indicates that in the three years that Judd was in medical work there, this was his favorite analogy.

39. "Wanted, More Men Like Judd," *Reader's Digest* (May 1947): 118. The editors reflect upon this aspect of Judd's career as pointed out in their early support of his efforts; cf. "Let's Stop Arming Japan," *Reader's Digest* (February 1940): 41.

40. Personal interview with Walter Bush in Minneapolis, July 16, 1968. Bush served as treasurer for the Judd Volunteer Committee through the twenty years of its existence and was one of the original sponsors of Dr. Judd's candidacy; Thomas von Kuster, personal interview, July 24, 1968 (von Kuster served as chairman of the Judd Committee in 1944 and 1946). Both men attested that, before Pearl Harbor, they thought that Judd, though an interesting speaker, was a religious fanatic.

41. Minneapolis *Tribune* (September 26, 1955): 18.

42. Lonning, interview, February 12, 1968.

43. "Let's Stop Arming": 41.

44. *New York Times* (April 21, 1939): 8.

45. Lonning, interview, February 12, 1968.

46. Ibid.

47. von Kuster, interview, July 24, 1968; personal interview with Ms. R. M. Crounse, in Minneapolis, July 21, 1968. Ms. Crounse served as chairwoman for the Judd Committee in 1946.

48. Bush, interview, July 16, 1968.

49. Minneapolis *Star* (February 12, 1952): 1.

50. Minneapolis *Tribune* (September 9, 1942): 1.

51. Minneapolis *Tribune* (November 5, 1942): 1.

52. Minneapolis *Tribune* (September 26, 1955, September 1, 1955).

53. "Walter Judd: Congressman," *Advance* (June 1945).

54. Judd, "I Believe": 27.

55. Ibid. Also see the foreword to the 1944 edition of Walter H. Judd, *A Philosophy of Life That Works* (New York, New York: n.p., 1944) for a strong pronouncement that his life work centered on Christian missions even though his profession temporarily was politics.

56. St. Paul *Shopper* (December 1942): 1.

57. *New York Times* (June 23, 1943): 15.

58. Richard H. Rovere, "Eight Hopeful Congressmen," *Nation* (February 27, 1943): 295.

59. *Congressional Record*, 78th Cong., 1st session, Vol. 89, Pt. 1 (February 25, 1943): 1342.

60. Ibid., 1345.

61. Ibid., 1346.

62. The influence that propelled Judd to the forefront as such an authority is pervasive and is dealt with in particular by Robert Dahl, *Congress and Foreign Policy* (New York: Harcourt, Brace and Company, 1950), pp. 60ff.

63. *Congressional Record*, 78th Cong., 1st session, Vol. 89, Pt. 3 (April 22, 1943): 3713.

64. Ibid., p. 3714. He made a similar argument on an economic basis three weeks later in ibid. (May 11, 1943): 4225.

65. Ibid., Pt. 1 (April 22, 1943): 3714.

66. Ibid.

67. Judd spent a considerable amount of time away from Washington in 1944 on a multinational fact-finding trip for Congress and as one of the main campaigners for the Republican ticket nationally; cf. *New York Times* (August 26, 1944): 6; (September 6, 1944): 6; (November 6, 1944): 16.

68. Lincoln *Evening Journal* (November 28, 1944): 1.

69. Chicago *Tribune* (October 8, 1945): 1. For the complete development of the theory as Judd saw it, see the *Congressional Record*, 80th Cong., 2nd session, Vol. 94, Pt. 9 (February 19, 1948): A1336–41 and his speeches in the House, especially in 1948.

70. "Walter Judd: Congressman," *Advance* (June 1945): 4.

71. St. Paul *Pioneer Post* (October 18, 1945): 1; *Congressional Record*, 79th Cong., 1st session, Vol. 91, Pt. 2 (March 15, 1945): 2294–95.

72. *New York Times* (December 1945): 15. For a continuation of the controversy see St. Paul *Dispatch* (November 1946): 1.

73. The seat on the House Foreign Affairs Committee was a prize for the congressman.

74. *Congressional Record*, 78th Cong., 1st session, Vol. 89, Pt. 6 (October 20, 1943): 8588–92

75. For his full argument see ibid., 79th Cong., 1st session, Vol. 91, Pt. 2 (March 15, 1945): 2294–2302.

76. These ideas are prominent in most of Judd's speeches regarding immigration reform; cf., *Congressional Record*, 80th Cong., 1st session, Vol. 93, Pt. 1 (January 3, 1947): 46; 80th Cong., 1st session, Vol. 93, Pt. 9 (December 19, 1947): 11764; 80th Cong., 2nd session, Vol. 94, Pt. 6 (June 4, 1948): 7116; 81st Cong., 2nd session, Vol. 96, Pt. 8 (July 24, 1950): 10899.

77. Marion T. Bennett, "The Immigration and Nationality (McCarron-Walter) Act of 1952, as Amended to 1965," *The Annals* (September 1966): 126–36. The *New York Times* (May 15, 1949): 35 and (May 24, 1949): 29 relates some of Judd's contributions to immigration reform. Also see Gerald T. White, "The Chinese and the Immigration Law," *Far East Survey* (April 5, 1950): 68.

78. During twenty years in Congress, Judd authored ninety-six distinct congressional bills. Fully 37 percent dealt with measures for health and safety; 16 percent with military or veterans' affairs; 12 percent with immigration; 5 percent with international cooperation; the rest were distributed throughout various endeavors. Data compiled by the author.

79. *Congressional Record*, 80th Cong., 1st session, Vol. 93, Pt. 2 (March 5, 1947): 1685; 80th Cong., 2nd session, Vol. 94, Pt. 5 (May 20, 1948): 6155; 81st Cong., 1st session, Vol. 95, Pt. 3 (May 9, 1949): 5927.

80. The examination of the congressional career of Walter Judd from published sources leaves many questions unanswered. Certainly future research must point to day-to-day activities and monitor his behind the scenes efforts in Congress.

81. *Congressional Record*, 81st Cong., 1st session, Vol. 95, Pt. 6 (June 7, 1949): 7357 reflects in particular his continuing desire to restructure the United Nations.

82. Walter H. Judd, "Control of Asia is Crucial Question," *Midland Schools* 62 (May 1948): 18–19. WHJ Papers, "America's International Expanding Role," in file of Judd

speeches at the Republican Research Center, Edina, Minnesota.

83. *Congressional Record*, 80th Cong., 2nd session, Vol. 94, Pt. 9 (February 19, 1948): A1336–41.

84. Judd, "Control of Asia": 18–19; *Congressional Record*, 81st Cong., 2nd session, Vol. 96, Pt. 18 (December 19, 1950): A7831.

85. Minneapolis *Tribune* (April 1, 1962; April 11, 1962): 4.

86. Basoco, "Rep. Walter Judd."

87. *New York Times* (August 4, 1959): 10; Walter Judd, "On the Announcement of Exchange of Visits of President Eisenhower and Khrushchev," in file of Judd speeches at the Republican Research Center, Edina, Minnesota.

88. Chicago *Tribune* (July 28, 1960): 2.

89. *New York Times* (July 26, 1960): 1.

90. For his support of the Peace Corps see the *Congressional Record*, 87th Cong., 1st session, Vol. 107, Pt. 15 (September 14, 1961): 20481; for that of religions or social emphasis, see "Personal Interview with Walter Judd," *Impact* (April 1962): 10.

91. Judd, "I Believe": 27.

92. Walter H. Judd, "The Professional Person's Place in Public Affairs," *Journal of Iowa Medical Society* 52 (May 1962): 268.

93. *New York Times* (October 29, 1961): 1.

94. Lincoln *Star* (April 9, 1962): 1.

95. Walter H. Judd, "What You Can Do for America," *Word Records* (1962), Minneapolis Public Library Record Collection.

15

CONCLUSION AND BIOGRAPHICAL NOTES

Patricia Neils

From the papers presented in this volume it is clear that the merits and extent of the influence of the missionaries individually and collectively are controversial and difficult to measure accurately. Nevertheless, they certainly demonstrate, as pointed out by Professor Richard Madsen at the San Diego conference, that international relations are determined by more than economic and political forces. Religion has been an important enterprise beyond its influence within American society and its impact on foreign cultures. It has represented America's quest for a moral ground to stand on when dealing with other countries. America needs to find for some way to deal with the world that is more meaningful than sending out pragmatists to do good works and fundamentalist nationalists to proclaim their faith. A study of the impact of American missionaries on U.S. attitudes and policies toward China may lead the way toward intercultural understanding.

Indeed, such efforts are already well underway. Since 1980 the United Board for Christian Higher Education in Asia, a private agency supported by the Protestant churches, has sponsored scholars from China to study in the United States and sent Western educators abroad.

Also, the School of World Missions of the Fuller Theological Seminary in Pasadena, California, which was established for the study of the processes of indigenization and church growth, has shown special interest in China since 1970; at Princeton Theological Seminary, Archie Crouch, for a number of years, has been preparing a guide to archival resources for the study of missions in China; the Luce Foundation in New York, established by the late Time-Life founder Henry R. Luce in memory of his missionary father Henry Winters Luce, is in its second year of a six-year project exploring the history of Christianity in China; and the Association for Asian Studies has recently given a China Missions group official standing within its organization.

This last group of scholars, under the leadership of Professor Kathleen Lodwick, addresses the fact that the China missionaries, who numbered conservatively at fifty thousand over a century (roughly from 1850 to 1950) had a profound influence on the Chinese nation of over a billion people. As demonstrated in this volume they not only served the poor and the down-trodden with their orphanages, schools, and hospitals, but they also trained China's elite.

In spite of his personal reservations about the overall merit of the missionary enterprise in China, John Fairbank has recognized the relevance of missionary studies in Sino-American relations and has led the way in promoting further scholarship. In his presidential address to the American Historical Association in 1969, Fairbank called for more interest in China-American relations in general, but emphasized a need to study American missionaries in particular. He said, "Americanists have studied the American end of our expansion: the rhetoric of manifest destiny, ideas of mission and empire, business interests and the Open Door for trade. Is it not time for a further step, the study of American activities abroad, our interaction with foreign peoples like the Chinese and Japanese, and the impact of all this experience abroad on our growth at home?" More recently Fairbank noted:

> Consciously or unconsciously, [the missionaries] imbued many Chinese with reformist ideals. Although by the 1930s, only 10 to 20 percent of the students attending missionary schools were Christian, they were learning Western democratic principles of liberty and equality. It has been postulated that the students thereby became prophets of reform inspiring both the Nationalist and Communist movements. In spite of their bitterness toward Christian missionaries, the Communist leaders have stressed the spread of literacy to ordinary people, the publication of journals and pamphlets in the vernacular, education and equality for women, the abolition of arranged child-marriages, the supremacy of public duty over filial obedience and family obligations, increased agricultural productivity through the sinking of wells and improved tools, crops, and breeds, dike and road building for protection against flood and famine, public health clinics to treat common ailments and prevent disease, discussion groups to foster better conduct, student organizations to promote healthy recreation and moral guidance, and the acquisition and sinification of Western knowledge for use in remaking Chinese life. Missionaries of the nineteenth century pioneered in all of these activities.... [I]n the Maoist message . . . ''serve the people,'' one can hear an echo of the missionary's wish to serve his fellow man.[1]

Thus recognizing the need for further study as well as new trends in the study of Sino-American relations, John Fairbank has himself led the way in encouraging graduate students at Harvard to pursue the study of American missionaries in China. For the last couple of decades he has readily acknowledged the positive aspects of missionary work in China and has been actively promoting the study of the impact of missionaries on China-American intercultural relations in general, and on American images of China in particular.

A number of his students at Harvard have written and published important works on mission history and the history of Christianity in China. Paul Cohen, for example, has emerged as a highly recognized scholar of Chinese studies in general and of Chinese resistance to Christian mission efforts in particular. Cohen's work, *and Christianity* (Cambridge: Harvard Univesity Press, 1963), was published in 1964. More recently he has been interested in the broader view, and authored *Discovering History in China: American Historical Writing on the Recent Past* (New York: Columbia University Press, 1984).

Kwang-Ching Liu has also made a seminal contribution to the field in his *Americans and Chinese: A Historical Essay and a Bibliography* (Cambridge: Harvard University Press, 1963) and his subsequent edition *American Missionaries in China: Papers from Harvard Seminars* (Cambridge: Harvard University, East Asian Research Center, 1966). Liu continued his involvement as a researcher and an organizer of research into the 1970s and 1980s.

In 1972 scholars interested in the American missionary enterprise in China convened at the small resort city of Cuernevaca outside Mexico city. The papers presented at that meeting were published two years later under the editorship and with an introduction by John K. Fairbank. The book that resulted, *The Missionary Enterprise in China and America* (Cambridge: Harvard University Press, 1974), is now regarded as one of the pioneering classics in this new field of study. Two years later Philip West published a history of the most famous of the missionary universities, *Yenching University and Sino-Western Relations, 1916–1952* (1976). In 1977, with funds from the Luce Foundation, Suzanne Wilson Barnett was able to organize a summer seminar on missions and mission writings. The papers presented then were reviewed and critiqued the following year at Harvard's Fairbank Center and eventually, resulted in the published volume, *Christianity in China: Early Protestant Missionary Writings* (Cambridge: Harvard University, Council on East Asian Studies, 1985), which was edited by Suzanne Barnett and John Fairbank. Additional contributions from the Harvard University Press in recent years include *Our Ordered Lives Confess: Three Nineteenth-Century Missionaries in East Shantung* by Irwin T. Hyatt (Cambridge: Harvard University Press, 1976), *The Home Base of American China Missions, 1880–1920* by Valentine H. Rabe (Cambridge: Harvard University, Council on East Asian Studies, 1977), and *The Missionary Mind and American East Asia Policy, 1911–1915* by James Reed (Cambridge: Harvard University, Council on East Asian Studies, 1983).

Meanwhile, beyond the Harvard efforts Jessie Lutz produced a masterful study of the evolution and demise of missionary educational institutions in China entitled *China and the Christian Colleges, 1850-1950* (Ithaca: Cornell University Press, 1971). Also, Adrian Bennett focused on the efforts of an individual missionary in his *Missionary Journalist in China: Young J. Allen and his Magazines, 1860–1883* (Athens, GA: University of Georgia Press, 1983). Examining the role of women in the American missionary enterprise have been Patricia R. Hill in *The World Their Household: The American Women's Foreign Mission Movement and Cultural Transformation* (Ann Arbor: University of Michigan Press, 1985) and Jane Hunter in *The Gospel of Gentility: American Women Missionaries in Turn-of-the-Century China* (New Haven: Yale University Press, 1984). Among the notable publications put out by religious and seminary presses is Leonard I. Sweet's edition, *The Evangelical Tradition in America* (Macon, GA: Mercer University Press, 1984).

Laying the groundwork for the study of Catholic missions in China were Rev. George H. Dunne's *Generation of Giants* (Notre Dame, IN: University of Notre Dame Press, 1962), which deals with the Jesuit efforts in late Ming China, and French Sinologist, Jacques Gernet's *China and the Christian Impact* (Cambridge: Cambridge University Press, 1985), which surveys Catholic efforts in Ming and Ch'ing and focuses particularly on the efforts of Matteo Ricci. Meanwhile George Minamaki, a Japanese-American Jesuit at Notre Dame published *The Rites Controversy, From its Beginnings to Modern Times* (Chicago: Loyola University Press, 1985). There is also Jonathan Spence's *The Memory Palace of Matteo Ricci* (New York: Viking Press, 1984), and Jean-Paul Wiest, the director of the Maryknoll Society History Program, has just written a monumental work entitled *Maryknoll in China: A History, 1918-1955* (Armonk, NY: M. E. Sharpe, 1988).[2]

With the recent emphasis on detente and rapprochement the American missionary enterprise in China is being reevaluated not only by the Americans, but by the Chinese as well. Although the missionary schools were closed, amalgamated, or renamed under Mao's regime, in recent years alumnae associations have started to form. The government's interest in rehabilitating the missionary legacy, however, is generally limited to the educational and cultural accomplishments. China is wary of allowing scholarly interest to become a catalyst for renewed efforts at evangelism and the reopening of a painful chapter of history.

Among the conference commentators in San Diego was Edward Xu (Xu Yihua) whose father, grandfather, and uncles all attended Yenching University, a missionary institution founded by the Rockefeller Foundation in 1898. Xu is now a graduate student of religion at Princeton University. The Chinese government is partially underwriting his tuition costs. Xu explained that the government's interest in the missionary enterprise really goes beyond promoting intercultural understanding. He said that on a more practical level it is also part of the overall effort "to attract foreign visitors and overseas investments." Franklin Woo, director of the China Program of the National Council of Churches, an organization of mainstream Protestant churches, agreed that the new openness benefits the Chinese because the government makes contacts all over the world through the international church network.

With support from the Luce Foundation's History of Christianity in China project, Dr. Arthur Waldron of Princeton University spent June of 1986 visiting six cities and seven universities in China to assess the condition and accessibility of the archives of former Christian colleges in China, and to meet interested faculty and students in order to evaluate the possibilities for cooperative research. He saw that in every place he visited, efforts were already underway to gather and organize school archives. Professor Waldron found that the faculties were uniformly enthusiastic, and a number of institutions were already compiling and publishing their siastic, and a number of institutions were already compiling and publishing their histories. The universities he visited in 1986 were Huazhong Normal University (Wuhan), Sichuan University (Chengdu), Beijing University, Beijing Normal University, Shandong University (Jinan), Fudan Univesity (Shanghai), and Sun Yat-sen University (Guangzhou).

In 1987 Xu Yihua was the leader of a similar mission. His trip was funded by the United Board for Christian Higher Education in Asia and resulted in even further detailed information and archival accessibility for American scholars. Universities visited in 1987 were Suzhou University, Fudan University, Nanjing University, Huazhong Normal University, St. John's University in Shanghai, Aurora University in Shanghai, and Shanghai University. Professor Xu, has been the principal Chinese scholar instrumental in locating archives in China and in working to gain wider access for Americans.

Recently, nearly two decades after Fairbank's appeal, Harvard Professor of Religion William Hutchinson reiterated Fairbank's argument for missionary studies, and placed it in the context of Professor Madsen's call for a higher sense or morality in intercultural interactions when he wrote:

> The foreign mission enterprise in its heyday (about 1880 to 1930) was a massive affair, involving tens of thousands of Americans abroad and millions at home. Even in the early nineteenth century, as a movement of huge aspiration but more modest dimensions, it exceeded most other reform or benevolent organizations in size and resources. It sent abroad, through most of its history, not only the largest contingents of Americans—dwarfing all other categories except that of short-term travelers—but also the most highly educated. Missionaries on the whole belonged to the tiny cohort of the college-trained; and male missionaries generally had been educated beyond college. If deficient from a modern point of view in sensitivity to foreign cultures they were measurably superior in that regard to most contemporaries at home or abroad.[3]

Hence the Christian, democratic ideals that the missionary enterprise as a whole represented are significant in the larger context of the general approach to American interactions with the world. A preponderance of evidence indicates that the attitudes of good will toward China that the American missionaries in general epitomized, offer a prospect of gradual osmosis, a "trickle up" theory as John Fairbank calls it, whereby American leadership could eventually become more understanding and appreciative of the Asian point of view and could then ultimately have the wit, wisdom, and conscience to promote more humanitarian policies in Asian-American relations.

Notes

1. John K. Fairbank, "Introduction: The Many Faces of Protestant Missions in China and the United States," John Fairbank, ed., *The Missionary Enterprise in China and America* (Cambridge, MA: Harvard University Press, 1974).
2. Murray Rubinstein of Baruch College in New York has recently prepared a compre-

hensive bibliographical essay which summarizes and analyzes the entire field of China Missionary studies in the English language. Also, Samuel Chow of Fuller Theological Seminary in Pasadena, California has just completed an annotated bibliography with a ten-page introduction surveying the influence of missionaries on Chinese women.

3. William R. Hutchison, *Errand to the World: American Protestant Thought and Foreign Missions* (Chicago: The University of Chicago Press, 1987), p. 1.

ABOUT THE CONTRIBUTORS

John C. Brewer is professor of history and director of Louisiana Tech at Barksdale. A specialist in American diplomatic history, Dr. Brewer's most recent work is *The Forgotten Ambassador: The Reports of John Leighton Stuart, 1946–1949,* which he coedited with Kenneth W. Rea. He is the editor of *U.S. Foreign Policy Since 1945* (forthcoming).

Margaret B. Denning is assistant professor of history and political science at Sioux Falls College, and the author of *The Sino-American Alliance in World War II: Cooperation and Dispute Among Nationalists, Communists and Americans.*

Arline T. Golkin is a lecturer in history at the University of Southern California. Her publications include *Famine: A Heritage of Hunger* (1987).

Lawrence D. Kessler teaches Chinese history and East Asian civilization at the University of North Carolina in Chapel Hill, North Carolina. His publications include *North Carolina's "China Connection," 1840–1949* and *K'ang-hsi and the Consolidation of Ch'ing Rule, 1661–1684* (1976).

Marjorie King is associate professor of history at St. John's University, Collegeville, Minnesota. Her past presentations and papers have focused on American missionary women in China, and currently she is completing a biography of Ida Pruitt.

Tony Ladd teaches at Wheaton College, Wheaton, Illinois. He has coached baseball in East Asia, led a study tour during the 1988 Olympics Games, and has written extensively in the area of sports and evangelism.

Kathleen L. Lodwick is director of academic affairs and associate professor of history at Pennsylvania State University, Mont Alto Campus, Mont Alto, Pennsylvania. Her publications include *The Chinese Recorder Index: A Guide to Christian Missions in Asia, 1876–1941* (1986).

Jessie Gregory Lutz is professor of history emeritus, Rutgers University. Her publications include *Christian Missions in China*, edited with introduction (1965); *China and the Christian Colleges, 1850–1950* (1971); and *Chinese Politics and Christian Missions: The Anti-Christian Movement of 1920–1928* (1988).

Patricia Neils teaches International Relations at United States International University in San Diego. She is the author of *China Images in the Life and Times of Henry Luce* (forthcoming).

John Rawlinson, son of Frank Rawlinson (editor of *Chinese Recorder*), is professor of history at Hofstra University. He is the author of *China's Struggle For Naval Development, 1839–1895* (1967) and has just completed a two volume biography of his father, *Rawlinson, The Recorder, and China's Revolution*.

Kenneth W. Rea is professor of history and vice-president for academic affairs at Louisiana Tech University. Among his many publications on China are *Canton in Revolution, Early Sino-American Relations, 1841–1911*, and *China: An Analytic Reader*.

Murray A. Rubinstein is associate professor of history at Baruch College, the City University of New York. He has written about the Protestant missionary enterprise in nineteenth- and twentieth-century China and is now studying the indigenization of Christianity on Taiwan. He is the author of *The Protestant Community on Modern Taiwan: Mission, Seminary, and Church* (forthcoming).

Charles W. Weber received his Ph.D. from the department of History of the University of Chicago. His research interest is in the strategy of mission education and its impact on Asian and African cultures. Currently Charles Weber is a Professor of History at Wheaton College in Wheaton, Ill. and directs the College's East Asia Study Program, which he initiated in 1974. His publications include *Dupage Discovery: A Bicentennial View* (1976), coedited with David Maas.

Edmund S. Wehrle is professor of history at the University of Connecticut. He has written *Britain, China and the Antimissionary Riots, 1891–1900* (1966), *International Politics in East Asia Since World War II*, with Donald F. Lach (1975), and coedited with Stephen L. Petersen, *Missionary Periodicals from the China Mainland* (1976).

Jean-Paul Wiest is research director for the Maryknoll Society History Program and professor at the Maryknoll School of Theology in Ossining, New York. He is the author of *Maryknoll in China: A History, 1918–1955* (1988), and the academic advisor of *Bibliographic Guide to the Microfiche Collection of Collectanea Commissionis Synodalis* (1988).